THE BIG LIE, EXPOSED!

THE BIG LIE, EXPOSED!

†

Thomas L. Copping

iUniverse, Inc.
Bloomington

The Big Lie, Exposed!

iUniverse books may be ordered through booksellers or by contacting:

iUniverse
1663 Liberty Drive
Bloomington, IN 47403
www.iuniverse.com
1-800-Authors (1-800-288-4677)

ISBN: 978-1-4620-0045-6 (sc)
ISBN: 978-1-4620-0044-9 (hc)
ISBN: 978-1-4620-0043-2 (ebk)

Library of Congress Control Number: 2011903663

Printed in the United States of America

iUniverse rev. date: 07/20/2011

CONTENTS

Introduction   1

Judaism, Christianity, Islam   29

The Lord's Appearing   45

Resurrection of the Dead   50

When You See All These Things, Know My Kingdom Is Near   80

The 10 Percent Tithe Lie, Exposed   99

Judgment upon Babylon (Iraq) in Our Time   106

The Genesis Account and the Historical Record   118

God's Word versus Man's Word   136

Notwithstanding, I Have a Few Things against Thee   166

The Never-Ending Dispute   186

God's Promise of Divine Intervention   211

Scripture That Proves There Is No Pre-Tribulation Resurrection   237

The True Time of the Resurrection of the Dead   272

Closing Comments   384

Bibliography   398

Introduction

To OPEN THIS MANUSCRIPT, I have one thought. If there is a pre-tribulation rapture of the living church to heaven, then who are these people about whom the Bible tells us? Let's note that the Holy Spirit thought it necessary to repeat this three times—in Matthew16:28, Mark 9:1, and Luke 9:27, which says, "There shall be some standing here, that shall not taste of death till they see the coming of the Lord." These who don't taste of death will see the Son of Man coming with his holy angels. Matthew tells us in 16:27 that this is when the Lord Jesus will reward every person according to his or her works. Who are the Christians who shall be changed at the last trumpet into their immortal bodies (1 Cor. 15:51–52, 54)? Revelation 17:2 says, "He that overcometh shall inherit all things; and I will be his God, and he shall be my son." Is this not the church of the Lord Jesus Christ, who prays for our "day of visitation" daily, "Thy kingdom come. Thy will be done on earth as it is in heaven," as instructed in Matthew 6:10? Luke 11:2 says, "Thy kingdom come, Thy will be done, as in heaven, so in earth." In light of these verses, who are they? This is what the tribulation is all about, to bring the people of the earth back to God. The Lord Jesus says in Matthew 23:39, "For I say unto you, Ye shall not see me henceforth, till ye shall say, Blessed is he that cometh in the name of the Lord." And during the tribulation period, Christians will pray with more intensity.

These are just a few verses of scripture that prove there is not a "rapture of the living church" to heaven. There will be no one "left behind" because the living church during the great tribulation will be protected by God here on this earth. And yes, Christians will die for their beliefs in the tribulation period. John tells us this in the book of Revelation and Paul warns in his epistles that all the churches will suffer tribulation. The twenty-first-century church is no exception.

The Bible is God's instruction manual. It is how God expects the people he created to act toward God and their fellow human beings. We should note that the language calls them "the Ten Commandments" and not "the Ten Suggestions."

The prophets in the Bible truly spoke the Word of God, because their predictions were precisely accurate. The words in the Old Testament are the same words given by the prophets in their day, and the Dead Sea Scrolls prove this. In my interpretation, I assume nothing, but I give you just the facts or the only possible conclusion of what the prophets of God say. Judge for yourself if this is the right conclusion, for my interpretation is unlike anything I have read or heard.

I started listening to pastors on the radio and on television in the early 1990s. It got to the point where that was all I did. I started at about eight thirty in the morning until twelve thirty in the afternoon five days a week for about eight years. On Saturdays, I would watch preaching on television on Saturdays from three o'clock to six o'clock, when local programming aired the prophecy pastors. I also started studying the Bible for myself. One spring morning, I picked up my Bible, sat on my back patio, and started to read Genesis. After reading through Abraham, Isaac, and Jacob, I closed the book, and I made this prayer to the Lord: "If you help me understand your Word, I will study every day." And I did.

After a few years of study, I realized I needed to be baptized again. So I called a friend who I knew was a churchgoer. In a few weeks, I was baptized at a First Christian Church. Now I know I am saved. I attended that church for several years, and for personal reasons, I left that church. For several more years I attended many church denominations. I attended one service where the lady pastor said, "We are a gender-friendly church, so you can pray to your father in heaven or your mother." I thought to myself, *Where did she get her degree in theology?* The more I listened to pastors and tried to match their interpretations to the Bible, the more I started to realize they did not match. This manuscript is the result of this study. It has taken me ten years and many thousands of hours to write this manuscript.

About twelve years ago, I sent out my interpretation to several pastors around the country. I asked them, "Is this what the Bible says? Just prove me wrong." At that time, I did not think there was no such thing as a pre-tribulation rapture but only that it was at a later date. I hand-printed the scriptures because I didn't own a computer at this time. I went to a copy store to make the copies. Only two of the pastors responded, just thanking me for my work, but they did not comment on its context. I did receive a donation envelope. I really did not expect them to answer my interpretation, because I don't go along with their teaching. None of them have come up with the same conclusion as I have.

I also passed this out to several pastors around the city in which I live. I know one of the pastors read what I wrote because he angrily stated on his program, "My church is the Philadelphia church, and we are not going through the tribulation period." I compare the pre-tribulation rapture pastors to the Pharisees. Both were and are blinded to the true time of the "day of visitation" and the "day of the Lord." In Matthew 21:43 the Lord Jesus says, "Therefore say I unto you, The kingdom of God shall be taken from you, and given to a nation bringing forth the fruits thereof." The kingdom of God was taken from the Jewish people, and note it says it's given to a "nation," one nation that is the Christian nation. Why did the Lord Jesus tell them this?

The answer is Luke 19:44: "Because thou knewest not the time of thy visitation." This is what the living Christian church is to watch for and instructed to pray for. This is the time of our visitation of the Lord Jesus. This is the answer to our daily prayer of Matthew 6:10: "Thy kingdom come. Thy will be done on earth, as it is in heaven." The rapture theory is just the opposite of the way we are told to pray. The rapture pastors tell us the church is called up to heaven when the Bible tells us the Lord Jesus will bring heaven to earth. They have their pulpits, their radio and television programs, and all I have is a manuscript with the Word of God. It was a relative who suggested to me to write a book, so that is just what I did. He suggested, "If they are wrong and you are right, put it in a book and let the people decide."

Since I got almost no response from any of these pastors, I decided I had not done a convincing job. That is when I quit listening to these pastors and devoted more time to my personal study. And I brought a *Strong's and Bullinger's* concordances. Since my only day off from work is Sunday, I quit attending church services and devoted the whole day to studying the Bible. That day of study started at eight o'clock in the morning and lasted until six o'clock in the evening. My only break from study was to take my two best friends for their Sunday afternoon walk.

And after several years of more study, I realized that not only was there not a pre-tribulation rapture but there was not a "rapture" at all of the living church to heaven. I was so blinded by the pastors' teachings. The "we which are live and remain till the coming of the Lord that meet the Lord in the air" of 1 Thessalonians 4:17 meant what it said. There is a special place of protection for part of the church during the wrath of God. This is where these people learn how they will rule with Christ. The Christians of Matthew 16:28, Mark 9:1, and Luke 9:27, which says, "There shall be some standing here, which shall not taste of death, till they see the Son of Man coming in his kingdom," are also protected on the earth. These are the sheep the Lord will separate from the goats when the Lord sits on his throne "on earth." The Lord will say to them, "Come, ye blessed of my Father, inherit the kingdom prepared for you before the foundations of the world" (Matt. 25:31–34). "Blessed are the meek, for they shall inherit the earth" (Matt. 5:5). It is only the dead who are resurrected at the Lord's appearing in heaven. The we who shall meet the Lord in the clouds are at his coming. And now, almost twenty years after that day on my back patio, I believe I have put together a manuscript that proves all things you will read in this manuscript.

I am also risking my eternal future with this interpretation. The book of Revelation states:

> For I testify unto every man that heareth the words of
> this prophecy of this book, If any man shall add unto
> these things, God shall add unto him the plagues
> that are written in this book. And if any man take
> away from the words of the book of this prophecy,
> God shall take away his part out of the book of life,
> and out of the holy city, and from things which are
> written in this book (Rev. 22:18–19).

I am willing to risk my eternal future on this interpretation. This is how important I believe this interpretation is. If your name is taken out of the "book of life" it means, "And whosoever was not found written in the book of life was cast into the lake of fire" (Rev. 20:15). This is taken very lightly by most pastors. The lake of fire is only reserved for Satan, his fallen angels, and the people who commit the unpardonable sin. There is a difference between "the Lamb's Book of Life" and "the book of life." This will be explained later.

When we read the meanings of words in Hebrew and Greek, sometimes they have various meanings. I will choose what each word's meaning is, and I will let you decide if it is the right one. I will give at least two to three prophets, when available, who say the same thing to prove the accuracy of my statements. Let's note now that the Old Testament relates to God's dealings with the tribes of Israel, from the beginnings to the Lord's return. The New Testament also relates to them but now includes the Gentiles, to whom the Jews were selling salvation at the temple. As the Lord Jesus states in Matthew 21:13, "It is written, My house shall be a house of prayer; but ye have made it a den of thieves."

I might add that the New Testament church has done the same thing. For it is by grace you are saved by faith, it is the gift of God that no man shall perish. Ephesians 2:8–9 tells us, "For by grace are ye saved through faith; and not of yourselves: it is the gift of God: Not of works, lest any man should boast." The church of the Lord Jesus Christ is not under the Mosaic Law of the 10 percent tithe. And I should note this: in the messages to the seven churches that are in Asia in Revelation 2:47, the Lord Jesus tells them, "I have somewhat against

thee." Revelation 2:14 says, "But I have a few things against thee," and
Revelation 2:20 says, "Notwithstanding, I have a few things against
thee." These are the messages to the twenty-first-century church. In
this manuscript, I will tell you what the Lord Jesus has against them.
This is why I named this manuscript *The Big Lie, Exposed.*

I reference the *Strong's Complete Word Study Concordance,* by
James Strong, LLD, STD; the Qur'an, by Muhammad Zafrulla Khan,
copyright by Olive Branch Press in Northampton, Massachusetts, 2005;
The Complete Works of Josephus, by William Whiston, 1999, by Kregel
Publications, Grand Rapids, MI; E. W. Bullinger's A *Critical Lexicon
and Concordance to the English and Greek New Testament,* published in
1999 by Kregel Publications, Grand Rapids, MI; J. M. Roberts's *The
New History of the World; A History Of The Modern World,* by R. R.
Palmer, second edition, revised with the collaboration of Joel Colton,
copyright 1950, 1956 in New York, published by Alfred A Knoff, Inc.;
A History of Civilization: Volume One: to 1715, copyright 1955, 1960
by Prentice-Hall, Inc., England Cliffs, New Jersey; and the *Webster's
Dictionary.*

This book is about sin and God's dealings with sin before history
and throughout history. Sin starts with Satan and his rebellion against
God in which a third of the angels of heaven followed him. Let's note
Jude 1:4, "For there a certain men crept in unawares, who were before
of old ordained to this condemnation, ungodly men, turning the
grace of our God into lasciviousness [*aselgeia,* which means from the
compound (as a negative particle) of *al,* which means the first; Alpha[1]],
and denying the only Lord God, and our Lord Jesus Christ." Note the
word "lasciviousness" means to worship the negative to the true God,
which means to worship the Antichrist. We should note the "before of
old." The word for old is *palai,*[2] which means ancient, great while ago,
in time past. These men's spirits rebelled against God before (the angels
that rebelled against God that took spirit human bodies). These certain
men are ordained into this condemnation because they deny the only
Lord God, the Lord Jesus Christ.

---

[1]   James Strong, *Strong's Complete Word Study Concordance,* 757.
[2]   Ibid., 2127.

But then we have these people in Ephesians 1:4–5, which says, "According as he has chosen us in him before the foundation of the world, that we should be holy and without blame before him in love: Having pre-designated us unto the adoption of children by Jesus Christ to himself, according to the pleasure of his will." Note the language. Now we have people pre-designated unto God before the foundation of the world. The angels who followed Lucifer in his rebellion against God are the angels who God made human spirits. The angels who are not rebellious then are not rebellious in this life, for we believe in the only true God, the Lord Jesus Christ. Note that Psalms 104:4 tells us, "Who maketh his angels spirits." And Hebrews 1:7 also says, "Who maketh his angels spirits." This is why God created man—to redeem the fallen angels who rebelled against God our Father. This is why the Lord Jesus died on the cross—for my sin and your sin. The Bible tells us this in Matthew 18:11, "For the Son of Man is come to save that which was lost." I was also one of the lost, but I am redeemed back to the Father through the Lord Jesus Christ.

We should note in Revelation 20:15, it states, "And whosoever was not found written in the book of life was cast into the lake of fire." It's only the angels who refuse life on this planet who are cast into the lake of fire. The spirits who follow after Satan who became humans on this planet are redeemed (the soul) back to God, but those who have their faith in the Lord Jesus (those who are written in the Lamb's Book of Life) receive eternal life on the earth. Those who refuse the Lord Jesus as their Savior do not have the eternal spirit and soul life, and this is the second death.

Let us also note 1 Corinthians 3:14–15, "If any man's work abide which he hath built upon, he shall receive a reward. If any man's work shall be burned, he shall suffer loss: but he himself shall be saved; yet so as by fire." Those who are saved by works have faith in the Lord Jesus; those who don't are also saved as yet by fire. This New Testament has its equivalent message in the Old Testament in Daniel 12:2, "And many of them that sleep in the dust of the earth shall awake, some to everlasting life, and some to shame and everlasting contempt." Those who inherit the earth have eternal life, and those who don't live in everlasting contempt in heaven.

When the Antichrist makes his appearance, he will appear in his angelic form. He will not be a human born on this planet. Revelation 12:9 says, "He was cast into the earth, and his angels were cast out with him." We should note that it says here that Satan was cast to the earth. It does not say his angels were cast to the earth, just that they were cast out of heaven into outer darkness. Just as Satan appeared and tempted the Lord Jesus (in the flesh) in the wilderness, he will tempt man in the last days. This is why Satan and the false prophet are cast into the lake of fire, as stated in Revelation 20:15, because they are never born on the planet.

The Bible gives us the key to unlocking its messages that God has sent to us through his prophet Isaiah, who lived during the eighth century BC, along with the other prophets of the Old Testament. I mention Isaiah mainly because he gives the most complete picture of prophecy. Together with the New Testament, we get the complete picture of God's plan for mankind. But we first must know what happened in the past to understand the future. Some of the Old Testament's prophecies match what is said in the New Testament of things yet to come. And when we put in the Hebrew and Greek word meanings, we will see they help match the old with the new. This is why the Old Testament is important. God gives us examples of things done in the past to reveal what he will do in the future. Let's note Ecclesiastes 1:9: "The thing that hath been, it is that shall be; and that which is done is that which shall be done: and there is no new thing under the sun." Those things that have been are the pre-tribulation rapture, the first and second rule of Satan on this planet, the Christian Christmas tree, and those things that shall be are Muhammad's Allah, the mosques on the Temple Mount, and many more things before they happen.

We should note that many of the New Testament saints refer to the Old Testament, just as the Lord did on many occasions. And at the time of the Lord's physical human appearance, his return was well documented in the Old Testament. And I will do this as Isaiah the prophet instructed.

Most people don't know this is in the Bible. This interpretation is not a reading of the Word of God but a study. To understand all I am about to give you, it's time to put on your thinking caps.

> Whom shall teach knowledge? And whom shall be made to understand doctrine? Them that are weaned from milk, and drawn from the breast. For precept must be upon precept, precept upon precept; line upon line, line upon line; here a little, and there a little (Isa. 25:9–10).

> Produce your cause saith the Lord; bring forth your strong reasons, saith the King of Jacob. Let them bring them forth, and show us what shall happen: let them show the former things, what they be, that we may consider them, and know the latter end of them; or declare us things to come. Show the things that are to come hereafter, that we may know that ye are gods: do good or do evil, that we may be dismayed, and behold it together (Isa. 41:21–23).

> Thus saith the Lord the King of Israel, and his redeemer the Lord of host; I am the first, and I am the last; and besides me there is no God. And who, as I, shall call, and shall declare it, and set it in order for me, since I appointed the ancient people? And the things that are coming, and shall come, let them shew unto them (Isa 44:6–7).

> I am the Lord. That is my name and my glory will I not give to another, neither my praises to graven images. Behold, the former things are come to pass, and new things do I declare before they spring forth I tell you of them (Isa. 42:8–9).

Isaiah tells us here that God has revealed the future from the very beginning to prove that he is God. The prophecies are given to us so we can know the future and what it brings. The past also reveals the future. But to understand all the prophecies, you must do as God has instructed. That is to put precept upon precept, line upon line, and here a little and there a little, which means to use all the prophets God has given us to fully understand Bible prophecy. And for me to come to the conclusions I have, I had to use just about every book in the Bible. This is why it took me ten years to write this manuscript. I did that so you will know that when I speak, I speak the Word from God.

I will give you examples of what happened in the past that reveals future events and the rapture of the dead. And since most people do not have the time to study God's words, I wrote this book in a short version. By following Isaiah's instructions on how to interpret its messages, I hope to prove the following.

The resurrection of the dead does not happen until the start of the battle of Armageddon, when the sun and the moon do not give their light. It's only the resurrection of the dead and not the living at his appearing. Those who are alive and remain shall be caught up together with them in the clouds to meet the Lord in the air, and so shall we ever be with the Lord. Revelation 21:3 says, "And I heard a voice from heaven saying, Behold, the tabernacle of God is with men, and he will dwell with them, and they shall be his people, and God himself will be with them, and be their God." This is how the Lord will shorten the days for his elect. Those who are caught up together with them (the dead) in the clouds, the living church on the earth, do this in 1 Corinthians15:52, "We shall be changed, this mortal puts on immortality." This is how the church is protected during the great tribulation period when the Lord shall be revealed from heaven in a flaming fire, taking vengeance on them that know not God.

And the equivalent verse of Revelation 21:3 found in the Old Testament is found in Psalms 27:5, "For in the time of trouble [tribulation] he shall hide me in his pavilion: in the secret of his tabernacle shall he hide me; he shall set me upon a rock." This is unlike what you have been promised by the pre-tribulation rapture pastors when they tell you alive church is raptured up to heaven. In both the

Strong's and the *Bullinger's* concordances, the word "rapture" is not given. We will note that John, in the book of Revelation, never tells us that he sees the church in heaven but only those who were killed. Let us note Revelation 6:9: "I saw the souls of them that were slain for the word of God, and for the testimony which they held." This is when the fifth seal is revealed and all John sees are the souls that were slain. The scriptures I will give you prove this theory of the living church rapture to heaven is wrong theology. If your Christian pastors knew the Bible, they would have known that this Armageddon battle is fought and won by the Lord Jesus Christ. It's God's rescue plan for his people. This is the greater gift of God to the meek that inherit the earth. The Lord Jesus says in Matthew 5:5: "Blessed are the meek: for they shall inherit the earth." This is the fulfillment to the promise that God gave to Abraham. Genesis 15:18, "Unto thy seed have I given this land, from the river of Egypt unto the great river, the river Euphrates." This prophecy has never been fulfilled, but it will be after the battle of Armageddon.

In my next manuscript, with Bible prophecy and the history books, I will prove that Ephraim and Manasseh are the house of Israel that became what is known today as England and America and that most of Europe is composed of the other eight tribes that were taken into Assyrian captivity. We should note what Josephus writes about the ten tribes of the northern kingdom. He says, "So the ten tribes of the Israelites were removed out of Judea nine hundred and forty-seven years after their forefathers were come out of the land Egypt two hundred and forty years, seven months, and seven days after they had revolted from Rehoboam. And such a conclusion over took the Israelites."[3] I could not find anywhere where Josephus writes that the ten tribes ever returned. But when we search the scriptures, we will read that God will guide the ten tribes where he wants them to go.

I believe I will prove that Adam and Eve were not formed first but were created in 5000 BC. God first created male and female in 7000 BC. The Lord Jesus could not come until he did to save men's spirits until seven thousand years after they were first created. which I found

---

3   William Whitson, *The Complete Works of Josephus,* 332.

in December 2010 under the title of "Hebrew word meaning seven," The Hebrew meaning for *seven* has a special symbolic significance. The number seven is a symbol of completion. That is exactly what the Lord Jesus said in Matthew 7:17: "Think not that I come to destroy the law, or the prophets: I am not come to destroy, but to fulfill." We will read later that the Greek word for fulfill means "to complete."

The Lord Jesus's return will not come until two thousand years after his first physical visitation. Hosea says in 6:2, "After two days [two thousand years] will he revive [the dead in Christ shall be raised first] us: in the third he will raise us up [we which are alive and remain will meet the Lord in the air], and we shall live in his sight." This would make this "third day" the tenth day (ten thousand earth years) since God first created male and female. The Hebrew meaning for *ten* is the perfect number, the completeness of order. The number and order are perfect, that the whole cycle is complete. The completion of the whole cycle is found in Revelation 10: 6–7 "that there should be time no longer" and "the mystery of God should be finished." This is the "last day" of John 6:39, 6:44, and 6:54. On this tenth day is when the Lord Jesus will rule and reign forever. This is the answer to our daily prayer, "Thy kingdom come. Thy will be done on earth as it is in heaven," the day for the twenty-first-century church's day of visitation.

I want the people who read this book to judge it. You have heard the pre-tribulation rapture pastors for years say that the church does not go through the tribulation period, that the people who are alive before the tribulation are called up to heaven in Revelation 4. These pastors include Tim LaHaye, Jerry Jenkins, John Hagee, Jack Van Impe, Perry Stone, Hal Lindsey, and most of the other pastors on radio and television. They have written many books and made movies promising a pre-tribulation rapture. Tim LaHaye and Jerry Jenkins have sold over sixty-six million books with the Left Behind series, which is based on a lie.

There is also the warning that is given in 2 Peter 2:1–3:

> But there were false prophets also among the people, even as there shall be false teachers among you, who privily shall bring in damnable heresies, even denying

the Lord bought them, and bring upon themselves swift destruction. And many shall follow their pernicious ways; by reasons of whom the way of truth shall be evil spoken of. And through covetousness shall they with feigned words make merchandise of you: whose judgment now of a long time lingered not, and their damnation slumbered not.

I believe these false teachers are the pre-tribulation of the living rapture pastors. The *Webster's Dictionary* definition of "feign" is "to invent; to pretend; to make a deceptive move." The word for feigned is *plastos*,[4] which means molded, that is (by implication) artificial or (figurative) fictitious (false), feigned. It comes from *plasso*, a primary verb, which means to mound, that is, shape or fabricate, form. I will prove that they invented their theory about a pre-tribulation and that the living rapture is not in scripture. We should note that Peter warns that they will "make merchandise of you" in 2 Peter 2:3. This is done when a pastor demands to see your W-2 form to check to see how much you earn before you can join that church. They demand 10 percent of your earnings, even from people who don't make much. This is one of the big lies you will read about in this manuscript.

Here is what the Bible says. Second Corinthians 9:7 says, "Every man according as he purposeth in his heart, so let me give, not grudgingly, or of necessity: for God loveth a cheerful giver." Paul tells pastors not to demand money if that money is necessary for that family to pay its bills. The Lord rebukes the Pharisees when he says in Matthew 15:2, "Why do thy disciples transgress the tradition of the elders?" Jesus goes on to tell them that instead of giving money to the temple it would be better served taking care of their father and mother.

This pre-tribulation rapture of the living church is the biggest hoax ever perpetrated on the church, and this manuscript will prove the pastors wrong. This is the big lie, exposed. It is time for the church of the Lord Jesus to know the truth. This secret pre-tribulation rapture is so secret that Matthew, Luke, Mark, John, and Paul do not mention it.

---

4   *Strong's*, 2136.

If the Lord Jesus is not revealed from heaven and his appearing is not until the scriptures tell us, then I say, "Rip these scriptures out of your Bible, because they don't tell the truth." They are all false teachers, just as the Bible tells us there would be. They may lead people to the Lord, which is a good thing, but they are promising something that is not in the Bible.

We should note here also that the Lord "will not give his glory to another" (Isa. 42:8). That should tell us that the worship of anything other than the Lord provokes the Lord. We should also note that the God of the Old Testament refers to himself as the Savior, such as in Isaiah 45:15: "Verily thou art a God that hidest thyself, O God of Israel, the Saviour." And in Isaiah 43:11, he says, "I, even I, am the Lord; and beside me there is no Saviour." The Old Testament also refers to the Lord as our Father, Savior, and Redeemer, just as the New Testament does. But when we examine the Qur'an, which claims to affirm the truth of previous revelations, we will read that Allah never claims to be the Savior, Redeemer, or Father.

The Jews had hundreds of years to study the scriptures to know when the Messiah's visitation was to happen. They missed it, and we will find out why. The Pharisees had an excuse, but the twenty-first-century church does not. The Lord's second coming is even more documented. Man has now had the scriptures for a least seventeen hundred years, and there not much agreement in their interpretation. This is why I call this manuscript, *The Big Lie, Exposed.* I will expose the lies the Christian pastors tell their congregations and the lies the liberal scientists tell us about global warming and the ape-man evolution.

The meaning of the words in Revelation 21:27, "or maketh a lie" is *pseudos*,[5] which means a falsehood The Bible even tells us that there are big lies, and two big lies are the pre-tribulation rapture and the alive church vanishing. There is one God of heaven, and his name is the Lord God of hosts, who is the Lord Jesus Christ, which makes Muhammad's Allah a lie. Just as the Lord blinded the eyes of the Pharisees to bring salvation to the Gentiles, the Lord Jesus Christ has also sent them a delusion because of their hatred for their brother. And this is the

---

[5]   *Strong's*, 2181.

warning to twenty-first-century man. Reject Christ now, when Satan is cast to the earth, and he will do this, as stated in 2 Thessalonians 2:11: "For this cause God shall send them strong delusion, that they should believe a lie." Isaiah 45:7 tells us, "I form the light, and create darkness: I make peace, and create evil: I the Lord do all these things."

The last of the big lies are ape-man evolution and mother-earth worship. And we will read what the Almighty Lord has to say to these people.

If there was a rapture of the living church at the time of the end, why would the Christians be instructed to pray daily in Matthew 6:10, "Thy kingdom come. Thy will be done on earth as it is in heaven"? If the church was not on the earth when the Lord returns, why are we instructed to pray this? This should be the first hint to Christians that the church will be on the planet when the Lord returns. In Luke 18:8, the Lord Jesus asks, "When the Son of man cometh, shall he find faith on the earth?" According to the pre-tribulation rapture pastors, the answer is no, because the church is in heaven and not "on the earth." The Bible tells us just exactly when the Lord's return to the earth is, and the Lord does not leave heaven in a pre-tribulation rapture to take his church to heaven.

Pastors of today completely ignore scriptures when they ignore this. We are told in Proverbs 10:30, "The righteous shall never be removed: but the wicked shall not inherit the earth." The word for "removed" is *mowt*,[6] which means to waver and by implication to slip, shake, and fall. We should note the word for removed means shake, to waver, to slip, and fall, and the righteous don't. Romans 14:4 says, "For God is able to make him stand." So why is this particular scripture given? The Lord God commands earthquakes for judgment. And if the righteous are never removed, there is no living church rapture. The New Testament equivalent verse is John 17:15. The Lord says, "I pray not that thou shouldest take them out of the world, but thou shouldest keep them from the evil." Just what did the Lord pray here? Not to take the church out of the earth, but to keep them from evil. Another part

---

6   *Strong's*, 1894.

of our daily prayer of Matthew 6:13 is "deliver us from evil." This is because blessed are the meek, for they shall inherit the earth.

Let's note Psalms 76:7, 9–10, "Thou, even thou, art to be feared: and who may stand in thy sight when once thou art angry? When God rose to judgment to save the meek of the earth. Surely the wrath of man shall praise thee: the remainder of wrath shalt thou restrain."

It tells us that the meek are able to stand, in God's sight. When? When God is anger. And why does God rise to judgment? To save the meek of the earth. When does an angry God rise to judgment? This is given in Ezekiel 38:18–20:

> And it shall come to pass at the same time when Gog shall come against the land of Israel, saith the Lord God, that my fury shall come up in my face. For in the jealousy and in the fire of my wrath have I spoken, and all men that are upon the face of the earth, shall shake at my presence.

We are told in 1 Corinthians 16:22, "If any man love not the Lord Jesus Christ let them be Anathema [which means "a thing devoted to destruction or given up to the curse"[7]] Maranatha [which means, "the or our Lord cometh. It is a solemn watchword, reminding them and us of the nearness of His coming, and the duty for being ready for it[8]]." Most pastors don't teach from the book of Revelation because they don't understand it. We are instructed in scripture to be watchful, to know when the scriptures are to be fulfilled. There is even this in Revelation 3:3: "If therefore thou shall not watch, I will come on thee as a thief." And who is given up to the curse? The answer is in Isaiah 34:5: "For my sword shall be bathed in heaven: behold, it shall come down upon Idumea [Edom], and upon the people of my curse, to judgment."

---

7   Bullinger, *E. W. Bullinger's Critical Lexicon and Concordance to the English and Greek New Testament,* 50.
8   Ibid., 482.

We are told again in Psalms 41:1–2, Blessed is he that considereth the poor: the Lord will deliver him in the time of trouble. The Lord will preserve him, and keep him alive, and he shall be blessed upon the earth: and thou wilt not deliver him unto the will of his enemies." First note that the same language is given in 2 Corinthians 9:9, "He hath given to the poor: his righteousness remaineth for ever." Let us note Psalms 41:2, "The Lord will preserve and keep him alive." This is the Old Testament equivalent to 1 Thessalonians 5:23, "And the very God of peace sanctify you wholly; and I pray God your whole spirit and soul and body be preserved blameless unto the coming of our Lord Jesus Christ."

We are told in this verse that God will preserve the whole body and soul and spirit until the coming of the Lord Jesus Christ. Note the language; it says here at his coming and not at his appearing. Also note in Psalms 41:2 it says, "He shall be blessed upon the earth." This is Old Testament equivalent of the verse where the Lord Jesus states in Matthew 5:5, "Blessed are the meek: for they shall inherit the earth." The alive church is blessed upon the earth and not taken to heaven in a rapture. Not once in the scriptures does it say that giving money to the church is righteousness. Let's note the word "trouble" here is *rah*, which means; bad (as a noun), evil (natural or moral), adversity, or affliction.[9] And the word "preserve" is *shamar*, which means properly to hedge about (i.e., guard), generally to protect, attend to, etc.[10] Note Psalms 41:1–2 says "to keep him alive" and when "in adversity and affliction" in the "time of trouble," in the time of tribulation.

Also note Psalms 34:16, "The face of the Lord is against them that do evil, to cut off the remembrance of them from the earth." The evil is cut off in the earth, because of this next verse. And again in the Sermon on the Mount, the Beatitudes, Matthew 5:5 says, "Blessed are the meek: for they shall inherit the earth." Blessed is *horao*, which means gazing at (i.e., by implication, of being seen, visible).[11]

---

[9]   *Strong's*, 1971.
[10]   Ibid., 1990.
[11]   Ibid., 2123.

We read here that in the time of trouble (tribulation), the Lord will preserve (put a hedge about) him and keep him alive, and God will not deliver the saints to the will of the Satan, for blessed are the meek that inherit the earth. We should also note that Psalms 41:2 says, "He shall be blessed upon the earth in the time of tribulation." And we are told that the Lord will "put a hedge about" us. And how shall we "blessed upon the earth"? In Acts 2:17 we are told, "It shall come to pass in the last days, saith God, I will pour out my Spirit upon all flesh." That hedge is the Holy Spirit, and it shall be poured out in the last days.

These are the last days just before the "last day" where John tells us this in John 6:39, "I should lose nothing, but raise it up again at the 'last day'" and in verse 40, "And this is the will of him that sent me, that every one which 'seeth' the Son, and believeth on him, may have everlasting life: and I will raise him up at the last day." Let's note the language of both these verses. In verse 39 it says "raise up again" (the dead) and in verse 40 it says "raise up" (the living). The dead are raised up again in verse 39 and the living are raised up that "seeth the Son" and this happens on the last day. This refers to the "we which are alive and remain shall be caught up together with them [the dead] in the clouds" in 1 Thessalonians 4:17.

When is the last day? When the seven thunders had uttered their voices in Revelation 10:6–7 we are told, "That there should be time no longer: But in the days of the voice of the seventh angel, when he shall begin to sound, the mystery of God should be finished, as he hath declared to his servants the prophets." This is the last day when there is time no longer. We should also note John 6:39–40 will match John 11:25–26. John 6:39, which says, "raise up again at the last day," matches John 11:25, "I am the resurrection, and the life: he that believeth in me, though he were dead, yet shall he live." John 6:40 says, "Everyone that seeth the Son and believeth on him, may have everlasting life," which matches John 11:26, "And whosoever 'liveth' and believeth in me shall never die." Those who are alive shall be changed, as stated in 1 Corinthians 15:52 and "see the coming of the Lord." This same "gazing at" is talked about in Matthew 24:30, "And then shall appear the Son of Man in heaven." These are the people that

John told us "seeth the Son." This is after the tribulation of those days, when the sun and moon don't give their light.

This is the bigger message the Bible is trying to tell us. Those who endure until the end will be the meek who inherit the earth with immortal bodies. There are estimates that say there are only one billion Christians on the earth of the six billion known inhabitants. That means the billions of people who survive the battle of Armageddon will continue to live and die as normal, while the Christians live the entire thousand-year reign of Jesus Christ. This is why I say this. Revelation 20:7–8 says, "When the thousand years are expired, Satan shall be loosed out of his prison, And shall go out to deceive the nations which are in the four quarters of the earth, Gog and Magog, to gather them together to battle: the number of whom is as the sands of the sea." After the thousand-year reign of Jesus Christ, Satan will again deceive a population as the sands of the sea. It's only the meek of the earth who get to enter into this new city. Revelation 21:11–12 says:

> And he carried me away in the spirit to a great and high mountain, and shewed me that great city, the holy Jerusalem, descending out of heaven from God, Having the glory of God: and her light was like unto a stone most precious, even like a jasper stone, clear as crystal; And had a wall great and high, and had twelve gates, and at the gates twelve angels, and names written thereon, which are the names of the twelve tribes of the children of Israel.

Notice the reference to the "twelve tribes of the children of Israel" here in the book of Revelation. All the gates to the city have names of the house of Israel and not one for Christians or Gentiles. I believe this tells us here that some of the Christian people of the world are the descendants of the "twelve tribes of the children of Israel." Let us note the language of Matthew 15:24: "I [Jesus Christ] am not sent but unto the lost sheep of the house of Israel." The Lord tells his apostles in Matthew 10:5–6, "Go not unto the way of the Gentiles, and into any city of the Samaritans enter ye not: But go rather to the lost sheep of the house of Israel." The gospel of Jesus Christ was to be preached to the lost tribes of the house of Israel. So where was the gospel spread? The gospel was taken mainly to Europe and to the Byzantine Empire.

I believe Zechariah tells us the direction most of lost tribes of the house of Israel when after the Assyrian captivity, "Thus saith the Lord of hosts; Behold, I will save my people from the east country [Israel], and from the west country [Christians and the house of Israel]." Note it says here "country" and not countries just as in Matthew 21:43: "The kingdom shall be taken from you, and given to a nation." Some of the Jews today have returned to the land of Israel. And this is when the Lord God fulfills Zechariah 8:8: "And I will bring them [house of Israel], and they shall dwell in the midst of Jerusalem: and they shall be my people, and I will be their God." Now let us note who is not allowed into Jerusalem. Revelation 21:27 says, "And there shall in no wise enter into it [Jerusalem] any thing that defileth, neither whatsoever worketh abomination, or maketh a lie: but they which are written in the Lamb's Book of Life." This means many unsaved people survive Armageddon. This is why Satan deceives a number as the sands of the sea. It is only the people who are written in the lamb's book of life who can enter Jerusalem and eat from the tee of life. This is the beginning of the fulfillment of the prophecy given in Genesis 49:10, "Unto him [the Jews] shall the gathering of the people be."

Its equivalent message is given in the Old Testament in Ezekiel 39:28-29:

> Then shall they [the house of Israel] know the Lord their God, which caused them to be led into captivity among the heathen: but I have gathered them unto their own land, and have left none of them any more there. Neither will I hid my face any more from them: for I poured out my spirit upon the house of Israel, saith the Lord God.

Note here that God poured out "my spirit" or the "Holy Spirit" upon the house of Israel. And this is after the battle of Armageddon. This is when God will gather the house of Israel and bring them back to the land of Israel. These are the people of whom Revelation 21:27 states "are written in the Lamb's Book of Life." These are the people of Revelation 22:4, "And they shall see his face; and his name shall be in their foreheads." The west country of Zechariah 8:7 is the Christian country, which are the lost tribes of the house of Israel, where the Lord Jesus told them to spread the gospel.

Ezekiel tells us in 43:4: "And the glory of the Lord came into the house [the holy Jerusalem of Revelation] by the way of the gate whose prospect is toward the east."

This is the greater message of the Bible. It's the people of "Blessed are the meek: for they shall inherit the earth." This is where 1 Corinthians 15:53 comes in: "And this mortal (body) must put on immortality." We will live for all eternity in the presence of the Lord. This is the answer to our daily prayer in Matthew 6:10: "Thy kingdom come. Thy will be done on earth as it is in heaven." Let's note 1 Thessalonians 5:23, "And the very God of peace sanctify [the Greek word meaning "to put into a state corresponding to the nature of God"[12]] you wholly; and I pray God your whole spirit and soul and body be preserved blameless unto the coming of our Lord Jesus Christ." This is 1 John 3:2, "When he shall appear, we shall be like him," for the church will have immortal bodies like his.

Let's note Revelation 21:7, "He that overcometh shall inherit all things, and I will be his god, and he shall be my son." The Christians who overcome all the judgments in this book will inherit all things. This is the message to the seven churches that are in Asia. These are the people of Revelation 21:27, "They which are written in the Lamb's Book of Life," who get to enter into this city.

Revelation 22:14 says "Blessed are they that do his commandments, that they may have the right to the tree of life, and may enter in through the gates into the city." This should be the goal of every Christian, to "do his commandments" and endure until the end. And how do the Christians do his commandments? In Matthew 22:37–40, Jesus says, "Thou shalt love thy God with all thy heart, and all thou soul, and all thy mind. This is the first and great commandment. And the second

---

[12]   *Bullinger's*, 660.

is like unto it, Thou shalt love thy neighbor as thyself. On these two commandments hang all the law and the prophets." Let's note here "thy heart," which I believe means the body. Then "thou soul" and "thy mind," which I believe is the spirit as three separate entities. These are the people who are "Blessed are those that inherit the earth." They are not involved in the environmentalists' nightmare and are not looking for this "big lie," the pre-tribulation rapture. We are also to note Psalms 104:35, "Let the sinners be consumed out of the earth, and let the wicked be no more. Blessed thou the Lord, O my soul. Praise ye the Lord." And why are the sinners consumed out of the earth? Because "Blessed are the meek, for they shall inherit the earth."

We also have the Lord Jesus telling us in John 17:15, "I pray not that thou shouldest take them out of the world, but that thou shouldest keep them from evil." The word "take" is *airo*,[13] which means to lift; by implication to take up or away; figurative to raise (the voice), keep in suspense (the mind). The Lord here is praying against this so-called pre-tribulation rapture where the Greek word means to take up or away. Note also what John 17:15 says, "Keep them from evil." This is the answer to our daily prayer in Matthew 6:13, "Deliver us from evil." We will see in scripture that this Greek word is not used when the Lord speaks to the church. The word for keep is *tereo*,[14] which means to guard (from loss or injury) properly by keeping the eye upon. This is the word mostly used when it speaks to the church, the meek that inherit the earth. This is told to us in Psalms 37:11, 76:9, Isaiah 11:4, 29:19, Zephaniah 2:3, and Matthew 5:5.

And to preachers who claim to be the Philadelphia church, the Lord says to the Philadelphia church that he will, "Keep you from the hour of temptation" in Revelation 3:10 and not take them out. This is even how the Lord instructed us to pray in Matthew 6:13: "And lead us not into temptation, but deliver us from evil." The word "deliver" is *rhuomai*,[15] which means to rush or draw (for oneself) (i.e., to rescue).

---

[13] *Strong's*, 2015.
[14] Ibid., 2164.
[15] Ibid., 2149.

Note the Greek word to rescue. If there was a pre-tribulation rapture, there would be no rescue.

First Timothy 3:5 says, "If any man teach otherwise, and consent not to wholesome words, even the words of our Lord Jesus Christ, and to the doctrine which is according to his godliness. He is proud, knowing nothing, but doting about questions and strifes of words, whereof cometh envy, strife, railings, evil surmisings [*huponoia*,[16] which means suspicion, surmising. From *huponoeo*, which means to think under (i.e., to surmise or conjecture), think, suppose, deem]."

This pre-tribulation rapture is nothing but conjecture. We should note that Timothy said, "Even the words of the Lord Jesus Christ." And what are the words of the Lord Jesus Christ? Jesus tells us in Matthew 34:13 and Mark 13:13, "But he that shall endure until the end, the same shall be saved." He also says:

> For the Son of Man shall come in the Glory of his Father with his angels; and then shall reward every man according to his works. Verily I say unto you, There shall be some standing here, which shall not taste of death, till they see the Son of Man coming in his kingdom.

It is not until we endure to the end and see the coming of the Lord that we don't taste death. Note the language says "standing here." This is the answer to our daily prayer, "Thy kingdom come." This means here on the earth. Romans 14:4 tells us, "For God is able to make him stand." And now let's finish with verse 5: "Perverse disputings of men of corrupt minds, and destitute of the truth, supposing that gain is godliness: from such withdraw thyself." You pre-tribulation rapture preachers are destitute of the truth, and the people who attend your churches are told, "Withdraw thyself." This is reason I named this manuscript *The Big Lie, Exposed*, because there is not a pre-tribulation, or the living church, rapture to heaven.

---

[16]   Ibid., 2170.

Another prophecy worth noting is in the next scripture, Luke 21:25–28. The Lord says:

> And there shall be signs in the sun, and in the moon, and in the stars; and upon the earth distress of nations, with perplexity; the seas and the waves roaring; Men's hearts failing them for fear, and for looking after those things which are coming upon the earth: for the powers of heaven shall be shaken. And then shall they see the Son of Man coming in a cloud with power and great glory. And when these things begin to come to pass, then look up your heads; for your redemption draweth nigh.

We should first note here that the Lord Jesus warns the church about the distress of nations. He warns that the seas and the waves would be roaring. And then the powers [*dunamis*,[17] which means force (literal or figurative), specifically miraculous power] of heaven shall be shaken, and then shall they see the Son of Man coming [*erchomai*,[18] which means to come or go, accompany, appear] in a cloud with power and great glory. And when these things begin to come to pass, what happens? Your redemption [*apolutrosis*,[19] which means ransom in full, (specifically) Christian salvation] draws nigh [*eggizo*,[20] which means; to make near] Once again, Christians will see the coming of the Lord in a cloud when Christian salvation is near. This is also the "meek which inherit the earth." These are those who don't taste death till they see the coming of the Lord. This is also the answer to our daily prayer, "Thy kingdom come, Thy will be done on earth as it is in heaven." The living Christian church is on the planet when the Lord returns, just as we are told in Joel 2:1, "Blow ye the trumpet in Zion, and sound an alarm in

---

[17] Ibid., 2058.
[18] Ibid., 2079.
[19] Ibid., 2032.
[20] Ibid., 2059.

my holy mountain: let all the inhabitants of the land tremble: for the day of the Lord cometh, for it is nigh at hand."

Was the tsunami of December 2004 not an example to us that this is just what the Bible tells us is going to happen before the return of the Lord? Were the hurricanes that hit Mississippi and Louisiana not examples of the seas and the waves roaring? Is this not a warning from the Lord that if you live on the coast, you are in greater danger during the tribulation period? This is when the seas will be roaring. We should note Matthew 8:26, which says, "And he saith unto them, Why are thou fearful, O ye of little faith? Then he arose, and rebuked the winds and the sea; and there was a great calm." Only God can control the weather. We think man can control the global weather, but this is nothing but utter stupidity on man's part. There is one thing, and I almost forgot to put it here. Get on your knees and pray to God, the only God, the Lord Jesus Christ.

We should note that 150 million people, a quarter of the total population of America, live in the coastal cities in America and are in the danger areas during the tribulation period. Is the Lord sending us messages in these signs that Bible prophecy is coming to pass? Revelation 6:14 says, "And the heaven departed as a scroll when it is rolled together; and every mountain and island were moved out of their places." The island of Sumatra was moved out of its place in 2004.

God is sending us warning signs that Bible prophecy is coming to pass. The church will see this happen, for it states in verse 28, "And when these things begin to come to pass, then look up, and lift up your heads; for your redemption draweth nigh." The word for nigh is *eggizo*,[21] which means make near (i.e., reflexive); approach, be at hand, come (draw) near. Who redeems us but the Lord? The Greek meanings show that he will be near or at hand. Notice our redemption draws near and the church is to look up. We are to look up to see the Son of Man appearing. And when does this redemption come? That would be in verse 27, "And then they shall see the Son of Man coming in a cloud with power and great glory." But if there is a pre-tribulation rapture where we don't see the coming of the Lord, then rip these scriptures out

---

21   Ibid., 2059.

of your Bible. And now to verse 31, which says, "So likewise ye, when ye see these things come to pass, know ye that the kingdom of God is nigh (near) at hand." The Lord tells us this twice, in verses 27 and 31, that we will see these things come to pass. And this is when the Lord will answer our daily prayer of Matthew 6:10, "Thy kingdom come. Thy will be done on earth, as it is in heaven."

When we get to verse 34, it states, "And take heed to yourselves, lest at any time your hearts be overcharged [*barus*,[22] meaning burdensome] with surfeiting [*kraipale*,[23] meaning properly a headache, probably *harpazo*,[24] which means to seize, a derivative to *aihreomai*,[25] meaning to take for oneself, probably akin *airo*,[26] which means a primary verb; to lift; by implication to take up or away]." Note the Greek word meaning "to take up." This is when 1 Thessalonians 4:17 says "Then we which are alive and remain shall be caught up together with them in the clouds, to meet the Lord in the air." And what is in the air? Revelation 21:3 says, "And I heard a voice from heaven saying, Behold, the tabernacle of God is with men, and he will dwell with them, and they shall be his people, and God himself shall be with them, and be their God." Let's finish 1 Thessalonians 4:17, "And so shall we ever be with the Lord." This matches Revelation 21:3, "God himself shall be with them."

The tabernacle is the place of protection from God's wrath, as stated in Psalms 27:5: "For in the time of trouble he shall hide me in his pavilion: in the secret of his tabernacle shall he hide me; he shall set me up upon a rock." And what is that rock of Psalms 27:5? Revelation 21:10 says, "And he carried me away in the spirit to a great and high mountain, and shewed me that great city, the holy Jerusalem, descending out of heaven from God." The rock of Psalms 27:5 is the great and high mountain of Revelation 21:10. And what does John see in Revelation 21:9? "Come hither, I will shew thee the bride, the

---

[22]   Ibid., 2041.
[23]   Ibid., 2103.
[24]   Ibid., 2034.
[25]   Ibid., 2015.
[26]   Ibid., 2015.

lamb's wife." This is the resurrected dead church. And when does John see this? Revelation 21:9 says, "And there come unto me one of the seven angels which had the seven vials full of the seven last plagues." John sees the resurrected dead church just as the lasts plagues are about to be poured out.

This is why Zechariah14:16 tells us, "And it shall come to pass that every one that is left of all the nations which came against Jerusalem shall even go up from year to year to worship the King, the Lord of hosts, and to keep the feast of tabernacles." And the New Testament equivalent verse is Revelation 21:24, "And the nations of them which are saved shall walk in the light of it: and the kings of the earth do bring their glory and honour into it." This is why everyone will keep the feast of tabernacles. It's because it was a place of protection from the wrath of God.

I also believe that the Christians who are called up to meet the Lord in the air are these people. Matthew 25:23 says, "Well done, good and faithful servant; thou hast be faithful over few things, I will make thee ruler over many things: enter the joy of the lord." In the parable of the laborers, the vineyard (earth) owner (Lord Jesus) paid the laborers the same penny whether they worked all day or just an hour. The ones who worked all day murmured. And the Lord Jesus tells them in Matthew 20:16, "So the last shall be first, and the first last: for many are called and few are chosen." The "we which are caught up in the air" come back to rule and reign and are the few that are chosen.

Now let's go to Matthew 24:39, "So shall also the coming of the Son of Man be." "Coming" in the *Strong's Complete Word Study Concordance* Greek is the word on page 2131, *parousia,* which means a being near (i.e., advent, physical aspect, coming presence). It is the Lord that is something near. Now let's finish the verse in Luke 21:34, "And drunkenness, and the cares of this life, and so that day come upon you unawares." "Unawares" in *Strong's Complete Word Study Concordance* Greek word on page 2015 is *aiphnidios,* meaning unexpected or suddenly. Christians will not expect to be here during the tribulation period. This is because of the pre-tribulation rapture, in which preachers teach we are not here at this time.

Let's check verse 35: "For as a snare shall it come on all them that dwell on the face of the earth." "Snare" is *pag-ece,*[27] meaning a trap, figuratively a trick or temptation. That temptation comes from Satan to trick us to take his mark. And then in verse 36 it says, "Watch ye therefore, and pray always, that ye may be accounted worthy to escape all these things that shall come to pass, and stand before the Son of Man." Who is the Lord telling to watch and pray but the church when this trick or temptation comes, and those who escape will stand before the Son of Man. That means the church is here during this time of temptation.

---

[27]   Ibid., 2127.

Judaism, Christianity, Islam

THIS CHAPTER WILL REVEAL these three religions, two of which are not known until hundreds years later. If the Jewish Pharisees in the time of Jesus knew the scriptures, they would have known this.

Let us note Isaiah 22. I will start with verse 17: "Behold, the Lord will carry thee away with a mighty captivity, and I will surely cover [*atah*,[28] which means to wrap (i.e., to cover, set aside)] thee." That captivity happened in AD 70 when Rome scattered the Jews throughout the Roman Empire. Note that Hebrew word means set aside.

Let us look at verses 18 and 19: "He will surely violently turn and toss thee like a ball into a large country: there shalt thou die, and there the chariots of thy glory shall the shame of thy Lord's house. And I will drive thee from thy station [*matstsab*,[29] which means a fixed spot; figurative an office, a military post], and from thy state shall he pull thee down."

The next verse proves the Roman Empire captivity is after the crucifixion of Jesus Christ. Look at the language. It says "a large country," one country, and that is the Roman Empire.

---

[28] Ibid., 1934.

[29] Ibid., 1906.

Verse 20 says, "And it shall come to pass in that day, that I will call my servant Eliakim [*Elyaqiym*,[30] which means God of raising, from the Hebrew word *el*,[31] which means as adjective mighty, especially the Almighty, God], the son of Hilkiah [*Chilqiyyah*,[32] which means portion of Jah, from *Yah*,[33] which means Jah–the Lord]." The God of raising is the Lord Jesus, who is the portion of (the Father) Jah. Note the term the God of raising. This is just what the Lord Jesus did after his crucifixion. He brought up all the spirits of men from the middle of the earth and took them to heaven. Also notice the Hebrew Jah–the Lord is found in Psalms 68:4: "Sing unto God, sing praises to his name: extol him that rideth upon the heavens by his name Jah, and rejoice before him."

Verse 21 says, "And I will clothe him with thy robe, and strengthen him with thy girdle, and I will commit thy government into his hands: and he shall be father to the inhabitants of Jerusalem, and to the house of Judah." The Lord Jesus in John 10:30 states, "I and the Father are one."

Verse 22 says, "And the key of the house of David will I lay upon his shoulders; so shall he open, and none shall shut; and he shall shut, and none shall open." It also says the "key to the house of David" is given in Revelation 3:7: "And the angel of the church in Philadelphia write; These things saith he that hath the key of David, he that openeth, and no man shutteth, and no man openeth."

Verse 23 says, "And I will fasten him as a nail in a sure place; and he shall be for a glorious throne to his father's house." That sure place is the cross. The Lord Jesus tells us of his father's house in John 14:2–3: "In my Father's house are many mansions: if it were not so, I would have told you. I go to prepare a place for you. And if I go and prepare a place for you, I will come again, and receive you into myself; that were I am, there ye may be also." And the next verse tells us, "I will come again."

---

[30] Ibid., 1812.

[31] Ibid., 1810.

[32] Ibid., 1857.

[33] Ibid., 1871.

Verse 24 says, "And they shall hang upon him all the glory of his father's house, the offspring [*tse' esta*,[34] which means issue (i.e., produce children, that which cometh forth)], and the issue [*tsphiah*,[35] which means an outcast thing], all vessels of small quantity; from the vessels of cups [*aggan*,[36] which means a bowl], even to the vessels of the flagons [*nebel*,[37] which means a skin-bag for liquids; hence, a vase]."

Note the Hebrew word that means a bowl and a vase is given in Revelation 16:1, "And I heard a great voice out of the temple saying to the seven angels, 'Go your ways, and pour out the vials of the wrath of God upon the earth.'" Now let's note the language of verse 25, "In that day, saith the Lord of hosts, shall the nail that is fastened in a sure place be removed, and be cut down, and fall; and the burden that was upon it shall be cut off: for the Lord hath spoken it." The sure place is faith in the Lord Jesus and the burden that was put upon it is cut off by its "burden removed." And that burden that was removed is the Law of Moses, because scripture tells us in Ephesians 2:8, "For by grace are ye saved through faith; and not of yourselves: it is the gift of God."

This message in Isaiah is recorded also by the prophet Zechariah, but the prophet Zechariah has added something new. The world today has three main religions: Judaism, Christianity, and Islam. All three are revealed in Zechariah. Isaiah told us to put precept upon precept, here a little and there a little, and we will begin at verse 8: "Three shepherds also I cut off in one month; and my soul lothed [*aster*,[38] which means to dock off (i.e., curtail), especially to harvest (grass or grain)] them, and their souls also abhorred [*bachal*,[39] which means to loathe me. Shepherds is *ra ah*,[40] which means to tend a flock, generally to rule]." We will see this is the Jewish, Christian, and Muslim religions. They have three different shepherds. God will cut off all three when he comes

---

[34]   Ibid., 1952.

[35]   Ibid., 1956.

[36]   Ibid., 1804.

[37]   Ibid., 1914.

[38]   Ibid., 1963.

[39]   Ibid., 1822.

[40]   Ibid., 1972.

and rules when as the Hebrew word meaning says at the harvest. Why does God say all three shepherds loathe me? The Jewish and Islamic religions reject the Lord Jesus Christ. The Christian churches have put their congregations under the curse of the law. This means they reject the work that the Lord Jesus did on the cross.

Also note the language here that it says to harvest (grain) the soul. Grain in Hebrew is turned into wheat in 1 Corinthians 15:37, "It may change of wheat, or some other grain." This leads us to the parable about the tares among wheat in Matthew 13:30, which states, "Let both grow together until the harvest: and in the time of the harvest I will say to the reapers, Gather ye together first the tares, and bind them in bundles to burn them: but gather the wheat into my barn." And to find out when the time of the harvest is to come, we go to Revelation 14:15, which states, "Thrust thy sickle, and reap; the time has come for thee to reap; for the harvest of the earth is reaped." And when is the harvest? Revelation 14:19 says, "And the angel thrust in his sickle into the earth, and gathered the vine of the earth, and cast it into the great winepress of the wrath of God." John sees another sign in heaven that is great and marvelous.

And what does John see? Revelation 15:2 says, "And I saw as it were a sea of glass mingled with fire: and them that gotten the victory over the beast, having the harps of God." And when will this sign in heaven appear? It is immediately after the tribulation of those days. The sun will be darkened, and the moon will not give her light, and then the sign of the Son of Man will appear in heaven. The Lord Jesus will be "Lord of lords and King of kings over all the earth." And it tells us it will happen at the harvest. This is the precept upon precept, line upon line that Isaiah told us to do to understand Bible prophecies.

Verse 10 says, "And I took my staff, even Beauty, and cut asunder, that I might break the covenant, which I had made with all the people." The Beauty and cut asunder is the house of Judah, and the covenant that is broken is the Law of Moses. Verse 11 says, "And it was broken in that day: and so the poor of the flock that waited upon me knew that it was the word of the Lord." That day is when the Messiah Jesus came to the earth. Note the poor of the flock.

This is the verse that is the precept to Zechariah in Isaiah 61:1, "The Spirit of the Lord is upon me; because the Lord hath appointed me to preach good tidings to the meek; he hath sent me to bind up the brokenhearted, to proclaim liberty to the captives, and the opening of the prison to them that are bound." The Lord Jesus preaches to the poor and the meek of the earth. To proclaim liberty to the captives, those who accept Jesus as the word and are no longer under the law of Moses, and to open the prisons of those who are bound. Jesus fulfilled this on the third day when he was raised from the grave. He brought up the dead who were the prisoners in the middle of the earth.

Verse 12 says, "And I said unto them, if ye think good, give me my price; and it forbear, So they weighed for my price thirty pieces of silver." Note the "if ye think good." This is Matthew 19:17. The Lord is speaking and says, "Why callest thou me good? There is none good but one, that is God: but if thou wilt enter into life, keep the commandments." Note Jesus states here one that is God—one God. So they weighed [*shaqal*,[41] which means to suspend or poise (especially in trade), pay, receive]. And this is Matthew 26:15, "And [Judas Iscariot] said unto them, What will ye give me, and I will deliver unto you? And they covenanted with him thirty pieces of silver."

Verse 13 says, "And the Lord said unto me, Cast it into the potter; a goodly price that I was prised at of them. And I took the thirty pieces of silver, and cast them to the potter in the house of the Lord." Matthew 26:15 says, "And he said unto them, What will ye give me, and I will deliver him unto you? And they covenanted with him for thirty pieces of silver."

Verse 14 says, "Then I cut asunder mine other staff [*maqqel*,[42] which means to germinate, a shoot (i.e., stick)], even Bands, that I might break the brotherhood between Judah and Israel." Note "mine other staff [stick]." The other stick is the reference to Ezekiel 37:19, "Behold, I will take the stick of Joseph, which is the hand of Ephraim, and the tribes of Israel his fellows, and I will put them with him, even with the stick of Judah, and they shall be one in my hand." This

---

[41] Ibid., 1994.
[42] Ibid., 1907.

brotherhood that is broken in Zechariah is unbroken in Ezekiel 37. We might want to note this is just before the battle of Armageddon in chapters 38 and 39. Also note "cut the bonds, that I might break" of Zechariah. This matches Psalms 2:3, "Let us break their bands asunder, and cast their cord from us."

Before we start with verse 15, remember in verse 8 there were three shepherds. The first shepherd, Jehovah, was the God of the Jews. The second shepherd is Jesus Christ, the God of the Christians, and verse 15 tells us what the Lord says about the last of the three shepherds.

Verse 15 says "And the Lord said unto me, Take unto thee yet the instruments of a foolish [*evility*,[43] which means silly, foolish, from *eviyl*,[44] which means to be perverse] shepherd." This third shepherd is perverse. Note the Hebrew word *eviyl*, which is pronounced ev-eel. This is the English evil. Compare this with 2 Timothy 1:15, "This thou knowest, that all they which are in Asia be turned away from me." The Greek word for turned means pervert, which is the same as the Hebrew word perverse. And then we are told in Acts 16:6, "Now when they had gone throughout Phrygia and the region of Galatia, and were forbidden of the Holy Ghost to preach the word in Asia." So why were the disciples forbidden by the Holy Ghost to go to Asia?

Asia during the Roman Empire days was the Middle East. Because of their hatred for the tribes of Jacob, God sent them a messenger to keep them in a strong delusion. This is the evil Isaiah tells us God created. And the Lord God's answer to why the disciples were not to allow the Word of God in Asia is in Malachi 1:4, "The people (Edom) against whom the Lord hath indignation for ever." Note that for indignation is *za-am*,[45] which means properly to form at the mouth (i.e., to be enraged, abominable, angry). And when will the Lord's indignation happen? We go to Isaiah 34:2, 5–8: "For the indignation of the Lord is upon all nations [Armageddon], and his fury is upon all their armies: he hath utterly destroyed them, he hath delivered them to the slaughter. For my sword shall be bathed in heaven: behold, it

---

[43] Ibid., 1806.

[44] Ibid.

[45] Ibid., 1849.

shall come down upon Idumea [Edom] upon the people of my curse, to judgment. For it is the day of the Lord's vengeance, and the year of recompences for the controversy of Zion." We should note here that scripture tells us that the wrath of God is against the armies, just as in Ezekiel 38. And the next verse will prove this is Muhammad's Allah.

Verse 16 says, "For, lo, I will raise up a shepherd in the land, which shall not visit those that are cut off, neither shall seek the young one, nor heal that is broke, feed that standest still: but he shall eat the flesh of the fat, and tear their claws into pieces." First note here that God said, "I raised up this shepherd." Note this shepherd will not seek the young one. Young is *na'ar*,[46] which means a boy, from the age of infancy to adolescence, by implication a servant. A boy means a son, and when the Lord Jesus became a man, he became a servant.

Muhammad's Allah declares he has no son. When people die, their souls go back to God, but the spirit of a man goes to the middle of the earth. Satan isn't in either place, so he will not visit them. Also note "feed that standest still." Note Matthew 24:45, which says, "Who then is a faithful and wise servant, whom his Lord hath made ruler over his household, to give them meat in due season." The Lord Jesus will feed his flock; Allah won't. Romans 14:4 says, "Who art thou that judgest another man's servant? To his own master he standest or fallest. Yea, he shall be holden up; for God is able to make him stand." The Lord Jesus will uphold so we are able to stand; Allah won't.

In Zechariah, God wants the friendship of the house of Israel and the house of Judah to end. If the house of Israel became Europe, England, and America, this prophecy was fulfilled. All during the dark ages, the Christians of Europe made the Jews second-class citizens. They had to live in the slums, and when they refused Christianity, they were forced to leave that country. Before the outbreak of World War II, about four hundred Jewish people got on an ocean liner trying to flee Hitler's Germany. Franklin Roosevelt would not let them emigrate to America. They were also turned down in other countries. When they got back to Germany, many were killed in the concentration camps. This was documented on the History Channel. Near the end of the

---

46   Ibid., 1921.

age, God will make the one in his hand, as stated in Ezekiel 37. This tells us that the house of Israel became the Christians of Europe and the Jews are who they are still. This is the same message.

Psalms 2:1–12 says:

> Why do the heathen rage, and the people imagine a vain thing? The kings of the earth set themselves, and the rulers take counsel together, against the Lord, and against his anointed saying, Let us break their bands asunder from us. He that sitteth in the heavens shall laugh: the Lord will have them in derision. Then shall he speak unto them in his wrath, and vex them in his sore displeasure. Yet have I set my king upon my holy hill of Zion. I will declare the decree: the Lord hath said unto me, Thou art my Son; this day have I begotten thee. Ask of me, and I shall give thee the heathen for thine inheritance, and the uttermost parts of the earth for thy possession. That shall break them with the rod of iron; thou shalt dash them in pieces like a potter's vessel. Be wise now therefore, O ye kings: be instructed, ye judges of the earth. Serve the Lord with fear and rejoice with trembling. Kiss the Son, lest he be angry, and ye perish from the way, when his wrath is kindled but a little. Blessed are all they that put their trust in him.

Note that Psalms tells us "the Lord will have them in derision." He is talking about the Pharisees where it states God anointed. Note that it says, "Let us break their bands asunder from us." The us is the Father and the Son. Bands here is *mowser*,[47] which means properly chastisement (i.e., by implication a halter). Also note the Lord Jesus will vex them with a sore displeasure. This was done when the Lord Jesus overturned the tables in the temple and in Matthew 23 where the Lord Jesus announced seven woes upon the Pharisees. Note in Psalms

---

[47]   Ibid., 1894.

it goes to the end of the age, when the Lord's wrath comes. Note it says, "Blessed are they that wait for him." We will read this many times in scripture, and it was given for a reason. We should note this is the same message given in Zechariah 11:11–14.

Isaiah, who lived during the eighth century BC, prophesied about the Lord Jesus seven hundred years before his appearance and about the prophet Muhammad fourteen hundred years before he appeared. We shall note Isaiah 44:5–8, which says, "One shall say, I am the Lord's; and another shall call himself by the name of Jacob [Jesus]; and another shall subscribe [*kathab*,[48] which means by implication to write, record], with his hand unto the Lord, and surname [*Kanah*,[49] which means to address by an additional name, hence, to eulogize, give flattering titles, surname (himself)], himself by the name of Israel." And this additional name would be Allah, whose flattering titles are: in the name of Allah, most gracious, ever merciful, the all seeing, the all knowing. He proclaims himself by the name of Israel. Muhammad claims that Allah led the Hebrews out of Egyptian bondage and Jesus is subject to the will of Allah. We should also note that Isaiah tells us that Jesus would come and after him would come the writings of Muhammad's Allah. Note that this prophecy given by Isaiah 44:5–8 will match what Jesus tells us in Luke 19: "But his servants hated him, and sent a message after him [the message that came after Jesus was Muhammad's Allah, which hates Jesus], saying, We will not have this man reign over us."

This is told to us in Revelation 2:9 and 3:8. These are the words of the Lord Jesus Christ. Revelation 2:9 says, "And I know the blasphemy of them that say they are Jew, and are not, but are the synagogue of Satan," and 3:9 says, "Behold, I will make them of the synagogue of Satan, which say they are Jews, and are not, but do lie; behold, I will make them to come and worship before thy feet, and to know that I have loved thee." The word "say" is the word[50] that means to lay forth (i.e., figurative), relate, affirming. Muhammad claims to affirm the

---

[48]   Ibid., 1887.
[49]   Ibid., 1884.
[50]   Ibid., 2107.

truth of previous revelations. These synagogues of Satan are among the churches of the Lord Jesus Christ, as noted here in the message to the churches. These are the people Jude warned us about in verse 4, which says, "For there are certain men crept in unawares, who were before old ordained to this condemnation, ungodly men, turning the grace of our God into lasciviousness, and denying the only Lord God, and our Lord Jesus Christ." Let us note that the Lord Jesus calls them synagogues of Satan. I just translated the scriptures.

Verse 6 says, "Thus saith the Lord the King of Israel, and his redeemer [*ga'al*,⁵¹ which means to redeem (i.e., to be the next of kin and to such to buy back a relative's property, marry his widow, etc., avenger, deliver, purchase)], the Lord of host: I am the first, and I am the last; and beside me there is no God." "The Lord, the King of Israel" is the Father, and the next of kin is the Son, and his redeemer is the Lord Jesus Christ, who redeemed us back to God the Father and purchased us back to God by dying on the cross for our sin. Isaiah tells us that the redeemer is the "Lord of hosts," which tells us that Jesus is the Father. Jesus states in Revelation 1:11, "I am the Alpha and Omega, the first and the Last." Let's note Isaiah 41:4, "I am the Lord, the first, and with the last; I am he." Note the language, "I am the Lord, 'with' the last, I am he." The Lord Jesus in John 10:30 states "I and the Father are one." Let us also note Matthew 23:34, "Wherefore, behold, I send unto you prophets." The Lord Jesus tells us here he sent the prophets, which makes him the Lord God, the Lord of hosts. Since scripture tells us here "beside me there is no God," then who are the Muslims praying to?

Verse 7 says, "And who, as I, shall call, and shall declare it, and set it in order for me, since I appointed the ancient people? And the things that are coming, and shall come, let them shew unto them." Isaiah tells us here that to prove that he is speaking the Word of God, he gives this message to the "ancient people," the people living over seven hundred years before it happened, of things that are to come.

Verse 8 says, "Fear ye not, neither be afraid; have I not told thee from that time, and have declared it? Ye are even my witnesses. Is there

---

⁵¹ Ibid., 1830.

a God besides me? Yea, there is no God; I know not any." The people of the eighth century BC were not to fear his words of the future; God is in control. The God Isaiah writes about in the previous verses is the only true God. Isaiah tells us again in 45:21, "There is no God else beside me; a just God and a Saviour; there is none beside me." We should note we are told in 45:23, "That unto me every knee shall bow, every tongue shall swear [*shaba*,[52] which means to be complete]."

We will compare these Old Testament scriptures with their New Testament equivalent in Philippians 2:9–11: "Wherefore God also hath highly exalted him, and given him a name which is above every name: That at the name of Jesus every knee should bow, of things in heaven, and things in earth, and things under the earth; And that every tongue should confess that Jesus Christ is Lord, to the glory of God the Father." The just God and Savoir to which every knee should bow to is the Savior revealed in Jesus Christ of the New Testament. Note the Hebrew word meaning to be complete. Jesus states in Matthew 5:17, "Think not that I am come to destroy the law or the prophets: I am not come to destroy, but fulfill," to be complete.

Now let's note Titus 3:10–11: "A man that is an heretick [aihretikos,[53] which means a schismatic, from *aihretizo*,[54] which means; to make a choice, from a derivative *nouthesia*,[55] which means; calling attention to (i.e., by implication mild rebuke or warning)." Let us note here what a schismatic means in the *Webster's Dictionary*: "one who creates or takes part in schism." Schism in *Webster's Dictionary* means "division, separation; also discord, disharmony; a formal division in or separation from a church or religious body"] after the first and second admonition [*nouthesia*,[56] which means calling attention to (i.e., by implication mild rebuke or warning). The Greek means "to put into mind to instruct, warn."[57] It refers to instruction by the word "reject."]

---

[52] Ibid., 1976.
[53] Ibid., 2015.
[54] Ibid.
[55] Ibid.
[56] Ibid., 2119.
[57] *Bullinger's*, 27.

knowing that he that is such is subverted [*ekstrepho*,[58] which means to pervert (figurative)], and sinneth, being condemned to himself." That man would be Muhammad, and he rebukes the first and second testaments of the Bible. We are told here that a man will reject the admonition that came after the first and second. He has perverted the people to believe that the God of heaven is Allah. Note that Titus says "being condemned to himself" and the Old Testament equivalent in Zechariah "which shall not visit that be cut off." In the book written by Muhammad Zafrulla Khan it states, "But it points out that the previous revelations have suffered from interpolations and perversions, at the hands of those whose duty it was to safeguard them" (2:80, 3:70). This is the spirit of the Antichrist.

In Luke 22:25–27, we have the words of the Lord Jesus.

Verse 25 tells us, "The Lord of the Gentiles exercise lordship [*kurieuo*,[59] which means to rule, have dominion, to rule, Lord] over them; and they that exercise authority upon them are called benefactors." The Qur'an tells us that the meaning of the Qur'an is the recited and rehearsed "He [Allah] created man from a clot of blood. Recite, for thy Lord is Most Beneficent, as quoted in the Qur'an in 96:2–6." This is exactly as the Lord Jesus tells us the lord of the Gentiles would say.

Then we have the parable of the long journey and the ten pounds in Luke 19:12–18. The Lord Jesus says:

> A certain nobleman [Jesus] went to a far country [heaven] to receive for himself a kingdom [the throne of God] and to return [Matthew 24:30 says, "And then shall the Lord appear in heaven"]. And he called his ten servants [ten tribes of the house of Israel], and he delivered them ten pounds [and five of them were wise, and five were foolish], and said unto them, Occupy [only given here in Luke; occupy

---

[58]   *Strong's*, 2066.

[59]   Ibid., 2105.

pragmateuomai,[60] which means to busy oneself with (i.e., to trade). From *pragma*,[61] which means a deed; by implication an affair, by extension an object; business, matter, work, which means to go about your normal business and to spread the gospel of Christ.] till I come [Luke 21:27 says, "And then shall they see the Son of Man coming in a cloud with power and great glory". This is the message the church needs to hear. We are to spread the gospel of Jesus Christ until when? Until the Lord Jesus comes.]

But the citizens [those who have not accepted Jesus as Lord] hated [*miseo*,[62] which means to detest (especially to persecute)] him, and sent a message [the message that came after Jesus was given by Muhammad in seventh century, that Allah is God] after him [Lord Jesus], We will not have this man [Jesus] rule over us. And it came to pass, that went he [Jesus] was returned [Luke 21:26 says, "And then shall they see the Son of Man coming in a cloud with power and great glory."], having received the kingdom [the kingdom here on earth] then he [Jesus] commanded these servants [the ten tribes of the house of Israel] to be called [back to the land of Israel] unto him [First Thessalonians 16:17 says, "For the Lord himself shall descend from heaven with a shout, with the voice of the archangel, and the trump of God: and the dead in Christ shall rise first: Then we which are alive and remain shall be caught up together with him in the clouds, to meet the Lord in the air: so shall we ever be with the Lord."], to whom he have given the money [the gospel], that he [Jesus] might know how much every man gained

---

60   Ibid., 2140.

61   Ibid.

62   Ibid., 2115.

by trading [spreading the good news of the gospel of Jesus Christ].

> Then came the first, saying, Lord thy pound [gospel] hath gained ten pounds [spirits, to the saving knowledge of Christ]. And he said unto him, Well, thou good servant: because thou hast been faithful in a very little, have thou authority over ten cities. And the second came, saying, Lord, thy pound hath gained five pounds. And he said likewise to him, Be thou over five cities.

It is only the servants who win spirits for the Lord who have remained alive until the coming of the Lord, because it is they who rule with Christ here. These are the people of 1 Thessalonians 4:15: "We which are alive and remain unto the coming of the Lord and meet the Lord in the air." In the air is where these people are instructed on how they shall use their authority over these cities.

Let's note Revelation 22:12: "And, behold, I come quickly; and my reward is with me, to give every man according as his work shall be." That reward and his work shall be of Revelation 22:12, which says, "Have thou authority over ten cities." One of these works is given in Ezekiel 39:14, "And they shall sever out men of continual employment, passing through the land to bury with the passengers those that remain upon the face of the earth, to cleanse it: after the end of seven months shall they search." Note the language of Ezekiel, "Those that remain upon the face of the earth." This is the reference to, "There shall be some standing here that shall not taste of death till they see the Son of Man coming in his kingdom" who don't taste of death.

I used the word "spirits" in the ten pounds because of 1 Corinthians 5:3, "That the spirit may be saved in the day of the Lord," and Acts 23:8, "For the Sadducees say that there is no resurrection, neither angel, nor spirit." The Lord tells us in verse 23, "Wherefore then gavest not thou my money [the gospel] into the bank [the world], that at my coming I might have required mine own with usury?" It is until the Lord's coming that we are to spread the gospel. In verse 27, we are told,

"But those my enemies, which would not that I should rule over them [Muslims], bring hither, and slay them before me." The enemies of Jesus Christ are the enemies Muhammad declared to be. In the Qur'an it states, "O ye who believe, make not friends with My enemy and your enemy." And the Lord Jesus says, "Slay them before me."

This parable matches the parable of the tares among wheat in Matthew 13:30, "Let them grow together until the time of the harvest I will say to the reapers, Gather ye together first the tares, and bind them in bundles to burn them: but gather the wheat into my barn." Note the language. Let them grow together until when? Until the time of the harvest. The time of the harvest is given in Revelation 14:14–15: "And I looked, and behold a white cloud, and upon the cloud one sat like unto the Son of man, having on his head a golden crown, and in his hand a sharp sickle. Thrust in thy sickle, and reap: for the time has come for thee to reap; for the harvest of the earth is ripe." This sounds to me like this is when the Lord shall appear in heaven.

The Lord appears in heaven immediately after the tribulation of those days when the sun and the moon don't give their light as given in Matthew 24:30. Also note it says in Matthew 13:30, "Gather the wheat into my barn," Barn is *apotheke*,[63] which means a repository. In *Webster's Dictionary* a repository means "a place, room, or container where something is deposited or stored." That "barn" is mentioned in Psalms 27:5: "For in the time of trouble he shall hide me in his pavilion: in the secret of his tabernacle shall he hide me" and this is when "his tabernacle shall hide me" in Revelation 21:3: "Behold, the tabernacle of God is with men, and he shall dwell with them, and they shall be his people, and God himself shall be with them." We will hear more about this later.

As you have just read, I believe the house of Israel is the ten servants. Why are there not six, twenty, thirty, or more virgins? It is because the Lord Jesus tells his disciplines, "Go ye to the ten lost tribes of the house of Israel," as stated in Matthew 10:6 and 15:24. Also, let's note 2 Thessalonians 1:13, "But we are bound to give thanks, always to God for you, brethren beloved of the Lord, because God hath from the

---

63   Ibid., 2030.

beginning chosen you to salvation through sanctification of the Spirit and belief of the truth." Who had God chosen from the beginnings? We go to Deuteronomy 7:6, which says, "For thou art an holy people unto the Lord thy God: the Lord thy God hath chosen thee to be a special people unto himself, above all people that are upon the face of the earth." The Lord God has not changed his mind. Although the Thessalonian people were not the lost tribes of the house of Israel, the message would get to them by this letter.

The Lord's Appearing

WE WILL ALSO NOTE in the scriptures that we are to wait for the appearing of Jesus Christ and coming. These are two different events in one. This is when the Lord will descend from heaven with a shout. Let's note that these scriptures are given to the church as the appearing message to them. Let us note Colossians 3:4, "When Christ, who is our life, shall appear." The word "appear" in the Greek is *phaneroo*,[64] which means to render apparent (literal or figurative), appear, manifestly declared, (made) manifest (forth), or show (self). Now let us finish the verse: "Then shall ye also appear with him in glory." To appear in glory is *doxa*,[65] which means glory (as very apparent) in a wide application (literal or figurative, object or subject), dignity, honor, praise. It is not until the Lord appears that the saints appear with him. We are also given this in Hebrews 9:28: "And unto them that look for him shall appear the second time."

The word for appear is *optanomai*,[66] which means properly to stare at, by implication, to discern clearly. It is from the word *optomai*, as an alternate *horao*, which means to gaze (i.e., with eyes wide-open, as at something remarkable). Let's note 1 John 2:28, "And now, little children, abide in him; that, when he shall appear, we may have

---

[64] Ibid., 2171.
[65] Ibid., 2057.
[66] Ibid., 2123.

confidence, and not be ashamed before him at his coming." John also tells the church to look for Jesus's appearing, and after his appearing is his second coming, at which we are told the church will not be ashamed. The church is the meek who inherit the earth. We should note that this matches Matthew 24:30, "And then shall appear the sign of the Son of Man in heaven, and then they shall see the Son of Man coming in the clouds of heaven with power and great glory." Let also note interpretation of the word "sign" is, "A sign, a signal; an ensign, a standard; a sign by which anything is designated, distinguished, or known; hence, used of the miracles of Christ as being the signs by which He might be known as the Christ of God: a sign authenticating His mission; a sign with reference to what it demonstrates."[67] That miracle is the resurrection of the dead.

Paul also told in 1 Thessalonians 2:19, "For what is our hope, or joy, or crown of rejoicing? Are not even ye in the presence of our Lord Jesus Christ at his coming?" And we are told a second time in 5:23, "And the very God of peace sanctify you wholly; and I pray God your whole spirit and soul and body be preserved blameless unto the coming of our Lord Jesus Christ." We should note here that the body with the whole spirit "and" soul be preserved until the coming of the Lord and not his appearing. First Thessalonians 4:15 says, "For this we say unto you by the word of the Lord, that we which are alive and remain [*perileipo*,[68] which means to leave all around (i.e., passive) survive] unto the coming of the Lord shall not prevent [*phthano*,[69] which means to be beforehand (i.e., anticipate or precede) them that are asleep. We should note the Greek word meaning to survive till the coming of the Lord]."

"For blessed are the meek, for they shall inherit the earth. Those that have died appear at his [the Lord's] appearing, and those who are alive will meet the Lord in the air [*aer*,[70] which means to breathe unconsciously (i.e., respire)] at his coming." The word "coming"

67 *Bullinger's*, 701.
68 *Strong's*, 2134.
69 Ibid., 2172.
70 Ibid., 2014.

is *parousia*,[71] which means a being near (i.e., advent, often return; especially of Christ to punish Jerusalem, or finally the wicked); by implication physical aspect—coming, presence. It is also from the presumed participle of *pareimi*,[72] which means to be near (i.e., at hand). It is from the neuter presumed participle (singular) time being. The key Greek word means being near, coming.

First Peter 5:4 says, "And when the chief Shepherd shall appear, ye shall receive a crown of glory that fadeth not away." Jesus is also near in Matthew 24:30: "And then shall appear the Son of Man in heaven." Heaven is *ouranos*,[73] which means the sky. Note that the word for chief is the word *archipoimen*,[74] which means a head shepherd. The Old Testament equivalent of calling the Lord Jesus the shepherd is Zechariah 11:8. But now he is the chief shepherd.

Let us also note 1 Timothy 6:14: "That thou keep this commandment without spot, unrebukeable, until the appearing of our Lord Jesus Christ." The word for keep is *tereo*,[75] which means to guard (from loss or injury) properly by keeping an eye upon. Titus 2:13 says, "Looking for that blessed hope, and the glorious appearing of the great God and our Saviour Jesus Christ." If the church is to wait for his appearing, which we are told eight different times, how can there be a secret pre-tribulation rapture? In Revelation 4, when John is called to heaven, the Lord is on the throne and is not appearing to the earth. Let's note scripture. First Thessalonians 4:16 states, "For the Lord shall descend from heaven: and the dead in Christ will rise first." The word for descent means to go, to come down, to descend from a higher to a lower place.[76]

The Lord is not descending in Revelation 4 but is on the throne. I don't see how this could be the time of the resurrection of the dead. Without the Greek meanings, in plain English, we are told to wait for

---

[71]   Ibid., 2131.

[72]   Ibid.

[73]   Ibid., 2125.

[74]   Ibid., 2035.

[75]   Ibid., 2164.

[76]   *Bullinger's*, 217.

his appearing and coming. So someone has made a mistake. Paul says to wait for his appearing and coming. The pastors today tell us the church vanishes in a pre-tribulation rapture. Who do you believe? Scriptures tell us this. His appearing is not until after the tribulation when the sun and the moon don't give their light. It is stated in Matthew 24:30 and in Mark 13:26, "And then shall they see the Son of Man coming in the clouds with great power and glory." Who are they who expect to "see the Son of Man coming" if it is not the church of the Lord Jesus Christ? This is the answer to our daily prayer of Matthew 6:10, "Thy kingdom come. Thy will be done on earth as it is in heaven."

We have in Acts 3:19–21, "Repent ye therefore, and be converted, that your sins may be blotted out, when the times of refreshing [*anapsuxis*,[77] which means a recovery of breath (i.e., figurative revival), from *anapsucho*,[78] which means properly to cool off (i.e., figurative relieve). It is from *psucho*,[79] which means to breathe] shall come from the presence [*prosopon*,[80] which means the front (as being toward view), aspect, appearing] of the Lord; And he shall send Jesus Christ which before was preached unto you; Whom the heaven must receive until the times of restitution [*apokatastasis*,[81] which means reconstitution, restitution] of all things, which God hath spoken by the mouth of his holy prophets since the world begin." We should note the word meaning "a recovery of breath, properly to cool," to have life again. This happens at the time of the Lord Jesus's appearing, and when we look at the prophets of the old time or the Old Testament, we learn when the Lord shall appear. Also note this "recovery of breath" and the Greek meaning in 1 Thessalonians 4:16, "we which are alive and remain till the coming of the Lord are caught up in the air" (which means to breathe unconsciously) match.

So how can the pastor teach this pre-tribulation rapture? The appearing of Jesus Christ is not until after the tribulation of "those

---

[77] *Strong's*, 2024.

[78] Ibid., 2024.

[79] Ibid.

[80] Ibid., 2145.

[81] Ibid., 2031.

days," when the sun and the moon don't give their light. This is proven in this book. In the hit television series *Touched by an Angel,* Della Reese sings the song, "I will walk with you till the sun don't even shine." God has angels watching over his own until when? Till the sun don't even shine. When the "sun don't even shine" is when the Lord shall appear, as stated in Matthew 24:29–30.

Let us also note this. When the Lord appears in heaven in Matthew 24:30, it says, "And then shall all of the tribes of the earth mourn." Here is the promise for the church of the Lord Jesus in Matthew 5:4: "Blessed are they that mourn: for they shall be comforted." The precept to this verse is 2 Corinthians 1:3–4: "Blessed be God, and the God of all comfort; Who comforteth us in all our tribulation." This includes the tribulation of the last days. So if there is this secret pre-tribulation rapture, I say then rip those books out of your Bible, because they are not correct scripture. Now let's note "the dead in Christ rise first" at his appearing, and his appearing is now until immediately after the tribulation of those days when the sun and the moon don't give their light. This proves in plain and simple language there is not the "pre-tribulation of the living church" as preached by many pastors.

Resurrection of the Dead

Let's start with Philippians 3:10–11, That I may know him and the power of his resurrection, and the fellow ship of his sufferings, being made conformable unto his death; If by any means I might attain unto the resurrection of the dead." so he might attain the resurrection of the dead. Paul says you have to be dead to be resurrected. First Corinthians 15:13, 21 says, "But if there be no resurrection of the dead, then Christ is not risen. For since man came death, by man come also the resurrection of the dead." It's the resurrection of the dead and not the living. In no place in the scriptures does it speak of a resurrection of the living. The word "resurrection" means from the dead.

This makes the whole theory of the pre-tribulation rapture (resurrection) of the whole church, even the living, before the tribulation bogus. Find one verse in scripture, outside of the two Old Testament prophets, where God called someone to heaven before dying. We will read in this manuscript that one day they will die. As quoted in the scriptures, "We which are alive and remain until the coming of the Lord" means the church, the living church, is on the planet when the Lord returns. Those are the ones who don't taste of death until they see the coming of the Lord as stated by Matthew, Luke, and Mark.

Let's note and notice there are two questions in First Corinthians 15:35–36:

> But some men will say, How are the dead raised up? And with what body do they come. Thou fool, that which thou sowest [*speiro*,[82] which means strengthened] is not quicken [*suzoopoieo*,[83] which means to reanimate conjointly with], except it die.

Note the language of Paul, "Thou fool." It is apparent that to me the Corinthian Church thought there was a resurrection of the living church before the tribulation of their day. Paul tells them the resurrection is for the dead and the living are strengthened. This is the language God will use against pastors who preach the pre-tribulation resurrection of the living church. The resurrection of the church is for the dead, not the living. Paul tells us here that the Lord will strengthen the living. Let's note verse 37, "And that which thou soweth, thou soweth not that body that shall be, but bear grain, it may change of wheat, or some other grain." That other grain is given in the parable of the wheat and the tares in Matthew 13:24–30, where the wheat will be gathered into the Lord's barn and the tares are burned. What the Lord strengthens is not quickened or raised. Its Old Testament equivalent is Joel 3:16, "But the Lord will be the hope of his people, and the strength to the children of Israel." Note Hebrew word for strength is *ma owz*,[84] which means a fortified place; figuratively, a defense, from *azaz*,[85] which means to be stout, prevail. Note the Hebrew word meaning prevail and fortified place. That fortified place is told to us in Psalms 27:5, "For in the time of trouble he shall hid me in his pavilion: in the secret of his tabernacle shall he hide me" and Revelation 21:3, "Behold, the tabernacle of God is with men."

Acts 23:6, 8 says, "But when Paul perceived that the one part were Sadducees, and the other part Pharisees, he cried out in the council, Men and brethren, I am a Pharisees, the son of a Pharisees: of the hope of the resurrection of the dead I am called in question." Note here it

---

[82]   Ibid., 2153.
[83]   Ibid., 2084.
[84]   Ibid., 1904.
[85]   Ibid., 1934.

says "resurrection of the dead." "For the Sadducees say that there is no resurrection, neither angel, nor spirit: but the Pharisees confess both." Also note here that it says the resurrection is of the "spirit." Note here that it also says it is the dead spirit that is raised from the grave and not the soul. And again note "neither angel" is raised from the dead. The angels that refuse to be born on this earth will not be raised from the outer darkness where they were cast, as Isaiah states and as stated in Jude 1:6, "And the angels which kept not their first estate, but left their own habitation, he hath reserved in everlasting chains under darkness unto the judgment of the great day."

This tells us at the resurrection of the dead, the body of the living have "not that body that shall be." This is the immortal body, the body that is strengthened. Note also the reference to "it may change of wheat, or so other grain." This is the parable of the wheat and the tares in Matthew 13:30, "Let them both grow together till the time of the harvest I will say unto the reapers, Gather ye together first the tares [the some other grain of 1 Corinthians 15:37], and bind them in bundles to burn them: but gather the wheat [it may chance of wheat of 1 Corinthians 15:37] into my barn." Who is the wheat but the church? They are on the planet when the Lord will reign.

Also note Matthew 22:31–32, "But as touching the resurrection of the dead, have ye not read which was spoken unto you by God, saying, I am the God of Abraham, and the God of Isaac, and the God of Jacob? God is not the God of the dead, but of the living." Note the language "resurrection of the dead." In Hebrews 6:2 it says, "And of the resurrection of the dead." It's only the resurrection of the dead and not the living church. To be resurrected, you have to be dead, in plain and simple language. You will never read in the scriptures about the resurrection of the living. Let's note the Greek meaning for resurrection is "a standing up, rising up, as from the dead; hence, Resurrection."[86]

Let us also note the Lord Jesus speaking in John 5:21, 24: "For the Father raiseth up the dead, and quickened them; even so the Son quickeneth whom he will. Verily, verily, I say unto you, He that heareth my word, and believeth on him that sent me, hath everlasting life, and

---

[86]   *Bullinger's*, 643.

shall not come into condemnation; but is passed from death unto life." Note we are told here that the Lord "raiseth up the dead" and they will "pass from death to life."

In the scriptures, the dead are only associated with the word "resurrection". And to prove this is a good interpretation of scripture, let's note John 11:25–26 and 1 Thessalonians 4:14–15. In John, the Lord Jesus says, "I am the resurrection, and the life: he that believeth in me, though he were dead, yet shall he live. And whosoever liveth and believeth in me shall never die. Believest thou this?" Now let's match verse by verse John and 1 Thessalonians. John says, "I am the resurrection, He that believeth in me, though he were dead, yet shall he live" and 1 Thessalonians says "for if we believe that Jesus died and rose again, even so them which sleep [died] in Jesus will God bring with him." Now John says, "Whosoever liveth and believeth in me shall never die" and 1 Thessalonians says "For this we say unto you by the word of the Lord [the word given by Jesus in John], that we which are alive and remain unto the coming of the Lord." It's those who remain "whosoever liveth shall never die," because "blessed are the meek: for they shall inherit the earth." This is the true message the Bible tells us.

Those who never die, as stated in John, are the people of 1 Corinthians 15:53, "this mortal must put on immortality." It is those of whom the Lord Jesus states in Matthew 24:13, "Those that endure unto the end, the same shall be saved." The end comes in the thunders in Revelation 10:6–7, "that there should be time no longer where the mystery of God should be finished." The mystery of God is the church age. This is where Psalms 81:7 says, "Thou callest in trouble and I delivered thee; I answered thee in the secret place of thunder." In the secret place of thunder where "I delivered thee" is where as the Lord Jesus tells us, "All that call upon the name of the Lord shall be delivered." And why is this a secret place? Revelation 10:4 says, "And when the seven thunders had uttered their voices, I was about to write: and I heard a voice from heaven saying unto me, Seal up those things which the seven thunders uttered, and write them not." The seven thunders are the seven spirits of God. This is why it is a secret—because John was told not to write what the seven spirits thundered.

In Matthew 16:28, Mark 9:1, and Luke 9:27, we are told, "Verily I say unto you, There be some standing here, which shall not taste of death, till they see the Son of Man coming in his kingdom." This is the answer to our daily prayer of Matthew 6:10: "Thy kingdom come. Thy will be done on earth, as it is in heaven." Those who don't taste death are on the planet when the Lord returns. These are the people of 1 Corinthians 15:51, "We shall all be changed," and in verse 53, "This mortal must put on immortality." Revelation 21:7 tells us, "He that overcometh shall inherit all things: and I will be his God, and he shall be my son." The church will overcome all things by, as Ephesians 6:11 says, "putting on the whole armour of God that ye may be able to stand against the wiles of the devil." Matthew 24:13 says, "But he that shall endure unto the end, the same shall be saved." This should be the ultimate goal of all Christians—to overcome all things that are written in the book of Revelation.

The basic fact of scripture is that the living church is on the earth when the Lord returns and is not taken in a resurrection because they will put on immortal bodies. I just hope that when the scriptures say, "He that overcometh shall inherit all things," the "all things" include the best golf courses in the world. That would be the only time I could afford to play them. To be able to play golf for all eternity in an immortal body, this is what I call heaven on earth. This is why I don't want to hear the words, "Come up hither," because I would have to be dead when the Lord returns. This is why I pray, "Thy Kingdom come. Thy will be done on earth as it is in heaven."

The Lord Jesus states this three times in Luke 12. Verse 37 says, "Blessed are those servants, whom the Lord when he cometh shall find watching." Verse 38 says, "And if he shall come in the second watch, or come in the third watch, and find them so, blessed are those servants." Verse 43 says, "Blessed is that servant, whom the Lord find when he cometh shall find so doing." Who are the Lord's servants but the church of Jesus Christ? In Mark 14:37, the Lord tells us, "And what I say unto you I say to all, Watch." The church is commanded by the Lord to know when his return to the earth is to happen. We should also note that it does not say here "at his appearing," which is immediately after the tribulation of those days.

The dead are to wait for his appearing and the living until his coming. John Hagee said in one sermon that I watched on his weekly service, at least four times, that the church is in heaven before the tribulation. Prove this in scripture. We should note that it says the second or third watch. We know these are the second and third watch at night, for Matthew 25:6 states, "And at midnight there was a cry made, Behold, the bridegroom cometh; go ye out to meet him." This tells us this sky is dark when the Lord comes.

The past reveals the future. Note Exodus 12:29, 31, which says, "And it came to pass, that at midnight the Lord smote all the first born in the land of Egypt. And he called for Moses and Aaron by night, and said, Rise up, and get you forth from among my people, both ye and the children of Israel; and go, serve the Lord, as ye have said." The New Testament equivalent is the parable of the ten virgins. Matthew 25:5 says, "And at midnight there was a cry made, Behold, the bridegroom cometh; go ye out to meet him." Go and serve the Lord. Those who are alive remain until the coming of the Lord and do this. This is the precept upon precept, line upon line. The past reveals the future study.

I believe these pastors miss the greater promise, for blessed are the meek, for they shall inherit the earth. This means those who survive the great tribulation period will inherit eternal life on the planet with the Lord Jesus Christ. The Lord will protect those who are truly his during this period. This is your basic failure of faith when you feel you have to be resurrected off the planet before the tribulation.

Another example is Paul, who complained about "the thorn in the flesh, the messenger of Satan to buffet me," but what does the Lord Jesus say in 2 Corinthians 12:9? "My grace is sufficient for thee: for my strength is made perfect in weakness." Note what Paul writes next in 2 Corinthians 12:9: "Most gladly therefore will I rather glory in my infirmities, that the power of Christ's sake may rest upon me." In 2 Corinthians 12:10 he says, "In distresses for Christ's sake; for when I am weak, then am I strong." This is who we who are alive and remain till the coming of the Lord should expect, because in the last days the Lord is going to send out his Holy Spirit on all flesh.

John tells us in Revelation 4 that the Lord was on the throne in heaven when he was called up to heaven to be given the revelation of Jesus Christ, and he did not meet the Lord in the air. We are also told in Matthew 24:39, "So shall also the coming of the Son of Man be." We are told in Matthew 24:40–41, "Then shall two be in the field; one shall be taken and the other left. Two women shall be grinding at the mill; the one shall be taken and the other left." These are the ones who are alive and remain until the coming of the Lord who meet the Lord in the air, which means to breathe unconsciously. Note the word for taken is *paralambano*,[87] which means to receive near, by analogy to assume an office, figurative to learn. Also note that the Greek meaning for appear also means to be near. "To assume an office" is the office of a judge with the Lord for a thousand years, as stated in Revelation 20:4, "They lived and reigned with Christ a thousand years." We are also told in Luke 19:17, "Well, thou good servant: because thou hast been faithful in very little, have thou authority over ten cities."

These are the Christians of whom Matthew, Mark, and Luke tell us, "There be some standing here, which shall not taste of death, till they see the Son of Man coming in his kingdom." It's because "this mortal shall have put on immortality." In 1 Corinthians 15:54, his coming is not until the "immediately after the tribulation of those days shall the sun be darkened and the moon shall not give her light" of Matthew 24:30. Then there is the sign in heaven of the Lord Jesus Christ.

Instead of the *Left Behind* series, Tim LaHaye and Jerry Jenkins should have written the *Stay Behind* series, for we are told in scripture to "stay behind, to bear the trials of the tribulation period, and to have fortitude." Romans 5:3 says, "We glory in tribulations: Knowing that tribulation worketh patience." Second Corinthians 1:4 says, "Who comforteth us in all our tribulation, that we may be able comfort them which are in any trouble, by the comfort wherewith we ourselves are comforted of God." This is how the Christians "are comforted by God." Mark says in 13:11, "Take no thought beforehand what ye shall speak, neither do ye premeditate: but whatsoever shall be given you in that

---

[87] Ibid., 2130.

hour, that speak ye: for it is not ye that speak, but the Holy Ghost." Note Mark's reference to "that hour." That is how long this happens.

Revelation 17:12 says, "And the ten horns which thou sawest are ten kings, which have received no kingdom as yet; but receive power as kings one hour with the beast." These kings have power for one hour and the Holy Ghost speaks for the church for one hour. What part of "all tribulation" is the twenty-first-century church no part of? Jeremiah tells the same thing in 20:12: "But, O lord of hosts, that triest the righteous, and seeth the reins and the heart, let me see thy vengeance on them, for unto thee have I opened my cause." Note that the word for triest is *bschan*,[88] which means to test general and figurative to investigate, examine, prove tempt, try. We should note that Jeremiah says God "triest the righteous" and your righteousness will be tried during the tribulation period. Look at the sentence "let me see thy vengeance." This vengeance is God's, and this is for later in this book.

We are told in Ephesians 5:6–7, "Let no man deceive you with vain words: for because of these things cometh the wrath of God upon the children of disobedience. Be not ye therefore partakers with them." The word "vain" is *kenos*,[89] which means, empty (literal or figurative); empty, vain. We should note that those who deceive you with this vain teaching receive the wrath of God. Let's note Revelation 2:22: "Behold, I will cast her into a bed, and them that commit adultery with her into great tribulation, except they repent of their deeds." We are not to be partakers with those who tell us the church is on the planet and not taken in a pre-tribulation resurrection. We should also note that the wrath of God is only upon the disobedient.

We are also told in Jude 1:14–15, "Behold, the Lord cometh with ten thousands of his saints. To execute judgment upon all, and to convince all that are ungodly among them of all of their ungodly deeds which they have ungodly committed, and of all their hard speeches which ungodly sinners have spoken against him." Notice that God executes judgment upon all. What part of all do the pre-tribulation resurrection pastors not understand? The "all" are the ungodly "among

---

[88]   Ibid., 1822.
[89]   Ibid., 2100.

them" (the meek that inherit the earth). Who are the ungodly among them but the church? We must always look to the past, as Isaiah tells us.

When the judgments came upon the Egyptians, it did not affect the Hebrews. Let's note Exodus 9:26, "Only in the land of Goshen, where the children of Israel were, was there no hail"; 10:22, "And there was a thick darkness in the land of Egypt three days"; and 10:23, "But all the children of Israel had light in their dwellings." When the judgments came upon the Jewish people in 586 BC, God put a seal upon his people. Let's note in Ezekiel 9:4 when the angels came to slay the people, an angel was to "set a mark upon the foreheads of the men that sigh and that cry for all the abominations that be done in the midst thereof." Then God tells these angels this in 9:6: "But come not near any man upon whom is the mark; and begin at my sanctuary." The past reveals the future. First Peter 4:17 says, "For the time is come that judgment must begin at the house of God." Those who "sigh and cry" in Ezekiel 9 are the past reference to the future people of Luke 18:7, "And shall not God avenge his own elect, which cry day and night unto him, though he bear long with them." When the fifth trumpet judgment of Revelation is upon the earth, this angel is commanded in 9:4 that they should hurt those men that "which have not the seal of God in their foreheads." We should also note that it states here that God will execute judgment upon all who have spoken against him (the Lord Jesus Christ). These include environmentalists, evolutionists, atheists, and Muslims.

Jude goes on to tell us this in verse 16:

> These are murmurers [Who are the murmurers? We are told in 2 Peter 3:3–4 they are those who, "Knowing this first, that there shall come in the last days scoffers, walking after their own lusts, And saying, Where is the promise of his coming?"] complainers, walking after their own lusts; and their mouth speaketh great swelling [*huperogkos*,[90] which means

---

[90] Ibid., 2169.

bulging over (i.e., insolent). The *Webster's Dictionary* meaning of insolent is "to grow haughty, arrogant in speech or conduct: overbearing, exhibiting boldness or effrontery." Effrontery in the *Webster's Dictionary* means shameless boldness] words, having men's persons in admiration because of the advantage. But beloved, remember ye the words which were spoken before of the apostles of our Lord Jesus Christ; How that they told you there should be mockers, in the last time, who shall walk after their own ungodly lusts. These be they who separate themselves, sensual, having not the spirit [Holy Spirit].

But ye, beloved, building up yourselves on your most holy faith, praying in the Holy Ghost, keep yourselves in the love of God, looking for the mercy of our Lord Jesus Christ unto eternal life. And on some have compassion, making a difference [*diakrino*,[91] which means to separate thoroughly (i.e., literal or reflexive, to withdraw). And the comment in *Strong's* concordance is particularly, spoken of physical separation in Jude 22: "And of some (i.e., those not Christians) having compassion, making a difference (i.e., separating yourselves from them.)] And others save with fear, pulling them out of the fire [Malachi 4:1 says, "For, behold, the day cometh, that shall burn as an oven"]; hating even the garment spotted by the flesh.

Those mockers of 2 Peter are the Muslim people, and their shameless boldness is to mock the Christian believer. And what does scripture tells us? "Separate yourself from them." Others are to try to save them by giving them the truth of the Word of God, that there is only one true God, the Lord of hosts of the Old Testament, which is

---

[91]   Ibid., 2053.

revealed in the Lord Jesus Christ of the New Testament. Note it says in 2 Peter, "Pulling them out of the fire." Here is the precept upon precept study. Matthew 13:49–50 says, "So shall it be at the end of the world: the angels shall come forth, and sever the wicked from among the just, And shall cast them into the furnace of fire: there shall be wailing and gnashing of teeth."

The Lord Jesus tells us when the "day cometh, that it shall burn as an oven." As the Lord Jesus states, we will save them from the "furnace of fire" or as Malachi states, "It shall burn as a oven." And to the pre-tribulation pastors, let us note, "Sever the wicked from among the just." The "just" is the church. Let us also note that this is where "the end of the world" comes, when it shall burn as an oven, and the Lord Jesus tells us, "Those that endure until the end, the same shall be saved." The just are not cast into the furnace of fire.

Revelation 1:10 states, "I was in the spirit on the Lord's day." This refers to the "Day of the Lord," the future. We should note first that he was in the spirit and not in his spiritual body. The spiritual body is what we receive at the resurrection of the dead. As we are told in scripture, the Lord will descend from heaven when the dead saints are caught up to meet him in the clouds. And in Revelation 4, the Lord is on the throne. And this is where 95 percent of the pastors teach that the resurrection happens. This is what I call stupid theology.

I believe we should note that John tells us that "one sat on the throne." Remember, the Lord told us, "I and the father are one." But there are seven lamps of fire burning before the throne, which are the seven Spirits of God. These seven manifestations are revealed in the Old Testament, which are El, Elah, or Elahim; Jehovah; Adon or Adonai; El Shaddai; El Elyon; El Olam; and El Gibbor. God can manifest himself into seven different beings. Let's note Revelation 5:6, "In the midst of the throne stood a lamb as it had been slain, having seven horns and seven eyes, which are the seven Spirits of God sent forth into all the earth." To give prophecy correctly, first we must forget about setting a date and focus on events. We have to wait on certain events to happen.

The Lord told us just what the signs would be at his near return in Matthew 24:6. Those signs are wars, famines, pestilence, and earthquakes. These are just the beginning of sorrows, and we are told to endure these things. This is where the pre-tribulation teachers are wrong again, for the Lord tells us, "He that shall endure unto the end, the same shall be saved" in Matthew 24:13. The word for endure here is *hupomeno*,[92] which means to stay under (behind), (i.e., remain, figurative to undergo, i.e., bear [trials]) have fortitude). Let us note that the word for judgment is the word *krisis*,[93] which means (subject or object, for or against) by extension a tribunal, by implication justice (especially divine law). This judgment is for or against, and we are to remain and endure the tribulation period. This is backed up by the psalms.

Psalms 25:9 says, "The meek will he guide in judgment: and the meek will he teach his ways." The word for judgment is *mishpat*,[94] which means, properly a verdict (favorable or unfavorable). This tells us the church (the meek who God will guide in the judgment) is on the planet when the judgments of God come in the book of Revelation. We are also told in Psalms 76:1, 7–9, "In Judah is God known: his name is great in Israel. Thou, even thou, art to be feared: and who may stand in thy sight when once thou art angry? Thou didst cause judgment to be heard from heaven; the earth feared, and was still, When God rose to judgment, to save the meek of the earth."

Note "who may stand in thy sight" is also found in Romans 14:4, "Who are thou that judgest another man's servant? To his own master he standest or falleth. Yea, he shall be holden up: for God is able to make him stand." We know this psalm is for the end time, for it states, "To save the meek of the earth." His judgments are heard from heaven, but when he is angry, who may stand in his sight? And why can we not stand in his sight? We go to Revelation 16:18: "And there were voices, and thunders, and lightnings, and there was a great earthquake, such as was not since men were upon the earth, and so great." It is not until God's wrath that he gets angry and leaves heaven. Then there is the great earthquake, and he is now in sight. We will read that when

---

92   Ibid., 2170.
93   Ibid., 2104.
94   Ibid., 1912.

God's presence is near, the earth shakes. Romans says, "God is able to make him stand." His judgments are to save the meek of the earth. Remember from Jeremiah 20:12 that to see the vengeance is to save the meek of the earth. These are two of many verses in Psalms that relate to the return of the Lord, and we will examine them later. This does not sound like a promise of a pre-tribulation resurrection from the Lord.

Here is another mistake of most pastors today. God's covenant with the Jews is an everlasting covenant. It remains until the Lord's return. Whatever the church is promised by Jesus is extended unto Jews. We should note this in scripture. When God leaves heaven in the latter days, this is the only time that the heavens and the earth shake together. I will prove this with this scripture. Haggai 2:2–9 says:

> Speak now to Zerubbabel the son of Shealtiel, governor of Judah, and to Joshua the son of Josedech, the high priest, and to the residue of the people saying, Who is left among you that saw this house in her first glory? And how do you see it now? Is it not in your eyes in comparison of it as nothing? Yet now be strong, O Zerubbabel, saith the Lord; and be strong Joshua, son of Josedech, the high priest; and be strong, all ye people of the land, saith the Lord, and work: for I am with you, saith the Lord of hosts: according to the word that I covenanted with you when ye came out of Egypt, so my spirit remaineth among you: fear ye not. For thus saith the Lord of hosts; Yet once, it is a little while, and I will shake the heavens, and the earth, and the sea, and the dry ground: And I will shake all nations, and the desire of all nations shall come: and I will fill this house with glory, saith the Lord of hosts. This silver is mine, and the gold is mine, saith the Lord of hosts. The glory of this latter house shall be greater than of the former, saith the Lord of hosts: and in this place I will give peace, saith the Lord of hosts.

In verse three, they compare the former house of God to the original, and it's not comparable. In verse 4, God encourages them to be strong in the land. God reminds them to remember the covenant he made with them when they came out of Egyptian bondage. Most of the prophets reference this time in history to the latter days. As Isaiah says, "The past reveals the future," and God's spirit remains with them. This is around 516 BC, and God says it will be a little while before he shakes the heavens and the earth when he comes back. The Lord has not done this yet, yet he calls it a little while. A little while is now over twenty-five hundred years, but it is only two days as far as God is concerned, for a thousand earth years is a day to the Lord.

We should note that this shaking of the heavens and the earth is given in Hebrews 12:26, "Whose voice then shook the earth: but now he hath promised, saying, Yet once more I shake not the earth only, but also heaven." It is also spoken of in Joel 3:16, "The Lord shall roar out of Zion, and utter his voice form Jerusalem; and the heavens and the earth shall shake: but the Lord will be the hope of his people, and the strength of the children of Israel." Note it states here he strengthens "his people" and the children of Israel.

This is the same strengthening God promises the church. In Revelation, it states a few times, "Which keep the commandments of God, and have the testimony of Jesus." His people of Joel are those who have the testimony of Jesus, and the children of Israel are those Jews who "keep the commandments of God." The latter house in verse 9 is the house in which the Lord will rule and reign a thousand years, because it says he "will give you peace."

This shaking of all nations, including the seas, is given to us in Ezekiel 38:18–19: "And it shall come to pass at the same time Gog shall come against the land of Israel, saith the Lord God, that my fury shall come up in my face. So that the fishes of the sea, and the fowls of the heaven, and the beast of the field, and all creeping things that creep upon the earth, shall shake at my presence, and the mountains shall be thrown down, and the steep place shall fall, and every wall shall fall to the ground." These Old Testament writers are trying to make a point—that when the Lord appears, his power is so great that it will affect everything on the earth, from the fowls of the sky to the smallest creature that creeps upon the earth, from the deepest sea to the highest mountain.

God reminds man though man has in his possession the silver and gold, it's God's; he made it. Haggai speaks of the latter house of God, and the greatest of it, just as Ezekiel does in chapter 40 of his book. In Exodus 15:3, God states, "The Lord is a man of war." Jesus tells us in Matthew 10:34, "I come not to the earth to bring peace, but the sword." But now, after the glory of this latter house, the Lord will bring peace to the earth as stated in Haggai 2:9. Just as Isaiah 2:4 says, "Nation shall not lift up sword against nation, neither shall they learn war any more."

We are also given this. John 4:17 says, "Herein is our love made perfect, that we may have boldness in the Day of Judgment." The word "boldness" is *parrhesia*,[95] which means all outspokenness (i.e., frankness, bluntness, publicity); by implication assurance, bold. The Day of Judgment is given in the book of Revelation, and John tells us here that we are to have boldness. If there is a pre-tribulation rapture, then rip this passage out of your Bible. This is backed up in the Old Testament. In Ezekiel 20:13, it says, "They walk not in my statutes, and they despised my judgments, which if a man do, he shall even live in them; and my Sabbaths they greatly polluted: then I will pour out my fury upon them in the wilderness, to consume them."

Are the pre-tribulation resurrection pastors despising "my judgments" when they promise their theory? Ezekiel 20:13 says, "Which if a man do he shall even live in them." The word for fury is *chemah*,[96] which means heat, figurative anger, poison (from the fever); anger, bottles, hot displeasure, furious (-ly, -ry), heat, wrath. This fury sounds like the fourth vial of wrath in the book of Revelation16:8, where it states, "And the fourth angel poured out his vial upon the sun; and power was given unto him to scorch men with fire." This is also a reference to the "heat" and the "wrath of God."

We have also greatly polluted the Sabbath day when we have businesses open every day and have not set aside one day in the week for the Lord. This is an example of many scriptures that prove that the pre-tribulation resurrection theory is wrong. We will note in scripture just when the end is.

And what does the Lord Jesus tell us in Matthew 24:13? "All that endure until the end, the same shall be saved." Also note Joel 3:16, "The Lord shall roar out of Zion, and utter his voice." The New Testament equivalent is 1 Thessalonians 4:16: "For the Lord shall descend from heaven with a shout." When does Joel tell us the Lord will roar out of Zion? "Multitudes, multitudes in the valley of decision: for the day of the lord is at near in the valley of decision. The sun and the moon shall be darkened, and the stars shall withdraw their shining." The New Testament equivalent is Revelation 15:16: "Behold, I came as a thief. And he gathered them together into a place in the Hebrew tongue called Armageddon." And when does this happen? Matthew 24:30 says, "Immediately after the tribulation of those days shall the sun be darkened, and the moon shall not give her light." And then shall the Son of Man appear in heaven.

Isaiah tells us in 1:26, "And I will restore thy judges as at the first and thy counselors as at the beginning; afterward thou shalt be called, the city of righteousness, the faithful city." This has not happened yet, so this still must be fulfilled. The judges in those days were appointed by the prophets of God, which were given by the Lord. We will see this is the same message given to the church when the Lord returns.

Malachi tells us when this happens. Malachi 3:16–18 and 4:1–2 says:

> Then they that feared the Lord spake often one to another: and the Lord hearkened [*qashab*,[97] which means to prick up the ears (i.e., hearken) attend, give heed, mark], and heard, and a book of remembrance [*zikkarown*,[98] which means memento, memorial, record, from *zakar*,[99] which means properly to mark]

97 Ibid., 1964.
98 Ibid., 1848.
99 Ibid., 1847.

was written before him that feared the Lord, and that thought upon his name. And they shall be mine, saith the Lord of hosts, in that day when I make up my jewels [*gullah*,[100] which means wealth]; and I will spare them, as a man spareth his own son that serveth him. Then shall ye return, and discern [*raah*,[101] which means to see, appear, gaze, mark, show, sight of others] between the righteous and the wicked, between him that serveth God and him serveth him not.

Before going to chapter 4, let's review chapter 3. When the Lord hearkens, which means prick the ears and mark those who are his, then they will return and appear to judge between the righteous and the wicked. The New Testament equivalent verse is in Matthew 13:38–43, where the good seed are the children of the kingdom and the tares are the children of the devil, and the tares are gathered and burned in the fire. The righteous shine forth as the sun in the kingdom of the father, and these are the meek, for blessed are the meek that inherit the earth. Also note in both verses the "righteous" are among the wicked.

Now for Malachi 4:1, which says, "For, behold, the day cometh, that it shall burn as an oven: and all that do wickedly, shall be as a stubble: and the day cometh shall burn them up, saith the Lord of hosts, that it shall leave them neither root or branch. But unto you that fear my name shall the Sun [*shemesh*,[102] which means from an unused root meaning to be brilliant; the sun; by implication the east; figurative a ray] of righteousness arise with healing in his wings; and ye shall go forth, and grow up as calves of the stall." Note the Hebrew word by implication means the east. This is stated in Matthew 24:27, "For as the lightning cometh out of the east, and shineth even unto the west; so shall also the coming of the Son of Man be." So why does Malachi use the words "sun of righteousness?" Second Thessalonians 1:7–8 says, "When the Lord Jesus shall be revealed from heaven with

---

[100]   Ibid., 1925.

[101]   Ibid., 1965.

[102]   Ibid., 1990.

his mighty angels, In flaming fire taking vengeance on them that know not God, and that obey not the gospel of our Lord Jesus Christ." Note the sun of righteousness, as a flaming fire.

I will match these Old Testament prophecy of Isaiah, "restore thy judges as of first," with the New Testament. Revelation 20:4 says, "And I saw thrones, and they that sat upon them, and judgment was given unto them that were beheaded for the witness of Jesus, and for the Word of God, and which had not worshiped the beast, neither his image, neither had received his mark upon the forehead, or in his hands; and they lived and reigned with Christ a thousand years." We read here it is only the people who were killed who got the victory over the beast and who rule and reign with Christ a thousand years. We should note, "And I saw thrones," which means there is more than one throne. The people who sat on those thrones got the victory over the beast and were killed.

Let's read scripture carefully. First Thessalonians 4:16-17 says, "And the dead in Christ shall rise first." This is Matthew 24:30, "And then shall appear the Son of Man in Heaven." First Thessalonians 4:15 says, "We which are alive and remain to meet the Lord in the air." This means the Christians remain on the earth until his coming. This is the second part of Matthew 24:30, "And they shall see the Son of Man coming in the clouds of heaven with power and great glory." Remain here is *perileipo*,[103] which means to leave all around, passive survive. But we meet the Lord in the air. Air in Greek is *aemi*,[104] which means to be unconscious. We are in a higher state of being. We are putting on immortality. The proof is in 1 John 3:2, which says, "When he shall appear, we shall be like him; for we shall see him as he is." Throughout the past scriptures, some (dead) were told to wait for his appearing and some (living) for the coming of the Lord.

Once again, Jesus tells us in Matthew 16:28, "Verily I say unto you, there be some standing here, which shall not taste of death, till they see the Son of Man coming in his kingdom." We should note here that it is not until "they see the Son of Man coming" that those "shall

103 Ibid., 2134.
104 Ibid., 2014.

not taste of death." "And they see his coming immediately after the tribulation of those days shall the sun be darkened and the moon shall not give her light, and the powers of heaven shall be shaken: And then shall appear the Son of Man in heaven and all the tribes of the earth shall mourn, and they shall see the coming of the Son of Man coming in the clouds of heaven of Matthew 24:30." Those who don't taste death are the ones who are alive and remain until the coming of the Lord. But what Matthew does not say are the words "great tribulation," because when the great tribulation starts is when God shortens the days for his elect, the ones who are alive and remain until the coming of the Lord of 1 Thessalonians 4:15.

Let us note Ezekiel 38:18–19: "And it shall come to pass at the same time Gog [Armageddon] shall come against the land of Israel, saith the Lord God, that my fury shall come up in my face. For in my jealousy and in the fire of my wrath have I spoken, Surely in that day there shall be a great shaking in the land of Israel." Spoken is *dabar*,[105] which means to speak, answer, destroy, or utter. Let's note the language. It says "at the same time" that Gog shall come against the land of Israel. It is not after but at the same time. It is an immediate response by the Lord.

And the response is given in Matthew 24:30, "Immediately after the tribulation of those days shall the sun be darken, and the moon shall not give her light, and the powers of the heavens shall be shaken: and then shall appear the Son of Man in heaven." And it is immediately in Revelation 22:12, "And, behold, I come quickly." The word for quickly is *tachu*,[106] which means shortly (i.e., without delay). It's immediately after the tribulation of those days that the great tribulation starts, and it's at the same time that Gog comes against the land of Israel that God's wrath begins.

Just as Daniel states in 12:1, "And there shall be a time of trouble, such as never was since there was a nation even to that 'same time': and at that time thy people shall be delivered, every one found written in the book." And this is where "the dead in Christ are risen, first and

---

[105]   Ibid., 1837.
[106]   Ibid., 2162.

we which are alive and remain until the coming of the Lord." The words "to be delivered" mean escape, preserve, speedily.[107] Note the Hebrew word meaning speedily. Revelation 22:13 says, "Behold, I come quickly."

Where else does the Bible tell us the Lord destroys? Revelation 11:18–19 says, "And the nations were angry, and thy wrath has come, and the time of the dead, that they should be judged, and that thou shouldest give reward unto thy servants the prophets, and to the saints, and them that fear thy name, small and great; and shouldest destroy them that destroy the earth." Note in this verse that at the time of God's wrath, only the dead are judged. We should also note that in here it says, "To give reward unto thy servants the prophets." This is the resurrection of the dead. Revelation 11:19 says, "And the temple of God was opened in heaven, and there was seen in his temple the ark of his testament: and there were lightings, and voices, and thunderings, and an earthquake, and great hail."

So let's note 2 Timothy 4:8: "Henceforth there is laid up for me a crown of righteousness, which the Lord, the righteous judge, shall give me at that day: and not to me only, but unto all them also that love his appearing." Paul tells us that his expectation of when he receives his crown is at the Lord's appearing. The Lord's appearing is not until Matthew 24:30: "Immediately after the tribulation of those days, shall the sun be darkened, and the moon shall not give her light, and then shall appear the Son of Man in heaven." Note the words "that day." This is the Day of the Lord. Also note the earthquake.

So we must conclude that the Lord's appearing is when the wrath of God comes. Revelation 11:19 tells us this is the time when the dead will be judged. John 5:25 also says, "Verily, verily, I say unto you, The hour is coming, and now is, when the dead shall hear the voice of the Son of Man: and they that hear shall live." Note the scripture says, "The dead shall hear." It doesn't say the living hear. His appearing is when the seventh trumpet is sounded in Revelation 11:18, and this is the last trumpet of 1 Corinthians 15:52. We should note that after his appearing in Matthew 24:30, "All the earth shall mourn," because this

---

[107]   Ibid., 1901.

is where the vials of wrath are poured out. And then after the seventh vial is poured out in Revelation 16:17, it states, "It is done." Verse 18 tells us, "And there were voices, and thunders, and lightings; and there was a great earthquake, such as was not since men were upon the earth, and so great." Matthew 24:30 says, "And they shall see the Son of Man coming in the clouds of heaven with power and great glory."

The great earthquake is the great earthquake of Zechariah 14:4: "And his feet shall stand that day upon the mount of olives, which is before Jerusalem on the east, and the mount of olives shall cleave in the midst thereof toward the east and toward the west, and there shall be a great valley; and half of the mountain shall remove toward the north, and half toward the south." One might ask, why did scripture tell us here there shall be a great valley? I believe the answer is in Revelation 21:10: "And he carried me away in the spirit to a great and high mountain, and he showed me that great city, the holy Jerusalem, descending out of heaven from God." That great valley is the foundation for the great mountain that descends out of heaven from God. God replaces the mountain of old Jerusalem with the mountain of the holy Jerusalem. God's prophets write in great detail so we can fully understand why they are given. This why Isaiah says in 28:10, "Precept must be upon precept, precept upon precept, line upon line; here a little there a little." Verse 5 tells us, "And the Lord my God shall come, and all of the saints with thee."

When in scripture does God utter his voice? It is found in Joel 2:10–11: "The earth shall quake before them, the heaven shall tremble: the sun and the moon shall be dark, and the stars shall withdraw their shining: And the Lord shall utter his voice before his army: for his camp is very great: for he is strong that executeth his word: for the day of the Lord is great and very terrible; and who can abide it?" Let's note the language of Joel, "For the day of the Lord is great." Matthew tells us that after the tribulation the Son of Man will appear in heaven. After the tribulation starts the great tribulation. It is God who makes the great tribulation great. Matthew and Joel tell us the same thing.

Now let's look at what is said in Revelation 11:18:

The Nations are angry [great tribulation], and thy
wrath has come [the fire of my wrath of Ezekiel
38:19], time of the dead [John 5:25 says, "The hour
is coming, and now is, when the dead shall hear
the voice of the Son of Man."], that they should be
judged, and to the saints, and that thou shouldest
give reward unto thy servants the prophets [Rev.
10:7]. But in the days of the voice of the seventh
angel, when he shall begin to sound, the mystery of
God should be finished, as he hath declared to his
servants and prophets and [2 Tim. 4:8] them that fear
thy name, small and great [Revelation 19:5 says, "And
a voice came out of throne, saying, Praise our God,
all ye servants, and ye that fear him, both small and
great (the meek that inherit the earth)], and shouldest
destroy them that destroy the earth [Ezekiel 38:22
says, "And I will plead against him with pestilence
and with blood; and I will rain upon him, and upon
his bands, and upon the many peoples with him, an
overflowing rain, and great hailstones.] [Revelation
16:21 says, "And there fell upon men great hail out of
heaven, fire, and brimstone"].

But if there is a secret pre-tribulation vanishing of the living, where
we don't see the coming of the Lord, when the sun and the moon don't
give their light, then rip these passages from your Bible, because it is
not scriptural. In the book of Revelation, it's not until "thy wrath has
come" that there is time "of the dead that they should be judged" (1
Thessalonians 4:16 says, "And the dead in Christ shall rise first") and
gave "reward unto thy servants the prophets," in the "days of the voice
of the seventh angel" where the "mystery of God should be finished,"
which is the end of the church age. It's in the days (more than one day)
of the voice of the seventh angel when this happens. As I say, note the
language. We are not told what day. No one knows the hour or the day,
but we will know when at is at the door, when the sun and the moon
don't give their light.

We are told in Philippians 1:6, 9–10, "Being confident of the very thing, that he which hath begun a good work in you will perform it until the day of Jesus Christ. And this I pray, that your love may abound yet more and more in knowledge and in all judgment; That ye may approve things that are excellent; that ye may be sincere and without offence till the day of Christ." We are told here twice that we are to wait until the day of Christ, or the day of the Lord. Our love is to abound, and we are to have more in knowledge in what? In all judgments.

In that passage, all judgments mean the judgments in the book of Revelation. I say this because in Revelation, all churches are told to endure until the end. Another reason not to believe the pre-tribulation resurrection is this. The Lord says, "And David himself saith in the book of Psalms 110:1, The Lord said unto my Lord, Sit thou on my right hand, Till I make thine enemies thy footstool." So let's go to Psalms 110:1, 5–7: "The Lord said unto my Lord, Sit thou at my right hand, until I make thine enemies thy footstool. The Lord at thy right hand shall strike through kings in the day of his wrath. He shall judge among the heathen, he shall fill the places with dead bodies; he shall wound the heads over many countries. He shall drink of the brook in the way: therefore shall he lift up the head."

So if the Lord is on the throne until the day of his wrath, how can there be a pre-tribulation resurrection? The word for judge in verse 5 is *diyn*,[108] which means to rule, by implication to judge, also to strive, contend, execute, judge, minister judgment, or plead. Brook is *nachal*,[109] which means to inherit, to occupy, distribute, or take as a heritage. And the word "lift" is *ruwm*,[110] which means to be high, active, to rise or raise, hold up, or breed worms. From the meaning of these Hebrew words, we see that when the Lord makes his enemies his footstool, he rules, executes judgment, raises the dead, takes as a heritage his land back that was promised Abraham, Isaac, and Jacob, and breeds worms.

---

[108]   Ibid., 1777.

[109]   Ibid., 1918.

[110]   Ibid., 1968.

And to prove he breeds worms, we go to Isaiah 41:12–16:

> Thou shalt seek them, and shalt not find them, even
> them that contend with thee; they that war against
> thee shalt be as nothing, and as a thing of nought.
> For I am the Lord thy God will hold thy right hand,
> saying unto thee. Fear not, thou worm Jacob, ye men
> of Israel; and thy redeemer, the Holy One of Israel.
> Behold, I will make thee a new sharp threshing
> [*mowrag*,[111] which means to triturate (*Webster's
> Dictionary* meaning crush, grind, to pulverize and
> comminute thoroughly by rubbing and grinding)]
> instrument having teeth: thou shalt thresh the
> mountains, and beat them small, and shall make the
> hills as chaff. Thou shall fan (*zarah*,[112] which means
> cast away, compass, or disperse) them, and the winds
> will carry them away, and the whirlwind shall scatter
> them: and thou shall rejoice in the Lord, and glory in
> the Holy One of Israel.

We know this is an end-time prediction because all Israel's enemies
are "nothing and a thing of nought." Isaiah says to "Fear not, thou
worm Jacob." Worm is *towla*,[113] which means a maggot (as voracious).
The *Webster's Dictionary* meaning of voracious is to devour, excessive
eager. When scripture uses the word "Jacob", it means all the tribes of
Israel, and they are excessively eager. God promises, "They that war
against thee shall be as nothing," and they shall rejoice in the Lord.

We are told in Ephesians 6:11, "Put on the whole armour of God
that ye may be able to stand against the wiles of the devil." Wiles is
methodeia,[114] which means traveling over. If the church is in heaven
before the devil appears, as pastors say, then rip this passage out of your

---

[111] Ibid., 1895.
[112] Ibid., 1850.
[113] Ibid., 1998.
[114] Ibid., 2112.

Bible. With the weapons of war man invented over the past decade, the battle of Armageddon can't last but a short time. And one may ask, "Why must there be a battle of Armageddon?" It is the restoration of Israel (all of the tribes of Israel) to the land God gave to Abraham, Isaac, and Jacob. Joel 3:2 says, "I will also gather all nations, and will bring them down into the valley of Jehoshapat, and will plead with them there for my people and for my heritage Israel, whom they have scattered among the nations, and parted my land." It is because they scattered "my people" among the nations, and they parted "my land." Our Lord told us if he didn't shorten those days, no one would be left. In Matthew 24:22, it says, "Except those days should be shortened, there shall no flesh be saved: but for the elect's sake those days will be shortened." The word "shortened" is *koloboo*,[115] which means to dock (i.e., figuratively, abridge, shorten). It is from the word *kolazo* (*drarf*), which means properly to curtail (i.e., figuratively to chastise [or reserve for infliction]) or punish. God shortens the days for his elect.

We should note the Greek meaning of to punish. And this is found in the Old Testament in Isaiah 26:21, "For, behold, the Lord cometh [*yatsa*[116] meaning to appear] out of his place to punish the inhabitants of the earth." We will read later that the shortening of those days is in the Old Testament. We are also told in Revelation 16:15, "Behold, I come as a thief." When does the Lord do this? Revelation 16:15 says "And he [God] gathered them together into a place called in the Hebrew tongue called Armageddon." The battle of Armageddon is not a war Christians fight.

This is the battle fought and won by our Savior, the Lord Jesus Christ. God will raise up his own army that will not be able to be killed. This is proven later in this book. But if there is a pre-tribulation resurrection, where the elect are already in heaven when this happens, then this cannot be correct scripture, so rip this scripture out of your Bible. This is the most important part of this book—to warn the church that there are very terrible times ahead for the church and they

---

must prepare themselves for the things to come. To prepare yourselves is to trust in the Lord Jesus Christ.

There are many promises from the Lord to help the church get through these tough times. This is our test. Do you trust in the Lord? James the apostle tells us in James 1:12, "Blessed is the man that endureth temptation; for when he is tried, he shall receive the crown of life, which the Lord hath promised to them that love him." The word "temptation" is *peirasmos*,[117] which means a putting to proof (by experience [of good], experience [of evil], solicitation, discipline, or provocation); by implication adversity, temptation, try. It is from *peirazo*,[118] which means to test (object), that is endeavor, scrutinize, or entice discipline. We should notice that this scripture in James matches what is given in Jeremiah 20:12. This scripture tells us we will be tried and tempted. But if there is the pre-tribulation resurrection, then rip this out of your Bible, because it is not scriptural. These are just the first pages of this book, and I have a question. Do you still believe all the pre-tribulation, the living church resurrection, pastors? There is more.

Not all scriptures were recorded in most Christian Bibles. Some were rejected. But some Christian books have them in their Bible, namely the Catholics and the Episcopalians. I still find them to be good reading. Maybe we should just take a quick read of some of them. This vision is for the last days in 2 Esdras 6:18–26.

> The time draws near when I come to judge the earth's inhabitants, the time when I shall enquire into the wickedness of the wrongdoers, the time when Zion's humiliation will be over, the time when a seal will be set on the age about to pass away. Then I shall perform these signs: the books will be opened out against the vault of heaven, and all will see my judgment at the same moment. Children only a year old will be able to talk, and pregnant women will give birth

---

[117] Ibid., 2133.
[118] Ibid.

prematurely at three or four months to babes who will survive and dance about. Fields that are sown will suddenly prove unsown, and barns that were full will suddenly be found empty. A loud trumpet-blast will sound, striking sudden terror into all who hear it. At that time friends will make war on friends as though on foes; the earth and its inhabitants will be terrified. Running streams will stand still, and for three hours cease to flow. Whoever is left after all I have foretold will be saved and see the salvation that I bring and the end of this world of mine.

They will see the men who were taken up into heaven without ever tasting death. They (the people of the earth) will literally see those taken to heaven without tasting death. This was told to us in Matthew 16:28, Mark 9:1, and Luke 9:27. Also note the "friends will make war on friends." Mark 13:12 tells us, "Now the brother shall betray the brother to death, and the father the son; and children shall rise up against their parents, and shall cause them to be put to death." And note, "Whoever is left after all I have foretold will be saved." This matches Matthew 24:13, "But he that shall endure unto the end, the same shall be saved."

We should note here that it tells us here that the judgments of God come on the wickedness of the wrongdoers. It is also a time when Zion's humiliation will be over, and is that true in our day? The United Nations and the world court rule against the state of Israel most of the time. In the current peace agreements, America is forcing Israel to give more land for peace, but it will be over when the Lord comes and reigns from Jerusalem. It will be a time when a seal will set on the age to pass away, the end of the church age. All will see the seal judgments of the book of Revelation. There will be the sound of the trumpet of God, striking sudden terror into all who are here.

Let us look to past. In Exodus 19:16, it says, "And it came to pass on the third day in the morning, that there were thunders and lightnings, and a thick cloud upon the mount, and the voice of the trumpet exceeding loud; so that all the people that was in the camp trembled." We should note that the same language is used for the day of the Lord in Joel 2:1–2: "Blow ye the trumpet in Zion, and sound an alarm in my holy mountain: let all the inhabitants of the land tremble: for the day of the Lord cometh, for it is nigh at hand; A day of darkness and of gloominess, a day of clouds and of thick darkness, as the morning spread upon the mountains: a great people and a strong; there hath not seen ever the like, neither shall it be and more after it, even to the years of many generations." This is the trumpet of 1 Corinthians 15:52.

Second Esdras 13 says, "How terrible it will be, to my thinking, for all those that survive to those days, but how much worse for those that do not! Those that do not survive will have the sorrow of knowing what the last days have in store, yet without attaining it. Those who do survive are to be pitied for the terrible dangers and many trials which those visions show they will have to face. But perhaps after all it is better to endure the dangers and reach the goal than to vanish from the world like a cloud and never see what will happen at the last."

To vanish from the world like a cloud is just how Jesus went to heaven in a cloud after his resurrection. It is also recorded here that it is better to endure until the end. Jesus tells us, "Those that endure till the end, the same shall be saved. And this is the meek that inherit the earth." This matches the writings in Isaiah 65:18–25. Some scriptures have been ripped out of the Bible, so let us continue the King James Version of the Bible.

James also tells us this in James 1:3, "Knowing this that the trying of your faith worketh patience."

This trying of your faith is during the tribulation period. All the signs tell us that those days are very near, for one of the signs is that terrorism will be happening around the world, just in the days of Noah, and that started back in the 1990s. I believe there will more attacks on American soil to come. September 11 was the first major attack on American soil since the attack on Pearl Harbor. We see on the news that the same people are making these attacks worldwide. The major Islamic jihad has begun, and this is happening worldwide. It will not end until the Lord comes back and destroys them all, although there will be three and a half years in our future when there will be peace made by the Antichrist.

But first the Bible tells us there is a major battle in the Middle East, and after this happens, the Antichrist makes this peace agreement. After three and a half years of peace, then comes Armageddon. This will come to pass, for it is told to us in scripture. This is the time when the world comes against the tiny nation of Israel, and as I see it, against the Christian world. This is where the Lord tells us he has had enough. We are told in Isaiah 66:16, "For by fire and by his sword will the Lord plead with all flesh: and the slain of the Lord shall be many." Isaiah 42:13–14 also says:

> The Lord shall go forth as a mighty man, he shall stir up jealousy like a man of war; he shall cry, yea roar; he shall prevail against his enemies. I have long time holden my peace; I have been still, and refrained myself: now will I cry like a travailing woman; I will destroy and devour at once.

We also see this in Jeremiah 25:32–33:

> Thus saith the Lord of hosts, Behold, evil shall go forth from nation to nation, and a great whirlwind shall be raised up from the coast of the earth. And the slain of the Lord shall be at that day from one end of earth even unto the other end of the earth: they shall not be lamented, neither gathered, nor buried; they shall be as dung upon the ground.

The evil that shall go forth from nation to nation is the Islamic jihad. Note the words of Jeremiah in "that day," the day of the Lord. This is when the Lord kills those who are bringing this evil. Let's note the words of the Lord Jesus, "But those that endure until the end, the same shall be saved." Most pastors only want to talk about the meek and mild Jesus, but the God of the Bible tells us different. We are told in Exodus 15:3, "The Lord is a man of War; the Lord is his name." In Matthew 10:34–38 we are told:

> Think not that I come to send peace on the earth:
> I came not to send peace but the sword. For I come
> to set a man at variance [*dichazo*,[119] which means to
> make apart, sunder (figurative) alienate] against his
> father, and the daughter against her mother, and the
> daughter in law against her mother is law. And a
> man's foes shall be they of his own household. He that
> loveth father or mother more than me is not worthy
> of me: and he that loveth son or daughter more than
> me is not worthy of me.

Jesus tells us in Matthew 22:37–38, "Thou shalt Love thy God with all thy heart, and with all thy soul, and with all thy mind [spirit]. This is the first and great commandment." The Lord tells us here to put God first in our lives.

This Islamic jihad has angered the Lord greatly, and when he has had enough, he will act. John 16:2 tells us, "The time cometh, that whosoever killeth you will think that he doeth God service." The only religion that teaches this is the Islamic religion. As Muhammad states, "The Christians and the Jews are your declared enemies." In the Qur'an, it states, "O ye who believe, make not friends with My enemy and your enemy." They are bringing this prophecy to pass. I believe we should have the faith that David had when he went against Goliath: "But I come to thee in the name of the Lord, for the battle is the Lord's." In Ezekiel 38 and 39 when Gog and his armies come against the land of the unwalled villages and the land of Israel, this is what is said. Ezekiel 38:19 says, "For in my jealousy and in the fire of my wrath have I spoken." In Revelation 16:15–16 when God gathers the two hundred million men to the battle of Armageddon, John tells us, "Behold, I come as a thief." This should be our attitude when the demonic forces come in the latter days. We will see in scripture just who the Lord's anger is directed at. We should note that Isaiah says that God refrains until he has had enough. The prophets tell us just when that happens in their books.

---

[119] Ibid., 2056.

When You See All These Things, Know My Kingdom Is Near

THERE ARE THESE MAJOR predictions in the Bible we must closely examine. When the two witnesses are killed in Jerusalem, the Bible tells us everyone in the world will see this happen. This was not possible until the invention of satellite television and the Internet. We know who the two witnesses are. They can only be Enoch and Elijah. These two prophets were the only ones who did not die in the flesh but were taken to heaven in their earthly bodies. The Bible tells us in 1 Corinthians 15:50, "Now I say, brethren, that flesh and blood cannot inherit the kingdom of God," so we must conclude that these two prophets must be returned to earth to die in the flesh.

There had to be a state of Israel and an Israel in control of the city of Jerusalem. This was not complete until 1967. This has happened in our generation. We should note what the scripture says in Mark 13:14 that the Lord tells us this that abomination of desolation, spoken by Daniel the prophet, standing where it ought not. The temple that the Jews of Israel will rebuild will not be where it should, and that is because of the Islamic mosque built there. The temple in the time of Jesus was on the Temple Mount, so this speaks of a temple in the future.

Note 2 Thessalonians 1:4, "Who opposeth and exalteth himself above all that is called God, or that is worshipped; so that he as God sitteth in the Temple of God, shewing himself that he is God." The Antichrist will stand in the temple of God, so we must watch for the building of this temple in Jerusalem. Ezekiel, the prophet who lived in the sixth century, said the same thing of the Islamic mosque in 36:2, where he writes, "Aha, even the ancient high places are ours in possession." We read here twice, once by Jesus and again in Ezekiel, that on the Temple Mount is something that should not be there. The mosque was built until AD 691. Ezekiel's prediction happened eleven hundred years after he gave his prophecy, and the Lord Jesus made this prediction over six hundred years before it was built.

The next sign I believe is in most people's wallet today. It's called your debit card. When all buying and selling is done electronically, this is how one man can control the economies of the world. I do not hear the churches in this country warning their people of this possibility. You even see television ads mocking people with cash. I believe this will get worse after the Antichrist is in control. The Lord Jesus warns us of this very thing in Mark 13:12, "Now the brother shall betray the brother to death, and the father the son; and children shall rise up against their parents, and shall cause them to be put to death." Will your brother betray you if you don't take the mark of the beast? One might ask, if there is a pre-tribulation resurrection, why is this in this book? If this is not a warning to the church, then who is this warning for?

We have this very warning from the Lord himself when he says in Mark 8:34–38:

> Whosoever will come after me, let him deny himself, and take up his cross, and follow me. For whosoever will save his life shall lose it; but whosoever shall lose his life for my sake and the Gospel's, the same shall be save it. For what shall it profit a man, if he gain the whole world, and lose his own soul? Or what shall a man give in exchange for his soul? Whosoever therefore shall be ashamed of me and of my words in this adulterous and sinful generation; of him shall the Son of Man be ashamed, when he cometh in the glory with his holy angels.

"Cometh" is the word *erchomai*,[120] which means appear. And as Matthew records, the Lord Jesus appears after the tribulation of those days, when the sun and the moon don't give their light. And if he comes as a thief, when he gathers the nations to the battle of Armageddon, in the book of Revelation, how can there be a pre-tribulation resurrection? But if there is a pre-tribulation resurrection, then rip this scripture out of your Bible. We should note here that not only did these pastors get the wrong time of the resurrection but also who is resurrected, for we who are alive and remain until the coming of the Lord don't taste of death and inherit the earth. Blessed are the meek, for they shall inherit the earth, as quoted in the scriptures. Just as the members of the first-century church were willing to lose their lives for the gospel's sake, this same command is required of the twenty-first-century church.

If this manuscript sounds like a broken record, it is because the church has heard this message of the pre-tribulation resurrection for at least a hundred years. Pastors like Tim LaHaye and Jerry Jenkins are writing books about people left behind, that the living church is resurrected to heaven before the tribulation, when it does not happen. I have used every scripture I can find to prove them wrong, and so far, I think I have done a good job. There is more.

We should first note here that we all have "a cross to bear." Above all things, when we read, "When he cometh in his glory, with his holy angels," this is when the church needs to look up. After Mark 13:12, where we are told that brother shall betray brother, verse 14 says, "And ye shall be hated of all men for my name's sake: but he that endure to the end shall be saved." And believers are to deny themselves of what? The mark of the beast. If you profit from the Antichrist, you will lose your own soul. And who is this adulterous and sinful generation? "Adulterous" is the word *moicheou*,[121] which means to commit adultery. It is from *moichos*,[122] which means perhaps from the primary a (male) paramour. To find out what a male paramour is, I had to go to my *Webster's Dictionary*. It means, "Me, par mour by the way of love, fr. of

---

[120] Ibid., 2079.

[121] Ibid., 2116.

[122] Ibid.

an illicit lover." You are an illicit lover if you take the mark of the beast. Until when are we to wait for the Lord? When he comes in the glory of his Father with the holy angels.

That is revealed in Mark 13:26–27, "And then they shall see the Son of Man coming in the clouds with great power and glory. And then shall he send his angels, and shall gather together his elect from the four winds, from the uttermost part of the earth to the utter most parts of heaven." But if there is a pre-tribulation resurrection, then rip this out of your Bible, because we are told by the pre-tribulation pastors that we just vanish and don't see his coming after the Lord. The question is, would we have a Bible if there was this pre-tribulation resurrection?

Are the international bankers and the banks in our country not pushing these cards instead of cash? This could be the way the Antichrist controls all spending when our governments take cash out of our society. If we see Europe go to this cashless society, will we in America do the same? Will Christians wake up and refuse this cashless system, knowing that this is how the Antichrist controls buying and selling? When I see most people in my area not having any cash but using a card for every transaction, they are prime candidates for the mark of the beast, for no one will be able to buy or sell unless he takes the mark of the beast. The Bible warns us that it is "the economy, stupid" when it warns not to take the mark of the beast. This card will possibly be turned into a computer chip in the hand or forehead. Remember what we are continually told it's "the economy, stupid." This is only possible in this generation. This is one of the signs that the Lord Jesus says, "When ye see all these things, know that it is near, even at the door."

We are told daily that we live in a global economy. Thanks to our politicians and the major corporations, American jobs have been sent overseas to tie the economies together and make all countries dependent on each other in trade. As we have seen the last few years, all it takes is one major market to crash to bring down all the markets in the world. Who is running the global economy? That would be the Bilderberg group, the Council on Foreign Relations, and the Trilateral Commission. These people don't get exposed by the press because they are owned by these people. The common citizens must know why these people must meet in secret. What are their plans for the future of the world? We all know about the G-8 meetings to discuss the global economy.

Will the G-8 become the G-10? Will these people working behind closed doors cause a worldwide economic depression to bring in the "New World Order"? Are we about to see the world placed into ten economic zones, just as the Bible tells us? Revelation 17:12 says, "And the ten horns which thou sawest are ten kings, which have received no kingdom as yet; but receive power as kings one hour with the beast." So we know there will be a global economic crash sometime in the future. What will happen to your IRA accounts when this crash happens? Are your treasures now invested in gold and silver?

In James 5:1–3, it says, "Go to now, ye rich men, weep and howl for your miseries that shall come upon you. Your riches are corrupted, and your garments are moth eaten. Your gold and silver is cankered; Ye have heaped treasure together for the last days." Your gold and silver will be worthless in the last days. So much for smart investments in gold and silver. One of these sellers of gold, Lear Capital on the Fox Business Network, tells us, "Gold has never been worthless." Once again, man's word is wrong. Let us note again that the past reveals the future. Ezekiel 17:19 says, "They shall cast their silver in the street, and their gold shall be removed: their silver and their gold shall not be able to deliver them in the day of the wrath of the Lord: they shall not satisfy their souls, neither fill their bowels: because it is the stumbling-block of their iniquity." The past reveals the future. When the judgments came upon the house of Judah, their gold and silver were worthless. Ezekiel tells us in verse 27, "I will do unto them after their way, and according to their deserts will I judge them; and they shall know that I am the Lord." This is the message the twenty-first-century people need to hear. Your only hope is in the Lord Jesus Christ.

When I read the obituary of a person who was a Baptist, Lutheran, or Catholic, does this mean they are they trusting in a denomination? When a soul gets to heaven, there will be no Baptists, Catholics, or Lutherans. Only the souls that are "saved by the blood of the lamb" who is the Lord Jesus Christ. For it's by faith in the Lord Jesus, and not of works; it's the gift of God. Are we all not but one church of the Lord Jesus? Europe is trusting in the pope of Rome more than God. When the pope of Rome visited New York City, I was watching it on Fox News. The commentator said, "It was like being in the presence of God." I couldn't believe she said that. He is just another man who needs a Savior.

This is how the Antichrist will appear unto man. But he will not be born on this planet. Revelation tells us "he was cast to the earth." He will be a man with great charisma that the Bible tell us, if it were possible he would fool the very elect. Matthew 24:24 says, "For there shall arise false Christs, and false prophets, and shall shew great signs and wonders; insomuch that, if it were possible, they shall deceive the very elect." I take this scripture as the church of the Lord Jesus Christ will not be fooled. If the elect are not deceived by these false Christs and prophets, then they will have to be on the earth when they appear. Daniel 11:24 tells us, "He shall enter peaceably even upon the fattest (a rich dish, a fertile field, a robust man) places of the province."

We should note that scripture tells us this happened in the past, because the past reveals the future. The Bible tells us that Satan was the real king of the city of Tyrus when it was wealthy and that Tyrus was the capital of the first global economy.

Ezekiel 28:11–14 says, "Moreover the word of the Lord came unto me, saying, [This is God giving Ezekiel the Holy Spirit knowledge of God to describe Satan] Son of man, take up a lamentation upon the king of Tyrus, and say unto him, Thus saith the Lord God; Thou sealest up the sum, full of wisdom, and perfect in beauty. Thy hast been in Eden the garden of God; every precious stone was thy covering, the sardius, topaz, and the diamond, the beryl, the onyx, and the jasper, the sapphire, the emerald, and the carbuncle, and gold: the workmanship of thy tabrets and thy pipes was prepared in thee in the day that thou was created." This is how Satan was clothed in heaven—with all the precious stones of heaven—and Satan rebelled against God. We should note that the saints of God, when they get to heaven, receive a linen garment but with certain crowns. "Thou art the anointed cherub that covereth and I have set thee so: thou wast upon the mountain of God; thou has walked up and down in the midst of the stones of fire."

Tyrus was as Ezekiel states in 27:3: "And say unto Tyre, O thou that art situate at the entry of the sea, which art a merchant of the people of my isles." Tyrus was the center of world trade in its day, and the king of it was Satan. And let's note all the nations that traded with Tyrus. There is Senir, Lebanon, Assurites, Chittim, Egypt, the isles of Elishah, Zidon and Arvad, Gebal, Persia and Lud, and of Put, Arvad, the Gammadims, Tarshish, Javan, Tubal, and Meshech, Togarmah, Dedan, Syria, Judah, and the land of Israel, Damascus, Dan, Arabia, Sheba and Raamah, Haran and Canneh, Eden, and Tarshish.

Ezekiel writes this to tell us that Satan was the king in Tyre, which was the center of world trade at this time. The past reveals the future. This is why the New Testament warns us not to take the mark of the beast. Satan again will be head of world trade. This is "when you see all these things come to pass, know that my kingdom is near" that the Lord Jesus stated in Matthew 24:33. Has anybody heard of the World Trade Organization? And why do we have this organization? It's because, "It's the world economy, stupid." John tells us in Revelation 17:12, "And the ten horns which thou sawest are ten kings, which have received no kingdom as yet; but receive power as kings one hour with the beast." One might ask, will the World Trade Organization place the world into ten economic zones?

Let's note Psalms 76:9, 12: "When God rose to judgment, to save the meek of the earth. He shall cut off the spirit of princes: he is terrible to the kings of the earth." And how terrible will it be? Revelation 19:20–21 says "And the beast was taken, and with him the false prophet that wrought miracles before him, with which he deceived them that had received the mark of the beast. These both were cast alive into a lake of fire burning with brimstone. And the remnant were slain with the sword of him that sat upon the horse." As the psalm stated that God "is terrible to the kings of the earth," this is how terrible it will be. And when are these kings slain with the sword? Revelation 19:15 says, "And out of his mouth goeth a sharp sword, and he treadeth the winepress of the fierceness and wrath of Almighty God." We should note that it is only "the beast and the false prophet" that are cast into the lake of fire. These other kings are slain with the sword. These are some of those that "came out of the great tribulation, and have washed their robes, and made them white in the blood of the lamb."

This is who the Lord used to destroy Satan and his first world economic center. Ezekiel 26:7 says, "For thus saith the Lord God; Behold, I will bring upon Tyrus Nebuchadnezzar king of Babylon, a king of kings, from the north." Note the title given to Nebuchadnezzar, king of kings. We know who else has only be given that title to destroy again Satan's kingdom in the last days. He is written about in Revelation 19:19: "And he (Almighty God) hath on his vesture and on his thigh a name written King of Kings, and Lord of Lords."

And if you didn't notice, it said Dan, Judah, and the land of Israel. Ezekiel lived in the sixth century. During Ezekiel's time, the state of Israel was known as the land of Judaea. The house of Israel was taken out of the land of Israel in the eighth century. And they are mentioned here as three separate people. The land of Israel of Ezekiel is the North Country that Jeremiah tells us is the wilderness that God caused Israel to rest in. Also note it said Dan. And Judges 5:17 says, "Why did Dan remain in ships." One might ask, why does Dan remain in ships? Maybe to go to another land? Does part of the tribe of Dan go to Greece, where the History Channel's "The Exodus, Exposed" tells us that there is evidence of a people that crossed over a parted sea? The Assyrians took the rest of the tribe of Dan in captivity later in history.

As the Lord Jesus states in Matthew 24:16, "Verily I say unto you, This generation shall not pass, till all these things be fulfilled." I believe this is happening in our generation. The European nation is trying to bring a new world government that will rule over all world trade. And just as the past reveals that Satan ruled the past world trade, he will rule over the last world trade. Will the next pope be the black pope that will take the name of Peter as prophecies claim? Not that the pope has done anything bad yet. But those of us who study the Bible know that in the future there will be the "false prophet," and that false prophet gives power to the Antichrist. And we know where that happens—in the city that is built on seven hills. That city is Rome. It scares me to think that this church brings in the rule of the Antichrist. But if Bible prophecy says it does, it will. I pray for all Christians, Catholics, and denominations that pray to the true God of heaven and for our brothers in faith, the Jews of Israel. They will see in the near future that Jesus was the Messiah. Zechariah 12:7 says, "And one shall say unto him, What are these wounds in thine hands? Then he shall answer, Those with which I was wounded in the house of my friends." God still loves the Jews of Israel. Although he has punished them, he will never lose his love for them, just as the Lord will never lose his love for his church.

But he will test the church just as he tested Israel. Let us note James 1:12: "Blessed is the man that endureth temptation: for when he is tried, he shall receive the crown of life, which the Lord hath promised to them that love him." Do you have the faith to go through what is about to happen in the near future? I believe that the judgments of God are our test on our faithfulness to him. After all that will happen on the earth will you keep your faith in God? We are warned many times by the Lord himself. We are also told this in the book of Revelation.

All seven churches are told, "He that hath an ear, let him hear what the spirit saith unto the churches." What is that message? They are to repent and overcome. We are to overcome the judgments and the wrath of Satan. Just as the first-century church had its persecutions by Nero (Satan), the twenty-first-century church will be persecuted by the Antichrist himself. But there are many promises from the Lord that the church will be able to endure until the end. The "we which are alive and remain till the coming of the Lord," will be the meek that inherit the earth, for blessed are the meek for they will inherit the earth, as said by the Lord Jesus himself. This is the greater message the scriptures tell us.

The American dollar value will be eaten up by inflation, for the Bible tells us in Revelation 6:6, "And I heard a voice in the midst of the four beasts say, measure of wheat for penny [a day's pay], and three measures of barley for a penny, and see thou hurt not the oil and the wine." The American dollar will be destroyed to bring in the new North American trade zone money. This is where all Christians will be required to take the mark of the beast and swear allegiance to him. Will it be caused by these secret societies? I am not a conspiracy writer. President George H. W. Bush spoke many times on the New World

Order. We are told every day on the news we live in a global economy. I give you world events with Bible prophecies.

After this crash, the Bible tells us who becomes the great economic leader who brings the world out of the collapse. He is none other than the Antichrist. Will you allow this man to completely restore your economic portfolio? These ten kings with the Antichrist head of the New World Order is where the mark of the beast comes in. Most of the world will not know who he is and will gladly take the mark of the beast if it wasn't for this. Revelation 14:9–10 says, "And the third angel followed them, saying with a loud voice, If any man worship the beast and his image, and receive his mark in his forehead, or in his hand, The same shall drink of the wine of the wrath of God." This is not an event Christians should fear, but if there is a pre-tribulation resurrection of the church, then rip this out of your Bible, because this is not a message to the church but to those who are left behind who don't read the Bible.

Iran, with the help of Russia, is developing nuclear weapons for the sole purpose of the destruction of Israel, as stated by Iranian President Mahmoud Ahmadinejad. This tells us that Armageddon can't be far off. Let's note Ezekiel 38:3: "Gog, the chief prince of Meshech and Tubal," and in verse 5, "Perish." In today's terms, this is the Russian and Iranian alliance that comes against the land of the unwalled villages and the land of Israel at the battle of Armageddon. The nations of the world do nothing about this. As Isaiah states, "The past reveals the future." The results of history tell us what will happen in the future. Not learning from past history is what I call stupid. The American government and Israeli prime minister being in negotiations with the Palestinian officials in the sharing of Jerusalem agreement tells us the end is near. Here is what the Word of the Lord has to say. Zechariah12:2 tells us, "And in that day will I make Jerusalem a burdensome stone for all people." We know that the Islamic militants Hamas will never agree to a sharing agreement but only call for the destruction of the state of Israel.

With the national debt of America now over ten trillion dollars and most of Europe in the same financial shape, I see a worldwide economic crash in just a few years. This is not just my opinion but the opinion of economists on Fox Business. Let us note Daniel 11:24, "He [the Antichrist] shall enter peaceably [*shalvah*,[123] which means security (genuine or false), abundance, peace, prosperity, quietness] even upon the fattest [*mishman*,[124] which means figurative and concrete, a rich dish] places of the province; and he shall do that which his fathers have not done, nor his fathers' fathers; he shall scatter among them the prey, and spoil, and riches: yea, and he shall forecast his devices against the strong holds, even for a time." Let us note here that it is in Daniel "for a time" and in the book of Revelation it's "an hour. And this is the tribulation period.

I have just finished reading a book by Daniel Estulin called *The True Story of the Bilderberg Group*. It is a must read by all Christians because he exposes the Council on Foreign Relations and the Trilateral Commission. He has done the research into the secret meetings of Bilderbergs and has pictures of the Bilderberg meetings. Note that John Kerry is there, and who is pushing to pass the carbon tax but John Kerry? In the photos of the 2004 meeting, who does he have a picture of? None other than John Edwards, the self-claimed champion of the poor, just as Bill Clinton claimed to be in the 1992 election. In the 1992 election, all we heard about was the homeless people of America. In the eight years Bill Clinton was president, can anyone tell me what legislation Bill Clinton initiated to help the homeless? None. We must note that when Jesus spoke, he asked us to help the poor. I don't believe the poor he relates to are the poor who refuse to work for a living, just the ones who cannot provide for themselves, like widows and orphans and the disabled.

Let us note scripture. In Mark 14:13–14, the Lord Jesus says, "But when thou makest a feast, call the poor, the maimed, the lame, the blind: And thou shall be blessed, for they cannot recompense thee: and thou shalt be recompensed at the resurrection of the just." The "unjust" are not resurrected until after the thousand-year reign of Christ at the great white throne judgment. Revelation 20:12 says, "And I saw the dead, small and great, stand before God; and the books were opened: and another book was opened, which is the book of life: and the dead were

123 Ibid., 1985.
124 Ibid., 1912.

judged out of those things which were written in the books, according to their works." This is how man can store up treasure in heaven. Note the word "resurrection", which means from the dead. This does not say that you can store up treasure in heaven by giving money to the church. Let us also note James 1:26–27, "If any man among you seem religious, and bideth not his tongue, but deceiveth his own heart, this man's religion is vain. Pure religion and undefiled before God and the Father is this, To visit the fatherless and the widows in their affliction, and to keep himself unspotted from the world." This is what the Word of God says to help the fatherless and widows in their afflictions. In the Bible, not one word about the 10 percent tithe is mentioned.

He also exposes the true story behind NAFTA to bring about the formation of the "American Union," similar to the European Union. Is this why none of the politicians want to secure the borders and grant amnesty to those who are here? Will Americans be willing to give up our sovereign rights under our constitution for the sake of the "New World Order"? When we hear from our politicians that change is coming, is this the change? Can American Christians trust any politician to tell us the truth? If the Bilderberg Group, the Council on Foreign Relations, and the Trilateral Commission all own the politicians of America, including the presidency, there is no stopping the New World Order from talking place. David Estulin exposes the New World Order, and I just match it to Bible prophecy. This is "when you see all these come to pass, know that my coming is near" as spoken by the Lord Jesus Christ.

America needs a new political party. It should be called the Constitution Party. Every candidate who runs for this office should be sworn to uphold the Constitution in the manner it was given and keep Americans from the power of the New World Order by paying down the national debt. America needs a wakeup call. The world is changing very quickly, and not to Christian values but to a New World Order that most Christians should fear. We, as Christians, are in deep trouble. As I am reading the newspaper today, I see that Congress has raised the debt limit to exceed twelve trillion dollars. This does not include their health care plan. The past reveals the future. The world powers of the past were not conquered but collapsed from within. This debt will be the downfall of America, and this debt is found in most countries around the world. The Lord Jesus prophesies, "When you see all these things come to pass." This worldwide debt is one of those things. This is insanity; this is stupid. I will visit the word "stupid" many times.

I believe American Christians will wake up and see what the one-world government people are trying to do. And they will act. But to pull this off, they must do one thing first. They must take away the second amendment, which is the right to bear arms, just as they have done in Europe and England. As Christian Americans, here is where we should make our stand. I will not accept the New World Order under any circumstances. My best guess is they will say I am one of those radical Christians who don't understand what is best for America. Even George Bush disappointed me when he gave in to global warming theory and the world court. The world court will be the tool of the Antichrist to persecute the twenty-first-century church, just as it rules against Israel even when they just defend themselves against Palestinian attacks.

Another book worth reading is *The Creature of Jekyll Island* by Edward Griffin. He exposes the truth behind the Federal Reserve. What really occurred in 1928 to bring about the 1929 stock market crash? It is apparent that many Wall Street investors were buying stocks on margin accounts, referred of as call loans, becoming very wealthy. This is when the Federal Reserve cut off the money supply to the banks, causing the bank to call in the call loans made to the investors. Panic selling started, and the market crashed on October 29.

We learn in Edward Griffin's book that there were warnings to certain individuals of the upcoming fed policy, and they were told to get out of the market. Those people were John D. Rockefeller, J. P. Morgan, Joseph P. Kennedy, Bernard Baruch, Henry Morganthau, and Douglas Dillon. Joseph P. Kennedy made a cool million dollars by shorting the market. The very rich don't lose a dime. Nice, huh? And who in history did President Franklin Roosevelt hire to reform the market? None other than the biggest crook, Joseph P. Kennedy. I believe they, the Trilateral Commission, the Council on Foreign Relations, and the Bilderberg Group, will do this again to bring in the New World Order. Will we see a stock market crash again?

The truth behind America's entry into World War I was that it wasn't about the sinking of the Lusitania but to bail out the New York bankers who lent money to Britain, France, and Belgium in their fight with Germany. They insisted they could not pay the debt unless they collected reparations from Germany. After World War I, the German mark was virtually worthless. Under the Dawes Plan of 1924, a great deal of American private capital was invested in the German government's bonds and industrial enterprises. In 1929, a new plan called the Young Plan, represented by J. P. Morgan, had the American banking system recalling loans and canceling credit to Europe, and the result of this, by 1933, was that two-thirds of world trade had vanished. The American government passed the Smooth-Hawley Act, which reduced world trade by adding tariffs to imported goods. These are the true reasons Americans experienced an economic depression. It's because of man's greed and stupidity.

Just about all wars are fought for no other reason than for money and world dominance. The war we are in today is a war against radical Islam that thinks Islamic people are to rule the world. We should also note that the governments around the world, with the help of these so-called global weather experts, are scaring people about global warming. There are more scientists telling us there is not global weather change other than what is natural than those who say this is caused by man.

Since that theory on global warming was totally proven wrong, it's now global weather change. If global weather is changing, maybe the Lord is trying to warn us about the coming judgments. There is nothing man can do about it except pray and fast. This is just an excuse to take away the individual liberties of the people of the world and get into the pocketbooks of the American people. All I can say about this theory of global warming is that it reminds me of the theory of evolution. There is not much evidence for either theory.

With all that I have read in books, seen in news stories of the things happening around the world, and read in Bible prophecy, I can believe that the closing days of man's rule of this earth are about to begin. All these things have come upon this generation, and one must also note Psalms 102:16, "When the Lord shall build up Zion he shall appear in his glory." The word for appear is *raah*,[125] which means a primitive root, to see, literal or figurative. When God returned the Jews back from the Babylonian captivity, he appeared to them in Jesus. In 1947, God returned the Jews to the land of Israel, and the state of Israel was formed. The Lord will soon appear to bring back all of the tribes of the house of Israel.

I believe and hope to prove to you that there is no pre-tribulation resurrection. There are just a few pastors out there who say there is no pre-tribulation rapture, and people call into their programs and tell them they're wrong. The old saying is true, "If you hear a lie long enough, you will believe it." The only problem is, if the resurrection of the church does not happen when most people think, it may be too late. Paul tells us in 2 Thessalonians 2:11, "And for this because God shall send them strong delusion, that they should believe a lie." The Bible gives many warnings to God's church to wait for him, to endure until the end. That is the message most pastors miss. To every one of the churches of Asia in the book of Revelation, they are told to endure until the end. The end is not in Revelation 4.

Throughout biblical history, before the Lord acted he had two prophets in the land telling them something was about to happen just like in the time of the judgments of the house of Israel and then on the house of Judah. They had false prophets telling them judgment was not coming when God's prophets said it was coming, and it came. The soon-coming judgments of the book of the Revelation are quickly going to come upon this generation. And what are Bible scholars telling us? They tell us not to worry; God is going to take us to heaven before this happens. I believe these scholars are wrong.

Peter even warns us about this wrong interpretation in 2 Peter 3:16, "As also in all his epistles [talking about Paul's epistles], speaking in them these things; in which are some things hard to understand, which they that are unlearned and unstable wrest, as they so also other scripture, unto their own destruction." The word for wrest is the word *strebloo*,[126] which means, to wrench (i.e., special) to torture (by the

125   Ibid., 1965.
126   Ibid., 2155.

rack), but only figurative to pervert, wrest. It is from *stepho*,[127] which means to twist (i.e., turn quite around or reverse) (literal or figurative), convert, or turn. Did we notice the Greek word meaning to pervert? They perverted the Word of God with the pre-tribulation resurrection. Also note the Greek word meanings to torture, (by the rack). This is exactly what the Christian churches did during the Dark Ages.

If the church is fooled by the pre-tribulation resurrection preachers, they will be easy pickings for the Antichrist. This is why Peter tells us that this brings on "their own destruction." We also should note Matthew 13:39, "The harvest is the end of the world." The end is the word *sunteleia*,[128] which means entire completion (i.e., consummation of a dispensation), end. We also read in Revelation 2:26, "And he that overcometh, and keepeth my works unto the end, to him will I give power over the nations." It is those who overcome until the end who come back to rule and reign with Christ. The pre-tribulation resurrection pastors must prove that the end of the dispensation is in Revelation 4.

Most pastors tell us that they are excited about the near return of Jesus Christ, when the Bible tells us this in Amos 5:18, "Woe into you that desire the day of the Lord! To what end is it for you? The day of the Lord is darkness, and not light." And in verse 20 it says, "Shall not the day of the Lord be darkness, and not light? Even very dark, and no brightness in it?" Man does not know when all the spirits in heaven are allowed to be made human beings to redeem them back to God.

And then you look at most of the other churches who are silent about this. They go on about how much God loves them, not warning their congregation that he is a God of judgment and wrath and that this could be the generation that sees the second coming of Jesus Christ. The Bible tells us through his prophets what God says about his watchmen and shepherds or in the term of today, his pastors. Isaiah 56:10–12 says:

---

[127]   Ibid.
[128]   Ibid., 2159.

His watchmen are blind: they are all ignorant, they are all dumb dogs, they cannot bark; sleeping, lying down, loving to slumber. Yea, they are greedy dogs which never have enough, and they are shepherds that cannot understand: they all look to their own way, every one for his gain, from his quarter. Come Ye, say they, I will fetch wine, and we will fill ourselves with strong drink; and to morrow shall be as this day, and much more abundant.

Remember, I did not say this, but it was Isaiah who got this from God. I did not want to originally put this scripture in this book, but I thought again, and if it is in the Bible, God wants us to hear it. This is what God has to say about his watchmen and shepherds or the pastors of his churches. Are they dumb dogs who cannot understand for promising a pre-tribulation and the alive resurrection? Does this not fit most of the television pastors when they continually ask for money, even from the very poor, saying, "Send me your money so God can bless you"? Are they not the greedy dogs that never have enough? In Matthew 21:1, 3 the Lord says, "It is written, my house shall be called the house of prayer; but ye have made it a den of thieves." Is this why the Lord overturns the tables in the temple? They too were selling salvation to whoever would give money to them.

I hear pastors on the radio and television say, "Send me some money so God can bless you." This goes against the Word of God. Let us note Acts 8:20, "But Peter said unto him, Thy money perish with thee, because thou hast thought that the gift of God may be purchased with money." This verse proves these pastors are wrong. Jesus was angered at the Jews in his time because they worshiped the temple instead of who the temple represented. Is this not what some of these pastors of today have done?

I was watching one of the television pastors say on his program that a ten-year-old girl who earned ten dollars by washing her grandmother's feet was going to send that ten dollars to them, and then he thanked her for her contribution to his ministry. Are they that greedy that they would accept that money? Another pastor is asking for a thousand-dollar contribution so he can buy a jet. Our Lord told us he didn't even have a place to rest his head, but this pastor needs his personal jet. This same pastor claims to heal the sick. If I had the power to heal the sick, I would be in every hospital in this country to do this. Is he? No. This is why I turned off my television and started studying the Bible for myself.

The rich young ruler came to Jesus and asked in Mark 10:17, "Good Master, what shall I do that I may inherit eternal life?" The response of the Lord Jesus in verse 21 was, "One thing thou lackest: go thy way, sell whatsoever thou hast, and give it to the poor, and thou shalt have treasure in heaven: and come, take up the cross, and follow me." Do we notice that Jesus did not say, "Sell what you have and give it to the temple," or in our time, the church. Giving money to the poor is where you will have treasure in heaven. Jesus has compassion for the poor and needy. Let's note 2 Corinthians 9:9, "He that given to the poor: his righteousness remaineth for ever."

In America, Americans pay over 40 percent of their income to local and federal taxes, and some of that money goes to the poor in this country and to many other counties in the world to feed the poor. The state has replaced the church in this manner. It is apparent to me that the temple was the government to the Jews in Jesus's day and had a lot of wealth. When the Romans destroyed the temple in AD 70, they used that money to build the coliseum in Rome. Were they providing for the poor, as instructed in the psalms?

The answer is in Luke. This is why this is recorded in the scriptures. When the Lord Jesus and his disciples were at the temple, they saw this. Luke 21:1 says, "And he looked up, and saw the rich men casting their gifts into the treasury. And he saw a certain poor widow casting in thither two mites." Note the language. The rich men were casting their gift and not a tithe. Note the poor widow cast in two mites. And what was the Lord Jesus's response? Verses 3 and 4 say:

> Of a truth I say unto you, that this poor widow hast
> cast in more than they all: For all these have of their
> abundance cast unto the offerings of God: but she

of her penury [*husterema*,[129] which means especially poverty] hath cast in all the living that she had.

This tells the twenty-first-century church not to demand that the poor give to the church. Did this happen before the Lord Jesus say in Matthew 23:14, "Woe into you, scribes and Pharisees, hypocrites! For ye devour widow's houses, and for a pretence make long prayer: therefore ye shall receive the greater damnation."

When the Lord Jesus returns, his mind will not have changed. He tells those who inherit the kingdom on earth the reason to give in Matthew 25:35–36: "For when I was hungered, and ye gave me meat: I was thirsty, and ye gave me drink I was a stranger, and you took me in: Naked, ye clothed me: I was sick, and ye visited me: I was in prison, and you came into me." Then in verse 40 he says, "Inasmuch, as ye have done it unto me of the least of them is my Brethren, ye have done it unto me."

That's plain and simple language. Provide the poor their necessaries, not so that you pastors can build monuments to their ministries, just as the temple was. I hear pastors telling their congregations the only way to salvation is to give their estates to the church, but this is the same as these Pharisees who devoured widows' houses. Not much has changed in two thousand years. This is why I named this manuscript, *The Big Lie, Exposed*—to expose these greedy pastors. This is why Zechariah 11:8 tells us, "Three shepherds also I cut off in one month." The Christian religion is one for the reasons revealed in this manuscript.

---

[129]   Ibid., 2171.

The 10 Percent Tithe Lie, Exposed

When Jesus died on the cross, the Christians were freed from the Mosaic Law. The scriptures that you will read in this chapter prove this. When the church of the Lord Jesus Christ realizes that giving money to the church in the form of the 10 percent tithe is not scriptural, then they can truly say this. And I will paraphrase Dr. Martin Luther King, "Free at last, free at last, thank God Almighty we are free at last." This is why I wrote this manuscript: to free the Christians from these greedy pastors.

Let's note Acts 15:24, "That certain which came out from us have troubled you with words, subverting your souls, saying, Ye must be circumcised, and keep the law: to whom we gave no such commandment." Luke tells us here we are not under the Law. Second Corinthians 3:17 says, "Now the Lord is that Spirit: and where the Spirit of the Lord is, there is liberty [*eleutheria*,[130] which means freedom, from *eleutheros*,[131] which means (genitive) exempt (from obligation or liability)]." In Galatians 5:1 it says, "Stand fast therefore in the liberty wherewith Christ hath made us free, and be not entangled again with the yoke of bondage." If we are under the Mosaic Law of the 10 percent tithe, then this would not be in scripture. Notice the Greek word meaning "exempt from obligation or liability."

---

[130] Ibid., 2068.
[131] Ibid.

Galatians 1:16 says, "Knowing that a man is not justified by the works of the law, but by the faith of Jesus Christ, even we have believed in Jesus Christ, and not by the works of the law: for by the words of the law shall no flesh be justified." Note in this one verse of scripture we are told that man is not justified by the Mosaic Law.

Galatians 2:21 says, "I do not frustrate the grace of God; for if righteousness come by the law, then Christ is dead in vain." Galatians 3:11–13 says, "But no man is justified by the law in the sight of God, it is evident: for, the just shall live by faith. And the law is not of faith; but, the men that doeth them shall live in them." Christ has redeemed us from the curse of the law. This is the same kind of warning to the people who want to live under the law when Paul writes, "The men that doeth them shall live in them."

We are told in verse 23, "But before faith came, we were kept under the law, shut up unto the faith which should afterwards be revealed." Romans 3:21 says, "But now the righteousness of God without the law is manifested, being witnessed by the law and the prophets." Paul goes on and writes in verse 27, "Where is boasting then? It is excluded. By what law? Of works? Nay: but the law of faith." And Paul writes in Romans 6:14, "For ye are not under the law, but under grace." I know that the Assemblies of God and the Pentecostal churches demand that their members pay the full 10 percent tithe, and that is of the gross income and not the net income. They even ask their members to give their estates to the church to receive true salvation. These churches are dens of thieves.

This is why Peter writes in 1 Peter 4:17, "The judgments must begin with the church of God." I believe it will start with pastors. The past reveals the future. When the judgments came upon the house of Judah, Ezekiel 9:6 says, "But come not upon any man upon whom is the mark; and begin at my sanctuary." Paul writes in Romans 16:1, "I commend unto you Phoebe our sister, which is a servant of the church which is Cenchrea." She was the pastor. Paul said in verse 17, "Now I beseech you, brethren, mark them which cause divisions and offences contrary to the doctrines which ye have learned; and avoid them." That doctrine they had learned was "for by faith ye are saved by grace, it's the gift of God" and not by the "works of the law," which is the 10 percent tithe. And what does Paul say? Avoid them. Now verse 18 says, "For they that are such serve not your Lord Jesus Christ, but their own belly; and by good words and fair speeches deceiver the hearts of the simple." This tells us that the churches that demand the 10 percent tithe serve not the Lord Jesus Christ. This is another big lie, exposed by this manuscript.

And what is the law of faith? These are the words of the Lord Jesus in Matthew 22:37–40:

> Thou shall love the Lord thy God with all your heart,
> and with all your soul, and with all your mind. This
> is the first and great commandment. And the second
> is like unto it. Thou shalt love thy neighbor as thyself.
> On these two commandments hang all the law and
> the prophets.

So which part of these two commandments on which "hang all the law" is the law of the 10 percent tithe? We should note this part of the scriptures "and their damnation slumbereth [*nustazo*,[132] which means to nod, (i.e., by implication) to fall asleep, figurative to delay] not." This tells us these pastors will not hear these words, "Come up hither," because their sleep will not delay.

We are told this in Romans 13:8–11:

> Owe no man any thing, but to love one another:
> for he that loveth another hath fulfilled the law. For
> this, Thou shalt not commit adultery, Thou shalt no
> kill, Thou shalt not steal, Thou shalt not bear false
> witness, Thou shalt not covet; and if there be any
> other commandment, it is briefly comprehended in
> this saying, namely, Thou shalt love thy neighbour as
> thyself. Love worketh no ill to his neighbour; therefore
> love is the fulfilling of the law.

---

[132] Ibid., 2119.

I think it is interesting that Paul says, "Owe no one anything." This means to get out of debt and basically puts us under the Ten Commandments. This is the fulfillment of the Law.

Acts 6:14 says, "For we have heard him say, that this Jesus of Nazareth shall destroy this place, and shall change the customs [*ethos*,[133] which means a usage (prescribed by habit or law)] which Moses delivered us." This is not good news to the Sanhedrin. This place is the temple. The custom of the people was the Law of Moses, and this was now being changed, because it is now "by faith are you saved, it's the gift of God." A gift cannot be paid for.

And talk about taking verses out of context. The biggest lie by these pastors is when they use Malachi 3:8, "Will a man rob God? Yet ye robbed me. But ye say, Wherewith have ye robbed me? In tithes and offerings." Now let's read what this verse is really all about.

In chapter 1, the Lord of hosts is speaking through Malachi to the priests in the temple and says:

> O priests, that despise my name. And ye say, Wherein have we despised thy name? Ye offer polluted bread upon my alter; and ye say, Wherein have we polluted thee? In that ye say, The table of the Lord is contemptible. And if ye offer the blind for sacrifice, is it not evil? And if ye offer the lame and sick, is it not evil? Offer it now unto thy governor; will he be pleased, with thee, or accept thy person? Saith the Lord of hosts.

So we read here that the Lord is not happy with the evil sacrifices of these priests.

Malachi also tells them in 2:9, "But have been partial in the Law." Then he says in verse 10, "Have we not all one Father? Hath not one God created us? Why do we deal treacherously everyman against his brother, by profaning the covenant of our fathers." It says in Malachi 2:17, "Every one that doeth evil is good in the sight of the Lord, and he

---

[133]   Ibid., 2061.

delighteth in them; or, Where is the God of Judgment?" It is apparent that the Jews were looking for their messiah in the fifth century BC. Malachi was talking to the priests when he said, "Will man rob God?

Note in 3:9 it says, "Ye are cursed with a curse: for ye have robbed me, even this whole nation." The people were giving gifts to the priests, because the priests were saying to the congregation, "Every one that doeth evil is good, in the sight of the Lord." God was not accepting the priests' evil sacrifices. The priests were robbing the Lord and the nation, and apparently when the Lord shows up almost four hundred years later, he has not changed his mind.

This account is recorded in Mark 11:15–18:

> And they come to Jerusalem: and Jesus went unto the temple, and began to cast out them that sold and bought in the temple, and overthrew the tables of the moneychangers, and the seats of them that sold doves; And would not suffer any vessel through the temple. And he (the Lord Jesus) taught, saying unto them, Is it not written, My house shall be called of all nations the house of prayer? But ye have made it a den of thieves. And the scribes and chief priests heard it, and sought how they might destroy him: for they feared him, because all the people was astonished at his doctrine.

When New Testament pastors put you back under the law of the 10 percent tithe, they have just made their church a den of thieves. Some of these pastors are so greedy that they are asking people even to leave their estates to the church. Let us note what Paul says in 2 Corinthians 12:13: "Behold, the third time I am ready to come to you; and I will not be burdensome to you: for I seek not yours, but you: for the children ought not to lay up for the parents but the parents for the children." Paul says, "I seek not yours, but you." I believe yours is not their money, because he says that money should be laid up for the children. First Peter 4:17 states, "For the time is come that judgment must begin at the house of God: and if it first begin at us." If the judgments begin at "the church," how can they teach the pre-tribulation resurrection? And when the judgments come I believe that they will begin with the church pastors. Once again, the Lord has not changed his mind.

In Matthew 7:21–23, it says:

> Not every one that saith unto me, Lord, Lord, shall enter into the kingdom of heaven; but he that doeth the will of my Father which is in heaven. Many will say to me in that day Lord, Lord, have we not prophesied in thy name? And in thy name cast out devils? And in thy name done many wonderful works? And then will I profess unto them, I never knew you: depart from me, ye that work iniquity.

Note that the word for iniquity is *anomia*,[134] which means illegality (i.e., violation of the law). The pastors who demand the 10 percent tithe are in violation of the new law of faith. This is why the Lord says, "I never knew you."

We should also note this in Matthew 5. In verse 5, we are told, "Think not that I am come to destroy the law, or the prophets; I am not come to destroy; but fulfill." Now let's notice what it says just a few verses later. This is the Lord Jesus speaking: "Therefore if thou bring thy gift to the altar." If we are still under the law of the 10 percent tithe, why does the Lord say here, "If thou bring thy gift"? Gift is *doron*,[135] which means a present; especially a sacrifice or offering. And to prove I didn't take this out of context, let's read this next scripture.

Matthew 5:23–24 says:

> Therefore if thou bring thy gift to the altar, and there rememberest that thy brother hath ought against thee; Leave thy gift before the altar, and go thy way ;

---

134 Ibid., 2026.
135 Ibid., 2059.

first be reconciled to thy brother, and then come and offer thy gift.

If now it's a gift to be sacrificed at the altar, it's no more the 10 percent tithe. This will probably end any church endorsement of this manuscript because I give you the truth of scripture. I would as well like to add that God had his own social security system in place. It's called children, for children are to honor their mother and father by taking care of them in their old age. That's one of the Ten Commandments with a promise.

Judgment upon Babylon (Iraq) in Our Time

I WAS WATCHING THE History Channel one night, and they used Jeremiah's prophecies to declare that this war in Iraq was predicted by him, but what they didn't do was prove that the North Country is America. This interpretation will. But I will show you that it was also the prophecies in Isaiah. I will prove that Bible prophecy is quickly coming to pass with the following scriptures.

Isaiah 13:1, 3–6, 9 says:

> The burden [divine judgment] of Babylon [Iraq], which Isaiah the son of Amoz did see . . . I have commanded my sanctified ones, I have also called my mighty ones for mine anger, even them that rejoice in my highness . . . The Noise of the multitude in the mountains, like as of a great people; a tumultuous noise of the kingdoms of nations gathered together: the Lord of Hosts mustereth the host of the battle . . . They come from a far country, from the end of heaven, even the Lord, and the weapons of his indignation, to destroy the whole land . . . Howl ye; for the day of the Lord is a hand; it shall come as a destruction from the Almighty . . . Behold, the day of the Lord cometh, cruel both with wrath and fierce anger, to lay the land

106

desolate: and he shall destroy the sinners thereof out
of it.

We know this battle in Babylon (Iraq) is at the time of the end,
for in verse 6 it states, "For the day of the Lord is at hand." Isaiah even
tells us that they are nations that rejoice in "My Highness." You should
also note "my sanctified ones." The only people who are sanctified are
the whole house of Israel. I do not know of any country who ever
invaded Iraq that was a Christian nation except America and England.
The country of Israel has never invaded Iraq except in the time of King
David. Isaiah lived and died long after King David. However, they did
destroy Iraq's nuclear power plant in the 1980s. So this day of the Lord is
for our time. Also notice that Isaiah says that I (God) called my mighty
ones for mine anger. It's with God's anger that he raises up nations to
do his will. Just as God has raised up a nation to take the house of Israel
into captivity, which was done by the Assyrians, and then another to
take the House of Judah into captivity for seventy years, which was
done by the Babylonians (Iraq). Then he raised up another kingdom
to bring them back into the land; this was done by the Medes and the
Persians. So is our war in Iraq not the purpose of God's judgment? We
should also note that in the last verse it says, "Behold, the day of the
Lord cometh." But now this destruction comes from God almighty.
Now let us finish the verses that describe this event.

Isaiah 13:9–13 says:

> Behold, the day of the Lord cometh, cruel both with
> the wrath and fierce anger, to lay the land desolate,
> and he shall destroy the sinners thereof out of it. For
> the stars of heaven and the constellations thereof shall
> not give their light: the sun shall be darkened in his
> going forth, and the moon shall not cause her light
> to shine. And I will punish the world for their evil,
> and the wicked for their iniquity; and I will cause
> the arrogancy of the proud to cease, and lay low the
> haughtiness of the terrible. I will make man more
> precious than fine gold; even a man than the golden

wedge of Ophir. Therefore I will shake the heavens, and the earth shall remove out of her place, in the wrath of the Lord of hosts, and in the day of his fierce anger.

We should note here that this scripture tells us that there is a time when the sun and moon don't give their light. This is when the Lord comes, and it is in his wrath. So there is no mistake of what this day is, Isaiah tells us twice it's the day of the Lord. And talk about global weather change: "The earth will be removed out of her place." God will also shake the heavens and the earth. This shaking of the earth is told to us in Hebrews 12:26–27: "Whose voice then shook the earth: but now he hath promised, saying, Yet once more I shake not the earth only, but also heaven. And this word, yet once more, signifieth the removing of those things that are shaken, as of things that are made, that those things that cannot be shaken may remain." Old Testament prophecy is reaffirmed in the New Testament.

Let us also note that on April 12, 2012, some of the planets in this solar system will line up in a row. The sun will be in the darkest place in the Milky Way. The Mayan prophecies and the scientists on the History Channel tell us that this will cause a great gravitational pull on the earth, possibly pulling the earth out of its orbit, causing an ice age to occur. The Mayan prophecies claim that there will be a worldwide flood. This goes against the Word of God. Genesis 9:11 says, "And I will establish my covenant with you; neither shall all flesh be cut off any more by the waters of the flood; neither shall there any more be a flood to destroy the earth." And we know, by the Lord God's prophets, that in the last days when God's wrath comes, "It shall burn as an oven." It is just the opposite. Christians should know that no one knows the hour or the day, but the Mayans predict an exact date. How stupid can pastors get? I heard even a television pastor give this some credence. We should also note that the movie based on this prophecy was a complete failure at the theater box office.

The scientists made this prediction once before when five of the planets a lined in May of 2000. Do you remember the book *5-5-2000?* Will they be right this time? I don't think so, because Jesus told us no one knows the hour or the day, but we will know when it is at the door.

The Lord Jesus tells us in Matthew 24:6, "And ye shall hear of war and rumours of wars: see that ye be not troubled: for these things must come to pass, but the end is not yet." This is why the Bible tells us not to take the mark of beast. It's because it will be the Antichrist who brings in a new world currency. And before leaving this note the language "see that ye be not troubled." Who is the Lord Jesus speaking to when he say ye if it is not the church? Everyone who sets a date is wrong. But there will be a time when it will be possible for the earth to be pulled out of its orbit. And this is predicted in the Bible.

Isaiah the prophet tells us this happens in Isaiah 13:13: "Therefore I will shake the heavens, and the earth shall remove out of place, in the wrath of the Lord of hosts, and in the day of his fierce anger." In Isaiah 24:20 it says, "The earth shall reel to and fro like a drunkard, and shall be removed like a cottage; and the transgression thereof shall be heavy upon it; and it shall fall, and not rise again." Those things that cannot be shaken should be our faith in the Lord, so we can boldly say verse 6, "The Lord is my helper, and I will not fear what man shall do unto me." This is the greater message of the Bible. "Fear not for I am with thee," for "Blessed are the meek, for they shall inherit the earth." It is "we which are alive and remain until the coming of the Lord" who are the ones who "don't taste of death till they see the coming of the Lord." This is the message of the Bible. And I will say this again: if there is a pre-tribulation resurrection, then rip this out of the Bible.

Let's also note of Jeremiah 50:9–11:

> For, lo, I will raise and cause to come up against Babylon an assembly of great nations from the north country; and they shall set themselves in array against her; from thence she shall be taken; their arrows shall be as of a mighty expert man; none shall return in vain . . . And Chaldea shall be a spoil: all that spoil her shall be satisfied, saith the Lord . . . Because ye were glad, because ye rejoiced, O ye destroyers of

mine heritage, because ye are grown fat as the heifer at
grass, and bellow as bulls.

Once again, we are told by Jeremiah that "God" would cause to
come against Babylon (Iraq) nations. Jeremiah also tells us of smart
weapons when he said, "Their arrows shall be as a mighty expert
[*sakal,*[136] which means to be circumspect and hence intelligent] man;
none shall return in vain." It is not until this time in history that man
has produced a weapon (we call them smart weapons) that can hit a
precise target as we have today. We should note that Jeremiah calls
them intellect weapons and that God sanctified this battle against Iraq.
Why? It is because they rejoiced at the destruction of God's heritage.

And to prove this is for the latter days of our time, let's read
50:12-13:

> Your mother shall be sore confounded; she that
> bare you shall be ashamed: behold, the hindermost
> [*achariyth,*[137] which means the last or end, hence
> the future (last, latter time)] of the nations shall be
> a wilderness, a dry land, and a desert. Because of the
> wrath of the Lord it shall not be inhabited, but it shall
> be wholly [*kol,*[138] which means properly the whole,
> hence all, any, or every] desolate: every one that goeth
> by Babylon shall be astonished, and hiss at all her
> plagues.

Babylon has been inhabited since recorded history, so this is for
the last days. We should also note that Jeremiah tells us of the wrath of
God in the latter days, which I believe is the wrath of God in the book
of Revelation. "And they became fat as a heifer." The word for fat here
is *puwsh,*[139] which means to spread, figuratively, to act proud.

---

[136]   Ibid., 1984.
[137]   Ibid., 1809.
[138]   Ibid., 1883.
[139]   Ibid., 1945.

This message is repeated in 51:43–48:

> Her cities are a desolation, a dry [*tsiyyah*,[140] which
> means to parch, aridity, concrete, a desert, barren,
> solitary place] land, and a wilderness, a land where
> no man dwelleth, neither doth any Son of Man pass
> thereby. And I will punish Bel in Babylon, and I will
> bring forth of his mouth that which had swallowed
> up: and the nations shall not flow together any more
> unto him: yea, the wall of Babylon shall fall. My
> people, go ye out of the mist of her, and deliver ye
> every man his soul from the fierce anger of the Lord.
> And lest your heart faint, and ye fear for the rumour
> that shall be heard in the land; a rumour shall both
> come in one year, and after that in another year shall
> come a rumour, and violence in the land, ruler against
> ruler. Therefore, behold, the days come, that I [God]
> will do judgment upon the graven images of Babylon:
> and her whole land shall be confounded, and all her
> slain shall fall in the midst of her.
>
> Then the heaven and the earth, and all that is therein,
> shall sing for Babylon: for the spoilers shall come unto
> to her from the north [*tsaphown*,[141] which means
> properly hidden (i.e., dark)], saith the Lord."

Spoilers *shadad*,[142] which means to be burley (i.e., figurative)
powerful (passive impregnable); by implication to ravage, dead,
destroy, utterly waste. Also note it describes this North Country as a
dark place. What is the forest called in Germany? It's called the Dark
Forest. The Angelo-Saxons came out of this dark forest in AD 400 and
overtook England. The rest of history I believe you know. This is what

---

[140] Ibid., 1954.
[141] Ibid., 1956.
[142] Ibid., 1978.

the History International Channel failed to prove. We should note that these spoilers come out of the dark and the words "destroy utterly."

Later in this book, we will read that the Lord God will raise his own army to fight in the battle of Armageddon. I believe this happens immediately after the tribulation of those days when the sun will be darkened, and the moon will not give her light, which is spoken of in Matthew 24:29. Once again, we are told by Jeremiah about "a land where no man dwelleth." And once again, "my people" are to leave the land because of the fierce anger of the Lord. We should note the Hebrew meaning properly hidden, in dark where the spoilers come from. And Jeremiah tells us something new. We should note the "violence in the land, ruler against rule." It is apparent there will be civil war in the country. We should also examine this phrase "all that spoil shall be satisfied, saith the Lord." Satisfied is *saba*,[143] which means to sate (i.e., fill to satisfaction).

And who is this North Country?

> But, the Lord liveth which brought up and which led the seed of the House of Israel out of the north country, and from all the countries I had driven them (Jer. 23:8).

> For thus saith the Lord; Sing with gladness for Jacob, and shout among the chief of the nations: publish ye, praise ye, and say, O Lord, save thy people, the remnant of Israel. Behold, I will bring them from the north country, and gather them from the coasts of the earth, and with them the blind and the lame, the woman with child and her that travaileth with child together: a great company shall return thither. They shall come weeping and with supplications will I lead them: I will cause them to walk by the rivers of waters in a straight way, wherein they shall not stumble: for

---

[143]   Ibid., 1976.

I am a father to Israel, and Ephraim is my firstborn
(Jer. 31:7–9).

Jeremiah tells us here in two separate verses that this North
Country is where God led the seed of the House of Israel after the
Assyrian captivity. That North Country is Europe, east of the Danube.
And after over nine hundred years, they are led into all the countries
that God will lead them. We should note the emphasis Jeremiah gives
to the tribe of Ephraim that is of this North Country, who received the
greatest blessings. Note: Ephraim is my firstborn. Ephraim, as we will
later read, is prophesied to be a military power in the last days. God's
plans in the future after the battle of Armageddon are to bring them
back from the coast of the earth to the land of Israel. This will be fully
explained later in the next manuscript.

There is still more, for Jeremiah 50:41–44 states:

> Behold, a people shall come from the north, and a
> great nation and many kings shall rise up from the
> coast of the earth. They shall hold the bow and the
> lance: they are cruel, and will not shew mercy: their
> voice shall roar like the sea, and they shall ride upon
> horses, every one put in array, like a man to the battle,
> against thee, O daughter of Babylon. The king of
> Babylon hath heard the report of them, and his hands
> waxed feeble: anguish took hold of him, and pangs
> as of a woman in travail. Behold, he shall come up
> like a lion from the swellings of the strong: But I will
> make them suddenly run away from her: and who is a
> chosen man that I might appoint over her? For who is
> like me? And who will appoint me the time? And who
> is that shepherd that will stand before me?

Jeremiah tells us of the war against Babylon (Iraq) twice, with
exactly the same words, in Jeremiah 49:19 and in 50:44: "But I will
make them suddenly run away from her." This tells us of the 1990
invasion of Iraq and the 2003 invasion. Jeremiah goes on and tells us

that this is not the time for his final judgment to happen. Man does not make that decision, but it will be in God's timing, so he (God) will cause this "north country" to suddenly leave. God will have this North Country leave to protect them from the wrath of God. And 50:46 says: "At the noise of the taking of Babylon the earth is moved [*ra ash*,[144] which means undulate (as the earth, the sky, etc.; also a field of grain, make afraid, quake, shake, tremble)], and the cry is heard among the nations." Note the reference to a field of grain. This grain is 1 Corinthians 15:37, "Thou sowest not that body that shall be, but bare grain, it may change of wheat." This leads us to the parable of the wheat and the tares of Matthew 13:30.

This is the same language again in Revelation 18:2–3:

> And he [angel] cried mightily with a strong voice, saying, Babylon the great is fallen, is fallen, and is become the habitation of devils, and the hold of every foul spirit, and a cage of every unclean [*akathartes*,[145] from *A*,[146] which means occasionally in the sense of union (as a negative particle) and a presumed derivative of *kathairo*, which means to cleanse; impure (ceremonial), moral (lewd)] and hateful bird. For all nations have drunk of the wine of the wrath of her fornication with her, and the merchants of the earth are waxed rich through the abundances of her delicacies. And I heard another voice from heaven, saying, come out of her, my people, that ye be not partakers of her sins, and that ye receive not of her plagues.

We see the same language used in the "but I will made them suddenly run away her" of Jeremiah and the "come out of her, my people" of Revelation. Both verses are at the time of the wrath of God.

---

[144]   Ibid., 1972.
[145]   Ibid., 2016.
[146]   Ibid., 2009.

In scripture, "my people" are the church in the New Testament, and in the Old Testament, they are the whole house of Israel.

The only thing Iraq has "abundances of delicacies" of is oil, and all nations have used her oil supply. The "merchants of the earth are waxed rich through the abundances of her delicacies" because all the economies of the world rely on oil. We should note this verse to Jeremiah 51:7–8:

> Babylon hath been a golden cup in the Lord's hand [this is when God commissioned Nebuchadnezzar to bring judgment to the surrounding area], that made all the earth drunken: the nations have drunken of her wine [oil]; there for the nations are mad [note Revelation 18:11, "And the merchants of the earth weep and mourn over her"]. Therefore shall her plagues come in one day, death, and mourning, and famine; and she shall be utterly burned with fire: for strong is the Lord God who judgeth her.

This equivalent message is told to us in Malachi 4:1: "For, the day cometh, that shall burn as an oven; And all the proud, yea, and all that do wickedly, shall be stubble: and the day that cometh shall burn them up, saith the Lord of hosts, that it shall not leave neither root nor branch."

Not that we were not justified in our action, for Saddam Hussein was a sponsor of terrorism by giving twenty-five thousand dollars to the families of the Palestinians who would send their sons and daughters to be suicide bombers against the Jewish people. The American government knows that he had weapons of mass destruction because they gave him the knowledge to produce them in the 1980s to use against Iran. Those weapons of mass destruction were well-documented in the news in the 1980s. Iran sent their children into certain battlefields to keep their soldiers safe from the chemicals, because they knew Hussein had those weapons. I have even seen the films of the dead in those battles on the History Channel. He was also a mass murderer of his own people. So you politicians who say he didn't have weapons of mass destruction, you do it for political reasons only. We know those weapons were delivered to Assyria. Israel's intelligence agency reported that. But God says, "I will have this north country to leave," so that his wrath will begin.

We should also note that this prophecy relates to the time of the end, for in 51:1–2, 6 it states:

> Thus saith the Lord; Behold, I will raise up against Babylon, and against them that dwell in the midst of them that rise up against me, a destroying wind. And I will send into Babylon fanners [*zuwr*,[147] which means; to turn aside (especially for lodging)] that shall fan her, and shall empty her land: for in the day of trouble they shall be against her round about. Flee out of the mist of Babylon, and deliver every man his soul: be not cut off in her iniquity; for this is the time of the Lord's vengeance; he will render unto her a recompense.

The her that is not cut off received this recompense (*shalam*,[148] which means to be safe; figurative to be complete, make amends, make restitution, reward). Let us note the Hebrew word meaning "be safe" when the wrath of God is poured out. I think this is also important to note that the people of Babylon "rise up against me" the Lord God. Jeremiah tells us that God's vengeance is against those that "rise up against me."

This North Country is to get out because the wrath of God takes over. Notice that Jeremiah tells us that "shall empty her land." This is in verse 33 of the same chapter, "For thus saith the Lord of hosts, the God of Israel; The daughter of Babylon is like a threshing floor [to be made smooth], it is the time to thresh her: yet in a little while, and the time of the harvest shall come." Both the "day of trouble" and "the day of the harvest" relate to the last days, just as the "Time of Jacob's trouble" of Jeremiah 30:7 and "time of trouble, such as never was" of Daniel

---

[147] Ibid., 1847.
[148] Ibid., 1987.

12:1. Jeremiah tells us here, "The time of the harvest shall come in a little while." This time of the harvest is Revelation 14:14–15: "And I looked, and behold a white cloud, and upon the cloud one sat like unto the Son of Man, having on his head a golden crown, and in his hands a sharp sickle. And another angel came out of the temple, crying with a loud voice to him that sat on the cloud, Thrust thy sickle, and reap; for the harvest of the earth is ripe."

Verse 39 says:

> In their heat I will make feasts, and I will make them drunken, that they may rejoice, and sleep a perpetual [*owlan*,[149] which means; properly concealed, (i.e., the vanishing point); generally time out of mind (past or future) (i.e., practical) eternity] sleep, and not wake [*quwts*,[150] which means to awake (literal or figurative), arise, wake, watch], saith the Lord.

It tells us here that those who sleep (die) sleep eternally in their heat (hell) and will not wake (to wake, arise) to eternal life.

If these last scriptures don't tell us the lasts days are close, I don't know what will. Jeremiah tells us that after this North Country leaves, which I believe is America and England, in a little while, the time of the harvest will come. We should also note that they sleep in eternal sleep in hell. Let us note Matthew 13:30, "Let both grow together until the time of the harvest: and in the time of the harvest I will say to the reapers, Gather ye together first the tares, and bind them in bundles to burn them: but gather the wheat into my barn." I am not a farmer, but I think the time of the crop harvest is in September.

---

[149] Ibid., 1933.
[150] Ibid., 1960.

The Genesis Account and the Historical Record

THE BIBLE TELLS US just what the world was like before God's creation of man after his own image when God first created the earth. Genesis 1:1 says, "In the beginning God created the heaven and the earth." My big bang theory is that God spoke it into existence. Let's quote the psalmist in Psalms 19:1, "The heavens declare the glory of God; and the firmament sheweth his handywork." The signs in the heavens are the Zodiac, and they are Aries, Taurus, Gemini, Cancer, Leo, Virgo, Libra, Scorpio, Sagittarius, Capricorn, Aquarius, and Pisces. These are the proof in the heavens that declare the glory of God. To believe all these came into existence by just chance is not logical. To believe that the earth came into place just by chance the exact distance from the sun to allow life is not logical. After billions of years, he created man upon the earth in the days of creation. In Genesis 1:2, it says, "And the earth was without form." Without is *tohuw*,[151] which means to lie waste, a desolation (of surface) (i.e., desert); figuratively a worthless thing. God waited for the natural process of the planet to run its course before he placed man upon it.

Let us note on page 39 of J. M. Roberts' *The New History of the World*, "By comparison with the upheavals of the hundreds of millennial preceding the end of the last ice age, climate, too, was from this time stable; from this point the historian need only regard its

---

[151]   Ibid., 1997.

short-term fluctuations." Global warming scientists should also regard its short-term fluctuations as just that. Let us note on page 18 of J. M. Roberts' *The New History of the World*, he writes, "Two famous European skulls seem to belong to the period between two Ice Ages about two hundred thousand years ago." Then he writes on page 19, "the next ice age then brings down the curtain. When it lifts, a hundred and thirty thousand or so years ago, in the next warm period, human remains again appear."

This makes Darwin's theory of the slow evolution process impossible. If there is a period of hundred and thirty thousand years where there is no evidence of man, how does the process of evolution continue? The earth was too chaotic for the human man to survive, so after the ice age of 10,000 BC is when the Lord God made man in his own image. Remember, Darwin said that between the older bones and the newer bones there was a missing link. This is quoted in another history book. In *A History of Civilization*, by Crane Brinton, John B. Christopher, and Robert Lee Wolff, on page 11 they write, "But there is no 'missing link' between man and ape, because there are no links of descent between them." This is your missing link, and it is found in the Bible.

The men of the earth before the ten thousand-year ice age, were created by Satan and his angels; 7000 BC is when God created man in his own image. This is why no missing link was found, because there is no missing link. Let us also note the historical record of the weather. Note its short-term fluctuations. The global-warming scientists are ignoring the true history of weather. Weather runs in cycles. There are warming periods and cooling periods, and the sun and sun spots have more effect on this earth than man.

But we will read that Satan and his angels tried to precede God. We should note in Genesis 1:28, where on the sixth day of creation God said, "God created man upon the earth male and female created He them and God said be fruitful, and multiply, and replenish the earth." To replenish means there was something here that was to be replaced. Is this prehistoric ape man? We should also note that Mr. Roberts in his *The New History of the World* said this is where the first species of the *Homo sapiens* appear. On page 27 he writes, "We have lived in a period of comparative topographical stability which has preserved the major shapes of the world of about 9000 BC. That world was by then firmly the world of *Homo sapiens*."

But in *A History of Civilization*, by Brinton, Christopher, and Wolff, they write on page 10, "Historical records—that is, written accounts that we can read—go back no more than 5,000 to 6,000 years." The historical record varies with each historian. Josephus writes, "But from the generation of Adam, until this befall the temple, there were three thousand nine hundred and thirteen years, six months and ten days."[152] Adding 3,913 years to the fall of the temple in 586 BC puts the generation of Adam at 4499 BC. Note it says the generation of Adam. Was Adam already 499 years old, and could he be formed around 5000 BC? Then add two thousand years to the generation when God created male and female on the sixth day, and this puts man on the earth around 6,499 years before the destruction of the temple. So this could put 7000 BC as the exact year when God first created male and female, when God first created man. I would say the Genesis account and the historical record match.

Let's note that on the sixth day, Genesis 1:26 says, "And God said, Let us make man in our image, after our likeness; and let them have dominion over the fish of the sea, and over the fowls of the air, and over the cattle, and over all the earth, and over every creeping thing that creepeth upon the earth." In 1:29, it says, "And God said, Behold, I have given every herb bearing seed, which is upon the whole face of the earth, and every tree, in which is the fruit of a tree yielding seed; to you it shall be for meat."

On the sixth day, God created people who were fishermen, hunters, shepherds, and gathers of the fruits of the earth. We should note when God created the fruits and the trees, he created them with seeds, so this food would be an everlasting supply of food for man. One must ask the evolutionist, which came first, the seed or the tree? If it was the seed, what did the seed evolve from? Was the chicken formed from the egg or the egg from the chicken? Or did this happen by chance? And this is where you put your faith.

---

[152] Whitson, *The New Complete Works of Josephus*, 346.

Let us note Genesis 2:2: "And on the seventh day God ended his work." Genesis 2:4 states, "These are the generations of the heavens and of the earth when they were created." There is more than one generation. A thousand years is as a day to the Lord God. Verse 5 tells us, "There was not a man to till the round." This fits the Genesis account with the historical account, for history tells us humans hunted and fished and gathered the fruits for two thousand years before they stated farming the land.

This is where Adam is formed. Verse 7 says, "And the Lord God formed man out of the dust of the ground, and breathed into his nostrils the breath of life; and man became a living soul." Let's first note the difference: on the sixth day, God created man, and on the eighth day, God formed man. Also note that this is where man receives a soul. Note: 1 Corinthians 15:45–46 says, "And so it is written, The first man Adam was made a living soul; the last Adam was made a quickening spirit. Howbeit that was not first which was spiritual, but afterward that which is spiritual." This tells us Adam was the first to have a living soul; however, he was not the first to have a spirit.

"And the Lord God planted a garden eastward in Eden; and there he put the man whom he had formed." We should note here that God put Adam in a garden, to dress it and to keep it (Gen. 2:15), that provided for all his needs, whereas on the sixth day when he created male and female, they were over all the earth outside of the garden. Genesis 2:18 says, "And the Lord God said, it is not good for man should be alone; I will make him a help meet for him." God did not form Eve for Adam when he first created him. Let's note in the Qur'an he writes, "Adam was not the first man. He was the first whose faculties had been developed to a degree he could become the recipient of revelation." God set aside Adam to commune with man, and I don't believe God would have man having sex with his siblings to start mankind. We should also note that there are distinct differences between descriptions of the men created on both of these accounts. God created men on the sixth day who were hunters, fishermen, and shepherds, and Adam was formed to farm the land. Let us also note Deuteronomy 4:32, "Since the day that God created man upon the earth." Note it says "created" and not formed.

121

I believe the inhabitants of the earth were the same people of Genesis 6:4: "There were giants in the earth in those days; and also after that, when the sons of god came in unto the daughters of men, and bare them children to them, the same became mighty men which were of old, men of renown." Old is *owlam,*[153] which means properly concealed (i.e., the vanishing point); generally time out of mind (past or future), (practical) eternity, lasting long time, (of) old time, perpetual, at any time, (beginnings of the) world. We should note here that the Hebrew word old means at the beginnings of the world. The giants in the land then and the giants in the land of Noah's days are the same. Renown is *shew,*[154] which means an appellation. Compare to the Hebrew word on page 1988 in *Strong's Complete Word Study Concordance shamayim,* which means the sky. These are the men of old.

Let's note John 12:31, where the Lord is speaking: "Now is the judgment of this world: now shall the prince of this world be cast out." We all know that Satan is the prince of this world and that he shall be cast out. The Lord tells us he has been cast out. Let's note that the word for prince is *archon,*[155] which means a first (in rank and power): chief, magistrate, prince, ruler. It is the present participle of the word *archo,*[156] which means to be first (in political rank or power); reign. It is from *arche,*[157] which means beginning, first, to begin, or to be first. This should confirm that Satan and his angels were in the beginning rulers of this planet. You have Moses telling you this, and now the very words of Jesus that the men of old were here first and they were Satan and his angels.

Mr. Roberts states, in *The New History of the World* on page 27, "About the groups in which upper Paleolithic man lived there is much unknown" (Hebrew word meaning properly concealed). "What is clear is that they were both larger in size than in former times and also more settled." We should note "larger in size," and the Bible says in Genesis

---

153 *Strong's,* 1933.
154 Ibid., 1988.
155 Ibid., 2036.
156 Ibid.
157 Ibid.

6:4, "there were giants in the earth in those days." We should also note that it states, "Which were men of old," but it also states, "And also after that." This is a reference that this created prehistoric man and the giants (Nephilim) in the world in Noah's day are the same. I believe that these "sons of God" were angels mixed with apes (since there were no daughters of men) creating the strange bones found in prehistory. And after millions of generations, they came to look more like man. This is how these people survived the chaotic upheavals of the past millennia.

A History of Civilization by Brinton, Christopher, and Wolf states on page 12: "From the scanty remains of bodies left from these ages of prehistory, the anthropologist has constructed a sequence of species that become progressively more humans. These hominids, labeled with long Latin-Greek names, are certainly not quite man, *Homo sapiens* of today." Then on page 13, they state, "Finally, still in the Old Stone Age, there are true men, *Homo sapiens*, men who breed with us today" and "The first appearance on earth of our species, *Homo sapiens*, cannot be dated very exactly."

That is because these people were not created by God but by Satan's angels. This history book says, "But there is no 'missing link' between man and ape, because there are no links of descent between them." This is because the sixth day of creation, which happened around 7000 BC, is when God created man in his own image.

Let us also note scripture. Jude 1:6–7 says:

> And the angels which kept not their first estate, but left their own habitation, he hath reserved in everlasting chains under darkness unto the judgment of that great days. Even as Sodom and Gomorrah, and the cities about them in like manner, giving themselves over to fornication, and going after strange flesh, are set forth as example, suffering the vengeance of eternal fire.

Note it says the angels who kept not the first estate; those are the angels of prehistory who had fornication with strange flesh.

If the Lord Jesus was made a little lower than the angels, as scripture says, this would be the only reason these early men could survive the upheavals of the past. Evolution is explained. These "sons of God" angels do that again when it says "also after that." That is the reason for the flood in Noah's day. Is this the vanishing point for what was here? Is what was here "properly concealed"? God did this with the ice age that affected the whole earth in 10,000 BC. In the ice age years, do you think anyone or any living plant could have survived those conditions? Scientists tell us that a two-degree change in the world temperature would be devastating to man's survival.

After the ice age, the six days of creation of the world we see today started. We will read later in the Bible that God again destroyed the human race, except for Noah and his family, in the story of the flood and for the same reason given in Genesis 6:4. This is where the hedge was put in between the male and female God created and Satan and his angels (Sons of God). But Noah's family is the seed of the "Sons of God" (Nephilim), and it is in Canaan, Ham's son. When we get to Numbers 13, we are told in verse 29, "The Amalekites dwell in the land of the south: and the Hittites, and the Jebusites, and the Amotites, dwell in the mountains: and the Canaanites dwell by the sea, and by the coast of Jordon." Verse 33 says, "And there were giants, the sons of Anak, which come of the giants: and we were in our own sight as grasshoppers, as so we were in their sight." Anak is a Canaanite, a descendant of Canaan, who Noah cursed after he slept with Noah's wife.

We should also note J. M. Roberts writes in *The New History of the World* on page 31:

> Farming truly revolutionized the conditions of human existence and it is the main thing to bear in mind when considering the meaning of Neolithic, a meaning once summarized as a period between the end of the hunting way of life and the beginning of the full metal-using economy, when the practice of farming arose and spread through most of Europe, Asia and North Africa like a slow-moving wave.

We should also note the Bible. Genesis 4:2 says, "But Cain was a tiller of the ground." The Bible gives us the direction Cain went in Genesis 4:16, which says, "And Cain when out from the presence of the Lord, and dwelt in the land of Nod, east of the garden." Now let's continue. *The New History of the World* on page 31 says:

> The accidents of survival and the direction of scholarly effort have meant until recently that much more was known about early agriculture in the near east than about its possible precursors in further Asia.

We should also note that on J. M. Roberts' map on page 32, he states that farming first started east of the Tigris and Euphrates Rivers. We should also note in the Bible that Cain left the garden and went east. So when Cain and later Adam and his family got kicked out of the garden, they started to teach the rest of world to farm the land. This is another match between Genesis and the historical record.

Note Genesis 3:22, which says, "And the Lord God said, Behold, the man is become as one of us, to know good and evil: and now, lest he put forth his hand, and take also of the tree of life, and eat, and live for ever." If Adam had not been kicked out of the garden, he would have lived forever. Now we will learn where farming starts in the Middle East. J. M. Roberts states in *The New History of the World* on page 32, "Both the predisposing conditions and the evidence point to the region later called the 'Fertile Crescent' as especially significant; this is the arc of territory running northwards from Egypt through Palestine and the Levant, through Anatolia to the hills between Iran and the south Caspian to enclose the river valleys of Mesopotamia." Farming started in the location of the Garden of Eden and the near east, where the Bible and the history books tells us.

God formed man on the eighth day to farm the land. We should note that the geological record proves this to be true. Man survived by hunting and fishing for thousands of years before he started farming. This tells us a thousand years is as a day in the Lord and the world is just what he says. Man was created on the earth two thousand years before God formed Adam. We should note that the Hebrew males are circumcised on the eighth day because Adam was formed on the eighth day of creation. This is why it says in Philippians 3:5, "Circumcised on the eighth day."

Let's also note that scripture tells us Noah was the eighth person or the eighth generation when God caused the flood. It was two thousand years later when God called Abraham out of Ur. It was two thousand years later when the Lord Jesus came to redeem man. It is two thousand years later when we expect the return of our Savior, the Lord Jesus Christ. This is another sign that proves we are living in the last days.

Josephus writes "But from the generation of Adam, until this befall the temple, there were three thousand nine hundred and thirteen years, six months and ten days."[158] Adding 3,913 years to the fall of the temple in 586 puts the generation of Adam at 4499 BC. Mr. Roberts states that farming started in the Mesopotamia area between 5200 BC and 4000 BC. The generation of Adam being in 4499 BC means that Adam was formed in 5000 BC. I would say that is a close match between the Genesis record and the historical record.

Just after the past ice age allowing the earth to replenish itself, Mr. Roberts states in *The New History of the World* on page 31:

> After the hunting way of life and the practice of farming begins. While some peoples pursed game across plains uncovered by the retreating ice, others intensified their skills needed to exploit new prolific river valleys.

It is when the ice age is ending that mankind starts to increase its territory.

We should notice here that Mr. Roberts states this is happening after the 10,000 BC ice age and the Bible states the same thing. Most pastors teach that man was only on the earth four thousand years before the birth of Christ based on mere speculation and not on Bible facts. Let's note J. M. Roberts in *The New History of the World* on page 45 who says, "Over population may seem a paradoxical notion to

---

[158] Whitson, *The New Complete Works of Josephus*, 346.

apply to a world whose whole population in about 4000 BC has been estimated only between eighty and ninety million." This is why God created Adam. The population of the earth was expanding so rapidly that man would starve if he did not learn ways to produce food. This is historical record and the Genesis account confirmation. We are told in Exodus 31:3, "And I [God] filled him with the spirit of God, in wisdom, and in understanding, and in knowledge, and in all manner of workmanship." Note the land of Nod where Cain went to after he was kicked out of the garden.

Let's note that the word "Nod" is *Nowd*,[159] which means vagrancy, from *nuwd*,[160] which means, a primitive root to nod (i.e., waver); figuratively to wander, flee, or disappear. Cain disappears off the pages of the Bible after he is kicked out of the garden.

Mr. Roberts tells us in *The New History of the World* on page 35:

> It was first being hammered into shape without heating and then smelted at Catal Huyuk, in Anatolia, though the earliest known metal artifacts date from about 4000 BC and are beaten copper pins found in Egypt. Once the technique of blending copper with tin to produce bronze was discovered, a metal was available which was both relatively easy to cast and retained a much better cutting edge It was in use in Mesopotamia soon after 3000 BC.

Now let's note the Bible. Genesis 4:22 says, "And Zellah, she also bare Tubal-Cain, an instructor of every artificer in brass and iron." Tubal-Cain was the fourth generation of the seed of Cain, and Cain was in the Mesopotamia area. We should also note that the Bible says first brass and then iron, just as the geological record tells us.

We see here that from the beginning, God sets apart man for himself to commune with, just as he chose the sons of Abraham, Isaac, and Jacob. We should note that when Cain was not allowed to live in

---

[159]   *Strong's*, 1917.
[160]   Ibid.

the garden after he killed Abel, he went to the land of Nod, where he "knew his wife." We should note that it was not until Cain went to Nod that he knew his wife. Where did Cain's wife come from if God had not created "male and female" on the sixth day? The Bible does not tell us that God kicked Cain's wife out of the garden. The garden was a special place on the earth, for it tells us when God kicked Cain out of the garden in verse 16, "And Cain went out from the presence of the Lord." The garden is the place on the earth that was God's territory, and Satan violated that in the form of a snake.

We will read later in history that God has another place on the earth that is special to him, and he calls it the land of milk and honey. He gave it to a man named Abraham and his descendants. God again has a place on the Temple Mount where he communes with man. They got kicked out of the land for the same reason. They lived in the presence of God, and they turned away from God to idols. God is going to get jealous for his land in the future.

The Bible makes a special note to tell us exactly when man on the earth started to call upon the Lord after receiving the "soul" in Genesis 4:26: "And to Seth, to him was born a son; and he called his name Enos: then begin men to call upon the name of the Lord." This should tell us that man was on the earth for a long period of time (Seth lived 105 years, and he begat Enos). The Bible doesn't tell us how old Enos was when he called upon the name of the Lord. God added to Adam and his descendants a spirit and soul. The soul was the ability to commune with God. If Adam and Eve were the first man and woman, this would not have been possible.

We are told in Genesis 4:15, "And he Lord said unto him, Therefore whosoever slayeth Cain, vengeance shall be taken on him sevenfold. And the Lord set a mark upon Cain, lest any finding him should kill him." If Cain was the first person kicked out of the garden, who was the Lord worried would kill him? We should also note that God "set a mark upon Cain." This same mark will be used again when God brings judgment to the House of Judah. And then again at the end of the age, God will put a seal upon his church just before he returns to the earth. This could be the only reason God refused Cain's sacrifice. We are told in 1 John 3:12, "Not as Cain, who was of that wicked one." Wicked is *poneros*,[161] which means (passive) ill (i.e., diseased), masculine (singular) the devil. Satan and his angels are at it again.

We should also note in Genesis 9:1, "And God blessed Noah and his sons, and said unto them, be fruitful, and multiply, and *replenish* the earth." The word "replenish" is used again after the flood. So God flooded the earth again to kill off the "Sons of Man." The Lord God tells us this. Genesis 6:17 says, "And, behold, I, even I, do bring the flood of waters upon the earth, to destroy all flesh, wherein is the breath of life, from under heaven; and every thing that is in the earth shall die." The Bible makes it clear that all flesh died except Noah and his family. If the Lord God can cause the rains to come and flood the earth, this tells us he controls the weather. Also note it says, "The same day the fountains of the great deep broke up." This sounds like God caused a strong earthquake on the ocean floor. We will see later in the scriptures that the Lord God uses the weather as a blessing or a curse.

Let us note that Mr. Roberts writes in *The New History of the World* on page 47 that around 4000 BC, this appears in history: "There are three major ethnic classifications of the species of *Homo sapiens*: Caucasian, Negroid, and Mongoloid, just as the Bible states the three sons of Noah. The 'Hamitic' stocks evolved in Africa north and northeast of the Sahara." Those would be the Bible's sons of Ham. The Semitic languages speakers of the Arabian peninsula would be the Bible's descendants of Shem. The peoples of the Indo-European language who spread to southern Russia to the Caucasians of Georgia would be the Bible's sons of Japheth. Another history book and Bible confirmation! The Bible is not the only record of the flood and the Garden of Eden. There are other accounts of the flood recorded in the Epic of Gilgamesh. This is another Genesis and historical match.

We read in scripture that God scattered man over all the earth. Genesis 11:9 says, "Therefore is the manner of it called Babel; because the Lord did there confound the language of all the earth: and from thence did the Lord scatter them abroad upon the face of all the earth." God once again scattered men over all the earth. And why were they scattered? Genesis 11:6 says, "And the Lord said, Behold, the people is

---

[161]   Ibid., 2140.

one, and they have all one language; and this they begin to do: and now nothing will be restrained from them, which they have imagined to do." The known world was under one ruler, and his name was Nimrod. It was a one-world government, just as the world leaders are trying to bring to the world today. This is why God scattered them. We will read in the Bible that God scattered many different tribes of people from the Mesopotamia area by Nebuchadnezzar, King of Babylon.

Mr. Roberts writes in *The New History of the World* on page 49:

> The best case for the first appearance of something which is recognizably civilization has been made for the southern part of Mesopotamia, the 700-mile-long land form by the two river valleys of the Tigris and Euphrates. This end of the Fertile Crescent was thickly studded with farming villages in Neolithic times.

It is important to note that the two rivers Mr. Roberts writes about here are where the Bible tells us the Garden of Eden is located. Second, the history book tells us that in Neolithic times, there were recognizable civilizations, and the Bible tells us that God called Abraham out of Ur of the Chaldees, which is in the southernmost part of Mesopotamia. Has anybody noticed that just after the flood, man's life span quickly shortened? For example, Genesis 11:12–27 says, "And Arphaxad lived five hundred and thirty years. And Eber lived four hundred and three years. And Serug lived after he begat Nahor two hundred years. And Nahor lived after he begat Terah a hundred and nineteen years, and Terah was the father of Abram."

So now we have the Bible's explanation of the past history, with my interpretation. We have Darwin's theory that man evolved from apes and we have God's Word that says that the men of old were created by the Son of God, the angels. This explains the strange ape-like man. Darwin's theory is close. He just leaves out who created the ape man in the beginning. Whom do you trust? The Word of God or Charles Darwin? If an asteroid hit the earth sixty-five million years ago, does the evolution process start all over again? If the extinction of dinosaurs came by this asteroid, how did man survive? How did anything living above ground survive? The result of this asteroid hit was an extended global deep freeze. Just fifty thousand years ago, another asteroid hit in the western part of the United States. This too must have caused a global freeze. How does the evolution of the ape man continue? Just ten thousand years ago, there was a global ice age. The history of the planet tells us even volcanic eruptions occurred that brought on many global weather freezes. So how can this slow evolution from the ape walking on all four legs to man walking on two legs continue? Darwin's theory is impossible. This is one of the "vain babblings, and oppositions of science falsely so called" given in 1 Timothy 6:20 that Christians are to avoid.

We should also note Matthew 26:24, which says, "And, Behold, there arose a great tempest in the sea, insomuch that the ship was cover with the waves. And the Lord Jesus awoke from his sleep and rebuked the winds and the sea, and there was a great calm." The Lord Jesus controls the weather. Now let's note Psalms 8:4–5:

> What is a man, that thou art mindful of him? And
> the Son of Man, that thou visitest him? For thou
> has made him a little lower than the angels, and hast
> crowned him with glory and honour.

If the Lord Jesus was made a little lower in power than the angels, does this not tell us that angels are powerful beings? This is how prehistoric man survived.

I believe that because of Darwin's hatred for God after his daughter died, he tried to destroy everyone's belief in God, and he did this with his theory. So let us refer to the *Webster's Dictionary* meaning of theory, "A hypothesis assumed for the sake of argument or investigation, conjecture, speculation." So why is Darwin's theory of evolution taught as fact and not speculation or conjecture? I believe if the Bible had been interpreted in this way in the court, Darwin's theory would have lost. The church lost the case when they could not explain where Cain's wife came from. I got this information about the court case from the History Channel. To find out more information, I turned to the Internet, and when I searched for "court case evolution," I found the website www. tungate.com/evo in December 2010.

The case cited by the History Channel was actually the "The State of Tennessee v. Scopes" that started on July 21, 1925. It was better known as the Scopes Monkey Trial. John Scopes violated the state's Butler Act that prohibited the teaching of evolution. The ACLU opposed the Butler Act on the grounds it violated the teacher's individual right and academic freedom, and that made it unconstitutional. My question to the ACLU is where is the Christian right to that same individual right of freedom of speech and expression? When William Jennings Byran was on the stand, famed attorney Clarence Darrow asked Byran, "Where did Cain get his wife?" Byran answered, "Leave the agnostics to hunt for her." To me, that was a bad answer. Then Darrow said to Byran, "You insult every man of science and learning in the world because he does not believe in your fool religion." It sounds like to me Mr. Darrow was not a Christian. Byran's response to that statement should have been Psalms 14:1, "The fool hath said in his heart, There is no God. They are corrupt, they have done abominable works."

Since you can see my explanation of where Cain's wife came from, how can we appeal this decision to a higher court? The evolutionists won that case, and then there is no creator. Maybe when we are sworn into court or when a politician is sworn into office, we should be sworn in by the ape, since the ape is our creator. So why would the president of the United States or any politician put his hand on the Bible when sworn into office? This is an acknowledgment of a religion.

The Bible is packed with lies. This makes the Lord Jesus the biggest liar ever to have lived, because he states in John 10:30, "I and the Father are one." He says he is God. God states he created man. To think that the founding fathers of this country, America, taught that there was a God makes the basic premise of the constitution bogus, because there is no God. The Declaration of Independence says, "All men are created equal, that they are endowed by their Creator with certain unalienable rights, that these are life, liberty, and the pursuit of happiness." If there is an unalienable right to life, how can killing a life in the womb be justified by the Supreme Court? Just as the house of Israel was taken into captivity for their sin against the Lord, America will experience the same judgment.

Thomas Jefferson's separation of church and state statement did not mean the state could not recognize God. Let us read the First Amendment: "Congress shall make no law respecting an established religion, or prohibiting the free speech thereof." Not allowing teachers to teach from the Bible is a direct violation of this free speech. Not allowing public prayer is a violation of free speech. Let us look at the historical facts about what happened in Europe over the past seventeen hundred years. In AD 800, Charlemagne was crowned king of the Holy Roman Empire by Pope Leo III. This started the rule of church and state in Europe. In sixteenth-century Europe, the state determined what churches would be allowed in the state. The king in England switched from the Catholic Church to the Protestant Church depending on the king or queen. During the medieval period, the Calvinists tortured and banished individuals they thought sinful, even denying the individuals much of their individualism and privacy. These people went as far as to use governmental power to prevent public worship in any form other than their own. The Catholic Church was just as guilty. It is the Catholic Church's influence on the governments of Europe that turned them to socialism and liberalism. It is the church's manipulation of the affairs of government that got the church and state form of government changed.

In 1296, Pope Boniface VIII wrote to Philip the Fair of England that it was necessary for salvation for every living person to be subject to the Pope, when we are told in the Bible that the Lord Jesus is the only way to salvation. It is only the Lord Jesus Christ who we will answer to at the judgment seat of Christ. We should also note that the Lord Jesus says in Matthew 24:21, "Render [*apodidomi*,[162] which means to give away, yield] therefore unto Caesar the things that are Caesar's [government]; and unto God the things that are God's [man's spiritual redemption]." God will allow man attempt to rule for now, but at the end of time, when man's rule fails, God will step in. He steps in when the world gathers at the battle of Armageddon.

---

[162]   Ibid., 2030.

The Jews of Europe were either forced to accept Christianity or forced from one country to another. It is Darwin's theory of evolution that started the secularism of Europe. In Darwin's time, the Old Testament was already regarded as symbolic. Well, I beg to differ. The Old Testament, as well as the New Testament, is the Word of God, and it outlines the future. With this book, I will prove it is. Let us note that history tells us that the Jewish first international Zionist congress met at Basel in 1897 in hopes of establishing a Jewish state in Palestine. Is this why also the Christians of Europe left in mass amounts of population, as the history books tells us?

The "ape-man cult" was having a dissolving effect upon Orthodox Judaism and Christianity in Europe. But let's go back to AD 33. When Jesus was tried by Pontius Pilate (the state), Pilate stated, "I find no fault in this man." But what was the Pharisees' (the church's) response? "Crucify him, crucify him." Under our constitution, elected officials make the laws and enforce them and govern and not the church. And after reading just what the church leaders in Europe did to their followers for almost seventeen hundred years, I thank God for separation of church and state. The people of Europe made America the place to be to worship God in any manner, without fear of the church. We should note what they printed on the money, "In God we trust." Maybe we should change this to, "In the ape man we trust."

Since the court ruled that there is no creator, why would anyone build a church? We have no God to pray to. So all you secular humanists who want God out of the picture, you may win in the courts on this earth, but God will have the final victory in the end. Nations that rule against God, God has this message to you.

Psalms 2:2, 4 says, "The kings of the earth set themselves, and the rulers take council together, against the Lord, and against his anointed, saying, He that sitteth in the heavens shall laugh: the Lord shall have them in derision." Psalms 9:17 says, "The wicked shall be turned into hell, and all nations that forget God." And the psalmist tells us in 11:6, "Upon the wicked he shall rain snares, fire and brimstone, and a horrible tempest: this shall be the portion of their cup." Now let us match this same language to what happens when Gog comes against the land of Israel. Ezekiel 38:22 says, "And I will plead against him with pestilence and with blood; and I will rain upon him, and upon his bands, and upon the many peoples that are with him, an overflowing rain, and great hailstones, fire, and brimstone."

The Lord Jesus tells us in Mark 8:38 and Mark 9:26, "For whosoever shall be ashamed of me and of my words, of him shall the Son of Man be ashamed, when he shall come in his own glory, and in his Father's, and of the holy angels." If you rule God out of your world, he will rule you out of his. There is proof in the scriptures that this happens in the next chapter of this manuscript.

We should note Deuteronomy 28:64, which says, "And the Lord shall scatter thee among all people, from one end of the earth even unto the other; and there ye shall serve other gods, which neither thy fathers have known, even wood and stone." God predicts the scattering of the tribes of Israel all over the earth. We should note that most of people of the world are not buying this global warming theory. It's mainly the liberal people of Europe, England, and America. This is another link to the theory that part of the people of Europe and America are the lost tribes of the house of Israel that are among the heathens.

God's Word versus Man's Word

LET US START THIS chapter with the words of the Lord Jesus in Matthew 12:36–37: "But I say unto you, That every idle word that men shall speak, they shall give account thereof in the day of judgment. For by thy words thou shalt be justified, and by thy words thou shalt be condemned." The day of judgment in 2 Corinthians 5:10: "For we must all appear before the judgment seat of Christ; that every one may receive the things done in the body, according to that he hath done, whether it be good or bad." Your words are recorded in heaven, and you will have to give an account of what you say. All sins are forgiven man if he asks for forgiveness, but there is one sin that will not be pardoned by God. This is given in plain and simple language in Matthew 12:31–32:

> Wherefore I say unto you, All manner of sin and blasphemy shall be forgiven unto men: but the blasphemy against the Holy Ghost shall not be forgiven unto men. And whosoever speaketh a word against the Son of Man, it shall be forgiven him; but whosoever speaketh against the Holy Ghost, it shall not be forgiven him, neither in this world, neither in the world to come.

In the future, God is going to bring heaven to earth. Note it says here "the world to come." The Lord Jesus will fulfill our daily prayer of Matthew 6:10, "Thy kingdom come. Thy will be done on earth, as it is in heaven." This is the time of visitation the church of the Lord Jesus prays for. This means those who blaspheme the Holy Ghost will not be in either place. In the time of the Lord Jesus, the Pharisees ascribed the works of the Lord Jesus to Satan. To ascribe in the *Webster's Dictionary* is to refer to a supported cause, source, or author; attribute. To blaspheme the Holy Spirit is to also blaspheme God's prophets. Luke says in Acts 7:51–52, "Ye do always resist the Holy Ghost: as your fathers did, so do ye, Which of the prophets, have not your fathers persecuted." Let's also note Acts 15:8: "And God, which knoweth the hearts, bare them witness, giving them the Holy Ghost, even as he did unto us."

Let's also note Acts 5:1–3:

> But a certain man named Ananias, with Sapphira his wife, sold a possession. And kept back part of the price, his wife also being privy to it, and brought a certain part, and laid it at the apostles feet. But Peter said, Ananias, why hath Satan filled thine heart to lie to the Holy Ghost, and keep back part of the price of the land?"

Just to lie to or about the Holy Ghost or the prophets of God is, as Acts 5:9 says, to "tempt the Spirit of the Lord." What did God do to Ananias and Sapphira? He took their lives, and they died. To show you just how bad this sin is, let's read first what sins God forgives. This is given in First Corinthians 6:9–11:

> Know ye not that the unrighteous shall not enter the Kingdom of God? Be not deceived: neither fornicators, nor idolaters, nor adulterers, nor effeminate, nor abusers of themselves with mankind, Nor thieves, nor covetous, nor drunkards, nor revilers, nor extortioners, shall enter the kingdom of God. And such were some

of you: but ye are washed, but ye are sanctified, but ye
are justified in the name of the Lord Jesus Christ, and
by the Spirit of our God.

This covers just about every sin known to man except, as Acts
5:9 says, "tempting the Spirit of the Lord," which is to blaspheme the
Word of God given by his Holy Prophets through the Holy Ghost.
And this warning is repeated again.

Second Peter 1:19–21 says:

We have a more sure word of prophecy; where unto
ye do well that ye take heed, as unto the light that
shineth in a dark place, until the day dawn, and the
day star arise in your hearts; Knowing this first, that
no prophecy of the scripture is of any interpretation.
For the prophecy came not in old time by the will of
man; but holy men of God spake as they were moved
by the Holy Ghost.

We are told here that we can trust the prophecies in this book
because they didn't come by mere men but by holy men the Holy
Ghost spoke through. If we heed their words, we will do well. The day
star that arises in your hearts is given in Acts 2:17, "And it shall come to
pass in the lasts days, saith God I will pour out my spirit on all men."

Let's note 2 Thessalonians 1:10–12:

And with all deceivableness of unrighteousness in
them that perish; because they receive not the love
of the truth, that they might be saved. And for this
cause God shall sent them strong delusion, that they
should believe a lie: That they might be damned
who believe not in the truth, but had pleasure in
unrighteousness.

Let us note that this same message was given in Psalm 2: "were
those that counsel together against the Lord and his anointed sayings,

the Lord shall have the in derision, then he shall speak to them in his wrath." The Lord's anointed sayings are recorded in the Bible. This is another sign we are living in the last days. This delusion is that we can save the planet by going green. The earth-first people think man and the animals are destroying the planet by their mere existence. The truth is that God created the planet for man and animals, and they will be here for all eternity, but those who believe not the truth will be damned. I didn't say this; Paul did.

The History Channel has a new program series called *Life after People*. I hate to be the bearer of bad news to these people, but human life is going to continue for all eternity on this planet. These people who worship mother earth will not be the ones who inherit "all things" because they have put their faith in mother earth instead of Father God.

Let us also note Romans 1:25, "Who changed the truth of God into a lie, and worshipped and served the creature more than the Creator, who is blessed for ever. Amen." Creator is *ktizo*,[163] which means (through the idea if the proprietorship of the manufacturer) to fabricate (i.e., found [form originally]) create, make. Who has changed the truth for a lie? The big-bang theorists and the ape-man theorists. It is God who created the heavens and the earth and who created man upon the earth. What does the Holy Spirit have to say? Verse 26 says, "For this cause God gave them up unto vile affections." Until when? That is found in 2:5–6: "But after thy hardness and impenitent heart treasurest up unto thyself wrath against the day of wrath and revelation of the righteous judgments of God: Who will render to every man according to his deeds." We should note the phrase "day of wrath" of the righteous God.

This is where I will give you my favorite Bible verse: "And ye shall know that I am the Lord God." This is when the world will know that there is a God, and he is listening. Let us note verse 7: "To them who by patient continuance in well doing seek for glory and honour and immortality, eternal life." These are the "we which are alive and remain until the coming of the Lord" of 1 Thessalonians 4:15. We are told here

---

[163]   Ibid., 2105.

to seek immortality. This is 1 Corinthians 15:51, 53: "We shall not all sleep (died), but we shall all be changed . . . For this corruptible must put on incorruption, and this mortal must put on immortality." These people are the blessed, for they shall inherit the earth. This is why the Christians pray daily, "Thy kingdom come. Thy will be done on earth, as it is in heaven" as instructed in Matthew 6:10. Most pastors today tell us we are to look for a church rapture to heaven. This is just the opposite of our daily prayer and this verse in the scriptures, where we are told to "seek immortality" until the coming of the Lord.

Since the Bible is just composed of fables and the story of Jonah and the big fish that swallowed him and then vomited him out on dry ground is not true, then you make the Lord Jesus a liar. The Lord Jesus says in Matthew 12:40, "For as Jonas was three days and three nights in the whale's belly; so shall the Son of man be three days and three nights in the heart of the earth." It literally happened, and the Lord of the universe had this happen on the planet later in history to prove to man that this was possible. Jonah 2:7 states, "When my soul fainted within me I remembered the Lord: and my prayer came unto thee, into thine holy temple."

Now let's read the *Princeton Theological Review*, volume XXV of 1927. The header at the top of the page is this: "THE SIGN OF THE PROPHET JONAH AND ITS CONFIRMATIONS." Oswald T. Allis opens with man's skepticism of the stories in the Bible, especially Jonah and the big fish. Mr. Allis goes on to prove that the great fish in the Bible is the sperm or cachalot whale and compares it to the whalebone whale. In the South Kensington Museum are the models of these sperm whales, with a mouth, "20ft. In length, 15ft. In height, and 9ft. In width." They have mouths big enough to accommodate twenty Jonahs standing up. He goes on to prove this was possible, but let's read some of the actual account.

> In Feb. 1891, the whaling ship "Star of the East" was in the vicinity of the Falkland Islands and the lookout sighted a large sperm whale three miles away. Two boats were launched.

The second boat attacked the whale but was upset by the lash of its tail and the men were thrown unto the sea, one man being drown, and another, James Bartley, having disappeared could not be found. The whale was killed and in a few hours was lying by the ship's side and the crew were busy with axes and spades removing the blubber. The next morning they attached some of the tackle to the stomach which was hoisted on deck. The sailors were startled by something in it which gave spasmodic signs of life, and inside was found the missing sailor doubled up and unconscious. He was laid on the deck and treated to a bath of sea water which soon revived him. He remained two weeks a raving lunatic. At the end of the third week he had entirely recovered from the shock and resumed his duties.

There is a lot more to this story, and for anyone with Internet access, visiting the online Princeton Seminary Library, which I found in 2005, is a good place to start for additional material worth reading on the subject. I believe this happened in history to prove the story of Jonah as a literal Bible fact. The last statement made in their review was, "Truly this was the Son of Man."

This happened around the time when Charles Darwin and the great Dr. Strauss came up with their theories. We should note the effects it had on Jonah and James Bartley. Jonah turned to God. My best guess is James Bartley didn't.

All you scientists who came up with the big bang theory and ape-man evolution, God has this message for you. Jeremiah 10:10–11 says, "But the Lord is the true God, He is the living God, and an everlasting king: at his wrath the earth shall tremble, and the nations shall not be able to abide his indignation. Thus shall ye say unto them, The Gods that have not made the heavens and the earth, even they shall perish [*abad*,[164] (causative destroy), not escape, be void of] which means from the earth, and from under these heavens."

Did you notice the "Gods," the Father and the Son? I believe "the Gods" are very angry at these people, and this tells us here they don't inherit eternal life because they blaspheme the "Spirit of the Lord." God will one day rule in both heaven and earth, and the people who teach falsely against the Lord will not be in either heaven or earth. That only leaves one place. So all you public school boards, professors, and school teachers who teach this ape-man evolution and the big bang theory, you will be utterly destroyed. We should note the phrase, "From the earth and under these heavens." You will not be one of the meek who inherit the earth or have eternal life because they blaspheme the words of the Holy Ghost that were spoken through the holy prophets. Ezekiel 18:4 says, "The soul that sinneth, it shall die." We should note 1 Corinthians 15:49: "And as we have borne the image of the earthly, we shall also bear the image of the heavenly." Yet Jeremiah tells us these people will "perish from this earth, and from the heavens." This is the second death.

Jeremiah also tells us this about this worry of the poles melting and flooding the coasts of the earth, which is part of Al Gore's global warming theory. Jeremiah 5:22–23 says:

> Fear ye not me? Saith the Lord: will ye not tremble at my presence, which have placed the sand for the bound of the sea by a perpetual decree, that it cannot pass it: and though the waves thereof toss themselves, yet can they not prevail; though they roar, yet can they not pass over it? But this people hath a revolting and a rebellious heart; they are revolted and gone.

Jeremiah tells us that the Lord set the bounds of the sea, which cannot be passed. These coasts of the earth are a perpetual decree, meaning an everlasting coast. Though the waves pass over them, they will not prevail. So to Al Gore and the global warming theorists, this

---

[164] Ibid., 1803.

is what the Lord says: "This people hath revolting and a rebellious heart. And here is the judgment. They are revolted [*sarar*[165] which means; to turn away, backsliding, rebellious)] and gone [*yalak*,[166] which means depart, vanish]." Jeremiah tells us that they are removed from the earth. And once again it tells us here, "They shall tremble at my presence." Second Corinthians 5:9 says, "For we all must appear before the judgment seat of Christ." The Hebrew words mean the rebels will be removed. Let us note Proverbs 10:30: "The righteous shall never be removed: but the wicked shall not inherit the earth."

Isaiah 45:9–12 says:

> Woe unto them that striveth [*riyb*,[167] which means; to toss (i.e., grapple); mostly figurative to wrangle (i.e., hold in controversy), contend] with his Maker! Let the potsherd [*cheres*,[168] which means a piece of pottery, earth(en)] strive with the potsherds of the earth. Shall the clay say to him that fashioneth [*yatsar*,[169] meaning to mound or to form] it, He hath no hands. Woe unto him that saith unto his father, What begettest thou? or to the women, What hast thou brought forth? Thus saith the Lord, the Holy One of Israel, and his Maker, Ask me of things to come concerning my son, and concerning the work of my hands command ye me. I have made the earth, and created man upon it: I even my hands, have stretched out the heavens, and all their host have I commanded.

First of all, I think we should notice there are two "woes" unto them who "hold in controversy" whether man evolved from ape or was created by God, who Isaiah states here is our heavenly Father,

---

[165]   Ibid., 1929.

[166]   Ibid., 1874.

[167]   Ibid., 1970.

[168]   Ibid., 1864.

[169]   Ibid., 1876.

and to the people who came up with the big bang theory instead of acknowledging it was God who created the heavens. Did you notice here that Isaiah writes that God says, "Concerning my son"? He formed man out of the clay of the earth and said it would be Adam. He created man upon the earth, and that's when he created male and female, on the sixth day. Instead of going to the scientist, the Lord says, "Ask me." Read the scriptures.

We should also note Ezekiel 20:32: "And that cometh into your mind shall not be at all, that ye say, We shall be as the heathens, as the families of the countries, to serve wood and stone." The environmentalists who put the earth above God he calls heathens. And this is how he will deal with man who does this. Verse 33 says, "As I live, saith the Lord God, surely with a mighty hand, and with a stretched out arm, and with fury poured out, will I rule over you." When the Lord's fury is poured out, it means you are under the punishments of the great tribulation period and it is ruling over you when the Lord comes back to rule and reign forever.

While we are here, let's look at the weather, but first let's note what Mr. Roberts recorded in *The New History of the World* on page 47:

> Drought or desiccation could dramatically and suddenly destroy an area's capacity to feed itself and it was to be thousands of years before food could be brought from elsewhere. The disturbances which resulted were the prime movers of early history; climate change was still at work as a determinant, though now much more local and specific ways. Droughts, catastrophic storms, even a few decades of marginally lower or higher temperatures, could force peoples to get on the move and so help to bring on civilization by throwing together peoples of different traditions.

As long as man has been on the planet, there has been climate change. Droughts as long as seven years were even recorded in the Bible, and the proof is still in Egypt today. All these forms of natural disasters are part of the natural characteristics of the planet, like it or not. In the 1980s, we were told of a hole in the ozone layer that was getting bigger every year above the South Pole that was going to melt it, causing a worldwide flood within the decade. Did it happen? No. Twenty years later, it's now the North Pole that is melting. These same scientists are now telling us that global weather change is happening, as if it was something man can control. This is where the word "stupid" comes in to play. There is only one person who can control the weather. That one person is the Lord God. Let also note this in history.

This is a quote from A *History of Civilization* by Brinton, Christopher, and Wolff on page 136: "The methods of the fourth century BC often still served the fourth century AD. Farm production may possibly have declined also because of a prolonged drought which dried up fertile grain lands. The evidence, however, suggests that change of climate probably occurred at an imperceptible pace." Climate change happened during the Roman Empire days over just an eight-hundred-year period. History tells us that the Romans' conquest of northern Africa started in the year 264 BC. I believe they went to North Africa for the food supply. They must have been putting a lot of greenhouse gases into the atmosphere at this time in history. So now we have change in climate in about the first century, we have climate change between the thirteenth and the eighteenth centuries, and we have change in climate at our time in history. This is history's inconvenient truth in answer to Al Gore's inconvenient truth. Let's ask one last thing. Can Al Gore produce a degree in climatology that makes him a climatologist? Or does he have a political agenda to help finance the New World Order? With Wall Street making a lot of money selling these carbon credits, this tells us it is all about the money because "it's the economy, stupid." It's time for American Christians to wake up. This is the big lie, exposed by this manuscript.

In the days of the Jews coming out of Babylonian captivity, they were commanded by God to rebuild the temple, but they were disobedient and God's discipline came. And this is what Haggai tells them in 1:10–11:

> Therefore the heaven over are stayed from dew [rain],
> and the earth is stayed from her fruit. And I [God]

called for a drought upon the land, and upon the mountains, and upon the corn, and upon the new wine, and upon the oil, and upon which the ground bringeth forth, and upon men, and upon the labour of their hands.

The Bible tells us that no matter what your occupation is, the weather is going to affect you. You can't escape God's judgment.

Even in Job we are told that God controls the weather. Job 37:6 says, "For he saith to the snow, Be thou on the earth; likewise to the small rain, and to the great rain of his strength." Job 37:9 says, "Out of the south cometh the whirlwind [hurricanes in Hebrew]: and cold out of the north." Job 37:10 says, "By the breath of God frost is given: and by the breadth of the water is straitened." Job 37:13 says, "He causeth it to come, whether for correction, or for his land, or for mercy." The mercy part is given in Ezekiel 34:26: "And I will make them and place them around about my hill a blessing; and I will cause the showers to come down in his seasons; there shall be showers of blessings." There was correction upon the house of Israel in Amos.

I will start with Amos 4:7–8:

And also I have withholden the rain from you, when there were yet three months to the harvest: and I cause it to rain upon one city, and cause it not to rain upon another city: one piece was rained upon, and the piece where upon it rained did not wither. So two or three cities wandered unto one city, to drink water; but they were not satisfied: yet have ye not returned unto me, saith the Lord.

The Lord God controls in every city how much rain it receives, so if your city suffers a drought, there is something that man can do about it. "Return unto me," saith the Lord. Let's also read verse 9:

> I have smitten you with blasting [*shdephah*,[170] which
> means blight, from *shadaph*,[171] which means to scorch]
> and mildew: when your gardens and your vineyards
> and your fig trees and your olive trees increased, the
> palmerworm devoured them, yet ye not returned
> unto me, saith the Lord.

Are your crops burning up in the fields, or is it raining so much you can't harvest your fields? There is something man can do about this. "Return unto me," saith the Lord.

Let's also read verse 10:

> I have sent among you the pestilence after the manner
> of Egypt: your young men have I slain with the sword,
> and I have taken away your horses; and I have made
> the stink of your camps to come up unto your nostrils:
> yet ye not returned unto me, saith the Lord.

We should note here that the pestilences used on the Egyptians were used on the Hebrews in the desert wilderness. They are used again on the house of Israel and again on the house of Judah. They are the same pestilences as in the book of Revelation. Do you want to be saved from these pestilences? There is something man can do. "Return unto me," saith the Lord.

Verse 11 says, "I have overthrown some of you, as God overthrew Sodom and Gomorrah, and ye were as a firebrand plucked out of the burning: yet ye not returned unto me, saith the Lord." In the last days, the Bible tells us, "For, behold, the day cometh, that it shall burn as an oven; and all that do wickedly, shall be stubble; and the day cometh shall burn them up." Do you not want to be scorched when it shall "burn as an oven"? There is something man can do about this. "Return unto me," saith the Lord.

Let's finish with verses 12 and 13:

---

[170] Ibid., 1979.

[171] Ibid.

Therefore thus will I do unto thee, O Israel: and because I will do this unto thee, prepare to meet thy God, O Israel. For, lo, he that formeth the mountains, and created the wind, and declareth unto man what is his thought, that maketh the morning darkness, and treadeth upon the high places of the earth, The Lord, The God of hosts, is his name.

Who is the "Lord of hosts"?

This is given to us in Isaiah 44:6: "Thus saith the Lord the King of Israel, and his redeemer the Lord of hosts." Isaiah 47:4 says, "As for our redeemer, the Lord of hosts is his name, the Holy One of Israel." And who is the redeemer? Isaiah 45:15 says, "O God of Israel, the Saviour," and Isaiah 45:21 says, "a just God and Saviour; there is none besides me." The Lord of hosts is the Lord Jesus Christ, who is man's redeemer and Savior. The "Lord of hosts" is a title of God given in Psalms, Isaiah, Jeremiah, Hosea, Amos, Micah, Nahum, Habakkuk, Zephaniah, Zechariah, and Malachi. The word for hosts is *tsaba* (or feminine *tseba'ah*[172]), which means a mass of persons, organized for war; by implication a campaign, literal or figurative: appointed time, army, battle, soldiers, waiting upon. It is from *tsaba*,[173] which means to mass (an army or servants), assemble, or fight. Not one Hebrew word means meek and mild. When the Lord of hosts appeared on the planet, he did not change his mind.

Then we have the Lord Jesus speaking in Luke 12:51: "Suppose ye that I am come to bring peace on earth? I tell ye Nay; but rather division." And the "mass of persons (soldiers) organized for war at the appointed time" are the soldiers of 2 Timothy 2:3: "Thou therefore endure hardness [*kakopatheo*,[174] which means to undergo hardships; be afflicted, endure afflictions, suffer trouble], as a good soldier of Jesus Christ." And we do this by Ephesians 6:11: "Put on the whole armour

---

172   Ibid., 1952.
173   Ibid.
174   Ibid., 2093.

of God, that ye may be able to stand against the wiles of the devil."
These Hebrew meanings don't speak of the meek and mild Jesus we are
told about by Christian pastors.

We should note that we are told here that God's presence is in the
high places of the earth, just as Jeremiah tells us in 23:23–24, "Am I
a God at hand, saith the Lord, and not a God afar off? Can any hide
himself in secret place that I shall not see him? saith the Lord. Do not
I fill heaven and earth? saith the Lord." Are you prepared to meet your
God and Father? And Jeremiah will tell us this in plain and simple
language.

Jeremiah 10:13–15 says:

> When he uttereth his voice, there is a multitude of
> waters in the heavens, and he causeth the vapours
> to ascend from the ends of the earth; he maketh
> lightnings with rain, and bringeth forth the wind out
> of his treasures. Every man is brutish [Hebrew word
> meaning stupid, foolish[175]] in his knowledge: every
> founder is confounded by the graven image: for his
> molten image is falsehood, and there is no breath in
> them. They are vanity, and the work of errors: in the
> time of their visitation they shall perish.

God tells in verse 13 that he controls the weather. Man's worship of
this earth [earth-first people] is stupid and foolish knowledge. I didn't
call you stupid and foolish; God did.

Who else does the Lord call stupid and foolish? This is given in
Isaiah 32:5: "The vile [*nabal*,[176] which means stupid; wicked and
foolish] person shall no more be called liberal." And why are these
liberal persons called stupid, wicked, and foolish? It is because they
utter against the Lord with this ape-man evolution and the big bang
theory. There will be more on liberal people later. They say that man is
destroying the earth just by his mere existence. We are told in scripture

[175] Ibid., 1827.
[176] Ibid., 1914.

this is why God created the earth. You are telling Almighty God he made a faulty planet if man is able to do this. And when God comes back (the time of their visitation) to reign, they will perish. This need to go green is "the work of errors" and is "vanity." These environmentalists and evolutionists will not inherit eternal life because they speak falsely against the Lord in their theories. History cannot be denied.

Was the small ice age from the 1300s to the 1800s caused by greenhouse gases before the 1300s? Just how many so-called fossil fuels were they putting into the atmosphere before 1300 to cause this massive weather change to happen? I would also like to ask scientists today this. Just how big did the Arctic ice cap get during this ice age?

Just forty years later, when the planet was on a warming trend, history tells us this. On April 15, 1912, an iceberg sank the *Titanic*, killing over one thousand five hundred people. There were reports of many icebergs. What heat wave hit the Arctic Circle? Maybe the ice cap got too heavy to be sustained. I think we should also note this. Here is a headline from a British newspaper: "This ship is unsinkable, even God Himself can't sink her." Did they "tempt the Spirit of the Lord" as Acts 5:9 says? Five days after her maiden voyage started, God sunk her with an iceberg. This tells us that the Lord God is still listening. But since there is no God, I think the blame should go to mother earth. The scientists tell us that human beings are the greatest threat to the planet, while the Bible tells us in Isaiah 45:18, "God himself that formed the earth and made it not in vain, he formed it to be inhabited." The scientists of today are in complete contradiction to what is told to us in the Bible, which is the Word of God.

Jeremiah 5:24–25 says:

> Neither say they in their heart, Let us now fear the Lord our God, that giveth rain, both the former and the latter, in his season: he reserveth unto us the appointed weeks of the harvest. Your iniquities have turned away these things, and your sins have withholden good things from you.

Once again, scripture tells us that the Lord God controls the weather. It's the Lord God who "giveth rain for the appointed weeks of the harvest." When man continually sins against the Lord, the Lord will use the weather against man. Let us also note Ezekiel 24:26, "And I [God] will cause the showers to come down in his seasons; there shall be showers of blessing." Let's note who are included with the environmentalists and the evolutionists mentioned in this "time of visitation."

Jeremiah 5:26, 29, 32 says:

> For among my people are found wicked [*rasha*,[177] which means moral wrong, concrete a bad person, condemned, guilty, ungodly] men: they lie wait, as he that setteth snares [*yaquwsh*,[178] which means entangled, passive participle of *yaqosh*,[179] which means to ensnare, and the *Strong's Concordance* comment on is this: "The bait of these snares is people's desire for other Gods"[180]] they set a trap [*mashchiyth*,[181] which means; destructive (i.e., as noun) destruction], they catch [*lakad*,[182] which means to capture or occupy] men. Shall I not visit [*paqad*,[183] which means to visit (with friendly or hostile intent); by analogy oversee, care for, avenge] for these things? saith the Lord: shall not my soul avenged on such a nation as this? A wonderful and horrible thing is committed in the land; The prophets prophesy falsely, and the priest bear rule by their means; and my people love to have it so: and what will you do in the end

---

[177] Ibid., 1974.
[178] Ibid., 1876.
[179] Ibid., 1877.
[180] Ibid.
[181] Ibid., 1911.
[182] Ibid., 1890.
[183] Ibid., 1949.

[*achariyth*,[184] which means the last or the end, hence the future: last, latter, end time] thereof?

First of all, we should note that chapter 5 of Jeremiah lists the reasons for judgment with all the indications of the last days. We should note it states that "my people" are still on the planet. There are ungodly men who "lie in wait." When we read the Qur'an in this book, we will see this is just what Muhammad instructed his followers. Let's note the Hebrew meaning for Arab is "to lurk (lie in) ambush, lay (lie in) wait."[185] We should note that there are false prophets and priests who rule by their means in the land and "my people love to have it so." That would be the pre-tribulation resurrection pastors and the pastors who put you under the Mosaic Law and their congregations who applaud that they don't go through the judgments of God. It's at the time of their visitation when the Hebrew word for "avenge" comes in. The Lord will avenge in scripture in 2 Thessalonians 1:7-8:

> And to you who are troubled [tribulation] rest with us when the Lord Jesus shall be revealed from heaven with his mighty angels, In flaming fire taking vengeance on them that known not God, and obey not the gospel of our Lord Jesus.

If the Lord Jesus is not revealed from heaven until his vengeance on them who know not God, how can there be a pre-tribulation resurrection? The church has been told differently for the past hundred years or so. It is time they learned the truth.

Jesus tells us that whosoever puts anything above him is not worthy of him. Isaiah tells us in 55:8–10:

> For my thoughts are not your thoughts, neither are your ways my ways, saith the Lord. For as the heavens are higher than the earth, so are my ways higher than

---

[184]   Ibid., 1809.

[185]   Ibid., 1816.

your ways, and my thoughts than your thoughts. For
as the rain cometh down, and the snow from heaven,
and returneth not thither, but watereth the earth, and
maketh it bring forth and bud, that it may give seed
to the sower, and bread to the eater.

God creates earthquakes at his command. It states this in Ezekiel 38:20, "All men that are upon the face of the earth, shall shake at my presence." Let us review the scriptures that deal with the PETA group. This is given to us in 1 Timothy 4:1: "Now the Spirit speaketh expressly, that in the latter times some shall depart from the faith, giving heed to seducing spirits, and doctrines of devils." To start, here it tells us this will be in the "latter times." What these people come up with are "doctrines of devils." Verse 2 says, "Speaking lies in hypocrisy; having their conscience [*suneidesis*,[186] which means co-perception (i.e., moral consciousness)] seared [*kauteriazo*,[187] which means to brand (cauterize), (i.e., by implication) to render insensitive] with a hot iron." This says nicely that their brains are fried. Verse 3 tells us who this scripture is against: "Forbidding to marry, and commanding to abstain from meats, which God hath created to be received with thanksgiving of them which believe and know the truth."

Are not the PETA people against people eating meat? They even demand that animals have equal rights. This is nothing but the cultic religion of Hinduism. Indian people believe that the soul of a person comes back, and if they lead ungodly lives, they come back as animals. This is why they don't eat their cattle. The PETA people also tell us that animals put out greenhouse gases that are destroying the earth. They go against the Word of God. I give you Genesis 1:25: "And God made the beast of the earth after his kind, and cattle after their kind, and every thing that creepeth upon the earth after his kind: and God saw it was good." The PETA people tell us cattle are bad for the earth when God says what he created was good. This is another contradiction to the Word of God.

---

[186] Ibid., 2158.
[187] Ibid., 2099.

Let's also note Psalms 104:14, which says, "He [God] causeth the grass to grow for the cattle, and herb for the service of man: that he might bring forth food out of the earth." And now let's finish with verses 4 and 5: "For every creature of God is good, and nothing to be refused, if it be received with thanksgiving: For it is sanctified by the Word of God and prayer." If eating meat is sanctified by the Word of God, I would think it is okay to eat meat. If you didn't receive the message, here it states "the latter times," the end of days. But later in this manuscript we will read there are restrictions. We should also note that it is "doctrines of devils" to forbid a man and a woman to marry. There is only one religion that has this doctrine.

This scripture in 1 Timothy has its equivalent scripture in Isaiah 66:1–5:

> Thus saith the Lord, The heaven is my throne, and the earth is my footstool: For all those things hath my hands made, and all those things have been, saith the Lord: but to This Man will I look, even him that is poor and of a contrite spirit, and trembleth at my word.

God says through Isaiah that he made all the things in the heavens and the earth. Note the scripture talks about this man who has a contrite spirit. Contrite is *nakeh*,[188] which means smitten (i.e., literally) maimed, or (figuratively) dejected. Basically, the Hebrew and the Greek meanings of 1 Timothy are the same. And as in 1 Timothy, let's read what Isaiah tells us about who has this maimed spirit. This is the Old Testament equivalent of what we read in 1 Timothy.

Verse 3 says:

> He that killeth an ox as if he slew a man he that sacrifice a lamb, as if he cutteth of a dogs neck; he that offereth an oblation, as if he offered swine's gift; he that burneth incense, as if he worship an idol.

---

[188] Ibid., 1949.

Yea, they have chosen their own ways, and their soul delighteth in their abominations.

Putting animals on the level of humans is an abomination to the Lord. What God has provided for man for food is given in Deuteronomy 14, and the dog is not included. Can anyone tell me what dogs evolved from? Now let's read what God says he will do to people with this contrite spirit.

Verse 4 says:

I will also choose their delusions, and bring their fears upon them; because when I called, none of them answered; when I spake, they did not hear; but they did evil before my eyes, and chose that in I delighted not.

Note here in Isaiah God says, "I will chose their delusion." This is the same message given in 2 Thessalonians 2:11: "And for this cause God shall send them strong delusion, that they should believe a lie." That lie is animals are not food for man, and they are not destroying the planet as the PETA claims. They did not hear what the Lord has said because God tells us in Isaiah 56:10, "His watchmen are blind; they are all ignorant, they are all dumb dogs." Pastors are not speaking out against these evolutionists, environmentalists, and members of PETA. And as always with God, there is judgment for those in delusion.

Verse 5 says:

Hear the word of the Lord, ye that tremble at his word; Your brethren that hated you, that cast thee out for my name's sake, say, Let's the Lord be glorified: but he shall appear to your joy, and they shall be ashamed.

Is this ever true in today's world! Christian people are looked down on as a people who don't fit in today's society. For those who trust in the Lord and his Word, when he appears, it will be to them a joy. To all those who trust in their theories, it will be a disappointment because the Almighty God is going to prove their theories wrong. I will allow the psalms to speak for me. Psalms 1:1–6 says:

> Blessed is the man that walketh not in the counsel of the ungodly, nor standeth in the way of the sinners, nor sitteth in the seat of the scornful. But his delight is in the law of the Lord; and his law doth he meditate day and night. And he shall be like a tree planted by the rivers of water, that bringeth forth his fruit in his season; his leaf also shall not wither; and whatsoever he doeth shall prosper. The ungodly are not so: but are like the chaff which the wind driveth away. Therefore the ungodly shall not stand in his judgment, nor sinners in the congregation of the righteous. For the Lord knoweth the way of the righteous: but the ungodly shall perish.

Always in the scriptures it is said "blessed" is the man who trusts in the Lord. The ungodly who trust in mother earth and all the earthly idols will not be able to stand in the judgment. That judgment is in the book of Revelation. Note the ungodly shall "not stand." Romans says that it is God who enables the righteous to stand in the judgments. This should also tell the church that they will be on the planet when these judgments come. This is when the church is to, as the psalms state, bring forth its fruit during this season. Also note it says, "The ungodly shall perish." This means they will not be the "blessed are the meek; for they shall inherit the earth." Also note the psalms mention "the wind." Ezekiel tells us it is the four winds that put the spirits in the dead, that they might live. When the resurrection of the dead happens, these people's spirits that are in the grave will not hear the words, "Come up hither." This is why this is written. And to the global warming and weather change scientists, the Bible tells us this in Genesis 8:22: "While the earth remained, seed time and harvest, and cold and heat, and summer and winter, and day and night shall not cease."

We should note that during the small ice age, people were still harvesting crops, although not as much as was needed. Millions of people perished during this period because of this shortage. But God says judgment falls on the just and the unjust. I believe this small ice age was the judgment on the church at this time because the church tortured and burned Christians on the stake. Even in America in the 1400s people who committed a sin were put in stocks. Man has a sin nature. This is why 1 John 2:1 says, "And if any man sin, we have an advocate with the Father, Jesus Christ the righteous." This is not following the words of the Lord Jesus where he states in Matthew 19:19, 7:22:39, and Mark 12:31, "Thou shalt love thy neighbour as thyself" and in Matthew 7:1 and Luke 6:37, "Judge not, that ye be not judged." I can't find it, but did this small ice age extend to the other parts of the northern hemisphere? Did it happen to the southern hemisphere at all?

Jeremiah 5:24 also says, "Neither say they in their heart, Let us now fear the Lord our God, that giveth rain, both the former and the latter, in his season: he reserveth unto us the appointed weeks of the harvest." It clearly states here that if you fear the Lord, there will always a guarantee of the appointed weeks for the harvest and winter. There are always conditions with God, and just as the house of Judah turned from God, this is given. Jeremiah 5:25 says, "Your iniquities have turned away these things, and your sins have withholden good things from you." Will this happen to the world for all their unbelief in our time? Man continues to rebel against God when we try to save mother earth instead of praying and fasting to Father God.

We are also told in 1 Timothy 6:20:

> O Timothy keep that which is committed to thy trust,
> avoiding profane and vain babblings, and oppositions
> of science falsely so called.

I watched part of Al Gore's *An Inconvenient Truth*. I couldn't stomach to watch much. His global warming theory is based on mere speculation, and his insufficient evidence is presented as fact. Man's puny efforts will not change what God has planned for the future.

We get this from a man who said when he was running for president that his favorite Bible scripture was John 16:3: "And these things will they do unto you, because they have not known the father, nor me." He meant to say John 3:16. He doesn't know the Bible well enough to quote the right verse. What God has created, man will not be allowed to destroy, and when I hear scientists say the very existence of man on the planet is destroying the earth, I would like to remind them that man was the reason God created the earth. These are the profane and vain babblings that Christians are to avoid.

We should note Zechariah 14:9, "And the Lord shall be king over all the earth: in that day shall be one Lord, and his name one." When the Lord comes to rule and reign, Zechariah 14:8 tells us, "And it shall be in that day, that living waters shall go out of Jerusalem; half of them toward the former sea, and half of them toward the hinder sea: in summer and in winter shall it be." When the Lord comes back, there will still be summer and winter. Your inconvenient truth is spoken by the Word who created the world.

I was watching the Science Channel, and they said that the earth has warming and cooling periods that happen over thousands of years, and we are in one of the warming periods. They also stated that the planet was warmer than now until the 1300s. The late 1300s is when the weather got cooler, and this is when the planet experienced what they said was the small ice age that lasted from around the 1370s to the 1870s. This is why the Vikings named their country Greenland—because it was green. This was around the year 1000. They said they lived mostly from its crops until the late 1370s, when they turned to the sea as their main food source. The small ice age that lasted from the 1370s to the 1870s was God's judgment on these people for the way they treated their fellow Christians and Jews.

By the way, oil is not fossil fuel. Oil is produced by the heat from the core of the earth on certain chemicals in the earth that produce oil. I believe the earth continues to produce oil naturally. A new theory found on the Internet at the website www.wnd.com is by Giora Proskuronski of the school of oceanography of Washington University. It's called the abiotic synthesis of hydrocarbons. I believe the creator of the planet knew man would depend on this oil as a resource for energy, and the earth will continue to make this vital resource. It is a natural product of the earth, such as natural gas, gold, silver, coal, and diamonds.

The Rocky Mountains are full of shale oil. Why shale oil? It didn't stay close enough to the heat source, which is the core, to make it liquid oil. If the Rocky Mountains came up from the deep parts of the core, which scientists tell us, how did the dinosaur oil get that deep through solid rock? Is the phrase "stupid" coming into play here? The deeper man drills, the bigger the oil resources he will find. A person I know who works in Saudi Arabia for a oil company told me, "We only drill for oil about ten miles in the earth." The core of the earth is four hundred miles deep. This tells us the deeper man drills, the bigger the oil reserves become.

And if the dinosaur bones are found near the earth's surface, how did their decomposing remains get through miles and miles of solid rock? Since most of the known oil supplies are in the Middle East. Did most of the dinosaurs go there to die? I have some questions. How many barrels of oil did we get from each dinosaur? They must have found thousands and thousands of dinosaur bones in the Middle East. How did so many dinosaurs die in one area of the world? Does anybody believe God would create a product in the earth to destroy the earth?

Isaiah tells us in 44:24–25:

> Thus saith the Lord, thy redeemer, and he that formed thee from the womb, I am the Lord that maketh all things; that stretcheth forth the heavens alone; that spreadeth abroad the earth by myself. That frustrateth the tokens of the lairs, and maketh diviners mad; that turneth wise men backward, and maketh their knowledge foolish.

This foolish knowledge is the need to go green. I will write this again if you didn't get it the first time. "I [God] am the Lord that maketh all things." That includes oil. We should note Psalms 50:10, "For every beast of the forest is mine, and the cattle upon a thousand hills." God says he created them; they're his. Everything in or on the earth is God's. He created them for man.

We are also told in Isaiah 42:5, "Thus saith God the Lord, he that created the heavens and stretched them out; he that spread forth the earth, and that which cometh out of it; he that giveth breath unto the people upon it, and the spirit to them that walk therein." And once again I will repeat scripture: "He [God]" that spread forth the earth and "that with cometh out of it." It is God who gives life to the spirit (humanity) that walks upon the earth.

It's the political parties that create the so-called crisis so that man is dependent on them to solve the so-called problems. This tax on energy use, the carbon tax, is nothing but a tax to fund the one-world government, which are the liberal politicians of the European Union. This is nothing more than the redistribution of wealth. How is the buying of carbon credits going to save the planet? All this is only going to drive up the cost of energy. To believe that solar and wind power are going to replace oil is completely stupid.

If man was destroying the earth with the use of oil, God says, "I destroy those who destroy the earth." That means God has to destroy me, because he created all things on the earth, and this includes the animals. When I heard a PETA person say we should not eat meat because animals put out greenhouse gases, which they say are destroying the earth, I see why God calls them stupid and foolish.

But if the environmentalist would turn to God, he would change things. And it is the same environmentalists who make us dependent on foreign oil and slaves to the Middle East. You hypocrites! I will say this in exchange for other words I would rather use. How fast would the price of oil drop if we had a president and Congress that commanded the oil companies in this country to drill, drill, drill everywhere? We should be drilling anywhere there is the possibility of oil, such as off the coast of California. But the liberal environmentalists don't want drilling even in areas where the ocean floor is leaking out oil. This need to grow our own energy is stupid. It takes up more resources to produce fuel out of food than to feed the starving people of the world. Since we started making food into fuel, food prices have been driven up. Is this not where the word "stupid" comes into play? Where is this saving people money? This need to grow our energy is nothing but pure greed on the part of farmers.

Maybe you tree-hugging, earth-first environmentalists should first set the example to save a tree and live in a mud hut. I'm talking to you, Al Gore. Sell your car and jet and walk or ride a bike everywhere you need to go. Turn off your power to your home if the electrical power is produced by coal or nuclear energy. Reduce your carbon imprint on the earth by killing yourself and save the planet. How dare any of you environmentalists have children, since man is destroying the earth, because God didn't create the earth for mankind. When I hear people make this statement about how we must save "mother earth," it is stupid. If we pray to Father God, then he will "heal our land." This need to go green is what Isaiah described as "their knowledge is foolish." We should start with the politicians in Washington. I make these outlandish statements to make a point. We can only use the resources God has provided for mankind in the earth. It's up to man to use them so it doesn't harm the environment. We are to be good stewards of the land but not stupid stewards.

This is one of the signs the Lord Jesus told us to look for in the last days. The environmentalists have made mother earth their idol by worshiping the earth. Because the environmentalists are more worried about saving mother earth than praying to Father God, the Bible tells us in 2 Thessalonians 1:10–11: "And for this cause God shall send them strong delusion, that they should believe a lie. That they all might be damned who believe not the truth, but had pleasure in unrighteousness." The unrighteous do not have faith in the Lord Jesus Christ but rather put their faith in mother earth. And look at the language: "That they all might be damned." I didn't say this; Paul did.

The environmentalists have nothing to worry about because of the next scriptures. Isaiah 65:17 says, "For, behold, I create new heavens and a new earth: and the former shall not be remembered, nor come unto mine." The God who created the heavens and the earth in the beginning will in the future create something new. We have this in the book of Revelation.

Revelation 21:3–5 says:

> And I heard a voice from heaven saying, Behold, the
> tabernacle of God is with men, and they shall be his

> people, and God himself shall be with them, and be
> their God. And God shall wipe away all tears from
> their eyes; and there shall be no more death, neither
> sorrow, nor crying, neither shall there be any more
> pain: for the former things are pass away. And he that
> sat upon the throne said, Behold, I make all things
> new. And he said unto me, Write: for these words are
> true and faithful.

God says he is going to make all things new. We should note
that it says here, "God himself shall be with them [his people]." This
is the answer to our daily prayer, "Thy kingdom come. Thy will be
done on earth as it is in heaven." Do you remember the commercial
with the Indian with the tear running down his face in the pollution
commercial? God is going to wipe away that tear.

Darwin's biological evolution taught that some peoples were naturally
superior to others, such as whites to blacks. Do any African American
teachers want to teach the ape-man evolution theory with Darwin's
theory that whites were superior to blacks? If you believe Darwin's
theory is true, you must believe the whole theory. You can't have it both
ways, that the strong should survive and the less-superior perish. When
a natural disaster such as an earthquake happens, maybe it's just mother
nature cleansing itself of evil humans, and we should not help people
survive. Darwin believed that everything adapted to its environment,
replacing virtue, and outside of his theory, there was nothing right.

This is the same kind of thinking that has brought us the concept
of global weather change and that man must do something to correct
it. It's man's fault that the weather is changing. These kinds of theories
are nothing but radicalism and theories to replace the true creator of
all things. We in the twenty-first century want to teach this madman's
theory and the theory of David Friedrich Strauss, who wrote the book,
The Life of Jesus, which explains that the miraculous works of Jesus were
just a myth. This is passed on to the nineteenth century, where German
Bruno Bauer wrote his criticism of the Bible, where he states that Jesus
never existed and that the Old Testament was nothing but an allegory.
All I can say about Mr. Strauss and Bruno Bauer is maybe you were not

as smart as you thought. If my interpretation is correct, the Bible tells us the history of the world before it happens.

These Darwinian evolutionists are the first to question the uniqueness of the creation story given by God. This manuscript was written to prove that Darwinism is wrong. The Bible is the Word of God, and the complete picture of man's existence on this earth is given in the Word of God. To think that this earth came into place in our universe at exactly the right place to sustain life takes greater faith than to believe that God created the earth. To think that a single cell in the ocean developed into the complex system called the human body takes greater faith than God creating male and female.

The liberals of the 1800s gave us the ape-man cult and the liberals of the twenty-first century the mother-earth cult, all to deny the existence of God. This is why God says the vile (stupid, wicked, foolish) person shall no more be called liberal. Let's note 2 Corinthians 2:14–17:

> Now thanks be unto God, which always causeth us to triumph in Christ, and maketh manifest the savour of his knowledge by us in every place. For we are unto God a sweet savour of Christ, in them that are saved, and in them that perish: To the one we are the savour of death unto death; and to the other the savour of life unto life. And we are not many, which corrupt the Word of God; but as sincerity, but as of God, in the sight of God speak we in Christ.

In the Day of Judgment they will not hear these words of the Lord Jesus Christ, "Well done, my faithful servant." Note the language that says, "Savior of all men." Those who corrupt the Word of God go from death to death. These souls are the, "And many of them that sleep in the dust of the earth shall awake, some to everlasting life, and some to everlasting contempt" of Daniel 12:2. The soul without the body is considered a "dead soul," as quoted by E. W. Bullinger (728). This is why Ezekiel tells us "the soul that sinneth, it shall die." These are those who awake to everlasting contempt. That soul will not be one of the meek who inherit the earth for all eternity.

If all manner of sin is forgiven man except "blasphemy of the Holy Spirit," can Christians show the same forgiveness? Even with this being written in the Bible, let's also quote it. The Lord Jesus says, "Render therefore unto Caesar the things which are Caesar's; and unto God the things that are God's." In today's world, we have a separation of church and state. The homosexual couples pay their taxes to the state and not the church, as in past history. So if these people pay their taxes to the state, they should get the same benefits the state pays the marriages sanctified by God. The homosexual couples should just not ask the church to sanctify this marriage before the Lord God. I say let them also pay the marriage penalty, which is sanctified by the state. I believe the church is wrong to fight them on these rights. Maybe some of you "holier than thou" people would like to bring back the Dark Ages and banish them from society or torture them into submission, or better yet burn a few on a stake.

Some pastors will also say, "But this is an abomination unto the Lord." So is abortion, which most Christian Democrats vote for. God tells Jeremiah in 1:5, "Before I formed thee in the belly I knew thee; and before thou camest forth out of the womb I sanctified thee." At conception, God knew Jeremiah. This is, "Thou shalt not kill." How many of you commit that abomination by your vote? So is eating the blood of animals and eating chicken eggs uncooked; in the next chapter, I will prove this to be an abomination unto the Lord, a false witness who speaks a lie, which are the alive church rapture pastors. And who among you have brought merchandise you could not afford on a credit card and then asked for credit-card relief? This is thief of merchandise, only done legally. There are many abominations unto the Lord. One abomination unto the Lord is no worse than another.

The Bible tells us in Matthew 7:1–2, "Judge not, that ye be not judged. For with what judgment ye judge, ye shall be judged: and with what measure ye mete, it shall be measured to you again." God tells us this: If you divorce your wife and marry another, you are guilty of adultery. All have sinned and have come short of the glory of God. John 8:7 tells us, "He that is without sin among you, let him cast the first stone." Are you without sin that you condemn these people? By the same standard, should the state not pay the same benefits to divorced couples? Both are living in sin in the eyes of the Lord. And the second reason is this when the "one of them which was a lawyer, asked him [the Lord Jesus], Master, which is the great commandment in the law?" And the response of the Lord Jesus was, "Thou shalt love thy neighbour as thyself." I don't believe I have to explain this verse in scripture.

Let's finish this chapter with Mark16:16. The Lord Jesus says, "He that believeth [in the gospel] and is baptized shall be saved; but he that believeth not shall be damned." This is plain and simple language. It does not say he who is a sinner is damned. This is why the Lord came to this earth, to save the sinners who believe in him. Let us note 1 John 2:1: "My little children, these things write I unto you, that ye sin not. And if any man sin, we have an advocate with the Father, Jesus Christ the righteous." Those who believe and are baptized have eternal life, and for those who don't, it is not going to be good. This is what the early church didn't understand, or they would have not tortured Christians as they did. And it has gotten much better in the twenty-first century.

The Lord Jesus is inclusive. In today's world, this statement is not politically correct. When people say that all religions lead people to God, it is a contradiction to the Bible. When the environmentalists and members of PETA tell us the existence of man on the earth is destroying the earth, they speak against the Lord. The Bible tells us God created the earth to be inhabited by man and created the animals, such as cattle, as food for man. You are in direct contradiction to the Bible. When man says man evolved from apes instead of being created by God, that is another contradiction. This includes the pre-tribulation and the living resurrection pastors. Why does man continue to rebel against the Word of God? God has given man a free spirit and soul. You can either stand with God and the words given to us by his holy prophets or not. We have just read actions and words God sees and hears, and they are recorded to be used for or against man at the Day of Judgment. Don't believe what I have written, because I am just one of those idiots who believe in God and that the Bible is the Word of God. Don't be destroyed because of the lack of knowledge.

Notwithstanding, I Have a Few Things against Thee

IN THIS CHAPTER, I will deal with the different church denominations and the church doctrine they follow. When they do not follow as Paul has instructed, there is a problem. The first commandment from God was, "Thou shall not have no other gods before me." Americans have many gods they worship. They worship their football, baseball, and basketball stars. For movie stars, rock and roll stars, and country music stars, people stand on their feet and cheer. There are many other things Americans, as well as most of the world, deem more important than studying the Word of God. They don't have time for God, who died on the cross for their sins. Those people can remember how many home runs athletes hit, how many yards one ran in a season, and how many goals were scored, but they cannot remember a verse in scripture. It is to my amazement how little most people know about what is in the Bible, yet they say they are Christians. They rely on what their pastor has interpreted it to say and do not search out the truth for themselves.

I was brought up in a Catholic Church and was never told to study the Bible on my own, but after fifteen years of going to church, I knew as little about the Bible as I did when I started, since back then most of the mass was done in Latin. In my late twenties, I quit going to church. It wasn't until I turned forty that my interest in the Bible returned and I started studying the Bible again. Then, after many hours of study, I could not go back to the Catholic Church.

Around the early 1990s, I turned off the television except for certain occasions to search for the truth. The result of that is this study. I believe the Catholic Church is wrong to pray to Mary, the mother of the Lord, for the Bible tells us there is one intercessor and that is the Lord Jesus. We see in Jeremiah 7:18, "The children gather wood, and the fathers kindle the fire, and the women knead their dough, to make cakes to the queen of heaven, and to pour out drink-offerings unto other gods, that they may provoke me to anger." I believe this tells us that only the Lord should be prayed to and prayer to anyone else provokes the Lord. First Timothy 2:5 says, "For there is one God, and one mediator between God and men, the man Christ Jesus." If there is only "one mediator between God and man," how can the Catholic Church's worship of Mary be justifiable?

Matthew 6:6 says, "But thou, when thou prayest, enter into thy closet, and when thou hast shut the door, pray to thy father which is in secret; and thy Father seeth in secret shall reward thee openly." In verse 13 in our daily prayer, we are told, "And lead us not into temptation, but deliver us from evil." We don't have to be "caught up" or in a resurrection to be delivered from the devil, as we will see in scripture. One example is when the prophet Jeremiah was prophesying against the House of Judah. He said in Jeremiah 1:19, "And they shall fight against thee; but they shall not prevail against thee; for I am with thee, saith the Lord, To deliver thee." The Lord delivered Jeremiah, and he was still on the earth, for the meek will inherit the earth.

Outside of your earthly father, the Bible tells us to call nobody your father except for father who is heaven, and this is given in Matthew 23:9: "And call no man your father upon the earth: for one is your Father, which is in heaven." The Catholic Church has brought their biggest problems by not adhering to scripture. First Timothy 3:2 tells us:

> A bishop then must be blameless, the husband of one wife, vigilant, sober, of good behaviour, given to hospitality, apt to teach; Not given to wine, no striker, not greedy of filthy lucre; but patient, not a brawler,

not covetous; One that ruleth will his own house,
having his children in subjection with all gravity.

All the Pentecostal and Assemblies of God pastors are guilty of being "covetous." In these churches, you are put under the 10 percent tithe and asked to give your estates to the church to find true salvation.

Let us note Ezekiel 44. When the Lord reigns in Jerusalem, after the battle of Armageddon, these are the instructions for the ministers in the Lord's sanctuary. Verse 22 says, "Neither shall they take for their wives a widow, nor her that is put away: but they shall take maidens of the seed of the house of Israel, or a widow that had a priest before." If it is commanded by the Lord God for the ministers before God to be married, then Catholicism's non-marriage policy is a doctrine of devils, as stated in 1 Timothy. When you have a church setting aside millions of dollars to settle lawsuits for child abuse by priests, there is scriptural condemnation. The Lord Jesus says in Matthew 18:6 and Luke 17:2, "But whoso shall offend one of these little ones which believe in me, it were better for him that a millstone were hanged about his neck, and that he were drowned in the depth of the sea."

I think it is important to note that Paul goes on to write to Timothy in 3:8, "Likewise must the deacons be grave, not double-tongue, not given to much wine, not greedy of filthy lucre." If Paul says it's okay with him that a deacon can have some wine, I don't know how the church can say that Jesus did not turn the water into wine at the wedding feast. To teach that was anything but wine, as the Baptist preachers teach, saying this was grape juice, is just a lie, for the master of the wedding feast said they saved the good wine for last. If it was not wine, that would make our Lord a deceiver.

I don't believe the Lord is this stick-in-the-mud God that he would not want man to enjoy life. If they found a word to describe all sin in the Bible, I think that would have found a word for grape juice. Noah found grace in the eyes of the Lord, and what did Noah do? He makes himself a vineyard and drinks the wine. Let's note Genesis 9:21, "And he drank of the wine, and was drunken." Did God make a mistake when he called Noah "a righteous man"? Let us note Ezekiel 44:21, which says, "Neither shall any priest drink wine, when they enter into the inner court." When the Lord Jesus Christ returns and rules on this planet, the priests can drink wine, but not when they enter the inner court.

I think we should also note that Matthew tells us in 6:17–18, "But thou, when thou fastest, anoint thine head, and wash thy face; That thou appear not unto men to fast, but unto thy father which is in secret: and thy Father, which seeth in secret, shall reward thy openly." Is this not a direct command from God to "fast"? Is this why prayers are not answered, because you don't fast? Instead of a "prayer breakfast," maybe a "prayer fast" would be more appropriate. When pastors call for a national day of prayer, should this also be a day of fasting too? Or is it too much for man to fast a whole day?

If the Baptist pastors want you to live under the law of no wine or strong drink, then maybe you should live under the whole law. Judges tells us in 13:4, "Now therefore beware, I pray thee, and drink not wine or strong drink, and eat not any unclean thing." I believe this to mean also you are not to eat of the pig. Does this pastor eat his steak raw, which is to eat the blood of an animal? Saul called this "an abomination unto the Lord." Remember, you can't pick and choose what part of the law you want to follow. James 2:10 says, "For whosoever shall keep the whole law, and yet offend in one point, he is guilty of all." This is why I don't attend church. All of the denominations tried to put me under some form of the Mosaic Law. And this is found in Numbers 6:2–7:

> Speak unto the children of Israel, and say unto them, When either man or woman shall separate themselves to vow a vow of a Nazarite, to separate themselves unto the Lord: He shall separate himself from wine and strong drink, and shall drink no vinegar of wine, or vinegar of strong drink, neither shall he drink any liquor of grapes, nor eat moist grapes, or dried. All the days of his separation shall he eat nothing that is made of the vine tree, from the kernels even to the husk. All the days of the vow of his separation there shall no razor come upon his head: until the days be fulfilled, in which he separateth himself unto the

Lord, he shall be holy, and shall let the locks of the hair of his head grow. All the days of his separateth himself unto the Lord he shall come at no dead body. He shall not make himself unclean for his father, or for his mother, for his brother, or for his sister, when they die: because the consecration of his God is upon his head. Drink not wine nor strong drink, and eat not any unclean thing.

To follow the rest of the Law, read for yourself verses 8–19. Then there is verse 20, which says, "And the priest shall wave them for a wave-offering before the Lord: this is holy before the priest, with the wave-breast and heave-shoulder: and after that the Nazarite may drink wine." We should note that after that procedure, it's okay even for a Nazarite to drink wine. That same Baptist pastor is filling his face with pig every morning when we are told in Isaiah 66:1, "They that sanctify themselves, and purify themselves in the gardens behind one tree in the midst, eating swine's flesh, and the abomination, and the mouse, shall be consumed together, saith the Lord." We should note that eating swine's meat is an abomination unto the Lord, and he compares eating swine's flesh to the mouse. I think we should also note Leviticus 3:17, "It shall be a perpetual statute for your generations throughout all your dwellings, that ye eat neither fat nor blood." Perpetual in *Webster's Dictionary* means continuing forever. Is this not a warning for the Lord that this is not good for you? And this warning is not just for the children of Israel. Let us note Leviticus 17:10, "And whatsoever man there be of the house of Israel, or of the strangers that sojourn among you, that eateth any manner of blood; I will even set my face against that soul that eateth blood, and will cut him off from among his people." You see that this warning is to even the stranger, and that means it is for everyone. Then it says in Leviticus 17:14, "For it is the life of all flesh; the blood of it is for the life thereof: therefore I say unto the children of Israel, Ye shall eat the blood of no manner of flesh: for the life of all flesh is in the blood thereof: whosoever eateth it shall be cut off."

But before leaving this, let's note this Genesis 9:1 when God blessed Noah and said unto them, "Be fruitful, and multiply, and replenish the earth." Noah is also instructed in verses 3–4, "Every moving thing that liveth shall be meat for you; even as the green herb have I given all things. But flesh with the life thereof, which is the blood thereof, shall ye not eat." This is a commandment from God not to eat the blood of any animals. In verse 12 we are told, "And God said, This is the token of the covenant which I make between me and you and every living creature that is with you, for perpetual generations." We should note that not only is this covenant between God and Noah, but it is also a covenant God made with every living creature and with you because the life is in the blood. We should note that it is for perpetual (always, eternal) generations.

Even the disciples taught the Gentiles in Acts 15:20, "But that we write unto them, that they abstain from pollutions of idols, and from fornication, and from things strangled, and from blood." It was important enough to repeat this a second time in verses 28 and 29:

> For it seemed good to the Holy Ghost, and to us, to lay upon you no greater burden than these necessary things. That ye abstain from meats offered to idols, and from blood, and from things strangled, and from fornication: from which if ye keep yourselves, ye shall do well. Fare ye well.

Did we get that? It was a necessary message from the Holy Ghost to us to abstain from blood, and if they do they shall do well. Where are the Bible scholars on this necessary message?

Let us also note what Flavius Josephus says:

> This was told to the king by the scribes, that the multitude were sinning against God as they sacrificed and were eating before the blood was well washed away, and the flesh was made clean. Then gave Saul the order that a great stone be rolled into the midst of them, and he made proclamation that they should kill

their sacrifices upon it and not feed upon it and not feed upon the flesh with the blood, for that was not acceptable to God.[189]

I believe that if it was not acceptable to God then, it is not acceptable to God now. I also believe that eating fat, rare red meat, and swine (pork is very fatty) are the real reasons there are people developing all kinds of cancers, especially in children. Pigs don't have sweat glands except for their nose, so they can't sweat out body toxins. I used to think why, if there was a loving Father in heaven, there would be all this suffering in these little children. When I see all the little children in the Danny Thomas Hospital suffering from cancer, it makes me think they are inheriting this from their parents' mistakes. Let's look at the definition of leukemia in *Webster's Dictionary*: "An acute or chronic disease of unknown cause in man and other warm-blooded animals characterized by an abnormal increase in the number of Leukocytes in the tissue and often in the blood." The unknown cause is in the blood (Leukocytes) of animals, as foretold by God when he said, "Whosoever eateth shall be cut off." The word for cut is the word *karath*,[190] which means to cut, by implication to destroy, perish. The life of an animal is in the blood, and mixing the life of an animal into a human blood does not work. Is this the cause of leukemia? If the life is in the blood, two lives can't survive in one body.

I think it is important to note what the second verse after 3:17 says. Leviticus 4:2 says, "Speak unto the children of Israel, saying, If a soul shall sin through ignorance against any of the commandments of the Lord concerning things which ought not be none, and it shall do against any of them." This is a direct warning from God that your ignorance to the commandments of the Lord causes your ailments and death. Note that the Bible calls this sin. So how many of you righteous people commit that sin? We are also told in Leviticus 7:26–27, "Moreover ye shall eat no manner of blood, whether it be of fowl or of beast, in any of your dwellings. Whatsoever soul it be that eateth any

---

[189] Whitson, *The Complete Works of Josephus,* 208.
[190] *Strong's,* 1886.

manner of blood, even that soul shall be cut off from his people." If you eat your chicken eggs sunny side up, you are eating the blood of that foul. God says to those who do this, "That soul shall be cut off [perish] from his people."

In all the years I have been in churches, and for over the past twenty years of listening to pastors on the radio and television, I have never heard a pastor warn his people about eating the blood of animals. Why were all these verses in scripture written, and why do all pastors just ignore them? These pastors demand that you live under the Law of Moses by demanding from their congregation the 10 percent tithe, the law of no wine or strong drink, and telling their people they are adulterers if they get remarried after divorce. Why are they not teaching this commandment? Remember, Luke said in Acts 15:28–29, "For it seemed good to the Holy Ghost, and to us to lay upon you no greater burden [the law] than these necessary things; abstain from blood, ye shall do well." That was one of the laws of Moses they were asked to do in the church age. Note the language used by Luke, "these necessary things" that the Holy Ghost was to lay upon you. To "abstain from the blood of animals and the blessing is ye shall do well." And to say this is not a necessary thing is to blaspheme against the Holy Ghost, which is the unpardonable sin. This is the only commandment the church has ignored.

Another good example is Judges 13:3–4:

> And the angel of the Lord appeared unto the woman,
> and said unto her, Behold now, thou are barren, and
> bearest not: but thou shalt conceive, and bear a son.
> Now therefore beware, I pray thee, and drink not wine
> nor strong drink, and eat not any unclean thing.

To bring healthy children into the world, women should do as the Bible tells us

The previous verses are what I have against the churches. Let us take a closer look at just what the messages are to some of the seven churches that are in Asia that John wrote to. To the church in Ephesus he says, "Remember therefore from whence thou are fallen, and repent, and do the first works; or else I will come on thee quickly, and remove thy candlestick out of his place, except thou repent." To fully understand when "I will come on thee quickly," we have to go to the message to Pergamos, where it states, "Repent; or else I will come on thee quickly, and will fight against them with the sword of my mouth." Why is it from this church that God would "remove thy candlestick"? This is because the church is to be the light to the whole word.

John tells these churches that they are on the earth unless they repent that the Lord will "fight against them with the sword of his mouth." When does this happen? In Revelation 19:15, it says:

> And out of his mouth goeth a sharp sword, that with
> it he should smite the nations: and he shall rule them
> with a rod of iron: and he treadeth the winepress of
> the fierceness and wrath of Almighty God.

So unless these churches repent, they are not protected from the wrath of God. If there is this so-called pre-tribulation resurrection, why does God not promise those who repent to be taken away before the tribulation begins?

Let us look at what God says about the Pergamos church that "I [God] hate." It's those "that hold the doctrine of Balaam, who taught Balak to cast a stumbling block before the children of Israel." Balak, the king of the Moabites, went to Balaam, a prophet of the Lord, to curse the children of Israel on their way to the land of milk and honey. Balak tells Balaam in Numbers 22:17, "For I will promote thee unto very great honour, and I will do whatsoever thou sayest unto me: come therefore, I pray thee, curse me this people." Balaam answered him in verse 18: "If Balak would give me his house full of silver and gold, I cannot go beyond the word of the Lord my God, to do more or less." This is a lesson for us today. We must stand with the state of Israel no matter how much the Arabs (Muslims) try to use oil as a weapon against us to go against Israel. Americans did not learn a lesson from the 1970s when there was the Arab oil embargo. The rest of the world should have said to those people, "Feed your people oil because we will cut off your food supply." We should have started drilling for oil everywhere oil is to be found. I thought that is why we have a federal department of energy—to find energy this country needs.

This is the second thing God hates in verse 15: "So hast thou also them that hold the doctrine of the Nicolaitans." Nicolaitans is *Nikolaites*,[191] which means a *Nicolaitre* (i.e., adherent of Nicolaus). It is from *Nikopolis*,[192] which means victorious city; *Nicopolis*. Is this where we get the word Saint Nicholas or Santa Claus? The *Webster's Dictionary* meaning of Santa Claus is, "Saint Nicholas, fourth-century bishop Myra, Asia Minor and patron saint of children." This church made saints who are nothing but idols to God. This worship to them is an abomination to the Lord. I did not make this statement; God did. And to replace God, who gives all gifts to man, with Santa is an abomination to the Lord. So how many of you righteous people do this thing that God says he hates? We should note that this is also in Revelation 2:6.

There is one church that has people praying to man-made saints. And who claims to be the mother of all churches? Let's note Revelation 17:5: "Mystery Babylon the great, the mother of Harlots and abominations of the earth." Harlots is *porneia*,[193] which means figurative idolatry, from *pornos*[194] (to sell), akin to *piprako*, which means to traffic (by travelling) (i.e., dispose of as merchandise or into slavery). All the churches that demand 10 percent of your earnings are nothing but harlots, just as 2 Peter 2:3 states, "Through covetousness shall they with feigned words make merchandise of you."

The message to the church at Thyatira states, "But unto you I say, and unto the rest of Thyatira, as many as have not this doctrine, and which have not known the depths of Satan, as they speak; I will put upon you none other burden." The word for burden is *Baros*,[195] which means "a weight which one my bear without it becoming a burden."

---

[191] Ibid., 2118.

[192] Ibid.

[193] Ibid., 2140.

[194] Ibid.

[195] Ibid., 2041.

To put upon you no other burden means that there is some burden on this church.

Let's note, "Notwithstanding I have a few things against you, Because thou sufferest that woman Jezebel, which calleth herself a prophetess to teach and seduce my servants to commit fornication, and to eat things sacrificed unto idols." This fornication is happening spiritually. Let's note 1 Kings 18:4: "For it was so, when Jezebel cut off the prophets of the Lord." And how she does this is given in 1 Kings 19:1–2: "And Ahab told Jezebel all that Elijah had done, and withal how he had slain all the prophets with the sword. Then Jezebel sent a messenger unto Elijah, saying, So let the gods do to me, and more also, if I make not thy life as of one of them by tomorrow about this time."

The Lord tells us he will send Elijah the prophet before the great and notable day of the Lord, along with one hundred and forty-four thousand prophets of all of the tribes of the children of Israel. Will this church in the twenty-first century do the same as Jezebel? Also note it says in Kings, "Let the gods." Acknowledging any God but the Lord Jesus is blaspheming the Holy Spirit. Let's also note, "To eat things sacrificed unto idols." Those things are vegetables, for the PETA tell us that we must save mother earth (idol) by "abstaining from meats" to save the planet, which 1 Timothy tells is a doctrine of devils.

We should note also that it is not promised to save the church from the tribulation period but from the great tribulation if they repent because there is not a pre-tribulation resurrection. The word for tribulation is *Thlpsis,*[196] which means to crowd (literal or figuratively); afflict, narrow, throng, suffer tribulation, or trouble. It is akin to *Tribos,*[197] which means to crowd (literal or figurative); afflict, narrow, throng, suffer tribulation, or trouble.

Is this the burden Jeremiah told us about where he states, "Then shall thou say into them, what burden? And he that overcometh, and keepeth my works unto the end, to him will I give power over the nations." This church, as well all the churches John writes to, is told

---

[196] Ibid., 2088.

[197] Ibid.

to overcome and keep God's works unto the end. This church was also told, "But that which ye have already hold fast till I come." Come is *heko*,[198] which means to arrive (i.e., be present) (literal or figurative).

The Lord is figuratively present in Matthew 25:30: "And then shall appear the sign of the Son of Man in heaven." His literal presence is, "And they shall see the Son of Man coming in the clouds of heaven with power and great glory." So, when does the Lord arrive? Second Thessalonians 1:7–8 says, "And to you who are trouble rest with us, when the Lord Jesus will be revealed from heaven. In flaming fire taking vengeance on them that know not God, and obey not the gospel of our Lord Jesus Christ." When will he literally be present? Ezekiel 38:18–20 says, "When Gog comes against the land of Israel, For in the jealousy and in the fire of my wrath, all men that are upon the face of the earth shall shake at my presence." Note that the "fire of my wrath" of Ezekiel matches the "in a flaming fire, taking vengeance" of 2 Thessalonians where the Lord's presence is. The end does not come in Revelation 4, where the pre-tribulation resurrection pastors say the church is caught up.

To Smyrna, he writes:

> Fear none of those things which thou shall suffer:
> behold, the devil shall cast some of you into prison,
> that ye made be tried; and ye shall have tribulation
> ten days; be thou faithful unto death, and I will give
> thee a crown of Life.

The church is told, "Fear none of those things thou shall suffer." It is similar to when we are told in 1 Peter 5:10, "But the God of all grace, who hath called us into his eternal glory by Jesus Christ, after that ye suffered awhile, make you perfect, stablish, strengthen, settle you."

We should also note 1 Peter 4:16, "Yet if any man suffer as a Christian, let him not be ashamed; but let him glorify God on this behalf." These verses do not sound like a promise of a pre-tribulation resurrection. The devil has not cast anybody into prison yet since he

---

[198]   Ibid., 2085.

has not yet been cast down from heaven to the earth. This is a warning to the church. This church is told be faithful until death and "He that overcometh shall not be hurt of the second death." This is into eternal life. If you are not willing to die for Christ, you are not living for Christ.

Even to the church at Laodicea it is said, "To him that overcometh will I grant to sit with me in my throne, even as I also overcame."

Now here is the message to the church all the pastors claim to be, the good Philadelphia church:

> Because thou hast kept the word of my patience,
> I also will keep thee from the hour of temptation,
> which shall come upon all the world to try them that
> dwell upon the earth.

According to *Strong's Complete Word Study Concordance*, the meaning of "keep" in the Greek is *tereo*,[199] which means to guard (from loss or injury), property by keeping a eye upon. And his comment is this for to keep, guard (e.g., a prisoner) (Matt. 27:36, 54; 28:4; Acts 12:5, 6; 24:23; 25:4, 21). It means figuratively to guard in the sense of keep one safe, preserving (John 17:11, 12, 15; 1 Thess. 5:23; Jude 1; Rev. 3:10). It means figuratively, to guard in the sense of preserving something (e.g., the faith). We should note here that there is not one word meaning to be raptured or caught up. Jack Van Impe says its meaning is to keep from, and this is why he says the church does not go through the tribulation period. As we see here, Jack Van Impe's interpretation is wrong. We should also note the word "try". The word is *pierazo*,[200] which means to test (i.e., to endeavor, scrutinize, entice, discipline). Even the Philadelphia church will be tested in their faith during the tribulation period.

I do not believe that the descendants of Esau have been a blessing to anyone, not even to them themselves, for the descendants of Esau have been killing each other since the time of Muhammad. Their religion was

---

[199] Ibid., 2164.
[200] Ibid., 2133.

spread by the sword, as instructed by Muhammad. Jacob's descendants' religion was to be spread by the love of God. But in the days of the Dark Ages, when the barbarian tribes first accepted Christianity, they did kill nonbelievers if they did not convert. People were tortured and burned on a stake if they did not conform to church doctrine. The judgment on these people was the small ice age that lasted from the 1300s to the 1800s. Millions of people died from starvation because of the weather because it is God who controls the weather. This is the reason Thomas Jefferson said there is a separation of church and state—to take away this power from the church. In the last days, Paul tells us the judgments must begin with the "house of God." Why? Revelation 17:6 says, "And I saw the woman drunken with the blood of the saints, and with the blood of the martyrs of Jesus." This woman is "Mystery Babylon the Great," who sits on seven mountains.

The apostles were told that if they did not want to hear the gospel of the Lord, they were instructed about what to do. Mark 6:10–11 says:

> And he [Jesus] said unto them, In what place whoever ye enter into an house, there abide till ye depart from that place. And whosoever shall not receive you, nor hear you, when you depart thence, shake off the dust under our feet for a testimony against them. Verily I say unto you, it shall be more tolerable for Sodom and Gomorrah in that Day of Judgment, than for that city.

Let's quickly look at the word for tolerable, which is *anektoteros*[201] and comparative to *anechomai*.[202] It means to hold oneself up against (i.e., figurative) put up with, endure, forbear, suffer. This should tell us that there are cities that will be more tolerable during the tribulation period than others. The Christian countries will be judged but won't receive the same degree of judgments as non-Christian countries. This

---

[201] Ibid., 2024.
[202] Ibid.

is the message of these scriptures. Note the Greek word meaning "to hold oneself up," for Romans 14:4 tells us, "God is able to make him stand."

Do not force anyone to accept the Lord Jesus as Lord and Savior. Tell people what he did for them at the cross. God has not forgotten about the ten tribes that were taken away into Assyrian captivity. God tells us that he watches and guides them to the lands where he wants them to go, and to prove that the ten lost tribes of Israel are not regathering until the last days, there is the following scripture. When we read and study the following scripture, we will find out when that regathering happens. Jeremiah tells us in 31:8, "Behold, I will bring them from the north country, and gather them from the coasts of the earth, and with them the blind and the lame, the woman with child and her that travaileth with child together: a great company shall return thither." This is the North Country that brought judgment upon Iraq before the time of the harvest.

Even after Judah saw what happened to the house of Israel, when God gave them the bill of divorcement, they still committed whoredom by going after other gods. Feignedly is *sheqer*,[203] which means an untruth, by implication a sham, without a cause. And stocks is *ates*,[204] which means a tree, hence wood. Jeremiah tells us they committed adultery with stone (earth) and stocks (wood). So how do you commit adultery with earth and trees? By worshiping them, just as the tree-hugging, earth-first people are doing today. You worship the environment more than you worship God. This brings God's judgment here, and it will bring God's judgment in the future. "I am God, I change not," saith the Lord. As Isaiah states, "The past reveals the future."

America needs to realize that God has given us the power to be the world's superpower today, and if we take him out of our society, judgment will come upon America. This is why American Christians must get off their rears and tell their politicians that they want God (the Lord Jesus) back in our public society, and as James D. Kennedy says, "re-claim America for Christ." Are Americans so ashamed of being

---

[203] Ibid., 1994.
[204] Ibid., 1993.

Christians we don't want to admit it in public because it might offend someone? If this offends the Muslim people, I don't care. If we can save his soul and spirit, we have just done him a big favor.

Jesus says in John14:6, "I am the truth and the light, and nobody comes to the Father but by me." As for a country, we have just read what God did to the house of Israel for unbelief. And this is what Jesus says in Luke 14:34:

> Salt is good: but if the salt lost his savour, wherewith shall it be seasoned? It is neither fit for the land, yet for the dunghill; but men cast it out. He that hath ears to hear, let him hear.

The Lord is asking, "America, are you deaf?" When we are no longer the salt to the world with the gospel, this land will be a dunghill. Jeremiah tells us in 25:14, "For many nations and great kings shall serve themselves of them also: and I [God] will recompense them according to their deeds, and according to the works of their own hands."

If America is to be continually blessed by God, we better acknowledge who he is, and if the rest of the world doesn't want to acknowledge the Lord Jesus, well, that is their destiny. America needs to acknowledge the God of the Bible. This is our only hope for survival in the last days. Will America turn back to God? Our only hope is in the Lord. Will we be the meek that inherit the earth? If we don't change the minds of the American people and end abortion on demand, will God not judge this country as he did Israel? Why have Americans become so blind?

When I watched the first Muslim sworn into office at the federal capitol, I realized how unchristian the Democratic Party has become. Are there any true God-loving people in Minnesota? They swore him into office with his hand on the Qur'an. Let's note the *Webster's Dictionary* meaning of the word "Antichrist": "One who denies or opposes Christ." The Qur'an is opposed to Christ, and this is proven in this book. The Bible tells us that God's people are not to be allied to those who hate the Lord. Second Chronicles 19:2 says, "Shouldest thou help the ungodly, and love them that hate the Lord? Therefore is wrath upon thee from before the Lord." Psalms 139:21 says, "Do not I hate them, O lord, that hate thee? and am I grieved with those that rise up against thee?" The Lord God has not changed his mind. These are the New Testament verses.

Second Corinthians 6:14–15 says:

> Be ye not unequally yoked together with unbelievers: for what fellowship hath righteousness with unrighteousness? And communion hath light with darkness? And what concord [*sumphonesis,*[205] which means accordance] hath Christ with Belial [*Belial,*[206] of Hebrew origin, worthlessness, Belial, as an epithet of Satan] or what part hath he that believeth with an infidel [*apistos,*[207] which means; disbelieving (i.e., without Christian faith)]?

An epithet in *Webster's Dictionary* means, "To put on, add, a characterizing word or phrase accompanying or occurring in place of a name of a person or thing." Allah is the name of a person in place of Jesus as Lord. This scripture tells us that is Satan. I was grieved in my heart when I witnessed the Democrats' smiling faces on this occasion. I think the Old Testament is still valid when you have the New Testament saying the same thing, because the Bible says, "I am God, and I change not." They will receive the wrath of God for their actions.

I am beginning to believe that these people would give their country to the Antichrist to stay in power. We are also told in Colossians 1:21, "And you, that were sometime alienated and enemies in your mind by your wicked work, yet hath he reconciled." To acknowledge that there is any God but the Lord Jesus makes you an enemy of God. As for the atheist, here is God's message to you. Psalms 14:1 says, "The fool hath said in his heart, There is no God. They are corrupt, they have

---

[205]   Ibid., 2157.
[206]   Ibid., 2042.
[207]   Ibid., 2029.

done abominable works, there is none that doth good." Fool is *nabal*,[208] which means stupid, wicked, vile person. Jeremiah will have something to say about these stupid, wicked, and vile people. Will this be said of America, as this is given in scripture? Genesis 15:16 says, "For the iniquity of the Amorites is not yet full." Will there be a time that the sins or "iniquity" of America will be full and our destruction comes?

Here is what Jesus tells his disciples in Luke 19:42–44:

> If thou hadst known, even thou, at least in this thy day, the things which belong unto thy peace! But now they are hid from thy eyes. For the days shall come upon thee, that thine enemies shall cast a trench about thee, and compass thee round, and keep thee on every side, And shall lay thee even with the ground, and thy children within thee; and they shall not leave one stone upon another; because thou knewest not the time of your visitation.

God is going to tell his twenty-first-century church the same thing. The Christians of the world do not understand their "time of visitation" because pastors tell them they are raptured to heaven before the Lord descends from heaven. So how can the twenty-first-century church know the time of their visitation? Isaiah says in 29:6, "Thou shall be visited of the Lord of hosts with thunder, and with earthquake, and great noise, with storm and tempest, and the flame of devouring fire." And when does Isaiah tell us this happens? Verse 7 says, "And the multitude of all the nations that fight against Ariel." Verse 8 continues, "So shall the multitude of all nations be, that fight against Zion." These two verses say to us that this visitation is at the time battle of Armageddon. What is the Lord's response? Verse 14 says, "Therefore, behold, I will proceed to do a marvellous work among the people, even a marvellous work and a wonder."

So what marvelous work is Isaiah telling us? That is found in Revelation 15:1–2: "And I saw another sign in heaven, great and

---

[208] Ibid., 1914.

marvellous, seven angels having the seven last plagues; for in them is filled up the wrath of God. [Both Isaiah and John say this is marvelous work God will do.] And I saw as if it were a sea of glass mingled with fire: and them that had gotten the victory over the beast, stand on a sea of glass, having the harps of God." Those standing on the sea of glass are the resurrected saints. When "sign in heaven" does John talk about in Revelation 15:1? Matthew 24:29–30 says, "Immediately after the tribulation of those days, shall the sun be darkened, and the moon shall not give her light, and the stars shall fall from heaven, and the powers of the heavens shall be shaken: And then shall appear the Son of Man in heaven."

This is the time of the twenty-first-century church's "day of visitation." I look at America today, and they do the same thing. How have we become so pagan? We allow judges in this country to decide whether we can have public knowledge of the Lord Jesus. Why? It's because they want to be all inclusive. When Jesus tells us, "I am the truth and the light and nobody comes to the Father but by me," the Lord Jesus is inclusive. Those who don't believe in Jesus don't have eternal life. That is plain and simple language. We do the nonbelievers injustice if we tell them of the Lord. This is the Christian's mission in life. If this is a country where the majority rule, then this is a Christian country. If Christian Americans want a Christian country, then they need to start voting true Christian men and women into leadership. Why do most Americans not want God back in their life? Do we know that we are living in sin and do not want to admit it? All Americans think of is what they can possess in this life.

Solomon had it right when he said it was all vanity. Your earthly wealth is nothing to the glory we have in Christ Jesus. Solomon had it all—knowledge of the Lord, wealth, and all the pleasures of this life—and he failed God. Even Solomon worshiped other gods and not the God of Israel. Even David, Solomon's father, failed when he had an affair with another woman and had her husband killed. But David knew that the Lord of heaven is a forgiving God, and David never turned to another God. If you ask for forgiveness and repent, God will forgive that sin. David never forgot who God was, and that is why God said David was a man after his own heart. David sinned and asked God for forgiveness. This is what made David special to God.

God only asks one thing of his children—to love him with all their hearts and with all their souls. Americans for the most part don't have time for God, even to thank him when times are good. We should notice that God sends his prophets to his people when the time of judgments is about to happen. God has done that throughout biblical history. He did it in the past, and God will do it in the future. This is why he tells us that he will send Elijah, the prophet, before the great and terrible day of the Lord. This is the sign that Christians should be looking for. The Lord Jesus tells us in Matthew 24:6, "And ye shall hear of wars and rumours of wars: see that ye be not troubled: for all these things must come to pass, but the end is not yet." It also says in verse 13, "But he that shall endure unto the end, the same shall be saved." Who is told to endure until the end if it is not the Christian church?

The Never-Ending Dispute

LET US NOTE ON scripture just how far back in history the Arab world has laid claim to the land God gave the descendants of Jacob. This is in the time of the Judges, and Israel had been in the land three hundred years. This is when the children of Ammon came to war against Israel. They had just conquered the land of the Amorites, Hittites, Perizzites, Jebusites, and Canaanites, which was west of the Jordan River. Jephthah pleaded with the kings of Ammon and the kings of Edom not to war against them. Jephthah said to them in Judges 11:26, "While Israel dwelt in Heshbon and her towns, and in Aroer and her towns, and in all of the cities that be along by the coasts of Arnon, three hundred years? Why therefore did ye not recover them within that time?" But they warred against Israel, and this is what the Bible says: "So Jephthah passes over unto the children of Ammon to fight against them; and the Lord delivered them into his hands, and there was a very great slaughter." To this day, twenty-five hundred years later, the dispute continues.

The only peace that will be seen in the Middle East is the peace agreement the Antichrist makes. I believe the Antichrist will look like a descendant of Edom. Isaiah 63:1 says, "Who is this that cometh from Edom, with dyed garments from Bozrah? This that is glorious in his apparel, travelling in the greatness of his strength? I that speak in righteousness, mighty to save." The word for travelling is *tsa ah*,[209] which means, to tip over (i.e., figurative) depopulate; by implication to imprison or conquer. And this is just how the Antichrist comes to power by the greatness of his power. This is how he rules after the first three and a half years of imprisoning Christians and conquering and depopulating the planet. Revelation 2:10 says, "the devil shall cast some of you into prison, that ye may be tried; and ye shall have tribulation ten days."

Let us note the Qur'an, which says, "A Messenger who will come after me whose name will be Admad." Since there has not been another prophet since Muhammad, I believe this will be the name of the Antichrist. But now let's read verse 3: "I have trodden the winepress alone; and the people there was none with me: for I will tread them in mine anger; and their blood shall be sprinkled upon my garments, and I will stain all my raiment." And we know whose blood shall be sprinkled on his garments. Revelation 19:13 says, "And he was clothed with a vesture dipped in blood: and his name is called The Word God."

He will last just three and half years—just enough time to give the Antichrist his power. Their religion tells them to kill the Jews of Israel and Christians in plain and simple language. In the Qur'an, chapter 60, pages 557–558, it states:

> O ye who believe, make not friends with My enemy and your enemy. You send them messages of affection, while they disbelieve in the truth that has come to you, and call out the Messenger and yourselves to battle solely because you believe in Allah, your Lord. When you go forth to strive in My cause and to seek My pleasure, some of you send friendly messages in secret; while I know well that which you conceal and that which you disclose. Whoever of you does so, has slipped from the right path. Should they gain mastery over you, you will realize that they are your enemies

---

[209] Ibid., 1956.

and are employing their hands and tongues to your injury; ardently desiring that you should become disbelievers.

And this is given next on page 558:

> We dissociate ourselves utterly from you and from that which you worship besides Allah. We totally reject you. Enmity and hatred have become manifest between you and us for ever, until you believe in Allah, the One.

As we read here, Muhammad, the prophet, declared that disbelievers are the enemies of anybody not Muslim. They are to battle solely because they believe in Allah. If Abraham is "a friend of God," who is this God Allah calls "my enemy" that are Jews and Christians? To find the enemy of this god, we will read Revelation 12:12–13:

> Woe to the inhabiters of the earth and of the sea, for the devil is come down unto you, having great wrath, because he knoweth that he hath but a short time. And when the dragon saw that he was cast unto the earth, he persecuted the woman [Israel] which brought forth the man child [Jesus].

The devil is the enemy of the Jews and Christians.

If the children of Israel are God's chosen people, then the enemy, "my enemy," can only be the Antichrist and Satan. We should also note that they are called to battle solely because they believe in Allah. And you think you can make peace agreements with this religion. We will read in the battle of Armageddon that our meek and mild Jesus is going to get very furious at these people, so this cannot be our sister religion. This is why I totally reject Islam and believe that the Lord Jesus will totally destroy these people at his return to the earth. We were not in Iraq when the twin towers came down, so this is not the reason continued attacks are planned against America and against any nation not Muslim. My prayer for America is that they hear what the Lord says to them. This is a bigger threat to the American people than they realize.

The world of Islam is against us. You do not hear this in the churches of God that this religion, started by Muhammad, is against the Jews of Israel and the Christians of the world. Why are even the churches of our Lord silent in this manner? For a Christian pastor to say he has many Islamic friends, he must not know what the Qur'an says to them or what the Bible tells us. You do not know their religion. This is their holy war (jihad) that is taught in their Qur'an. Their goal is to bring Islam to the whole world, but first they must destroy the state of Israel.

Wake up, America! Are we this stupid? I am beginning to believe we are when I hear politicians say Islam is our sister religion. There is nothing in the Islamic religion that is close to Christianity or Judaism. We will review more of just what is said in the Qur'an to prove that this book was inspired by God to be the people of Isaiah 34:5, "the people of my curse," which is "Idumea," and its equivalent message in the New Testament is Mathew 13:38–39, "The tares are the children of the wicked one; The enemy that sowed them is the devil." Political correctness is not found in the Bible, and it won't be found in this interpretation.

For the people who want to take Christianity out of America, you need to look at what the Supreme Court has already ruled in the 1800s. America is a Christian nation. This establishes America as a Christian nation. I found this in December 2010 Princeton Seminar Library information on the Internet while searching under "Supreme Court Christian Country," which led me to the following website: vftonline. org/endthewall/trinit.[210] Let's quote the Supreme Court: "But, beyond, all these matters, no purpose of action against religion can be imputed to any legislation, state or national, because this is a religious people." What did I just read here? No action or legislation can be imputed

---

[210] The Supreme Court of the United States. Holy Trinity Church v. The United States. 143 U.S. 457, S.Ct. 511, 36 L.Ed. 226 (February 28, 1892).

against religion by any state government or the national government. This makes public display of the cross or the Ten Commandments protected by this Supreme Court decision. And what religion is that? And I will skip some of the writings to get to this. "The first colonial grant, that was made to Sir Walter Raleigh in 1584, was from 'Elizabeth, by the grace of God of England, Fraunce and Ireland, defender of the faith,' etc.; and the grant authorizing him to enact statutes of the government of the purposed colony provided that 'they be not against the true Christian faith nowe professed in the Church of England.'" The money granted them to colonize America was to enact statues of the government that they be not against the Christian faith.

The Supreme Court also says this: "The first chapter of Virginia, granted by King James I. In 1606, after reciting the application of certain parties for a charter, commenced the grant in these words: 'We, greatly commending, and graciously accepting of, their Desires for the Furtherance of so noble a Work, which may, by the Providence of Almighty God, hereafter tend to the Glory of his Divine Majesty, in propagating of Christian Religion to such people, as yet live in Darkness and miserable ignorance of the true Knowledge and Worship of God, and many in time bring the Infidels and Savages, living in those parts, to Human Civility, and to a settled and quiet Government; Do, by these letters-Patents, graciously accept of, and agree to, their humble and well-intended Desires.'" And next the Supreme Court writes: "Language of similar import may be found in the subsequent charters of the colony, from the same king, in 1609 and 1611; and the same is true of the various charters granted to the other colonies. In language more or less emphatic in the establishment of the Christian religion declared to be one of the purposes of the grant." I believe I just read here that the Supreme Court ruled that the purpose of the grants to colonize America was to make it a Christian country. So why have you Bible scholars not taken this ruling to court and to the ACLU?

Here is the test that John tells us to use to check to see if a spirit comes from God. First John 4:1–4 says:

> Beloved, believe not every spirit, but try the spirits
> whether they are of God: because many false prophets

are gone out unto the world. Hereby know ye the spirits of God: Every spirit that confesseth that Jesus Christ is come in the flesh is of God: And every spirit that confesseth not that Jesus is come in the flesh is not of God: and this is the spirit of Antichrist, whereof ye have heard that it should come; and even now already is it in the world. Ye are of God, little children, and have overcome them: because greater is he that is in you, than he that is in the world.

As we see here, if anyone comes and says that Jesus Christ is come and is not of God, that this is the spirit of Antichrist. This is just what Muhammad did in the seventh century. We should note the "it should come." The Muslim religion is the only new religion. Is John not also warning the church that the Antichrist will come and the church is still here? He tells us we have to overcome them and we are able because greater is he (Holy Spirit) who is in you, than he (Antichrist) who is in the world. And we should note that John had to write a second letter and 2 John 1:7, 10 says:

For many deceivers are entered into the world, who confess not that Jesus Christ is come in the flesh. This is a deceiver and an Antichrist . . . . If there come any unto you, and bring not this doctrine, receive him not into your house, neither bid him God speed.

So all you pastors who say you have many Muslim friends, you are going against the Word of God. You are friends with people who worship the Antichrist and the devil, and you are not to be friends of theirs. This "receive him not in your house" also refers to your country. Let's note the word for speed is *chairo*,[211] which means to be cheerful (i.e., calmly happy or well off). Then we are told in verse 8, "For he that biddeth him God speed is partaker of his evil deeds." The Lord knew what was going to happen in the near future. The belief in Islam

---

[211] *Strong's*, 2176.

was coming in history in just about another six hundred years. The Qur'an tells us that the Jews who were still in the Middle East in the time of Muhammad totally rejected his teachings—and with good reason. Muhammad had to war against his Arab brothers to force them into accepting his teachings. With the teaching of Muhammad, the never-ending war against the Christians and Jews started.

As we will soon see, their religion is against the Christians and the Jews. This is why I think Muhammad's prophecy is the same as the Bible, because he copies all the prophecies of the Old Testament and puts them in terms for the Muslim world. This is just the way Satan works. He takes God's Word and twists it to fit his plan for mankind. This is why Revelation tells us of the synagogues of Satan among the churches.

Let us note what *Strong's Complete Word Study Concordance* says is the meaning of Antichrist in the Greek: "an opponent of the Messiah."[212] His comment is:

> Noun from anti, instead of or against, and opposer of Christ. Found only in John's epistles, and there defined to be, collectively, all who deny that Jesus is the Messiah come in the flesh. What class of persons the apostle had in mind is unknown; probably Jewish adversaries.

We should also *Strong's Complete Word Study Concordance* writes this about the word "anti": "A primary particle, opposite (i.e., instead or because of, rarely in addition to), for, in the room of. Often used in composition to denote contrast, requital, substitution, correspondence, etc."[213] And his comment is:

> Preposition with the general meaning of over against, in the presence of, in lieu of. Spoken metaphorically either in a hostile sense, meaning against, or by way of

[212]   Ibid., 2027.
[213]   Ibid.

comparison, where it implies something of equivalent
value, and denotes substitution, exchange, requital.

And this is just what Muhammad did in the seventh century. That
unknown adversary *Strong's* is referring to is the message of Muhammad.
The opponent of the Messiah Jesus is Allah, but God's people will not
be fooled. If the Muhammad prophecies were from the God of heaven,
where is his second witness? The reason Muhammad didn't record his
message was he could not read or write, yet all the prophets in the Bible
wrote their own prophecies down. When the Lord speaks, he always
gives his message to two witnesses. We are also told this in the Qur'an
in chapter 4, page 96:

> We did kill the Messiah, Jesus son of Mary, the
> Messenger of Allah; whereas they slew him not, nor
> did they compass his death upon the cross, but he
> was made to appear to them like one crucified to
> death; and those who have different in the matter
> of his having been taken down alive from the cross
> are certainly in a state of doubt concerning it, they
> have no definite knowledge about it, but only follow
> a conjecture; they certainly did not compass his death
> in the manner they allege; indeed, Allah exalted him
> to himself; Allah is Mighty, Wise, and there is none
> among the People of the Book but will continue to
> believe till his death that Jesus died on the cross,
> and on the Day of Judgment Jesus shall bear witness
> against them; and their taking interest, though they
> have been forbidden it; and their devouring people's
> wealth wrongfully; because of all the transgressions of
> the Jews, and the hindering many from Allah's way.

And you are going to tell me this is our sister religion when
Muhammad himself denies that the Lord died on the cross for man's
sin? Muhammad says there is a state of doubt to the people who believe
the Lord died on the cross. This is the spirit of the Antichrist, plain and

simple. Muhammad himself was confused, for he states that both the Jews and the Christians disagree with each other "on the firm truth," that firm truth being that Jesus was their messiah, yet they read the same book. We should also note that Muhammad acknowledges that the temple of the Jewish people was destroyed twice.

This is another reason the Muslim world should have no claim to the Temple Mount. So should I care what a Muslim thinks about me? I believe the Lord died on the cross for my sins. If the Muslim world wants to say that the Day of Judgment is where Jesus shall bear witness against us, this is an all-out lie from the devil. Let us review more of just what an ungodly book the Qur'an is. In chapter 5:110–112, page 115, it states this:

> Allah will also say to Jesus son of Mary: Call to mind My favour upon thee and thy mother, when I strengthened thee with the spirit of holiness, so thou didst talk to the people of things divine in thy early and late years.

Our response to the Qur'an should be what "late years" is Muhammad talking about? Muhammad lived six hundred years after our Lord, and he is going to state that Allah saved him from the cross. There was no Allah before Muhammad's time. First John 2:22 says, "Who is a liar, but he that denieth that Jesus is the Christ? He is Antichrist, that denieth the Father and the Son."

Now read what Muhammad writes. In chapter 19, page 296, he alleges:

> The Gracious One has taken unto Himself a son. Assuredly, you have uttered a Monstrous thing! The heavens might well-nigh burst thereat, and the earth cleave asunder, and the mountains fall down in pieces, because they ascribe a son to the Gracious One to take unto a Son.

This is stated in chapter 6 (101–104) on page 130: "How can He have a son when he has no consort." Chapter 2 page 20 states, "They allege Allah has taken unto Himself a son." Chapter 17, page 275 says, "All praise belongs to Allah Who has taken unto Himself no son." Chapter 39:5–7 page 456 says, "If Allah had desired to make any one His son, He could have chosen whom He pleased out of his creation." I do not think I need to make any comments on these statements because it is plain and simple language; Allah has no Son. As President Bush said, we all pray to the same God. But Muhammad tells us differently on page 632. "Proclaim: Hearken ye who disbelieve! I do not worship as you worship, nor do you worship as I worship. I do not worship those that you worship, nor do you worship Him Whom I worship; that is because you follow one faith and I follow another faith."

This again is plain and simple enough for anyone to understand. Allah says he had no son. And if they do not worship who the Christians worship, then they worship the Antichrist.

Chapter 5, page 113 says: "Call to mind also when the disciples asked Jesus son of Mary: Has thy Lord power to send down to us from heaven a table spread with food? He rebuked them." The Qur'an goes on to say, "Thereupon Jesus son of Mary prayed: Allah, our Lord. I will certainly send it down to you but whosoever of you is ungrateful thereafter, such as him I will surely punish with torment wherewith I will not punish any other of the peoples." How could have Jesus prayed to Allah when Allah was not known until the seventh century? Jesus did feed the five thousand, because of his passion for his people with no conditions, as stated here by Muhammad.

Chapter 6:94, page 129 says:

> Who is more unjust than one who deliberately fabricates a lie against Allah: or says: I am the recipient of revelation, while nothing has been revealed to him; or says: I will surely send down the like of that which Allah has sent down?

Muhammad denies the book of Revelation of our Bible as being inspired by God through John. Chapter 6:123, page 132 says:

Can he who was as dead and We gave him life and appointed for him a light whereby he walks among people, be like one who is, as it were, in utter darkness whence he can by no means come forth? In like manner have the doings of the disbelievers been made to seem fair to them.

Muhammad denies that our risen Lord walked among the people after he was crucified in this statement. Muhammad states that he gets his message from messengers from Allah, when the Bible tells us this in Numbers 12:5–6:

And the Lord came down in the pillar of the cloud, and stood in the door of the tabernacle, and called Aaron and Miriam: and they both came forth. And he said, Hear now my words: If there be a prophet among you, I the Lord will make myself known unto him in a vision, and will speak unto him in a dream.

Muhammad claims he got his vision from Gabriel, the archangel. But I believe it was another archangel.

Chapter 6:165, page 139 says:

Ask them: Shall I seek someone other than Allah as Lord, while He is the Lord of all things? Every one must bear the consequence of that which he does, and no bearer of a burden can bear the burden of another. Then to your Lord will be return, and He will inform you of that wherein you used to differ.

Muhammad again denies that Jesus died on the cross for man's sin. This makes these statements from none other than the Antichrist. This book by Muhammad denies all that is told us in the New Testament. Christians are also to consider what is written in 2 Corinthians 4:3–4:

But if our gospel be hid, it is hid to them that are lost: In whom the God of this world hath blinded the minds of them which believe not, lest the light of the glorious gospel of Christ, who is the image of God, should shine unto them.

The God of this world is Satan. As said in Ephesians 2:3, "The prince of the power of the air, the spirit that now worketh in the children of disobedience." Disobedience is *apeitheia,*[214] which means disbelief (obstinate and rebellious), from *apeitheo,*[215] which means to disbelieve (willfully and perversely), not believe, obey not. If you remember in the second chapter of this manuscript, we learned that the gospel of Christ was forbidden by the Holy Ghost to be taken to Asia. Is the Muslim world not fulfilling this prophecy with this blindness? Also note the Greek word meaning "obey not." When the Lord Jesus is revealed from heaven, the scriptures tells us in 2 Thessalonians 1:8, "Taking vengeance on them that know not God, and that obey not the gospel of our Lord Jesus Christ." Muhammad also writes in chapter 5:76 on page 111: "The Messiah son of Mary was only a Messenger; many Messengers have passed away before him."

This statement by Muhammad classifies him as an Antichrist because he states that the Messiah was just a messenger. Once again, Muhammad is wrong. The Lord Jesus is alive and has not passed away. We should all note in chapter 5:13–15, pages 101–102 Muhammad writes:

For those who say: We are Christians; we also took a covenant, but they too have forgotten a portion of that which they were exhorted. So, we have put enmity and hatred between them till the Day of Judgment.

If this new English version of the Qur'an written by Muhammad Zafrulla Khan is more precise in its meaning, here is what *Webster's*

---

[214] Ibid., 2028.
[215] Ibid., 2029.

Dictionary says about enmity, "The quality of be an enemy; hostile or unfriendly disposition; hatred; rancour; hostility." The Qur'an tells Muslims to be hostile to Christians until the Day of Judgment. They are told to "lie in wait in every ambush." The Bible tells us the mouth of the upright will deliver them. And you say this is our sister religion. This should be a warning to all who are not Muslim. This is why this is a never-ending dispute. In the Day of Judgment, the Lord Jesus will come as a flaming fire, taking vengeance on those who know not God and who obey not the gospel of our Lord Jesus Christ. I have also noticed one thing about the Qur'an. It likes to point out all of the failures of Isaac's people. Muhammad's writings make a lot of references to the Bible, and he changes the God of heaven to Allah.

Talk about copyright infringement. Muhammad states this on several occasions: "Allah does not guide the unjust people." If Allah does not guide the unjust people, why does the Qur'an say Allah guided the Hebrews out of Egyptian bondage? Why are there all these writings about Jacob's descendants and not the descendants Esau? Why does the Qur'an not talk about what the God of the Islamic people is doing to guide the descendants of Ishmael and Esau during this time in history? What recorded miracle did Muhammad do that would classify him as a man of God? What miracle does Allah do for his people? The Qur'an likes to bring up all the sins of Israel during the Exodus, just like Satan is before God daily reminding God of our sins.

The Qur'an devotes a lot of scripture to "a day of judgment" and "the last day." The next set of verse in the Qur'an and the previous is where the pope of Rome should have questioned the mullahs. The next sets of verses that are taken out of the Qur'an are very disturbing to me as a Christian. There is this starting with 5:18:

> They are indeed disbelievers who say: Allah is the Messiah son of Mary. Say to them: Who can have any power against Allah, if He should desire to bring to naught the Messiah son of Mary, and his mother that are in the earth?

Is this not a direct attack on our Lord? This is the spirit of the Antichrist.

There is also this in chapter 5, starting with verse 117, on page 116:

> Keep in mind, when Allah will ask Jesus son of Mary;
> Didst thou say to the people: Take me and my mother
> for two Gods besides Allah? And he will answer: Holy
> are Thou. It behooves me not to have said that to
> which I have no right.

And in chapter 3 starting in verse 55, on page 54 it says:

> The enemies of Jesus devised their plan and Allah
> devised His plan; Allah is the best of planners. Allah
> reassured Jesus: I shall cause thee to die a natural
> death, and shall exalt thee to Myself, and shall clear
> thee from the calumnies of those who disbelieve.

These are just a few of the many attacks against our Lord. These are the same things Satan said to the Lord in his forty days in the wilderness—that the Lord Jesus should worship him and he would give him the earth. The enemies of Jesus are the followers of Allah, and we should note that Allah has a plan other than Jesus. Any other plan than that of Jesus is the work of the Antichrist. I think we should note that Muhammad says, "Take me and my mother as two gods." This is because of the teaching of the Catholic Church, where Mary worship is taught.

It is apparent that the Catholic Church started Mary worship very early in its formation. I think we should note Matthew 12:48, 50. The Lord says, "Who is my mother? And who are my brethren? For whosoever shall do the will of my Father which is heaven, the same is my brother, and sister, and mother." It does not sound to me in scripture that worship is required or demanded.

In chapter 6:159 on page 138, there is this:

> The day some of thy Lord should come, it shall not profit any one who had not believed before, nor earned any good by his faith, to believe in them. Say to them (Christians): Wait on, we too are waiting.

As we see here, they are waiting for their messiah to return, just as the Christians are waiting for the return of our Lord and Savior, the Lord Jesus. Their messiah is the Antichrist, and he is coming soon. In chapter 31:3–12 it says, "The revelation of this Book is from the Lord of the worlds; this is the truth beyond dough." Jesus tells us in John 18:36:

> My kingdom is not of this world: if my kingdom were of this world, then would my servants fight, that I should not be delivered to the Jews: but now is my kingdom not from hence [*enteuthen*,[216] which means on both sides, hence, on either side].

It's either Jesus or Allah. The Qur'an sickens me greatly because of its attacks on the Lord Jesus. The author of this book, the Qur'an, could only be by the devil himself. We are told in 2 Timothy 1:15, "This thou knowest, that all they which are in Asia be turned away from me." We see today that most of the countries in the Middle East and the Far East are Muslim.

The island peoples of Indonesia were told by the Muslims that Krakatoa blew because they allowed the Dutch people to live in their islands. We should note that the Dutch were Christian. They were told this was the judgment from Allah, and they believed this. I read this in a book on Krakatoa, *Krakatoa, The Day The World Exploded: August 27, 1883* by Simon Winchester.

In chapter 4, starting with verse 172, on page 97 the Qur'an says:

> People of the Book! Exceed not the limits in the matter of your religion, and say not of Allah anything

---

[216]   Ibid., 2072.

but the truth. Indeed, the Messiah, Jesus son of Mary, was but a Messenger of Allah and the fulfillment of glad tidings which He conveyed to Mary and a mercy from him. So believe Allah and His Messengers and say not: There are three Gods. Desist, it will be better for you. Indeed, Allah is the only one God. His holiness brooks not that He should have a son.

If Muhammad would have read the scriptures in the Bible more closely, he would see that the Lord Jesus said, "I and the father are one." Mark 12:29 says, "The first of all commandments is, Hear O Israel; The Lord our God is one Lord." It's only that he manifested into two people while he was on the earth. He calls himself the son of God because he was born in a fleshly body on this earth. Christians are instructed to pray to the Father, the Son, and the Holy Ghost. We should note in Revelation 4 John sees "a throne was set in heaven, and one sat on the throne." There is one God, the true God of heaven, and his name is not Allah.

There is also this in the "Qaf":

The disbelievers exclaim: This is a thing strange. Is it that when we are dead and have become dust, we shall be raised up again? That is a return which passes understanding. They rejected the truth when it came to them, so they are in the state of confusion.

The only one in the state of confusion is Muhammad. Muhammad here is denying the "resurrection of the dead." These attacks by the Qur'an on our Lord qualify the sayings in this book called the Qur'an to be the work of the Antichrist. Referring to the Islamic religion as a great religion is to blaspheme the Word of God. This is where the pope of Rome should have questioned the mullahs of the Middle East. It's time for the Christian world to quit cowering to the Muslim world and make a stand for the Lord Jesus Christ as the true God of heaven. For those who don't know what cower means, the *Webster's Dictionary* says, "To crouch down through fear, shame, cold, uncertain." Note the

Greek word meaning "cold." This is what the Lord Jesus has against the Laodicean church. The Lord Jesus says, "So then because thou art lukewarm, and neither cold nor hot, I will spue thee out of my mouth."

I will not make any apologies to the Muslim world for my belief, and I will never be a worshiper of Allah. I will prove this. Hebrews 10:38 says, "Now the just shall live by faith: but if any man draw back, my soul shall have no pleasure in them." To draw back *hupostello*,[217] which means to withhold (out of sight), [i.e., (reflexive) to cower or shrink (figurative), to conceal]. Scripture tells us here that we are not to withhold our faith and not to cower as the Hebrew meaning says. I don't know why the pope and his group of cardinals didn't stand up to the mullahs of the Middle East and tell them they are worshiping the devil.

And the just should live by faith until when? That is in verse 37: "For yet a little while, and he that shall come will come, and will not tarry." To come is *heko*,[218] which means to arrive (i.e., be present). And when is his appearing? It is immediately after the tribulation of those days, when the sun and the moon don't give their light, and then shall appear the Son of Man in heaven. And when does this happen? In Hebrews 10:30 it says, "For we know him that hath said, Vengeance belongeth unto me, I will recompense, saith the Lord. And again, The Lord shall judge his people." Hebrews makes it clear that the church goes through the judgments of God, because they are his people. We are also told in 2 Kings 1:3:

> Then Moeb rebelled against Israel after the death of Ahab. And Ahaziah fell down through a lattice in his upper chamber that was in Samaria, and was sick: and he sent messengers, and said unto them, Go, enquire of Baal-zebub the God of Ekron whether I shall recover of this disease. But the angel of the Lord said to Elijah the Tishbite, Arise, go up to meet the

---

217 Ibid., 2170.
218 Ibid., 2085.

messengers of the king of Sameria, and say unto them,
Is it not because there is not a God in Israel, that ye go
to enquire of Baal-zebub the God of Ekron?

We know who Baal-zebub is, for scripture tells us in Mark 3:22:

And the scribes which came down from Jerusalem
said, He hath Beelzebub, and by the prince of the
devils casteth he out devils.

We are also told in 2 Corinthians 11:14–15:

And no marvel; for Satan himself is transformed
into an angel of light. Therefore it is no great thing
if his ministers also be transformed as the ministers of
righteousness; whose end shall be according to their
works.

Webster's Dictionary meaning of marvel is "a wonderful or
astonishing thing." John tells this is no marvel. We should also notice
in Revelation 17:7, "And the angel said unto me, Wherefore didst thou
marvel?" We should note that Satan's ministers also will be as ministers
of righteousness. Here's the difference: "Whose end shall be according
to their works." Christians are saved according to faith. The Muslim
world teaches that if they die killing a Jew or a Christian, it gets them
seventy-two virgins in heaven. Does this make them think they are
ministers of righteousness when they die; is this martyrdom? This is
what they are taught at a very young age. We should note that John
told us this would happen. John 16:2–3 says:

The Lord speaking: They shall put you out of the
synagogues; yea, the time cometh, that whosoever
killeth you will think that he doeth God service. And
these things they will do unto you, because they have
not known the Father, nor me.

We should note that Jesus warned us there would come a time when those who kill us think they do God's service because they do not know the Father or Jesus. So who do the Muslims pray to?

Is this what inspired the nineteen Arabs to hijack the airlines and fly them into the twin towers on 9/11? They thought that killing the infidels (Christians) is what they are instructed to do in the Qur'an. But their works, we know, get them something much different than they think. And then in John 16:4, the Lord says:

> But these things have I told you, that when the time
> shall come, ye may remember that I told you of them.
> And these things I say not unto you at the beginning,
> because I was with you.

Is the rising threat of radical Islam coming to pass in our generation, just as the Lord told us this would happen? I like the "ye may remember that I [God], Jesus told you of them. And these things I say not unto you at the beginnings, because I was with you." The Jews were to have no fear of this happening to them because Jesus was among them. But most churches have forgotten this or just don't want to face the facts. I do not believe the cut-and-run Democrats would have won so big in November 2006 if the churches in this country would wake up. Christian Americans, wake up.

The radical Muslim world thinks they are here to rule the world, and if you don't accept the teachings of Islam, you will be killed. Jesus warned us this was going to happen, and is this not happening in our generation? I believe the closing days that we were told about are coming in the next few years. Some of the Arab world tells us that this is not what most of the Arab world wants, but do they condemn their fellow Muslims for their actions? I have not seen this. Let's not forget that Muhammad believed the Muslim world is in a perpetual state of jihad or holy war against any country not Muslim, and the proof is in their actions.

Throughout history, you either converted to Islam or were killed with the sword. Did they not attack the state of Israel after the very day it was announced to the world that the state of Israel was formed? Only with help from God did the state of Israel survive. The Muslim world has come against them in many wars since 1948, only to be defeated by the Jews. Even in 1973, when the Jews thought that the Arabs would win the battle, God stepped in. These people will not be destroyed by the Muslim world.

I have heard of a new book by former President Jimmy Carter. He is a bigger fool than I thought he was. I cannot believe I was fooled into voting for him. Like I told you before, I am not a college-educated person, but I believe that if you call yourself a Christian you are. But when you take the side of the Arab world against the Jewish people, you are going against the Lord. Jimmy Carter has lost all credibility as a Christian. He did not stand up against the radical Muslim world in his days as president, and I would like to say to Jimmy Carter, "No one cares what you think." Forgive my words. Jimmy Carter, you are a complete idiot.

Any politician who is not willing to stand up against the Muslim world is a chicken—but I will leave off the second part of that. Our only protection comes from God, and when you go against him, you are asking for more than you can bear. More terrorism hits America because of their blindness or better said undiscerning ignorance of the facts. Israel has lived with this threat their entire history. But now the radical Islamic world is bringing their jihad to the entire world. If you think you can make a peace agreement with these people, let's look at the past.

Did not England, France, and Russia make peace agreements with Hitler before World War II? They thought if they gave Czechoslovakia back to the Germans, that would keep them from German aggression. Did this happen? No! Will making peace agreements with radical Islamic people not produce the same result? As we see what is happening in Iran, they are developing nuclear power for one reason only: to destroy Israel. And what is the United Nations doing about this? Nothing. Will the state of Israel allow Iran to acquire a nuclear weapon? The answer is no, for their very survival. Could this start the battle of Armageddon? This is why studying history is important. What man has done in the past he will do in the future. America needs to open its eyes and see there is an enemy out there to destroy us. It's by the followers of the Antichrist, and those people are the Islamic people.

We are also told in Galatians 1:8–9:

> But though we, or an angel from heaven, preach any other gospel unto you than that which we have preached unto you, let him be accursed. As we said before, so say I now again, If any man preach any other gospel unto you than that ye have received, let him be accursed.

So was that angel from heaven that visited Muhammad in the seventh century AD from God or from the devil? I believe the latter is the more likely person. We are also told in 1 John 4:6: "We are of God: he that knoweth God heareth us; he that is not of God heareth not us. Hereby know we the spirit off truth, and the spirit of error." Error is *plain*,[219] which means object fraudulence; subject of straying from orthodoxy or piety. It is the feminine of *planos*,[220] which means roving, (i.e., by implication) an impostor or misleader. And since the Muslims refuse to hear the gospel of Christ, they believe in an impostor. First John 4:10–11 states:

> He that believeth on the Son of God hath the witness in himself: he that believeth not God hath made him a liar; because he believeth not the record that God gave his Son. And this is the record, that God hath give us eternal life, and that life is in his Son.

It's only in the belief in the Son of God that is there eternal life, and Allah has no Son. We see in scripture that God's vengeance is against Idumea. If you think a Muslim is your friend, here is what the Qur'an says to them.

Surah 5:52, page 107 says:

---

[219] Ibid., 2136.
[220] Ibid.

O you who believe! Do not take the Jews and the Christians for helpers, for they are helpers of one another. Whoso from among you takes them as helpers will indeed be one of them. Verily, Allah guides not the unjust people.

Al-Tauba, page 173 3–6 says:

When the period of four months during which hostilities are suspended expires, without the idolaters having settled the terms of peace with you, resume fighting with them and make them prisoners and beleaguer them, and lie in wait for them at every place of ambush.

Do you see this "lie in wait for them at every place of ambush"? David tells us in Psalms 59:3, "For, lo, they lie in wait for my soul: the mighty are gathered against me; not for my transgression, nor my sin." Then he tells us in 63:9, "But those that seek my soul, to destroy it, shall go into the lower parts of the earth." Now let's go to Proverbs 12:3,13: "The words of the wicked are to lie in wait for blood: but the mouth of the upright shall deliver them . . . . The wicked is snared [*mowqesh*,[221] which means a noose, by implication a hook] by the transgression [*pesha*,[222] which means to revolt (national, moral, or religious) rebellion, sin] of his lips [praise Allah]: but the just come out of trouble [tribulation]." So what were Muhammad's instructions? "To lie in wait for them at every ambush." What is told to us in Proverbs? That the "Wicked are to lie in wait for blood." Note also it states here that the "just" come out of trouble (tribulation), and not before the tribulation. This is just another verse that proves there is not a pre-tribulation rapture.

---

[221] Ibid., 1895.
[222] Ibid., 1951.

Does this sound like they will live up to any peace agreement? This ambush is the style of terrorism they use. Christians are in more danger than ever because they are living in our neighborhoods. Which one of them will be the next suicide bomber? Which one of them wants to die in martyrdom for the cause of Allah, as they are instructed? We are told by liberal people that we can't use racial profiling. The Lord Jesus will be the biggest racial profiler at his return. There is a religion preached by the Muslims to hate and kill anyone not Muslim. The days of Noah have returned upon this generation, and our Lord's return is very near. Are these statements by the Qur'an, as well as the actions taken by the descendants of Esau when the Hebrew children came out of Egypt, the reason for this next scripture?

Malachi 2:2–3 says:

> I have loved you, saith the Lord. Yet ye say, Wherein hast thou loved us? Was not Esau Jacob's brother? saith the Lord: yet I loved Jacob, And I hated Esau, and laid his mountains and his heritage waste for the dragons of the wilderness.

This is affirmed in Romans 9:13, "As it is written, Jacob have I loved, but Esau have I hated." We should also note Hebrews 12:16, "Lest there be any fornicator, or profane person, as Esau, who for one morsel of meat sold his birthright." The word "profane" is *bebelos*,[223] which means accessible (as by the cross, the doorway), (i.e., by implication of Jewish notions) heathenish, wicked. And the comment is, "Spoken of persons: profane, i.e., impious, a scoffer (2 Tim. 1:19; Heb. 12:16)."[224] We will read later in this book why I think God has this hatred for these people. I believe that the Greek meaning for a profane and wicked person is one who refuses Jesus Christ as the only doorway to heaven.

There must be a reason for God to have this predestined hate for Esau's descendants. And if God hates these people, I believe we

---

[223]   Ibid., 2042.
[224]   Ibid.

should feel the same way unless they turn from their worship of Allah. We should note Psalms 104:4, "Who maketh his angels spirits," and Hebrews 1:7, "And of the angels he saith, Who maketh his angels spirits." God made the angels into the human spirit to redeem them back to God.

These who God has this predestined hate for are the angels who rebelled against God with Satan. The angels who were not rebellious are explained in Ephesians1:3–4:

> Blessed be God and Father of our Lord Jesus Christ, who hath blessed us with spiritual blessings in heavenly places in Christ: According as he hath chosen us in him before the foundation of the world, that we should be holy and without blame before him in love.

This is affirmed in Matthew 13:38–40:

> The field is the world, the good seed are the children of the kingdom; but the tares are the children of the wicked one [Satan]; The enemy that sowed them is the devil; the harvest is the end of the world; and the reapers are his angels. And therefore the tares are gathered and burned in the fire; so shall it be in the end of this world.

If you want to save a Muslim friend, lead him or her to the saving knowledge of Jesus Christ.

I will not be friends with people who worship the Antichrist. Their hatred for the children of Israel has brought us to this. We were told of this hatred that started back around 1500 BC. This hatred continues to this day. To affirm this hatred, Muhammad wrote the Qur'an. So how we have two books, and both tell us one destroys the other. So we must ask ourselves, who's right? My trust is in the Lord of the Bible, and it is his Word that will prevail. Israel was told not to come against Esau's people when they came out of Egyptian bondage but to go through the land. The hatred begins here and continues until this day.

Is this a religion of peace? Or is this a religion of hatred for the Jews and Christians of the world today? I do not care if the Muslim world hates me. I know what the intent of a Muslim person's heart is, and that is to destroy the Jews of Israel and then the Christians. When will American Christians wake up to the fact that the Arab world is out to destroy Israel and America? You can stick your heads in the sand to this threat, but it is not going away.

If Iran gets the bomb, they will use it. We know what the final ending is, for I know who the God of heaven is, and he is the God of the Bible. Should not Christians take this same message to the rest of the world? Psalms 63:9 states, "But those that seek my soul, to destroy it, shall go into the lower parts of the earth." David tells us here that the soul goes to the lower parts of the earth. This was very confusing to me, and then I realized that the spirit of man was not revealed from God to David. It is the spirit of man that goes unto the lower parts of the earth. We will study this matter later in this book, for we are told in Revelation 5:3, "And no man in heaven, nor in the earth, neither under the earth, was able to open the book, neither to look thereon." These are the spirits of man waiting for the resurrection, and the proof is in the scripture.

God's Promise of Divine Intervention

This next set of verses in Ezekiel are an example of the reasons I don't believe in pre-tribulation resurrection. I believe the past reveals the future. The time period I am about to give you is when Babylon came, with God's guidance, to destroy the house of Judah in 586 BC. There was a great slaughter in the land of Judah because they would not listen to the prophets, Jeremiah and Ezekiel, to return to the God of heaven. The Lord gave the house of Judah many years to return to him and to stop child sacrifice, but God did something to protect the faithful inhabitants of the land. We should also notice this in Jeremiah 15:8, "She that hath borne seven languisheth: she hath given up the ghost; her sun is gone down while it was yet day." We see here that it is dark during the daylight hours when the wrath of God comes.

We will see this same darkness just before the Lord's return, but we are also told in verse 11, "The Lord said, Verily it shall be well with thy remnant; verily I will cause the enemy to entreat thee well in the time of evil and in the time of affliction." This is the same intervention spoken to the church in the latter days. They did not have to be resurrected off the earth to be protected by God. Let's look at just what Ezekiel prophesies to the house of Judah. I believe it was promised by other prophets that there was a pre-tribulation resurrection.

Ezekiel 13:17–20 says:

> Likewise, thou Son of Man, set thy face against the daughters of thy people, which prophecy out of their own heart; and prophecy thou against them, And say, Thus saith the Lord God; Woe to the women that sew pillows to all armholes, and make kerchiefs upon the head of every stature to hunt souls! Will ye hunt the souls of my people, and will ye save the souls alive that come unto you? And will ye pollute me among the people for handfuls of barley and for pieces of bread, to slay the souls that should not die, and save the souls alive that should not live, by your lying to my people that hear your lies? Wherefore thus saith the Lord God; Behold, I am against your pillows, wherewith ye there hunt the souls to make them fly, and I will tear them from your arms, and will set the souls go, even the souls that ye hunt to make them fly.

This is the first pre-tribulation resurrection theory given by these daughters of thy people. We should note here that they prophesy out of their own heart. They were prophesying that they would "save the souls alive that they shall live" and "make them fly." The word for kerchief is *Mispachath,*[225] which means scurf (as spreading over the surface). This sounds like to me that these women were prophesying that when judgment came, they would fly away, most likely referring to how God took Elijah to heaven. These women were doing this for "handfuls of barley and for pieces of bread."

In today's terms, this is about pastors teaching the pre-tribulation resurrection when we fly to heaven before the judgment of God. This is important to note. It says it is the soul and not the spirit that flies away. When we read the resurrection of the dead chapter, this will be explained. Let's note Ezekiel 13:22: "Because with lies ye have made the heart of the righteous sad, whom I have not made sad; and strengthened the hands of the wicked, that they should return from

---

[225]   Ibid., 1904.

their wicked way, by promising him life [*chayah*,[226] which means to live, whether literal or figurative; causative to revive]." Instead of telling the people to repent, they were promising them "save the souls alive that should live." Let's note the Hebrew word meaning in English to revive. In *Webster's Dictionary* that means, "To restore to consciousness or life." This fits Ecclesiastes 1:9, "The thing that hath been, it is that which shall be; and that which is done: and there is no new thing under the sun."

The past reveals the future. It was not until the 1800s when Margaret MacDonald, who fell into a trance, got this pre-tribulation vision. Let's note in the scriptures when we read "resurrection" the word "dead" follows. It never says the living. John Nelson Darby started teaching the pre-tribulation resurrection to the churches. Let's look at all the great theories that came out of the 1800s besides this resurrection theory: Darwin's ape-man evolution. Oil is a fossil fuel. The Bible is only a myth. I can't say too much, as this is the age of enlightenment.

Ezekiel 7:1–6 says:

> Moreover the word of the Lord came unto me, saying, Also, thou Son of Man, thus said the Lord God unto the land of Israel; An end, the end is come upon the four corners of the land. Now is the end come upon thee, and I will send mine anger upon thee, and will judge thee according to thy ways, and will recompense upon thee all thine abominations. And mine eyes shall not spare thee, neither will I have pity: but I will recompense thy ways upon thee, and thine abominations shall be in the midst of thee: and ye shall know that I am the Lord. Thus saith the Lord God; An evil, an only evil, behold, is come. An end is come: the end has come: it watcheth for thee; behold, it is come.

---

[226] Ibid., 1855.

We should note that Ezekiel announces of "the end of the first temple age" is come upon you before God's wrath. As we will see later in this book, there is another time when "an end" will be given in scripture. The Lord Jesus tells us, "All those that endure until the end, the same shall be saved." The past reveals the future. God uses other nations to bring his wrath on a people here in scripture, just as he will do at the end of the age. Who does God use to bring this wrath of the house of Judah? This is found in Ezekiel 23:22:

> The Babylonians, and all the Chaldeans, Pekod, and
> Shoa, and Koa, and all the Assyrians with them: all of
> them desirable young men, captains and rulers, great
> lords and renowned, all them riding upon horses.

Ezekiel gives us exact description of the tribes of people God brings against the house of Judah. We should take a special notice that the Assyrians are among them. The house of Israel was taken into captivity by these people before. The absence of the house of Israel should be noted. I believe this also proves they were released from Assyrian captivity when Babylon destroyed the Assyrian Empire. If the ten tribes of the house of Israel knew the Babylonians were on the way to take the house of Judah into captivity, they would have gone in another direction. Even with this great army, God gets involved.

Jeremiah warned King Zedekiah that the Lord was bringing Nebuchadnezzar, king of Babylon, to destroy the house of Judah. But he told them to go peacefully and live or fight and die. This was their option. Jeremiah tells us in 21:5, "And I myself (the Lord) will fight against you with an outstretched hand and with a strong arm, even in anger, and in fury, and with great wrath." And Ezekiel the prophet tells us exactly what the Lord does to help them destroy the house of Judah.

Ezekiel 9:1–6 says:

> He cried also in mine ears with a loud voice, saying,
> Cause them that have charge over the city to draw
> near, even every man with his destroying weapon in

his hand. And, behold, six men came from the way of the higher gate, which lyeth toward the north, and every man a slaughter weapon in his hand; and one man among them was clothed with linen, with a writer's inkhorn by his side: and they went in, and stood at the brazen altar. And the glory of the God of Israel was gone up upon the cherub, whereupon he was, to the threshold of the house. And he called to the man clothed with linen, which had the writer's inkhorn by his side; And the Lord said unto him, Go through the midst of the city, through the midst of Jerusalem, and set a mark upon the foreheads of the men that sigh and cry for all the abominations that be done in the midst thereof. And to the others he said in my hearing, Go ye after him through the city, and smite: let not your eye spare, neither have ye pity: slay utterly old and young, both maids, and little children, and women: but come not near any man upon whom is the mark; and begin at my sanctuary. Then they began at the ancient men which were before the house.

These six men are six angels that accompany the Lord, and we should note that they are armed with a slaughter weapon. But there is one man dressed in linen who had the writer's inkhorn by his side to seal the foreheads of the people who sigh and cry for all the abominations done in the land. These people are protected by this seal from the great slaughter that is coming to Jerusalem. These are the people taken into Babylonian captivity.

I believe this will happen in the latter days as well, for we see in the book of Revelation that many are sealed by the angels to protect them from the wrath of Antichrist. John 6:27 says, "Labour not for the meat which perisheth, but for that meat which endureth unto everlasting life, which the Son of Man shall give unto you: for him hath God the Father sealed." I believe this seal is to protect them from the effects of the judgments in the book of Revelation. An equivalent verse is found in Revelation 9:15 where angels will have slaughter weapons: "And the four angels were loosed, which were prepared for an hour, and a day, and a month, and a year, for to slay the third part of men." The past reveals the future. It's all a matter of faith, and I believe our faith will be tested.

I think it is also important that we should also notice that the judgments begin at the temple. Just as we are told in 1 Peter 4:17, "For the time is come that judgment must begin at the house of God." First Timothy 3:5 states, "The house of God, which is the church of the living God." The word "house" here is *oikos*,[227] which means, "Metaphorically: The house of God, i.e., the Christian church, Christians (1Tim. 3:15, Heb. 3:6, 10:21, 1Pet. 4:17); The Jewish assembly (Heb. 3:25)." Also, the word for judgment is *Krima*,[228] which means in reference to future reward and punishment. The past reveals the future. This is why I believe the church is still on the earth—to learn righteousness. We should also note the Greek meanings of reward and punishment. This is just another strike against the pre-tribulation resurrection, if the judgments must begin with the house of God. This will be proven later. So we will continue with verse 7:

> And he said unto them, Defile the house, and fill the courts with the slain: go ye forth. And they went forth, and slew in the city. And it came to pass, while I was left, that I fell upon my face, and cried, and said, Ah Lord God! Wilt thou destroy all the residue of Israel in thy pouring out of thy fury upon Jerusalem? Then he said unto me, The iniquity of the house of Israel and Judah is exceeding great, and the land is full of blood, and the city is full of perverseness: for they say, The Lord hath forsaken the earth, and the Lord seeth not. And as for me also, mine eye shall not spare, neither will I have pity, but I will recompense their way upon their head. And, behold, the man

---

[227] Ibid., 2121.
[228] Ibid., 2104.

clothed with linen, which had the inkhorn by his side, reported the matter, saying, I have done as thou hast commanded me.

Let us first notice why God's wrath came on these people. The sins of the house of Israel and Judah were exceedingly great, and the land was full of blood and perverseness. It sounds like America today. Note that they say here, "The Lord has forsaken the earth." Today we call this destroying mother earth. Not much has changed for thousands of years. We should note here that the Babylonian army needed help from the Lord for the destruction of the house of Judah. And the reason for this is told in Ezekiel 5:7–8:

> Therefore thus saith the Lord; Because ye multiplied more than the nations that are round about you, and have not walked in my statutes, neither have kept my judgments, neither have done according to the judgments of the nations that are round about you; Therefore thus saith the Lord God, I, even, I, am against thee, and will execute judgments in the midst of thee in the sight of the nations.

The house of Judah is so strong that even with this great army that the Lord commanded to come against them, they still needed help from God. This will happen again at the battle of Armageddon, only this time God will be on the side of the house of Judah. We should also note the same language is used at the battle of Armageddon in Ezekiel 38:23, "Thus will I magnify myself, and sanctify myself; and I will be known in the eyes of many nations, and they shall known that I am the Lord." When the wrath of God comes on a people, the Lord wants the rest of the world to know he is bringing the judgments upon these people.

We are told in Ezekiel 7:14–19:

They have blown the trumpet, even to make all ready;
but none goeth to the battle: for my wrath is upon all
the multitude thereof.

We should note that a trumpet is sounded before the wrath of
God. Keep this stored in your mind for future reference. I think you
should note that Ezekiel says, "But none go to the battle." Is this an
example of the way Americans today are? The polls around the country
tell us Americans want this war over, but we cannot end a war until we
kill the enemy that is bent on our destruction.

Have America's iniquities become so great that the Lord cannot
save America? Is our land also not full of innocent blood (abortion)
and perverseness? And we think that God is going to take us off the
earth before his judgments come. We are saying today that the use of
coal and gas are causing global warning, which the Lord created. Has
the Lord forsaken the earth? I believe those who have put their faith
in the Lord Jesus will be sealed during these judgments so we too can
witness what the Lord does to the unbeliever just as the Lord has done
before.

Ezekiel 7:15–19 says:

The sword is without, and the pestilence and the
famine within: he that is in the field shall die with the
sword; and he that is in the city, famine and pestilence
shall devour him. But they that escape of them that
escape, and shall be on the mountains like doves of the
valley, all of them mourning, every one of his iniquity.
And all hands be feeble, and all knees shall be weak as
water. They shall also gird themselves with sackcloth,
and horror shall cover them; and shame shall be on
all faces, and baldness upon all their heads. They shall
cast their silver in the streets, and their gold shall be
removed: their silver and their gold shall not be able to
deliver them in the day of the wrath of the Lord: They
shall not satisfy their souls, neither fill their bowels:
because it is the stumbling block of their iniquity.

We should notice that all that affected the house of Judah in 586 BC are the same in the book of Revelation. Note the reference to "all of them mourning." The New Testament equivalent verse is in Matthew 24:30: "And then shall appear the Son of Man in heaven: and then shall all of the tribes of the earth mourn." When the wrath of God only affected the house of Judah, they only mourned. In the last days, all the world will mourn. This proves one thing: that God changes not. Whether he is dealing with man in the BC period of time or whether he is dealing with man in the twenty-first century, it is the same. We should also notice that man thought then as man thinks now, that somehow it doesn't matter how we live; God will forget it. Man has always thought his wealth will save him in the time of trouble, for man trusts more in his silver and gold. Just as in the past when they threw their gold and silver in the streets, James tells us, "Your gold and silver is cankered which ye heaped treasures for the last days." Isaiah tells us in 41:42, "Let them bring them forth, and shew us what shall happen; let them shew the former things, what they be, that we may consider them, and know the latter end of them; or declare us things for to come." The past reveals the future, but our trust should be in the Lord. We should also note here the spirit of the Lord leaving the temple and what accompanies the Lord.

Ezekiel 10:4 says:

> Then the glory of the Lord went up from the cherub, and stood over the threshold of the house; and the house was filled with the cloud, and the court was full of the brightness of the Lord's glory.

The cherub accompanied the Lord in the temple on earth, just as we are told about in Revelation 4. And how does the Lord depart the temple on earth? This is in Ezekiel 11:22–23:

> Then did the cherubim's lift up their wings, and the wheels beside them, and the glory of the God of Israel was over them above. And the glory of the Lord went

up from the midst of the city, and stood upon the mountain which is on the east side of the city.

We see here the Lord leaving the temple, and he goes to the Mount of Olives when he goes back to heaven. The Lord comes back to this very mount at his return to the earth where he will reign forever. The Arabs went as far as to close the eastern gate to the city of Jerusalem by bricking the eastern entrance to the city of Jerusalem, as if that would stop our Lord from fulfilling prophecy. The prophecy in Ezekiel 43:4 says, "And the glory of the Lord came to the house by the way of the gate whose prospect is toward the east." Because of this, the Muslims bricked the eastern gate and only the eastern gate to the city of Jerusalem.

To see for myself just what the Qur'an says, I brought the book written by Muhammad Zafrulla Khan. He is also the president of the world court of Hague, and Americans will be in big trouble if our leaders put us under the rules of this court. This is an anti-Jewish, anti-Christian organization. We must, as Christians, demand from our president and Congress that we have no affiliation with this organization. This was the warnings from our founding president, George Washington. To unite the Arab world, Muhammad wrote the Qur'an. The stage is set for the final showdown between God and the ungodly. How can Allah be God?

Isaiah 34:1–10 says:

Come near, ye nations, to hear; and hearken, ye people: let the earth hear, and all that is therein; the world, and all things that come forth of it. For the indignation of the Lord is upon all nations, and his fury upon all their armies: he hath utterly destroyed them, he hath delivered them to the slaughter. Their slain also shall be cast out, and their stink shall come out of their carcasses, and the mountains shall be melted with their blood. And all the host of heaven shall be dissolved, and the heavens shall be rolled together as a scroll: and all their hosts shall fall down, as a leaf falleth off from a vine, and as a falling fig from the fig tree. For my sword shall be bathed in heaven: Behold, it shall come down upon Idumea, and upon the people of my curse, to judgment. The sword of the Lord is filled with blood, it is made fat with fatness, and with the blood of lambs and goats, with the fat of the kidneys of rams: for the Lord hath a sacrifice in Bosrah, and a great slaughter in the land of Idumea. And the unicorns shall come down with them, and the bullock with the bulls; and their land shall be soaked with blood, and their dust made fat with the fatness. For it is the day of the Lord's vengeance, and the year of recompenses for the controversy of Zion. And the streams thereof shall be turned to pitch, and the dust thereof into brimstone, and the land thereof shall become burning pitch. It shall not be quenched night nor day; the smoke thereof shall go up for ever: from generation to generation it shall lay waste; none shall pass through it for ever and ever.

In the first verse, Isaiah tells us that the nations of the world should listen to what he is about to say. For God's indignation (indignation is *qutseph*,[229] which means figurative rage or strife: wrath) is against all nations, and armies, and he utterly destroyed them all. The New Testament equivalent verse is Revelation 11:18, "And the nations were angry [they at war with one another], and thy [God's] wrath has come, and the time the dead be judged [the resurrection of the death], and destroy those who destroy the earth." We should also notice that this anger of the Lord is directed upon Idumea, where Isaiah tells us there will be a great slaughter in the land and that the land is turned into burning pitch. Note that Isaiah tells us, "The sword of the Lord is filled with blood." The New Testament equivalent verse is Revelation 19:15, "And out of his mouth goeth a sharp sword, that with it he should

---

[229] Ibid., 1963.

smite the nations: and he shall rule them with a rod of iron: and he treadeth the winepress of the fierceness and wrath of Almighty God."

We should also note here that Isaiah says, "Upon the people of my curse." The people of God's curse are also given in Galatians 1:8–9, where it is stated:

> But though we, or an angel from heaven, preach any other gospel unto you than which we have preached unto you, let him be accursed. As we said before, so say I now again, If any man preach any other gospel unto you than that ye have received, let him be accursed.

The people of God's curse are the Muslims, and their gospel is the Qur'an. Note that Galatians says, "An angel from heaven preach any other gospel." Muhammad claims Gabriel gave him his gospel. We know that this is the last days, for it is stated in verse 8, "For the day of the Lord's vengeance, and the year of recompences for the controversy of Zion." Why are these people destroyed? For the controversy of Zion. The Arab world wants Israel to be wiped off the face of the earth, but just the opposite happens. And we should note that "Idumea's lands the smoke thereof shall go up for ever: for one generation to generation it shall lie waste."

And if you think that this is not going to happen as Isaiah says, let's look at what he has to say in the same chapter.

Verse 16 says:

> Seek ye out of the book of the Lord, and read: no one of these shall fail, none shall want her mate; for my mouth it hath commanded, and his spirit it hath gathered them.

> And when I shall put thee out, I will cover the heaven, and make the stars thereof dark; I will cover the sun with a cloud, and the moon shall not give her light. All the bright lights will be dark over thee, and set

darkness upon thy land, saith the Lord God (Ezek.
32:7–30).

First Ezekiel gives us the world conditions at the time this happens.
We see here that the sun, the moon, and the stars above are darkened
by a cloud. We see here and many times throughout scripture that
these conditions exist during the time that God brings judgment to
the nations. The Egyptians experienced the same darkness for three
days. The Jews experienced this darkness when they crucified the Lord.
Mark 15:33 says:

> And when the sixth hour [noon] was come, there was
> darkness over the whole land until the ninth hour
> [3.00 p.m.]
> This darkness is also predicted for the end of days.

Now let's continue with Ezekiel 32:9–12:

> I will also vex the hearts of many people, when I
> shall bring thy destruction among the nations, into
> the countries which thou hast not known. Yea, I will
> make many people amazed at thee, and their kings
> shall be horribly afraid for thee, when I shall brandish
> my sword before them; and they shall tremble at
> every moment, every man for his own life, in the day
> of thy fall. For thus saith the Lord God; The sword
> of the king of Babylon shall come upon thee. By the
> swords of the mighty will I cause thy multitude to
> fall, the terrible of the nations, all of them: and they
> shall spoil the pomp of Egypt, and all the multitudes
> thereof shall be destroyed.

We see here that God rose up the Babylonian Empire to bring
judgment to the world. As we see here, "By the swords of the mighty
will I," meaning God causes this to happen. It is in this verse that
Ezekiel tells us that God scatters these people into countries they did

not know. I will skip verses 13–17 to get to the point more quickly, so we will start with verse 18.

> Son of Man, wail for the multitude of Egypt, and cast them down, even her, and the daughter of the famous nations, unto the nether parts of the earth, with them that go down into the pit. Whom dost thou pass in beauty? Go down, and be thou laid with the uncircumcised. They shall fall in the midst of thee that are slain by the sword: she is delivered to the sword: draw her and all her multitudes. The strong among the mighty shall speak to him out of the midst of hell with them that help him: they are gone down, they lie uncircumcised, slain by the sword. Asshur is there and all her company: his graves are about him: all of them slain, fallen by the sword: Whose graves are set in the sides of the pit, and her company is round about her grave: all of them slain, fallen by the sword, which caused terror in the land of the living.

Ezekiel tells us here why God raised up the Babylonian empire. It was to bring judgment to these nations that "caused terror in the land of the living." Is this why Babylon is the head of gold and the king of kings that is given us in the book of Daniel? God promised never to flood the world again, so now he raises up nations to stop terror in the land of the living. Scripture tells us this happens throughout history. Let us continue.

> There is Elam and all her multitude round about her grave, all of them slain, fallen by the sword, which are gone down uncircumcised into the nether parts of the earth, which caused their terror in the land of living; yet they have borne their shame with them that go down to the pit.

The pit here is *bowr*,[230] which means a pit hole (especially one used as a cistern or prison). This cistern is in the lower parts of the earth where all the spirits of men go. This lower part of the earth is the middle of the earth where Jesus went after he was crucified. Let's note 1 Peter 3:18–19, "For Christ also hath once suffered for sins, the just for the unjust, that he might bring us to God, being put to death in the flesh, but quickened [*zoopoieo*,[231] meaning; to (re) vitalize (literal or figurative) make alive, give life.] by the spirit: By which also he went and preached unto the spirits in prison." Jesus also died for the sins of all the just and unjust spirits of the past. Jesus went into the prison to revitalize their spirits unto God. Remember when we learned that the souls of men would fly away in the first part of the chapter. Now we are told hear that the "spirits" here go to the nether parts of the earth. I will give more on this when we get to the next chapter.

Let's skip to verse 25:

> There is Meshech, Tubal, and all multitude; her graves are round about him: all of them uncircumcised, slain by the sword, though they caused their terror in the land of the living. And they shall not lie with the mighty that are fallen of the uncircumcised, which are gone down to hell with their weapons of war: and they laid their swords under their heads, but their iniquities shall be upon their bones, though they were the terror of the mighty in the land of the living. Yea, thou shalt be broken in the midst of the uncircumcised, and shalt lie with them that are slain with the sword.
>
> There is Edom, her kings, and all her princes with their might are laid by them that were slain by the sword: they shall lie with the uncircumcised, and with them that go down to the pit. There be the princes of

---

230 Ibid., 1822.
231 Ibid., 2084.

the north, all of them, and all the Zidonians, which
are gone down with the slain; with their terror they are
ashamed of their might; and they lie uncircumcised
with them that be slain by the sword, and bear their
shame with them that go down to the pit.

Do most of these tribes of people who are bringing terror to the
land during this time in history sound familiar? These same tribes of
people are given to us in Ezekiel 38:3, "And say, Thus saith the Lord
God; Behold I am against thee, O Gog, the chief prince of Meshech
and Tubal." The same people who brought terror to the world back
then are bringing terror to the world at the time of Armageddon, only
this time Babylon is with them. God used Nebuchadnezzar, king of
Babylon, and named him king of kings to bring peace to the land.
The next time the Lord himself, who is the true King of Kings, will
bring in eternal peace. This is when they were scattered out of the
Mesopotamian area and went into the lands of present day.

One day I was studying the Bible in my business and an Arab, in
an angry way, asked me, "I guess you think that your God is the God
of heaven?" I said, "Yes he is, and we will soon see who the true God
of heaven is in a very short time." He did not like my answer, but I do
not care. I am proud that I am a child of the Lord Jesus, and I thank
him every day that he died for me on a cross for my sins. I could never
be good enough to enter the kingdom of heaven without him. I say
praise the Lord. America is a Christian nation, and if an Arab does not
like it, I say go back to the Middle East. They don't want us in their
country or any of their countries that are Muslim. They should stay out
of countries that say they are Christian countries.

If you have it so good there with your rulers, I say go back to
the Middle East. Live under Sharia law. Don't bring it to America.
As you can see, I am not a politically correct person. I call it as I see
it. Americans need to arm themselves, because our government is not
going to protect us from this threat for sake of political correctness.
Recently William Long, who died, was gunned down by Abdulhakim
Mujahid Muhammad at a recruiting center in Little Rock, Arkansas.
Muhammad was a recent convert to Islam while in Yemen. Remember

the Christmas Day bomber? Remember the Yom Kippur War, which is the holiest day for the Jew? The Muslim terrorists seem to want to make the attacks around Christian and Jewish holidays. The government doesn't even want to secure our borders. This should be the number-one concern for all Christian Americans. What is being preached in mosques in America? Are they preaching to live peaceably with the Christians around them, or are they saying to do the same thing that is told to them in Muslim countries? And if they are preaching this hatred for Christians, deportation should be immediate. This is hate speech, which is now against the laws of this country.

This is one of the main prophecies in our Bible that proves we are living in the last days, for terrorism is happening around the world, just as in the days of Noah. But the Lord himself will end this worldwide terrorism. Jeremiah tells us this 25:33, "And the slain of the Lord shall be at that day from one end of the earth even unto the other end of the earth." Why from one end of the earth to the other? It's because the Muslim people are scattered around the world.

Part of the Arab world, namely the president of Iran, says they will destroy the Saturday people first, meaning the Jews of Israel, and the Sunday people next, meaning the Christian people. But we see here what God is going to do. "I [God] will lie thy cities waste, and thou shall be a desolate, and thou shall know that I am the Lord. And I will make thee perpetual desolations, and thy cities shall not return." We will remember that this same warning was given in Numbers 24:20: "Amalek was the first of the nations; but his latter end shall be he shall perish forever." We should also note that God said he heard their blasphemies they had spoken, for their words were against God. Ezekiel 36:2–8, 10 says:

> Thus saith the Lord God: because the enemy hath
> said against you, Aha, even the ancient high places are
> ours in possession: therefore thus saith the Lord God;
> surely in the fire of my jealousy have I spoken against
> the residue of the heathen and against all Idumea,
> which have appointed my land into their possession
> with joy in their heart, with despiteful minds, to

cast it out for a prey. Therefore thus saith the Lord God; I have lifted up my hand, Surely the heathen that are about you, they shall bear their shame. But ye, O mountains of Israel, ye shall shoot forth your branches, and yield your fruit to my people of Israel, even all of it; and the cities shall be inhabited.

In verse two, Ezekiel tells us that the Muslims would control the Temple Mount, and as we see today, there are two mosques on the mount instead of the Jewish temple. Also note here Idumea has appointed "my land," God's land. It also tells us they have it there with "despiteful minds." God is not happy about this. He tells us when he has had enough, "In the fire of my jealousy," and that happens in Ezekiel 38:19 when Gog will come against the lands that come against Israel.

Let's also look at what Mr. Roberts, the historian, tells us on pages 329 and 330 of *The New History of the World*:

Muhammad died in the year 632. The Islamic people did not control the Temple Mount until 638. It was controlled by the Byzantine Empire until 638.

That should tell us that Muhammad did not ascend to heaven from the Temple Mount, because the Muslims did not control the area until six years later. This proves the Islamic people have no claim to the temple mount. The Muslim religion from the beginning is packed with lies, just as Satan is the father of all lies.

President Clinton and Ehud Barak of Israel met with Yasser Arafat for the Oslo peace accords. When President Clinton asked Arafat why Bethlehem should be part of the Palestinian state when our Lord was born in that town, Arafat answered, "Because Jesus was a Palestinian." A person who was in the room at the time said Bill Clinton was just stunned and could not comment. Since the signing of the Oslo peace accords, the Palestinian people have not lived up to any of their obligations while the Jews have given back more land for peace. However, they have not received any peace. This is why America comes under some of the judgments from God, for demanding that Israel give away more land for peace. And there will be no peace as long as there is a Palestine. Hamas, Hezbollah, the Muslim Brotherhood, and Al Qaeda have all sworn to the destruction of Israel. And there is not a peace agreement they will agree to. War is coming whether we like it or not. Some day in the near future there will not be a Palestinian state or a Palestinian person.

Ezekiel 39:6 says, "And I will send a fire on Magog, and among them that dwell carelessly in the isles: and they shall know that I am the Lord." And we know that only the bones of these people are left, for in verse 12 it says, "And seven months shall the house of Israel be burying of them, that they may cleanse the land." We should note the words "the house of Israel." This is all of the tribes of Israel and not the Jews of the land of Israel today. After they cleanse the land around Israel, we are told in verse 14:

> And they shall sever out men of continual employment,
> passing through the land to bury with the passengers
> those that remain upon the face of the earth, to cleanse
> it: after the end of seven months shall they search.

After the seven months, they will cleanse the rest of the world. Note the scriptures say here, "Those that remain upon the face of the earth." Those are the meek who inherit the earth.

Most pastors tell us that the plague of Zechariah is nuclear weapons, but when we read the scriptures carefully, we will see that this is the wrath of the Lord. The scriptures say, "The Lord will smite." This matches what Isaiah says in 66:15–16:

> For, behold, the Lord will come with fire, and with
> his chariots like a whirlwind, to render his anger with
> fury, and rebuke with flame of fire. For by fire and by
> his sword will the Lord plead with all flesh: and the
> slain of the Lord shall be many.

This matches the New Testament prophecy in 2 Thessalonians 1:7–8:

And to you who are troubled rest with us, when the Lord Jesus shall be revealed from heaven with his mighty angels. In flaming fire taking vengeance on them that know not God, and that obey not the gospel of our Lord Jesus Christ.

Many preachers teach that there is a coming destruction to America and that Americans will be a part of the last days' events. I believe this will not happen for two reasons. First of all, I don't think God will allow that to happen to a country that supports Israel and is a Christian nation. Remember, God would not destroy Sodom and Gomorrah for just five righteous people. Let's look at the sins of Sodom as described by Ezekiel in 16:49–50

Behold, this was the iniquity of thy sister Sodom, Pride, fullness of bread, and abundance of idleness was in her and in her daughters, neither did she strengthen the hand of the poor and the needy. And they were haughty, and committed abomination before me: therefore I took them away as I saw good.

We should notice that the first thing listed is pride. Is boasting that we are the only superpower in the world pride? Yes. Second, fullness of bread is listed. Americans have more than enough to eat, since too many of the American people are overweight. The third thing mentioned is abundance of idleness, and Americans have more time off from work than any past generation thanks to all the modern conveniences we have today. They do not help the poor and needy. The last thing mentioned is they were haughty and committed abominations before God. Well, we have plenty of that in our country also.

But 1 Peter 4:8 says, "And above all things have fervent charity among yourselves: for charity shall cover the multitude of sins." Thank God for Peter telling us this. We are guilty of all those sins, and I was about to think that America should be destroyed by God. But America is a blessing to most of the world because of our foreign aid programs.

We help many people in impoverished countries. America hands out more aid to other countries in distress than any nation in the world. We send aid even to countries that hate us. Americans were the first to help the many people when the tsunami of 2004 affected many countries of southeast Asia, mostly Muslim countries. Where were the rich Muslim countries? Did they send food and medicine to help those people? The answer is no.

When the twin towers of New York came down, did the people of Palestine celebrate in the streets of Gaza? Do we still send aid to them through the United Nations? What a misnomer the name "United Nations" is. The only thing most of the nations of the world are united about is that they are against the state of Israel and America. Most of the world votes against America and Israel in the general assembly of the United Nations. It is a fact that 181 nations of the 192 nations in the general assembly vote against America and Israel 95 percent of the time. This is backed up in a story by Fox News.

There is also this to be forgiven of sin in James 5:19–20:

> Brethren, if any of you do err from the truth, and one
> converts him; Let him know, that he which converteth
> the sinner from the error of his way shall save a soul
> from death, and shall hide a multitude of sins.

I believe this is for the individual, as well as for the nations. This is America's second hope of forgiveness from God, because we are taking the message of the gospel to the world. The more people we bring to the saving knowledge of our Lord and Savior, the more of our national sin God will hide. People I talk to tell me they have Muslim friends and they hope that their Muslim friends are saved. And I tell them, "I am the truth and the light, nobody comes to the father, but by me," as quoted by the Lord Jesus. If you want to save your Muslim friends, tell them of Jesus Christ who died for all men. Let's note James, which tells us "save a soul from death." The soul without a body is considered a dead soul.

My big problem is with the Christians of America today. Did not our Lord and Savior suffer die on the cross for our sins, and we are so righteous we don't go through a tribulation period. Are we more worthy that this will not happen to us? Are we more worthy than the apostles of our Lord who died and were persecuted for their belief? Are we more worthy than the first-century Christians who were killed for their faith? In 2 Timothy 2:18 it says, "Who concerning the truth have erred, saying that the resurrection is past already; and overthrow the faith of some." Did the early church think they would be taken off the earth before any persecutions began? This message from the Bible tells us that this is just what this church was thinking because they thought that the resurrection of the just had already happened and they were still here.

Revelation 21:23–27 says:

> And the city had no need of the sun, neither of the moon, to shine in it: for the Glory of God did lighten it and the light is the light thereof. And the nations of them which are saved shall walk in the light of it; and the kings of the earth do bring their glory and honor into it.

We should note here that there are nations saved out of the all the plagues from God. The word "saved" is *sozo*,[232] which means to save (i.e., deliver or protect) (literal or figurative), heal, preserve, save, or do well. These are the people protected by God on the planet. This tells us that the countries that don't come against Israel don't receive the wrath from God. When the people of the world see what God does to those nations that come against Israel, there will be this great desire as stated in Revelation 21:27, "And the kings of the earth do bring their glory and honour unto it" and that of Isaiah and Micah speak of: "many people shall go to the mountain of the Lord, and he will teach us his way."

Let's note that both Isaiah and Micah refer to "the mountain of the Lord." That mountain they are referring to is found in Revelation 21:10: "And he carried me away in the spirit to a great and high mountain,

---

[232]   Ibid., 2161.

and shewed me that great city, the holy Jerusalem, descending out from heaven from God." This makes this a literal mountain of the Lord. Let's refer to scripture and note that Micah and Isaiah are exactly the same, except Micah says "many nations" and Isaiah says "many peoples." Many people of many nations will come to this mountain of the Lord, where God will teach the people his ways. The word "last" in the verse is *achariyth*,[233] which means the last or end, hence the future; also posterity (last, latter), end (time, hinder, utter) most, remnant, or reward. Should we notice the word "reward" and the last or end. This happens on the last day or the end. The end comes in Revelation 10:6–7: "There is time no longer, the mystery of God should be finished." These are the ones spoken about by Matthew 16:28, Mark 9:1, and Luke 9:27: "There shall be some standing here, which shall not taste of death, till they see the coming of the Lord."

Let's note Isaiah 2:2–5:

> But in the last days it shall come to pass, that the mountain of the house of the Lord shall be established in the top of the mountains, and it shall be exalted above the hills; and the people shall flow unto it. And many nations shall come, and say, Teach us of his ways, and we will walk in his paths: for the law shall go forth of Zion and the word of the Lord from Jerusalem. And he shall judge among many people, and rebuke strong nations afar off; and they shall beat their swords into plowshares and their spears into pruning hooks: nation shall not lift up sword against nation neither shall they learn war any more. O house of Jacob, come ye, and let us walk in the light of the Lord.

This relates to after the battle of Armageddon, when these people from around the world come to Jerusalem to praise the Lord for protecting them during the battle of Armageddon. Note the language

---

[233] Ibid., 1809.

in Isaiah "in the last days." The last days is when Acts tells us the Lord will pour out the Holy Spirit upon all men. And the "Lord shall judge among the people" are the parables of the wheat among the tares, the just and the unjust, and the sheep and the goats of the New Testament given by Matthew. The equivalent in the Old Testament is Ezekiel 30:20, "I will judge between the fat cattle and the lean cattle," and 20:38, "And I will purge out from among you the rebels, and them that transgress against me."

Note in Isaiah, "O Jacob, come ye and let us walk in the light of the Lord." This is the re-gathering of all the tribes of Israel back to the land that God promised Abraham. The New Testament equivalent is Revelation 21:24: "And the nations of them which are saved shall walk in the light of it [the Lord Jesus Christ]." Note Revelation 22:14: "Blessed are they that do his commandments, that they may have right to the tree of life, and may enter into the city [of God]." For blessed are the meek, for they shall inherit the earth. This is the greater message the church needs to hear, instead of this pre-tribulation resurrection.

Isaiah continues in 2:7–8:

> Their land also is full of silver and gold, neither is there any end of their treasures; their land is also full of horses, neither is there any end of their chariots; Their land is also is full of idols; they worship the work of their own hands, that which their own fingers have made.

Is America the richest country in the world today, "their land is full of silver and gold"? I believe Isaiah describes America to the tee when he says, "Neither is there any end of their chariots," for Americans have more cars per person than any country in the world. Americans live better than most of the world today, and all they do is gripe. This is why most of the world hates us, because we are the most blessed people on the planet. Our status as the only superpower and world leader in the world makes them look like second-class powers to the rest of the world.

Spain was a superpower at one time; so were the French, during the time of Napoleon Bonaparte; so were the Germans, during the early days of the Holy Roman Empire. And so were the people of England from the 1600s until now. Is that why they are against us now? They would like to be known as the world's superpower. America's role in the world has always been to bring justice and freedom to the world, not to be conquers of nations.

We should notice that when the first four trumpet judgments of Revelation are given, that will only affect a third part of the world. That third part of the world is wherever Satan and his followers are.

I also base this on Romans 1:8, "First, I thank my God through Jesus Christ for you all, that your faith is spoken of throughout the whole world." As we know today, the whole earth is more than what was known in Paul's day. This is why I think America and the rest of the world where the house of Israel are at the time of the tribulation period do not come under the wrath of God.

Now let's note verses 4 and 5 of Isaiah 64: "For since the beginning of the world men have not heard, nor perceived by the ear, neither hath the eye seen, O God, besides thee, what he hath prepared for him that waiteth for him." The meek who inherit the earth are those who have waited for him. This should tell us that the earth be all new. Isaiah 65:17 says, "For, behold, I create a new heavens and a new earth: and the former shall not be remembered, nor come into mind."

> Thou meetess [*paga*,[234] which means to impinge, make intercession, intercessor] him [Lord Jesus] that rejoiceth and worketh righteousness, those that remember thee in thy ways: behold, thou are wroth [*qatsaph*,[235] which means to crack off (i.e., figurative), burst out in rage, wrath]; for we have sinned: in those is continuance [*owlam*,[236] which means properly concealed (i.e., vanishing point), eternity], and we

---

[234] Ibid., 1944.

[235] Ibid., 1963.

[236] Ibid., 1933.

shall be saved [*yasha*,[237] which means to be safe, defend, deliver] (Isa. 64:5).

This tells us that the Lord Jesus will make intercession for those who rejoice and work in righteousness. He does this at the time of God's wrath. Those who the Lord makes intercession for will live for all eternity. This also matches Zephaniah 2:3: "Seek ye the Lord, all ye meek of the earth, which have wrought his judgments; seek righteousness, seek meekness: it may be ye shall be hid in the day of the Lord's anger." Wrought is *paal*,[238] which means to do or make, especially to practice; commit, ordain, work. We are instructed to do the work (ordain work) of God in his judgments and we will be hid in the days of the Lord's wrath. Note here it says "seek meekness."

The New Testament tells us, "Blessed are the meek, for they shall inherit the earth." This is what the pre-tribulation pastors don't understand. This is why Revelation 21:7 says, "He that overcometh shall inherit all things, and I will be his God, and he shall be my son." The church is to overcome, to fight the wiles of the devil. The church will have this power given by the Holy Spirit.

This is what faith is all about. And as it usually is with God, there are conditions. Revelation 21:8 tells us:

> But the fearful, and unbelieving, and the abominable, and murderers, and whoremongers, and sorcerers, and idolaters, and all liars, shall have their part in the lake of fire which burneth with fire and brimstone: which is the second death.

So if you are fearful that you cannot overcome all the judgments in the book of Revelation because of unbelief, you will have your part in the lake of fire. This should be the message pastors should be teaching. This should be the goal of every Christian—to overcome and become one of these people to inherit the earth.

---

[237] Ibid., 1879.
[238] Ibid., 1948.

Scripture That Proves There Is No Pre-Tribulation Resurrection

IF THERE WAS A pre-tribulation resurrection, then the next set of verses would not need to have been written. Scripture proves that the church goes through the judgments of God, and as stated in scripture, "So we can be counted worthy to enter the kingdom of God." We should also note throughout the book of Revelation, there are those who "have the testimony of Jesus." The word for testimony is *marturia*,[239] which means evidence given (judicially or generic), record, report, testimony, witness. It is from *martus*,[240] of uncertain affinity; a witness (literal [judicially] or figurative [genitive]); by analogy a martyr; martyr, record witness.

This is when the Lord will send the Holy Spirit to help his saints. Matthew 12:31 says, "Wherefore I say unto you All manner of sin and blasphemy shall be forgiven unto men: but the blasphemy against the Holy Ghost shall not be forgiven unto men." To reject this from God is the unpardonable sin. I think we will know when the Holy Spirit comes in us. In Luke 24, when the risen Lord was revealed to the disciples, this is what the scripture says. Verses 31–32 say:

---

[239] Ibid., 2111.
[240] Ibid.

And their eyes were opened, and they knew him; and he vanished out of their sight. And they said to one another, Did not our hearth burn within us, while he talked with us by the way, and while he opened to us the scriptures?

This same burning is recorded in Jeremiah 20:9, "But his word was in mine heart as a burning fire shut up in my bones." I would expect this same burning spirit in the tribulation period be given to the saints, or to the church.

Let's read Matthew 24:21–22:

For then shall be great tribulation, such as was not since the beginning of the world to this time, no, nor shall ever be. And except those days be shortened, there should no flesh be saved: but for the elect's sake those days should be shortened.

The elect is *eklektos*,[241] which means select, by implication favorite, chosen, elect. If the days are shortened for the elect, they would have to be on the planet. These shortened days are given to us in the Old Testament. Malachi 4:5 says, "Behold, I will send you Elijah the prophet before the great and dreadful day of the Lord." The word for great is *gadowl*,[242] which means shortened. It is from the word *gadal*, which means properly to twist (i.e., to be [causative make] large [in various senses]), as in body, mind, estate, or honor, also in pride. Even in the Old Testament, we are told that the days would be shortened, and the prophet will be on the planet before the Day of the Lord.

What does James, the brother of the Lord, tell us? James 1:2–4 says:

My brethren count it all joy when ye fall into divers temptations; Knowing this, that the trying of your

---

[241] Ibid., 2066.
[242] Ibid., 1831.

faith worketh patience. But let patience have her perfect work, that ye may be perfect and entire, wanting nothing.

Throughout the book of Revelation, it is stated, "Here is the patience and the faith of the saints." If the saints are to have patience, why are we told here they are still on the planet if there was a pre-tribulation rapture? James continues in verse 12 to tell us: "Blessed is the man that endureth temptation: for when he is tried, he shall receive the crown of life, which the Lord hath promised to them that love him." James tells us, "When man is tried." Our faith is going to be tried during the tribulation period, and after we are tried, if we have the patience and the faith to overcome until the end, we will receive the "crown of life."

The word "blessed" is *makarious*,[243] which means supremely bless, by extension fortunate, well off; blessed, happy (-ier). The word "endureth" is *hupomeno*,[244] which means to stay under (behind) (i.e., remain; figurative to undergo, i.e., bear [trials]), have fortitude, preserve, abide, endure, (take) patient (-ly), suffer, tarry behind. We should note the words "to stay behind". The word for "temptation" is *peirasmos*,[245] which means a putting to proof (by experiment [of good], experiment [of evil], solicitation, discipline or provocation) by implication adversity, temptation.

This is a crown every true Christian should hope for. We would not receive this crown if there was a pre-tribulation resurrection. I think it is important to note that James states in verse 1, "James, a servant of God and of the Lord Jesus Christ, to the twelve tribes which are scattered abroad, greeting." James acknowledges that the twelve tribes are scattered throughout the world. I will start with the book of Revelation because I think we should carefully study what John really says.

Revelation 13:7–8 says:

---

243   Ibid., 2110.
244   Ibid., 2170.
245   Ibid., 2133.

And it was given unto him to make war with the saints, and to overcome them: and power was given him over all kindreds, and tongues, and nations.

Stop here! Now comes the verse that proves not everybody is overcome.

And all that dwell upon the earth shall worship him, whose names are not written in the book of life of the lamb slain from the foundation of the world.

This tells us that there are people who will not worship the beast, because their names are written in the Lamb's Book of Life (the church), and they are still on the planet. Their names are written in the Lamb's Book of Life before the foundation of the world. They are the angels God made human spirits on this earth who did not rebel against God. If Satan is to make war with the saints (sanctified ones), they would have to be on the planet to war with them. Verse 9 says, "If any man have an ear, let him hear." Let's check the Greek word for hear. It is the word *akouo*, which means to hear (in various senses), be reported, understand (*Strong's* 2017). This tells us the pre-tribulation teachers are deaf, and as Isaiah states, "dumb dogs." Let us note what is told to us in this next verse.

Second Timothy 2:26 says, "And that they recover themselves out of the snare [*pagis*,[246] which means trap] of the devil, who are taken captive [*zogreo*,[247] which means to take alive (make a prisoner of war), (i.e., figurative) to capture or ensnare] by him at his will." This is another example of scripture that tells us the church is on the planet when the devil makes his appearance. This warning is to the church.

Zechariah 12:7–9 says:

The Lord also shall save the tents of Judah first, that the glory of the house of David and the glory of the

---

[246] Ibid., 2127.

[247] Ibid., 2084.

inhabitants of Jerusalem do not magnify themselves against Judah. In that day shall the Lord defend the inhabitants of Jerusalem; and he that is feeble among them at that day shall be as David; and the house of David shall be as God, as the angel of the Lord before them. And it shall come to pass in that day, that I will seek to destroy all the nations that come against Jerusalem.

Zechariah tells us that the Lord saves the tents of Judah first. What part of "first" do we not understand? We should also note that Zechariah tells us that the "angel of the Lord is before them," just as Daniel tells us, "And at that time Michael stand up, the great prince which standeth for the children of thy people." We should also note that God says here that he will seek to destroy all nations that come against Jerusalem. So if America stands with Israel, we will not receive the wrath of God. We should note the house of David shall be as God. How will they be as God? This is told us in 2:7–9:

They shall run like mighty men; they shall climb the wall like men of war; and they shall march every one on his ways, and they shall not break their ranks. Neither shall one thrust another; they shall walk every one in his path: and when they fall upon the sword, they shall not be wounded. They shall run to and fro in the city; they shall run upon the wall, they shall climb upon the houses; they shall enter in at the window like a thief.

Look what this verse says: "When they fall upon the sword, they shall not be wounded." This is just as Daniel tells us in 11:34, "Now when they shall fall, they shall be holpen with a little help." "Holpen" is *azar*,[248] which means a primitive root; to surround (i.e., protect or aid). Isaiah tells us in 54:17, "No weapon that is formed against thee

---

[248]   Ibid., 1934.

shall prosper; and every tongue that shall rise against thee in judgment thou shall condemn. This is the heritage of the servants of the Lord, and their righteousness is of me, says the Lord." Just as the church, so are all of the tribes of the house of Israel, including the Jews; their righteousness is of the Lord. Just as the church questions, "Where is the promise of his coming?" the Jews in the land of Israel will do the same. Here is the response of the Lord as the prophet Joel tells us in 2:12–23:

> Therefore also now, saith the Lord, turn ye even to me with all your heart, and with fasting, and with weeping, and with mourning: And rend your heart, and not your garments, and turn unto the Lord thy God: for he is gracious and merciful, slow to anger, and with great kindness, and repenteth him of this evil.

We should note here that this message given by Joel about "ye turn to me with all your heart, and with fasting" is the same message given to the church in Mark 12:30. The Lord says, "And thou shalt love the Lord thy God with all thy soul, and with all thy mind, and with all thy strength: this is the first commandment." And how is this done? Mark 9:29 says, "This kind can come forth by nothing but by prayer and fasting." We should always note in scripture that when prayer is mentioned, fasting is attached. Now let us continue in Joel.

> Who knoweth if he will return and repent, and leave a blessing behind him; even a meat-offering and a drink-offering unto the Lord your God? Blow a trumpet in Zion, sanctify a fast, call a solemn assembly: Gather the people, sanctify the congregation, assemble the elders, gather the children, and those that suck the breast: let the bridegroom [the Lord Jesus; *chathan*,[249] which means a relative by marriage] go forth of his

---

[249]   Ibid., 1866.

chamber [the throne room], and the bride [the church, and all the tribes of Israel. Also *kallah*,[250] which means a bride (as if perfect); hence the son's wife.] out of her closet. Let the priest, the ministers of the Lord, weep between the porch and the altar, and let them say, Spare thy people, O Lord, and give not thy heritage to reproach, that the heathen should rule over them: wherefore should they say among the people, Where is their God?

These scriptures in verse 17 tells us these people are greatly distressed that the heathen should rule over them. We should note that there is the question, "Where is their God?" And the church is given the same message.

Second Peter 3:3–4 says:

Knowing this first, that there shall come in the last days scoffers [*empaiktes*,[251] which means a derider (i.e., by implication) a false teacher. From the word *empaizo*, which means to jeer at. *Webster's Dictionary* meaning of derider is, "To laugh at contemptuously, to subject to ridicule.], walking after their own lust, And saying, Where is the promise of his coming?

Now back to Joel, starting with verse 19.

Then will the Lord be jealous for his land, and pity his people. Yea, the Lord will answer and say unto his people, Behold, I will send you corn, and wine, and oil, and ye shall be satisfied therewith: and I will no more make you a reproach among the heathen. But I will remove far off from you the northern army, and drive him into a land barren and desolated, with his

---

[250]   Ibid., 1883.
[251]   Ibid., 2069.

face toward the east sea, and his hinder part toward
the utmost sea, and his stink shall come up, and his
ill savour shall come up, because he hath done great
things.

We should note that God gets jealous for his land, when the
northern army (Gog) invades Israel, and God promises to remove them
far off. This is precept to Ezekiel 38:19, "For in my jealousy and in
the fire of my wrath" and Ezekiel 39:2: "And I will turn thee back,
and leave but the sixth part of thee." As God destroys this army, God
is going to provide for their needs by supplying the corn, wine, and
oil. Let us note the *Webster's Dictionary* meaning of the word "corn":
"a small hard seed, and in the New World and Australia Indian corn."
Joel, who wrote his scriptures in the ninth or eighth century, spoke
of corn over two thousand years before it was discovered in America.
Note that Joel says "He [God] hath done great things." This is why I
say the great tribulation is the wrath of God. This is the precept upon
precept, line upon line, here-a-little-there-a-little study Isaiah 28:13
told us to do. Now let's finish.

Fear not, O land; be glad and rejoice: for the Lord will
do great things. Be not afraid, ye beast of the field: for
the pastures of the wilderness do spring, for the tree
beareth the fruit, the fig tree and the vine do yield
their strength. Be glad then, ye children of Zion, and
rejoice in the Lord your God: for he hath given you
the former rain moderately, and he will cause to come
down for you the rain, and the latter rain in the first
month.

Joel tells us "fear not" and "be not afraid" here that God is going to
protect the land, the beast of the field, and the children of Zion. And
once again the Lord will do great things. And in the next verse Joel tells
us when this happens. God tells us again that he controls the weather.

In verse 27, Joel tells us, "And ye shall know that I am in the midst
of Israel, and that I am the Lord your God, and none else: and my

people shall never be ashamed." Midst is *qereb*,[252] which means properly the nearest part (i.e., the center, e.g., center of a battle). This tells us that God will be in clouds in the middle of the tribulation period and do great things. And when is that middle? Matthew 25:29–30 says, "Immediately after the tribulation [and the start of the great tribulation] those days shall the sun be darken and the moon shall not give her light, and then shall the Son of Man appear in heaven." This is because God shortens the days for his elect, the meek who inherit the earth.

Romans 1:16–18 tells us:

> For I am not ashamed of the gospel of Christ: for it is the power of God unto salvation to every one that believeth; to the Jew first, and also the Greek. For therein is the righteousness of God revealed from faith to faith: as it is written, The just shall live by faith. For the wrath of God is revealed from heaven against all ungodliness and unrighteousness of men, who hold the truth in unrighteousness.

Why would not the Lord save the Jews of Judah first, since he was born of the house of Judah? We should also note that we are to live by faith, until the wrath of God is revealed. The wrath of God is revealed in Ezekiel 38:19, "For in jealousy and in the fire of my wrath have I spoken, Surely in that day shall be a great shaking in the land of Israel." In the New Testament, it's 2 Thessalonians 1:7–8: "When the Lord Jesus is revealed from heaven, In flaming fire taking vengeance on them that know not God." We should also note that it tells us here that the wrath of God is against all ungodliness and unrighteousness of men. So if you are a righteous man, the wrath of God will not affect you. This is just another mistake by the pre-tribulation resurrection preachers who say that is why the church is resurrected up because of how bad it will be on the planet.

We know Paul is writing to the church because he tells us in verse 7, "To all that be in Rome, beloved of God, called to be saints: Grace

---

[252] Ibid., 1963.

to you and peace from God our Father, and the Lord Jesus Christ." We need to realize the church is not found guiltless and must go through the judgments of God. They must repent, and if they do, they won't receive the wrath of God. No matter how good you are, the Bible tells us in Romans 2:11 that with God, "There is no respect of persons." Paul goes on to tell us that we have no excuse not to understand in verses 19 and 20: "Because that which may be known of God is manifest in them; for God hath shewed it unto them. For the visible things of him from the creation of the world are clearly seen, being understood by the things that are made, even his eternal power and Godhead; so they are without excuse."

First Peter 4:13–19 says:

> Beloved, think it not strange concerning the fiery trail which is to try you, as though some strange things happen unto you: but rejoice, inasmuch as ye are partakers of Christ sufferings; that when his glory is revealed, ye may be glad also with exceeding joy. Yet if any man suffer as a Christian, let him not be ashamed; but let him glorify God on his behalf For the time has come judgment must begin with the house of God; and if it first begins at us, what shall the end be of them that obey not the gospel of God? And if the righteous scarcely be saved, where shall the ungodly and the sinner appear? Wherefore let them suffer according to the will of God commit the keeping of their souls to him that well doing, as unto a faithful Creator.

We see here that the judgment must begin with the "House of God," and what is the house of God but his church? And if "any man suffer as a Christian" tells us there is no pre-tribulation resurrection. If the "righteous scarcely be saved," does this not tell us that it is at the last moment or better said "the last day," as stated in John 6:29, 40, 44, 54? The *Webster's Dictionary* meaning of scarce is "not plentiful; deficient;

wanting." The word "scarcely" is *molis*,[253] which means with difficulty, hardly, scare (-ly), and with much work. This should tell the church that it must go through some tough times ahead.

This is why I put in this manuscript the verses in Ezekiel when the judgments of God came upon the house of Judah. God started with the temple. Twenty-five hundred years later, the Lord God has not changed his mind.

Let us also note that it says here, "When his glory is revealed." His glory is revealed in 2 Thessalonians 1:6-8: "Seeing it is a righteous thing with God to recompense tribulation to them that trouble you; And to you who are troubled rest with us, when the Lord Jesus shall be revealed from heaven with his mighty angels, In flaming fire taking vengeance of them that know not God, and that obey not the gospel of our Lord Jesus Christ." Who is the you? It is the church.

The Lord Jesus is going to recompense (which means give the same treatment) on them that trouble you (the church), and this is the righteous with God. There is no promise of a pre-tribulation resurrection. Someone needs to tell the congregations at the pre-tribulation resurrection churches, such as John Hagee, Tim LaHaye, Jerry Jenkins, and Jack Van Impe, to unpack their bags, because they are not going up to heaven in a pre-tribulation resurrection.

This is just as the judgments of the house of Judah, where it is stated that the judgments began at the temple. Here is the verse in Ezekiel 9: "Slay utterly old and young, both maids and little children, and women: but come not near any man upon whom is the mark; and begin at my sanctuary."

And we read in Revelation 9:4, "But only those men which have not the seal of God in their foreheads." So we are in the fifth trumpet judgment, and there are men who have the seal of God in their foreheads. Let us note Isaiah 41:22, "Let them bring them forth, and shew us what shall happen: Let them shew the former things, what they be, that we may consider them, and know the latter end of them; or declare us things for to come." Isaiah tells us to look to the scriptures to see how God acted in the past to know the latter end. Just as God

---

[253]   Ibid., 2116.

put a mark on his people in Ezekiel, God will put a mark on his people in the book of Revelation.

First Peter 5:10 says:

> But the God of grace, who hath called us unto his eternal glory by Christ Jesus, after that ye suffered a while, make you perfect, establish, strength, settle you.

Peter tells us here that the judgments begin with the "house of God." Is not the church the house of God? We should note that it says here, "After ye suffer." Suffered is *pascho*,[254] which means to experience a sensation or impression (unusually painful); feel, passion, suffer, vex. This is to "make you perfect." The word for perfect is *katartizo*,[255] which means to complete thoroughly (i.e., literal or figurative) or adjust; fit, frame, mend, (make) perfect (-ly), join together, prepare, restore. And to "stablish you" is *sterizo*,[256] which means to set fast (i.e., literal), to turn resolutely in a certain direction, or (figurative) to confirm; fix, (e-) stablish, steadfastly set, strengthen. To "strengthen" is *sthenoo*,[257] which means to strengthen (i.e., figurative) confirm (in spiritual knowledge and power); strengthen. To "settle" is *themelioo*,[258] which means to lay a basis (i.e., literally erect, or figuratively consolidate); (lay the) found (-ation), ground, settle. Those are the reasons man goes through the judgments of God. The scriptures tell us by these Greek words "to turn resolutely in a certain direction, strengthen." This is the same message Paul gave to the Corinthian Church in 15:36 where he told us the dead are raised and the living are strengthened. The spiritual knowledge is the Holy Spirit that the Lord pours out in Acts 2. When the pre-tribulation resurrection pastors use 1 Thessalonians 4:16 to

---

254   Ibid., 2130.
255   Ibid., 2098.
256   Ibid., 2154.
257   Ibid., 2151.
258   Ibid., 2087.

teach the resurrection of the church, they fail to use chapter 3, which states in 1 Thessalonians 3:3–5, 16:

> That no man should be moved by these afflictions: for yourselves know that we are appointed there unto. For verily, when we were with you, we told you before that we should suffer tribulation; even as it came to pass, and ye know. For this cause, when I could no longer forbear, I sent to know your faith, lest by some means the tempter have tempted you, and our labour be in vain . . . To the end he may stablish your hearts unblameable in holiness before God, even our father, at the coming of our Lord Jesus Christ with all of his saints.

Paul is warning the church that they will go through and suffer in tribulation, and he tells them that this will come to pass. He even states here that we are appointed unto these afflictions. He was asking the church if their faith in the Lord was helping them to bear it. Paul was worried that all his preaching to them was in vain if their faith was failing them. And how long was their faith to last? To the end and the coming of our Lord. The Lord's coming is not until after the great tribulation of those when the sun and the moon don't give their light. Will the twenty-first-century church lose its faith if there is not a pre-tribulation resurrection?

So let's check out the parable of the sower and the soils. This is Mark 4:15–20:

> And these are they [the Christians] by the way side, where the word is sown; but when they have heard, Satan cometh immediately, and taketh away the word [of God] that was sown in their hearts. And these are they likewise which are sown on stony ground; who, when they heard the word, immediately received it with gladness; And have no root in themselves, so they endure but for a time [he that endure till the time of

the end he shall be saved]; afterward when affliction or persecution ariseth [the tribulation period of the book or Revelation] for the word's sake, immediately they are offended [offended is *skandalizo*,[259] which means to entrap (i.e., trip up, figurative stumble [transitive] to entice to sin, apostasy or displeasure.)].

And these are they which are sown among thorns; such as hear the word, And the cares of this world, and the deceitfulness of riches [take the mark of the beast] and the lust of other things come in, choke the word [God's Word], and become unfruitful. And these are they which are sown on good ground; such as hear the word, and receive it, and bring forth fruit [bring people to the Lord]. Some thirtyfold, some sixty, and some an hundred.

The church has a big mission during the tribulation. They are to be the light to the world. Are you in the good ground (or a good church) so that you will bring forth fruit so when Satan comes you will endure? We are to have roots deep enough so that when affliction and persecutions arise, we endure. Jesus gives us this parable to warn the church this is going to happen to the church. If there is a pre-tribulation resurrection, then rip this passage out of your Bible.

Let us note a few passages in the Bible that tell us we are to endure until the end. The end is not in Revelation 4.

Then cometh the end, when he shall delivered up the kingdom to God, even the father; When he shall put down all rule and all authority and power (1 Cor. 15:24).

_____

[259] Ibid.,

> But Christ as a son over his own house; whose house are we, if we hold fast the confidence and the rejoicing of the hope firm unto the end (Heb. 3:6).

> For we are made partakers of Christ, if we hold the beginning of our confidence steadfast unto the end (Heb. 3:14).

> And we desire that every one of you shew the same diligence to the full assurance of hope unto the end (Heb. 6:11).

> And ye shall be hated of all men for my name's sake: but he that endureth to the end shall be saved (Matt. 10:22).

> But he that shall endure unto the end, the same shall be saved (Matt. 24:33).

We should note that the end does not come until the seven thunders utter their voices, which John was told not to write, and this is where scripture tells us, "That there should be time no longer, The end." The end generally is *telos*,[260] which means (to set out for a definite point or goal); properly the point aimed at as a limit (i.e., by implication), the conclusion of an act or state (termination [literal, figurative, or indefinite], result [immediate, ultimate, or prophetic], purpose), especially an impost or levy (as paid); continual, custom, end(-ing), finally, uttermost. The word "endureth" generally is *hupomeno*,[261] which means to stay under (behind) (i.e., remain); figurative to undergo (i.e., bear [trials]), have fortitude, persevere, abide, endure, (take) patient(-ly), suffer, tarry behind.

Scripture tells us to stay behind, bear the trials, and have fortitude. Until when? Until the conclusion of an act. The conclusion of an act is

---

260   Ibid., 2163.
261   Ibid., 2170.

given in the next scripture. Verse 7 says, "But in the days of the voice of the seventh angel, when he shall begin to sound, the mystery of God should be finished, as he hath declared to his servants the prophets." We should note here that it is in the "days" of the voice of the seventh angel that the mystery of God should be finished. "Finished" is *teleo*,[262] which means to end (i.e., complete, execute, conclude, discharge [a debt]); accomplish, make an end. This is just the opposite of what the pre-tribulation pastors teach.

This is given to the church in Romans 2:5–6: "The day of wrath is the righteousness judgments of God according to his deeds." The end came to the house of Judah at the time of the wrath of God, and when it came to an end, Ezekiel 7:14 says, "They have blown the trumpet, even to make all ready; but none goeth to the battle: for my wrath is upon all the multitude thereof." We should note that the trumpet is not blown until "the end," just before the wrath of God. In Revelation, there is a trumpet to announce an end. We should also note Ezekiel 9:4, "Set a mark upon the forehead of the men that sign and that cry for all the abominations that are done in the midst thereof." The past reveals the future. Let us note Revelation 17:8: "And they that dwell on the earth shall wonder, whose names were not written in the book of life from the foundation of the world." This tells us there are names written in the book of life that dwell on the earth.

Luke 18:7 says, "And shall not God avenge his own elect, which cry day and night unto him, through he bear long with them." In Ezekiel's day, God set a mark upon the forehead, and this is given in Revelation 22:4: "And they shall see his face; and his name shall be in their foreheads." These are the meek who inherit the earth. What the Lord has done in the past should be a sign to us of what he will do in the future. Before we leave this, let's read this. Ezekiel 2:19 says, "They shall cast their silver in the street, and their gold shall be removed: their silver and their gold shall not be able to deliver them in the day of the wrath of the God: they shall not satisfy their souls, neither fill their bowels: because it is the stumbling block of their iniquity." James 5:3 says, "Your gold and silver is cankered; and the rust of them shall be

---

262   Ibid., 2163.

a witness against you, and shall eat your flesh as it were fire. Ye have heaped treasure together for the last days." Once again, the future is revealed in the past.

Let us note that Paul wrote in 2 Thessalonians 1:3–4:

> We are bound to thank God always for you, brethren, as it is meet, because that your faith growth exceedingly, and the charity of every one of you all toward each other abounded. So that we ourselves glory in you in the churches of God for your patience and faith in all your persecutions and tribulations that ye endure.

Paul was thanking God that this church was growing in its faith. How did Paul know this? It was by the charity they had one another and that they had patience and kept the faith in the Lord during persecutions and tribulations they endured. The Lord is going to expect the same kind of faith in the twenty-first-century church. Let's continue in this letter with verses 5–8:

> Which is a manifest token of the righteous judgment of God, that ye may be counted worthy of the kingdom of God, for which ye also suffer: Seeing it is a righteous thing with God to recompense tribulation to them that trouble you; And to you who are troubled rest with us, when the Lord Jesus shall be revealed from heaven with his mighty angels, In flaming fire taking vengeance on them that know not God, and that obey not the gospel of our Lord Jesus Christ.

Paul tells us here that the churches of God go through the judgments of God, so they are counted worthy of the kingdom of God and that God will recompense (which means to pay back with the same treatment) those who put the church in tribulation. We should note that Luke writes in Acts 14:21, "Confirming the souls of the disciples and exhorting them to continue in the faith, and that we must through much tribulation enter into the kingdom of God." If the first-century church must go through tribulation to enter the kingdom of heaven, then the twenty-first-century church must go through the tribulation to enter the kingdom of heaven. The only difference in the twenty-first century is, "Blessed are the meek; for they shall inherit the earth." These are those who don't taste death.

Paul goes on to tell the church that the Lord will be revealed from heaven when he comes in a flaming fire, taking vengeance on them who know not God. In the first letter, he tells the Thessalonian church when the Lord shall descend from heaven. The second letter tells them when it happens. This same language is used in Isaiah 26:21, "For behold, the Lord cometh out of his place to punish the inhabitants of the earth for their iniquity" (them who do not obey the gospel of our Lord Jesus Christ).

Also note Isaiah 30:27–28, 30:

> Behold, the name of the Lord cometh from afar, burning in his anger, and the burden thereof is heavy: his lips are full of indignation, and his tongue as a devouring fire. And his breath, as an overflowing stream, shall reach to the midst of the neck, to sift the nations with the sieve of vanity: and there shall be bridle in the jaws of the people, causing them to err. And the Lord shall cause his glorious voice to be heard [come up hither], and shall shew the lighting down his arm, with the indignation of his anger, and with the flame of a devouring fire, with scattering, and tempest, and hailstones.

When the Old Testament matches the New Testament, it's a pretty good assumption it means the same thing. Isaiah says the Lord comes as a devouring fire and 2 Thessalonians tells us as a flaming fire. This should tell anyone who can read that the Lord will not be revealed from heaven until his wrath. This is another mistake of the pre-tribulation teachers.

Second Thessalonians 2:7 says, "For the mystery of iniquity doth already work: for only he who now letteth will let, until he be taken out of the way." The "he that now letteth will let, until he be taken out of the way" is not the church, because in the time of Job, there was a restrainer called the hedge that kept Job from the wrath of Satan. In the time of the judges of Israel, when they did right in the sight of the Lord, they lived in peace and safety surrounded by their enemies and in the time of the two kingdoms, but that hedge was taken away from the northern kingdom first. Isaiah 4:5 says, "And now go to; I will tell you what I will do to my vineyard [Israel]: I [God] will take away my hedge thereof, and it shall be eaten up; and break down the wall thereof, and it shall be trodden down."

To find the true "he that letteth will let," let's read Daniel 10:13, "But the prince of the kingdom of Persia withstood me one and twenty days: but, lo, Michael, one of the chief princes, came to help me: and I remained there with the Kings of Persia." The word for remained is *yathar*,[263] which means to jut over or exceed; by implication to excel; (intransitive) to remain or be left; causative to leave, cause to abound, preserve, let. The *Webster's Dictionary* meaning of the word "jut" is "something that juts: protection."

Daniel 10:21 says, "But I will shew thee that which is noted in the scriptures of truth: and there is none that holdeth with me in these things, but Michael your prince." The word "holdeth" is *chazaq*,[264] which means to fasten upon; hence to seize, obstinate, to bind, restrain, conquer. It is Michael the archangel that restrains Satan and not the church. We have this in Jude 1:9: "Yet Michael the archangel, when contending with the devil he disputed about the body of Moses, durst not bring against him a railing accusation, but said, The Lord rebuke thee." So the person who is the "he that letteth will let" is Michael the archangel and not the church.

Notice that Paul has the same problem with the Corinthian church. In the first letter, he writes this about the mystery of the resurrection in 15:51–52:

---

[263] Ibid., 1880.
[264] Ibid., 1853.

> Behold, I shew you a mystery; We shall not all sleep,
> but we shall all be changed, In a moment, in the
> twinkling of an eye, at the last trump: for the trumpet
> shall sound, and the dead shall be raised incorruptible,
> and we shall all be changed.

And Paul has to write a second letter to them, and he tells them in 2 Corinthians 1:4–5, "Who comforteth us in all our tribulations, that we may be able to comfort them which are wherewith we ourselves are comforted of God." "Comforteth" is the word *paraklesis*,[265] which means imploration, exhortation, from *parakaleo*,[266] to call near (i.e., invite). Note the Greek word meaning "to call near." The Lord is near when he descends from heaven and appears in the heaven in Matthew 24:30. We are to comfort other people during the tribulation period, and God will comfort the church. So does God neglect to hear our cries during the tribulation period? Yes. Note the Greek word meaning "to call near." It is during the tribulation period that this happens. To all the churches in Asia this is given: "He that hath ear, let him hear what the Spirit saith unto the churches." And they are to hear that they are to overcome.

First John 4:17–18 says:

> Herein is our love made perfect, that we may have
> boldness in the day of judgment: because as he is, so
> are we in this world. There is no fear in love; but perfect
> love casteth out fear: because fear hath torment. He
> that feareth is not made perfect in love.

First John tells us that our love for God is made perfect in the "day of Judgment" and "perfect love casts out fear." Let us note again 1 John 4:17 tells us "in the day of judgment" is when Peter tells us in 1 Peter 4:17, "For the time is come that judgment must begin at the house of God." It does tell us that the judgments of the tribulation should not

---

265 Ibid., 2129.
266 Ibid.

be feared by the church. The word for boldness is *parrhesia*,[267] which means all outspokenness (i.e., frankness, bluntness), publicity; by implication assurance. This is because he says, "We are in the world." The period of the tribulation is to test the church. Are you who you say you are? This is a time when the church is tested. Do you really trust in God?

Luke 18:1–8 says:

> And he spake a parable unto them to this end, that men ought always to pay, and not to faint; Saying, There was in a city a judge, which feared not God, neither regarded man: And there was a widow in that city; and she came unto him, saying avenge me of my adversary. And he would not for awhile: but afterward he said within himself, Though I fear not God, nor regard man; Yet because this widow troubleth me, I will avenge her, lest by her continual coming she weary me. And the Lord said, Hear what the unjust judge saith. And shall not God avenge his own elect, which cry day and night unto him, though he bear long with them? I tell you that he will avenge them speedily. Nevertheless when the Son of Man cometh, shall he find faith on the earth.

First of all, this is an unjust judge who fears not God, nor regards man. This speaks only of one person—the Antichrist. This is the same language used by Daniel 11:37 to describe the Antichrist. The widow in that city is without a husband (as in without Christ). These are the Muslims. They want the Antichrist to avenge them, but they continually ask for revenge, and he does it. Our Lord said this is what the unjust judge tells them. When there is much tribulation (which cry day and night), he (God) will avenge them speedily when the Son of Man comes. Then the Lord questions if he will find faith on the earth. It's when he comes that God will find faith on the earth.

---

[267] Ibid., 2131.

The general word for cometh is the word *erchomai*,[268] which means to come or go, appear. His appearing is immediately after the tribulation of those days when the sun and the moon shall not give their light. Then shall appear the Son of Man in heaven. The word "bear" here is *makrothumeo*,[269] which means to be long-spirited (i.e., forbearing, patient, endure). The Lord is having patience until the time he can return. His church is to have the same patience and to endure. Other scriptures tell us when the Lord will avenge them speedily. The word "speedily" is *tachos*,[270] which means a brief space (of time), in haste To preach the pre-tribulation resurrection theory, most pastors say "the elect" is not a reference to the church, but here it says, "God avenge his own elect." This and other scriptures will prove that the elect is the church. Let's also note Luke 17:22, 29–30, which says:

> And he [the Lord Jesus] said unto his disciples, The days will come, when ye shall desire to see one of the days of the Son of Man, and ye shall not see it. But the same day that Lot went out of Sodom it rained fire and brimstone from heaven, and destroyed them all. Even thus shall it be when the Son of Man is revealed.

Is that desired day the resurrection of the church because there is so much tribulation on the earth? The Lord Jesus tells us here, "Ye shall not see it." The same day Lot went out of Sodom God's judgment happened. We know when God rains down fire and brimstone, and that is in Ezekiel 38:22. It's on those who come against Israel in the battle of Armageddon. And this is when the Lord shall be revealed from heaven. "Revealed" here is *apokalupto*,[271] which means to take off the cover (i.e., disclose). And that cover is found in Isaiah 60:1–2: "Arise, shine; for thy light is come, and the glory of the Lord is risen

---

[268] Ibid., 2079.

[269] Ibid., 2110.

[270] Ibid., 2162.

[271] Ibid., 2030.

upon thee. For, Behold, the darkness shall cover the earth, and gross darkness the people: but the Lord God shall arise upon thee, and his glory shall be seen upon thee." We should note that it is not until the "darkness shall cover the earth" that the "Lord God shall arise upon thee." And Luke tells us when the Lord shall be revealed there is fire and brimstone. Ezekiel tells us in 38:20, "all men that are upon the face of the earth shall shake at my presence" and 38:22 tells us what happens: "I will rain upon him, and upon his bands, and upon the many people that are with him, an overflowing rain, and great hailstones, fire, and brimstones." This "gross darkness" of Isaiah 60:2 will match Matthew 24:29–30:

> Immediately after the tribulation of those days shall the sun be darkened, and the moon shall not give her light, and the stars shall fall from heaven, and the powers of the heavens shall be shaken. And then shall appear the Son of Man in heaven.

Hebrews 12:6–8 says:

> For whom the Lord loveth He chasteneth, and scourgeth every son whom he receiveth. If ye endure chastening, God dealeth with you as a son; for what a son is he whom the father chasteneth not? But if ye be without chastisement, whereof all are partakers then ye are bastards, and not sons.

Let us note the word for chastened, *paideuo*,[272] which means to train up a child, (i.e., educate or [by implication] discipline [by punishment]), chasten(ise), instruct, learn, or teach. Let us also note Psalms 94:12–13:

> Blessed is the man whom the thou chastenest, O Lord, and teachest him out of thou law; That thou

---

[272]   Ibid., 2127.

mayest give him rest for the days of adversity, until
the pit be digged for the wicked.

And when is the "pit digged for the wicked"? Blessed is the man
who God will give rest (the rest in Jeremiah in the time of Jacob's
trouble) in the days of adversity (Tribulation) when the pit will be dug
(the lake of fire of Revelation 19:20).

Revelation 19:20 says, "And the beast was taken, and with him
the false prophet that wrought miracles before him, with which he
deceived them that had received the mark of the beast, and them that
worshipped his image." These both were cast alive into the lake of fire
burning with brimstone. The word for chastenest is *yasar*,[273] which
means a primitive root; to chastise, literal (with blows) or figurative
(with words); hence to instruct, reform, reprove, sore, or teach. We
should note that we are told here in the psalms, "Blessed is the man
whom thou chastenest." This should also tell us that we go through the
judgments of God in the book of Revelation.

And then we should note the next verse: "And then if a man shall
say unto you, Lo, here is Christ; or, Lo, he is there; believe him not."
There is only one group of people looking for the return of the Lord
Jesus Christ. If the church is still looking for him when the Lord
shortens the days, that means they are still on the planet. If you are a
true Christian, this is where you expect him to return. This is how the
Lord will keep the Philadelphia church from the hour of temptation.
There is the passage in Mark 13:11, "But when they shall lead you,
and deliver you up, take no thought beforehand what ye shall speak,
neither premeditate; but whatsoever shall be given you in that hour,
that speak ye; for it is not ye that speak, but the holy spirit." Instead of
being resurrected off the planet, God gives the Philadelphia church the
Holy Spirit to deal with Satan.

This is the same spirit that the Lord gave to Jeremiah in 1:9, "Then
the Lord put forth his hand, and touched my mouth. And the Lord
said unto me, Behold, I have put my words in thy mouth." Ezekiel 2:2
says, "And the spirit entered into me when he spake unto me, and set

---

[273]   Ibid., 1875.

me upon my feet, that I heard him that spake unto me." This tells us the church is still on the planet when the devil makes his appearance. To the Philadelphia church, it is also stated, "Behold I come quickly: hold that fast which thou hast, that no man taketh thy crown."

And when does the Lord come quickly? Revelation 22:12 says, "Behold I come quickly; and my reward is with me, to give every man according as his work shall be." Where is the reward given? Revelation 11:18 says:

> And the nations were angry, and thy wrath has come,
> and the time of the dead, that they should be judged,
> and that thou shouldest give reward unto thy servants
> and prophets, and to the saints, and them that fear
> thy name, small and great; and shouldest destroy
> them which destroy the earth.

The Lord is not coming quickly in Revelation 4, where it is said that the Lord is on the throne. And I shall repeat this again and again till you understand this. Here is where "the dead" are judged. This is when the Lord descends from heaven to destroy those who destroy the earth. When I was looking for a publisher, I brought the book *The Writer's Market*. One of the publishing firms said it doesn't accept books on religion unless you have a degree in theology. If your theology is wrong, what good is it? The Philadelphia church is also told, "Him that overcometh."

I do not see a promise of a pre-tribulation resurrection for this church or any church. Let us note the word for overcometh *nikao*:[274] to subdue (literal and figurative), conquer, overcome, prevail, or get the victory. The church is promised in Mark that the Holy Spirit will help them overcome (get the victory) Satan. Mark tells us here that it will be given to the saints what they shall speak by the power of the Holy Spirit. As the pastors say, Jesus overcame death, hell, and the grave on the cross; the church is also to overcome the devil.

---

[274]   Ibid., 2118.

Paul warned in 2 Thessalonians 1:4: "So that we ourselves glory in you the churches of God, for your patience and faith in all your persecutions and tribulations that ye endure." Is this the same message John gives in the book of Revelation in his messages to the churches? All seven churches of God are to endure to the end. Every church is told, "He that hath an ear, let him hear what the spirit saith unto the churches." We all go through persecutions and tribulations, but if we endure, which I think means to keep our faith in the Lord during this horrible time on the earth, we will be saved. Second Peter 3:2-5 says:

> That ye may be mindful of the words which were spoken before by the holy prophets, and of the commandment of us the apostles of the Lord and Saviour: Knowing this first, that there shall come in the last days scoffers, walking after their own lust, And saying, Where is the promise of his coming? For since the fathers fell asleep, all things continue as they were from the beginning of the creation. For this they willingly are ignorant of, that by the Word of God the heavens were of old, and the earth standing out of water and in the water.

This scripture tells us the church is in great distress and the Lord has not taken the church off the earth. Does Peter not tell us here that we should look to the Old Testament prophets as well as the apostles to understand true Bible prophecy? Why is there a question of the promise of his coming? The word "delayeth" is *chronizo*,[275] which means to take time (i.e., linger); delay, tarry. This is because of the pre-tribulation resurrection pastors who teach that the church is not on the earth at this time. This is why if you are in a church that teaches the pre-tribulation rapture, you should leave that church. The Bible states in Matthew 24:48–51:

---

[275]   Ibid., 2180.

> But and if that evil servant shall say in his heart, My
> Lord delayed his coming; And shall begin to smite
> his fellow servants, and to eat and drink with the
> drunken; The Lord of that servant shall come in a day
> when he looketh not for him, and in a hour that he is
> not aware of, And shall cut him asunder, and appoint
> him his portion with the hypocrites: there shall be
> weeping and gnashing of teeth.

This is exactly why I say there is no pre-tribulation resurrection. These statements by Peter and Matthew would not be in the Bible if the church was caught up to meet the Lord in the air before the tribulation period. Here is why teaching that there is a pre-tribulation resurrection is not right. Why would the church say, "My Lord delayed his coming" or "Where is the promise of his coming" if they were are taken off the planet before the tribulation? Is this why there are the warnings to the prophets that teach this is the punishment that they receive because of their teaching?

Jeremiah says the same thing when he states, "I will punish that man and his house." This is given in Jeremiah 23:34: "And as for the prophet, and the priest, and the people, that shall say, The burden of the Lord, I will even punish that man and his house." I think this argument about a pre-tribulation, middle-tribulation, or an after-tribulation resurrection is kind of stupid. The Bible says the resurrection of the dead happens some time when the sun and the moon are darkened. As we will see in scripture, there is a time when the Lord leaves heaven, and we will soon see in this book when it happens.

I continued to watch some of the pre-tribulation resurrection pastors who preach this lie, and their congregations get up and cheer that they don't go through the tribulation period. I think, *Man are they in for a rude awakening.* When I see this happening around the country, I ask myself, *Does anybody study the Bible?* We are told in 2 Timothy 2:15–16, "Study to shew thyself approved unto God, a workman that needeth not to be ashamed, rightly dividing the word of truth. But shun profane and vain babblings: for they will increase unto more ungodliness." These "vain babblings" are the teaching of the pre-tribulation resurrection.

We are also told in James 5:10, "Take my brethren, the prophets, who have spoken in the name of the Lord, for example of sufferings, affliction, and of patience." The word "patience" is *makrothumia*,[276] which means (i.e., objective) forbearance or (subjective) fortitude; longsuffering, patience. Also Revelation 14:12 says, "Here is the patience of the saints."

The prophets and the disciples all suffered persecutions and trials, but now in the twenty-first century, the church has become so holy that they don't go through any persecutions or trials. This goes against what is given in scripture. There is a set time for the Lord to come back to this earth, just as there was a set time for him to come and save the world. That set time is "the time of the end" and the "last day." I want to say again, prove the last day or the end is in Revelation 4.

We should also note 2 Timothy 4:1, "I charge thee therefore before God, and the Lord Jesus Christ, who shall judge the quick and the dead at his appearing and his kingdom." The word for quick is *aqzao*,[277] which means to live (literal or figurative); life. This is "we which are alive and remain until the coming of the Lord" who don't taste of death until they see the coming of the Lord. It is not until his appearing that the Lord will judge the dead. We should note that it says here "and his kingdom." The Lord's kingdom on the earth is where he judges the living and where he will divide the wheat from the tares, the wicked from the just. It is after the tribulation of those days. If the Lord shall descend from heaven with a shout, the voice of the archangel, and the trumpet of God, this should tell us that the whole world will know of his soon return to earth and not this secret resurrection that the pre-tribulation pastors teach. This secret pre-tribulation church resurrection is so secret I can't find one verse that pertains to this prophecy.

We should also note 1 Thessalonians 5:23, "And the very God of peace sanctify you wholly; and I pray God your whole spirit and

---

[276] Ibid., 2110.

[277] Ibid., 2084.

soul, and body be preserved blameless unto the coming of our Lord Jesus Christ." Once again we read in scripture that the body will be preserved until the coming of the Lord. The Lord comes in Revelation 16:15: "Behold, I come as a thief." When? Verse 16 says, "He gathered them in a place called Armageddon." We should note the three distinct characteristics of man. The spirit is *pneuma*,[278] which means the vital spirit of life, the principle of life residing in man. It is the breath breathed by God into man and again returning to God, the spiritual entity in man The soul is *psuche*,[279] which means specifically as the sentient principle, the seat of the senses, desires, afflictions, appetites, passions, the lower aspects of one's nature. It refers to the disposition, feeling, temper of mind (e.g., the spirit of gentleness) as understanding, intellect. The body is *soma*,[280] which means body (as a sound whole) used in a very wide application, literal or figurative. To have your whole body, soul, and spirit until the coming of the Lord means you are one of the blessed who inherit the earth.

We should note that John writes in Revelation 1:3, "Blessed is he that readeth, and they that hear the words of this prophecy, and keep those things which are written therein: for the time is at hand." Many people I talk to tell me that their pastor never teaches from the book of Revelation. Why? It's because they don't understand its meaning. If pastors are blind to the coming of the Lord, how in the world will their congregations know? The signs of the end are all around us today. If the pastors don't want to study to show themselves approved unto God, then maybe they should find a new profession.

I talked with one pastor who said that the Old Testament was not taught in his church because it was not important. This was also told to me by many Catholics. This is how Isaiah can justify saying, "His [the Lord's] watchmen [pastors] are blind: they are all ignorant, they are all dumb dogs." They are the pre-tribulation resurrection pastors. It is just as Jeremiah told the false prophet Hananaih, "The Lord hath not sent thee, but thou makest this people to trust in a lie." The word for

---

278   Ibid., 2137.

279   Ibid., 2181.

280   Ibid., 2161.

"lie" is *sheqer*,[281] which means an untruth by implication, sham (often adverbial). It is from *shaqar*,[282] a primitive root; to cheat (i.e., be untrue [usually in words]); fail, deal falsely, lie. That trust in a lie also relates to the pre-tribulation resurrection. Let's note what Ezekiel writes in 2:7: "And thou shall speak my words unto them, whether they will hear, or whether they will forbear: for they are most rebellious." The Jews of Ezekiel's day believed that the Lord would not bring judgment on Jerusalem, just as the twenty-first-century church believes in the pre-tribulation rapture.

Jeremiah tells us in 4:28, "For this shall the earth mourn, and the heavens above be black." When the judgments came upon the house of Judah, the sky was black. This is the same message to today's church, as told in Matthew 24:30. The Lord says in Matthew 13:21, "Yet hath he not root in himself, but dureth for a while: for when tribulation or persecution ariseth because of the word, by and by he is offended." If the Lord is not speaking to the church, then who is this message for? When tribulation and persecutions come, this is what Christians are to do. In verse 23, the Lord says, "But he that received seed into good ground is he that heareth the word and understandeth it; which also beareth fruit, and bringeth forth, some a hundredfold, some sixty, some thirty." The church that is on good ground is to bear fruit during the tribulation period. This is the mission of the church during this time and not to be resurrected out.

This tells us when the Lord leaves heaven. It is when he brings his wrath upon the earth. If the wheat (the church) is to grow with the tares (Muslims), or every unsaved person, until the time of the harvest, there can't be a pre-tribulation resurrection. We should note that the word for tares is *zizanion*,[283] which means of uncertain origin; damned or false grain: tares. Note the Greek word meaning damned. Who is damned? Mark tells us who is damned in 16:16: "He that believeth and is baptized shall be saved; but he that believeth not shall be damned." This is again plain and simple language. We should also note that there

---

[281]   Ibid., 1994.
[282]   Ibid.
[283]   Ibid., 2084.

is not one verse in scripture I can find where the Lord leaves heaven for his church before the wrath of God.

I think it is very important to note that when John is called up to heaven in Revelation 4, the Lord is on the throne. He does not come down to meet the saints in the air. I think it is also important to refer to this verse in 2 Timothy 3:12, "Yea, and *all* that will live godly in Christ Jesus shall suffer persecution." Does this "all" exclude the twenty-first-century church? If it does, then I say rip this passage out of the Bible. This would not be in scripture—"My Lord delayed his coming"—if the church was called up in a pre-tribulation resurrection. There would not be, "Come out of her, my people" in Revelation 18. Who are my people but the church? The word for "my people" is *Laos,*[284] which means specifically of the Jews as the people of God's choice, figuratively of Christians as God's spiritual Israel. This so-called pre-tribulation resurrection is so secretive that it was not given to any of the prophets in the Bible.

Let's finish the verse, "That ye receive not of her plagues." The plagues are only referenced in scripture as the vial judgments. We should also note in Acts 12:11, "And when Peter was come to himself, he said, Now I know of a surely, that the Lord hath sent his angel, and hath delivered me out of the hand of Herod, and from all the expectation of the people of the Jews." Peter was delivered as were Paul and Daniel, and they were still on the earth. Revelation 13:7 says, "And it was given unto him [Satan] to make war with the saints." Who are the saints but the church?

Most pastors say the conditions on the earth are going to be so bad that God will take his church off the planet before the coming judgments of the book of Revelation. However, the Lord tells us six times in Matthew, Luke, and Mark, twice in each book, "Verily I say unto you, It shall be more tolerable for the land of Sodom and Gomorrah in the day of judgment than for that city."

There will be places on the earth that don't receive the judgments of God, just as none of the plagues on the Egyptians affected the Hebrews, and just as God sealed the Jews when the judgments came

---

[284] Ibid., 2106.

upon them when they were taken into Babylonian captivity. In the book of Revelation, we read that when God returns to the earth, there will be people whose names are written in the Lamb's Book of Life still on the planet. God's wrath is against all those nations that come against Jerusalem in the Old Testament. First Thessalonians 1:8 says, "When the Lord Jesus is revealed from heaven taking vengeance on them that know not God, and obey not the gospel of our Lord Jesus Christ" of the New Testament.

We told in Philippians 1:6, 10, 16:

> Being confident of this very thing, that he which hath begun a good work in you will perform it until the day of Christ. That ye may approve things that are excellent; that ye may be sincere and without offence till the day of Christ. Holding forth the word of life; that I may rejoice in the day of Christ, that I have not run in vain, neither laboured in vain.

We are told here three times that the church is to wait for the "day of Christ" or the day of the Lord. Then we are told this in 1:9, "And this I pray, that your love may abound yet more and more in knowledge and in all judgment."

We are then told in 1:29, "For unto you is given in the behalf of Christ, not only to believe in him, but also to suffer for his sake." We should note here "all judgment." What part of "all judgment" and "suffer for his sake" do the pre-tribulation pastors not understand? Then Paul tells us in 1:13–15:

> For it is God which worketh in you both to will and to do of his good pleasure. Do all things without murmurings and disputings: That ye may be blameless and harmless, the sons of God, without rebuke, in the midst of a crooked [*skolios*,[285] which means warped (i.e., windings), figurative perverse] and perverse

---

[285] Ibid., 2152.

[*diastrepho*,[286] which means to distort (i.e., figurative) misinterpret, or morally corrupt] nation, among whom ye shine as lights in the world.

That perverse and morally corrupt nation is the Islamic nation. Second Timothy 1:14 confirms this: "This thou knowest, that all they which are in Asia be turned away from me [the Lord Jesus Christ]."

This is just as the Lord Jesus instructed in Matthew 5:16, "Let your light so shine before men, that they may see your good works, and glorify your Father which is in heaven."

I will close this chapter of this book with the epistle Paul wrote to the Romans.

Romans 8:35–39 says:

> Who shall separate us from the love of Christ? Shall tribulation, or distress, or persecution, or famine, or nakedness, or peril, or sword? As it is written, For thy sake we are killed all the day long; we are accounted as sheep for the slaughter.

It is written in Psalms 44:22:

> Yea, for thy sake are we killed all the day long; we are counted as sheep for the slaughter. Nay, in all things we are more than conquerors through him that love us. For I am persuaded, that neither death, nor life, nor angels, nor principalities, nor powers, nor things present, nor things to come, nor height, nor depth, nor any other creature, shall be able to separate us from the love of God, which is in Jesus Christ our Lord.

---

[286] Ibid., 2054.

Paul tells us here that no matter what this present and evil world in which we live throws at us, we are more than conquerors, because none of these trials will separate us from the love of the Lord Jesus Christ. I want to make scripture clear and precise.

I was listening to a preacher on the radio who changed his mind on the pre-tribulation resurrection. This pastor, by the way, was one of the pastors to whom I sent my interpretation. A caller called and said he was wrong because the church doesn't go through the tribulation. The pastor did not do a convincing job in his explanation. This is why I wrote this manuscript. This is why I named this manuscript *The Big Lie, Exposed.*

Another pastor said on his program that he got a vision from God about the lost tribes of the house of Israel and next week's program would explain it. When I called his church office and told them I am not God, they said his next week's program was pre-recorded. He even questioned a fellow pastor if there was a pre-tribulation resurrection in the weeks after.

Several people have said to me "Why do you listen to television pastors?" Then someone told me that after his grandmother died, his parents went through her checkbook, and they found checks made out to all kinds of television pastors. She gave money they could not afford. And I know why. It's because these pastors say on their programs, "Send me your money so God can bless you."

When a young lady stopped me as I was walking my dogs, she said to me that her husband told her that I studied the Bible. I told her, "Yes, what would you like to know?" She told me her mother-in-law gave all her estate to the Pentecostal Church. She gave her entire estate to that church because that pastor told her that was the only way to receive true salvation. I told her that her mother-in law was brainwashed by that pastor, and it was not biblical. Proverbs tells us in 13:22, "A good man leaveth an inheritance to his children's children: and the wealth of the sinners is laid up for the just." This is why I wrote this manuscript—to expose the greedy, dumb dogs Isaiah told us of. This same Pentecostal church assigns each member of their congregation a family counselor. They tell them just how much they are to tithe each week. This makes this church a cult, and any church that puts you under any part of the Mosaic Law is a cult and not a church of the Lord Jesus Christ. This includes the Baptist churches that put you under the Nazarite Law. This is why scripture tells us that the judgments begin with the house of God. And it will begin with church pastors. This is not my interpretation; this is what the Word of God says.

The True Time of the Resurrection of the Dead

LET US FIRST START with the scriptures that refer to the resurrection of the (dead) church in the New Testament. I said the dead church because it is only those who are in the grave who hear, "Come up hither." You also should notice that I said the new because there are many scriptures in the Old Testament that refer to the same thing. Surprised? Most people are. We will see in scripture that God has revealed from the beginning to the end of days just what his plan for mankind is and his plan of man's continued existence in the millennium. I believe the churches of today have missed the bigger picture. Most churches say it is not important to teach from the Old Testament because Jesus changed everything when he died on the cross. This is why they miss the bigger picture. There is not one scripture in either the Old Testament or the New Testament that relates to this so-called pre-tribulation resurrection or the living church resurrection. There is only one second coming of our Lord Jesus. As we have seen throughout history, God always has prophets warning of coming judgment and when God is going to act. This will be true at the end of days.

Just as the Lord came down from heaven in the times before, I think these times were missed by most pastors. The Bible tells us this. When there is judgment coming, God's prophets appear, just as he has done in the past. "I change not," saith the Lord. This is why the prophets tell us Elijah the prophet comes before the great and terrible day of the Lord. Let us note what Jesus said in Luke 4:18–19:

The spirit of the Lord is upon me, because he hath appointed me to preach the gospel to the poor; he hath sent me to preach deliverance to the captives, and recovering of sight to the blind, to set at liberty them that are bruised, To proclaim the acceptable year of the Lord.

But he leaves off this part of Isaiah 61:3: "And the day of vengeance of our God; to comfort all who mourn." Jesus tells us in the Beatitudes in Matthew 5:4, "Blessed are they that mourn: for they shall be comforted." "Comforted" is *parakaleo*,[287] which means to call near. Do you not see this to call near? The Lord makes the call in the day of vengeance to comfort all who mourn. This is the same mourn in Matthew 24:30: "And then shall appear the sign of man in heaven; and then shall all the tribes of the earth mourn." It is when the tribes of the earth mourn the Lord will make the call. The Hebrew meanings prove this.

This year in Isaiah is *shenah*,[288] which means a year (as a revolution of time). It is from the word *shanah*, duplicate (literal or figurative), do a second time, repent, reward. It's when the earth mourns that the Lord Jesus comes the second time to give the reward. The reward is given at the marriage supper of the lamb. Also, it is from the Greek word *eniautos*, prolonged from the primary. In this "Day of the Lord," the word for day is *yown*[289] from an unused root meaning to be hot; a day (as the warm hours), whether literal or figurative (from sunrise to sunset), or figuratively (a space of the defined by associated term). Did we notice that it is not until "all of the tribes of the earth mourn" that the Lord will "do a second time" or come back to earth, and to do what? Give the reward.

Now let's put precept upon precept, line upon line, as Isaiah has instructed. Isaiah tells us that the day of vengeance is to comfort all who mourn. Second Corinthians tells us in 1:4 when we are comforted:

---

287 Ibid., 2129.
288 Ibid., 1991.
289 Ibid., 1872.

"Who comforteth us in all our tribulations, that we may be able to comfort them which are in any trouble, by which wherewith we ourselves are comforted of God." It is in the tribulation period when the Christians are to comfort those who are in trouble, because the Christians are comforted by God. He strengthens by the Holy Spirit, as stated in 1 John 3:2: "When he shall appear, we will be like him; for we will see him as he is." When will the Lord seek vengeance? That would be 2 Thessalonians 1:7–8:

> And to you who are troubled [tribulation] rest with us, when the Lord Jesus will be revealed from heaven with his mighty angels, In flaming fire taking vengeance on them that know not God, and obey not the gospel of Jesus Christ.

This tells us just who God's wrath is against, them who know not God; that would be the Muslims. They obey not the gospel of Christ. When the nations come against the land of Israel, they are not obeying the commandment, "Thou shall love thy neighbour as thyself." Even though Christians sin, if we have our faith in the Lord Jesus Christ, we will be saved from the wrath of God. Note 1 Thessalonians 1:10 says, "And to wait for his Son from heaven, who delivered [*rhuomai*,[290] which means to rush or draw (for one-self), i.e. rescue] us from the wrath to come." Romans 14:9 says, "For to this end Christ both died and rose, and revived, that he might be Lord both of the dead and the living."

We know who the second prophet will be, for the Bible tells us in 1 Corinthians 15:50, "Now I say, Brethren, that flesh and blood cannot inherit the kingdom of God." There was no other prophet taken to heaven before death but Enoch and Elijah. Let us note Genesis 5:24, "And Enoch walked with God; and he was not; for God took him." If flesh and blood cannot enter the kingdom of God, then Enoch and Elijah have to die, and that is done by the Antichrist in Revelation 11:7 where the two witnesses are killed.

---

[290]   Ibid., 2149.

If the prophets come before the Lord, there cannot be a pre-tribulation resurrection. We are told in 2 Thessalonians 2:9, "Even him [Lord Jesus] whose coming is after the working of Satan with power and lying wonders." The Bible reveals to us in the book of Revelation that there are two prophets in Jerusalem, but there are also the one hundred and forty-four thousand prophets of God in the world, and there are still angels warning people not to take the mark of the beast. The one hundred and forty-four thousand are not just Jews but of all of the tribes of Israel that were scattered around the world. The Lord does all he can to save every child on the earth at the time of the end.

Let us note this passage in Matthew 24:13: "But they that endured unto the end, the same shall be saved." The word "saved" here is *sozo*,[291] which means "safe"; to save (i.e., deliver or protect) (literal or figurative): heal, preserve, save (self), do well, be (made) whole. We should note here that there is no reference to resurrection or being caught up. one of the ones caught up to heaven are "the dead in Christ" and not the whole church, as you have been promised by most pastors. I will prove this in scripture. The end is, as we will see, when God says the end is, and the end is not in Revelation 4, when the pastors say the resurrection happens. This is for later in this manuscript. Let's start with the mystery of the resurrection.

First Corinthians 15:51–52 says:

> Behold, I shew you a mystery; We shall not all sleep, but we shall all be changed, In a moment, in the twinkling of an eye, at the last trump: and the dead shall be raised incorruptible, and we shall be changed.

This establishes the time. This happens at the last trump. This is where we get our incorruptible bodies just like the Lord Jesus after he was crucified. Ask a pre-tribulation pastor, the ones who say this come up hither in Revelation 4:1, to prove that this is the last trump. They cannot prove this. If you cannot prove your interpretation of the

---

[291] Ibid., 2161.

Bible, then maybe you are wrong. This is told to us in First Corinthians 15:52. But we should notice this verse, "But we all shall be changed." Verse 53 says, "For this corruptible must up on incorruption, and this mortal must put on immortality." Mortal is *thnetos*,[292] which means liable to die. The word "immortality" is *athemitos*,[293] which means deathlessness. First John 3:2 says, "Beloved, now are we the sons of God, and it doth not yet appear what we shall be: but we know that, when he shall appear, we shall be like him; for we shall see him as he is." Note the scripture, "the dead shall be raised." It does not say the living are raised but "we shall be changed."

And when does the Lord appear? Revelation 1:7 says, "Behold, he cometh [cometh is another word for appear] with clouds: and every eye shall see him, and they also which pierced him: and all kindreds of the earth shall wail because of him." We should note, "And they also which pierced him." Zechariah 12:10 says, "And they shall look upon me whom they have pierced, and they shall all mourn."

This is what happens to the meek which are baptized and confess Jesus Christ as Lord. Those who inherit the earth are the people who inherit immortality. The nations and the people of those nations that don't come against Israel at the battle of Armageddon are the nations of Revelation 23:24: "And the nations of them which are saved [preserved] walk in the light of it [glory of God]." They will survive in their earthly bodies. Even in Ezekiel when Gog's armies come against Jerusalem, God leaves a sixth part. In Revelation, when the two-hundred-million-man army comes, the angels slay but a third part of men. Human life continues even after the battle of Armageddon.

Zechariah14:16 says:

> And it shall come to pass, that everyone that is left
> of all the nations which come against Jerusalem shall
> even go up from year to year to worship the King, the
> Lord of hosts [which is the Lord Jesus Christ], and to
> keep the feast of tabernacles.

---

[292]   Ibid., 2088.
[293]   Ibid., 2014.

Note the language here.

> Everyone that is left of all nations that came against Jerusalem. Human life continues. This is what you don't hear from pastors. Why will the people of the earth keep the feast of tabernacles? The answer is in Psalms 27:5: "For in the time of trouble he shall hide me in his pavilion: in the secret of his tabernacle shall he hide me." This is how the Christians are protected from the wrath of God.

Zechariah tells us in verse 9, "And the Lord will be king over all the earth: in that day shall there be one Lord, and his name one." The Lord Jesus states in Revelation 1:8, "I am Alpha and Omega, the beginning and the end." We are told this in Ezekiel 43:7: "And he [the Lord] said unto me, Son of Man, the place of my throne, and the place of the soles of my feet, where I dwell in the midst of the children of Israel forever." Thy will be done on earth as it is in heaven. Does this sound familiar?

This is given in Isaiah 65:18–25. During the millennial reign of Christ, this is how the body is changed in verse 20: "There shall no more thence an infant of days, nor an old man that hath not filled his days: for a child shall die a hundred years old; but the sinner being an hundred years old shall be accursed." God brings back the life span to the like of Adam. Why would a child die at an hundred years old? Just as in the Garden of Eden, Adam and his family were living in the presence of God, and Cain killed Abel. The punishment to those who kill or unjustly behave is the job of those who come back to rule and reign with Christ. This is in Isaiah 1:26, "I will restore thy judges as at the first." But during the millennial reign this happens. Isaiah 65:24 says, "And it shall come to pass, that before they call, I will answer; and while they are yet speaking, I will hear."

It was important enough for Isaiah to tell us twice about the meek that inherit the earth. Let's note Isaiah 11, starting with verse 4: "But with righteousness shall he judge the poor, and reprove with equity for the meek of the earth: and he shall smite the earth with the rod of his mouth, and with his breath of his lips shall he slay the wicked." This equity for the meek of the earth is the word *miyshowr*,[294] which means a level (figurative) justice, uprightness. It is from *yashar*,[295] which means, to be straight or even; figurative to be (causative to make) right, pleasant, prosperous, direct, fit, seem good. The meek of the earth receive justice, uprightness, and for it to be pleasant. But he shall slay the wicked. And this is during the thousand-year reign of Christ.

Let's continue with verses 5 and 6:

> And righteousness shall be the girdles of is loins, and faithfulness the girdle of his reins. The wolf shall dwell with the lamb, and the leopard shall lie down with the kid; and the calf and the young lion and the fatling together; and a little child shall lead them.

Do we not see here what a different earth this will be when the Lord returns? What is required of man to be one of the meek who inherit the earth? Micah 6:8 says: "He hath shewed thee, O man, what is good; but to do justly, and to love mercy, and to walk humbly with thy god." Now let's go to 1 Thessalonians 4:15-17:

> For this we say unto you by the word of the Lord, that we which are alive and remain until the coming of the Lord shall not prevent them with are asleep. For the Lord himself shall descend from heaven with a shout, with the voice of the archangel, and the trump of God: and the dead in Christ shall rise first: Then we which are alive and remain shall be caught up together with them in the cloud, to meet the Lord in the air: and so shall we ever be with the Lord.

First let's note that it says here, "We which are alive until the coming of the Lord will follow some time later after the Lord's appearing."

"Remain" is *perilupos*,[296] which means to leave all around (i.e., passive) survive. This means the living church is not resurrected to heaven. These are the last days when Acts 2:17 states, "And it shall come to pass in the last days, saith God, I will pour out my Spirit upon all flesh." And after the Lord's coming is when the Lord shall separate the sheep from the goats, or the wheat from the tares. And the word for prevent is *phthartos*,[297] which means to be beforehand (i.e., anticipate or precede). The dead arise at the appearing of the Lord. Now let's note the word for air is *aer*,[298] which means to breathe unconsciously (i.e., respire). Those who remain are the meek who inherit the earth, and as quoted in Zephaniah 2:3, "Seek ye the Lord, all ye meek of the earth, which have wrought his judgment; seek righteousness, seek meekness: it may be ye shall be hid in the day of the Lord's anger." Note the "all ye meek of the earth," which have wrought (*poal*,[299] which means ordain work) did work during God's judgments.

Between the appearing of the Lord and his coming is the wrath of God. This is why Matthew tells us in 24:30, "And then shall appear the sign of the Son of Man in heaven: and then all of the tribes of the earth shall mourn [the wrath of God is poured out], and then shall they see the Son of Man coming in the clouds of heaven with power and great glory." Let's also note the word meaning for this sign in Matthew 24:30:

> A signal, a standard; a sign by which anything is designated, distinguished, or known; hence use of the miracles of Christ as being the signs by which He might be known as the Christ of God: a sign authenticating His mission; a sign with reference to what it demonstrates.[300]

---

296 Ibid., 2134.
297 Ibid., 2172.
298 Ibid., 2014.
299 Ibid., 1948.
300 *Bullinger's*, 701.

The sign is a reference to what is given in verse 31, which states, "And he shall send his angels with the sound of a trumpet, and they shall gather together his elect from the four winds [which Ezekiel 37:9 tells us that the four winds put the spirits into the dead], from one end of heaven to the other." Note it does not say the earth. It's one end of heaven (the heaven in space) to the other (the paradise under the earth).

The way God is going to hide the "we which are alive and remain" and the meek who are hid in the day of the Lord's anger is found in Psalms 27:5: "For in the time of trouble [tribulation] he [God] shall hide me in his pavilion [*sok*,[301] which means a hut; also a lair (*Webster's Dictionary* definition, 'A place of protection')]; in the secret of his tabernacle shall he hide me; he shall set me up upon a rock." This is why this is given in Revelation 15:5: "And after that I looked, and, behold, the temple of the tabernacle of the testimony in heaven was opened." Is it opened by being brought to the clouds, as stated in Revelation 21:3? "And I heard a great voice out of heaven saying, Behold, the tabernacle of God is with men, and he will dwell with them, and they shall be his people, and God himself shall be with them, and be their God." These are those who are alive and remain by meeting the Lord in the air (which means to breathe unconsciously). So shall they ever be with the Lord of 1 Thessalonians 4:17.

And what was this after? Revelation 15:2 says, "And I saw as it were a sea of glass mingled with fire: and them that got the victory over the beast, stand on a sea of glass, having the harps of God," because the dead in Christ rise first in 1 Thessalonians 4:15. We know these of Revelation 15:2 who got the victory over the beast are the dead who are raised first because Revelation 20:4 says:

> And I saw thrones, and they sat upon them, and judgment was given them: and I saw the souls of them that were beheaded of the witness of Jesus, and for the Word of God, and had not worshiped the beast: and they lived and reigned with God a thousand years.

---

[301] *Strong's*, 1927.

Revelation 20:5 states, "This is the first resurrection."

It's only the dead in Christ who rise first, "at his appearing," and we who are alive and remain until the "coming of the lord." As stated in Matthew 16:27–28: "For the Son of Man shall come in the glory of his Father with his angels; and then he shall reward every man according to his works at his appearing. Verily I say unto you, There be some standing here, which shall not taste of death." These are the "we which are alive and remain until the coming of the Lord," and in 1 Corinthians 15:54, "this mortal shall put on immortality till they see the Son of Man coming in his kingdom." The living church puts on immortality.

We should also note here what is really said in 1 Corinthians 15:51: "Behold, I shew you a mystery, We shall not all sleep [dead], but we all shall be changed." Let's read this very carefully. "The dead shall be raised incorruptible." It is only the dead who are raised out of the grave, not the alive church, for the living church this is the prophecy "and we all shall be changed." How is the living church changed? "This mortal must put on immortality," the meek that inherit the earth. This is why verse 55 was written, "O death, where is thy sting?" The mortals who put on immortality know there is no sting and death, and "O grave, where is thy victory?" refers to the dead who shall be raised incorruptible.

For blessed are the meek, for they shall inherit the earth. This is the message pastors should be teaching their congregations. I will state this again so the church of the Lord Jesus Christ will realize there is no pre-tribulation resurrection, mid-tribulation resurrection, or after-tribulation of the living church as promised by the pre-tribulation resurrection pastors. Scripture tells us to wait for his appearing, and his appearing is not until "after the tribulation of those days." It's only the dead who shall arise, because we who are alive and remain until the coming of the Lord don't taste death. The dead taste death.

Let us refer to scripture to see why the "dead in Christ" shall rise first. According to *Strong's Concordance*, the Hebrews believe in a place called hades. This is *sheh-ole*;[302] from the word *shaw-al*;[303] hades or the world of the dead (as if a subterranean retreat) including its accessories and inmates. One of the words for hell is *haides*,[304] which means properly unseen (i.e., "hades") or the place (state of) departed souls; grave, hell. The abode of hades, orcus, was a vast subterranean receptacle where the souls of the dead existed in a separate state until the resurrection of their bodies. The region of the blessed during this interval, the inferior paradise, was supposed to be the upper part of the receptacle, while beneath was the abyss or Gehenna, in which the souls of the wicked were subjected to punishment.

This is one part where I don't agree with *Strong's Concordance*. In Revelation, John sees the souls of those who were killed in heaven. In 1 Corinthians 5:5, it states, "That the spirit may be saved on the day of the Lord." First Peter 3:19 states "By which also he went and preached unto the spirits in prison." Acts 3:8 says, "For the Sadducees say there is no resurrection, neither angel, nor Spirit." Romans 8:10 says, "If Christ be in you, the body is dead because of sin; but the spirit is life because of righteousness." Verse 23 says, "Not only they, but ourselves also, which have the first fruits of the Spirits." It is the spirit that rises from the grave and not the soul. God made his angels human spirits. The soul was created to that spirit when that person is born on this planet. The soul of a man is not part of the pre-designated death because the soul was not created until Adam was formed. Verse 49 states, "And as we have borne the image of the earthly, we shall also bear the image of the heavenly."

This is why this is given in Philippians 3:5: "Circumcised on the eighth day." Jewish children are to be circumcised on the eighth day because Adam was formed on the eighth day. First Corinthians 15:45 says, "The first Adam was made a living soul." Verse 46 says, "Howbeit that was not first to be spiritual." He was not first to have a human spirit. Adam was formed on the eighth day. God created male and female on the sixth day.

---

302 Ibid., 1974.
303 Ibid., 1975.
304 Ibid., 2013.

We should note that Paul writes the first letter to the Thessalonians in 4:16, "For the Lord shall descend from heaven with a shout, with the voice of the archangel and the trumpet of God: and the dead shall rise first." Paul writes the second letter to the Thessalonian church and tells them just when the Lord shall descend from heaven with the shout for the dead church, and here is the verse 2:1:7–8

> And to you who are troubled [*thilbo*,[305] which means afflict, suffer tribulation] rest with us, when the Lord Jesus shall be revealed from heaven with his mighty angels, In flaming fire, taking vengeance on them that know not God, and obey not the gospel of Jesus Christ.

It's those who are in tribulation. Not before the tribulation, not after the tribulation but in tribulation. This is when the Lord is revealed. This is when Matthew 24:30 says the Lord will appear in heaven. The Lord didn't come down to take Christians to heaven for vengeance. That vengeance is against those who "know not God" and who "obey not the gospel of Jesus Christ." That is anybody who is not a Christian.

And the verses in 1 and 2 Thessalonians match the Old Testament prophet Isaiah in 26:19, 22, where it states, "Thy dead men shall live, together with my dead body shall they arise, and the earth shall cast out the dead. For, behold, the Lord cometh out of his place to punish the inhabitants of the earth." This tells us that the dead arise when the Lord comes out of his place. We will read in Ezekiel that God will use an earthquake to "cast out of their graves." Also when we get to Ezekiel, we will see that God has different plans for the tribes of Jacob. But for "my people" of verse 20, scripture says, "Enter thou into thy chambers, and shut thy doors about thee: hide thyself as it were for a little moment, until the indignation be overpast." These my people are the meek who inherit the earth.

---

[305] Ibid., 2088.

Let's note what Paul wrote in 2 Thessalonians 1:10: "When he shall come to be glorified in his saints, and to be admired in all them that believe (because our testimony among you) was believed." Paul's testimony was that Jesus would raise the dead. Look what it says here: "when he the Lord Jesus comes," which means appear. The people (among you) on the planet when this was to happen believed this would happen. This is the message to the twenty-first-century church. This is the answer to our daily prayer of Matthew 6:10, "Thy kingdom come." This is when we get our immortal bodies.

When Jesus died on the cross, he told the thief on his cross, "Today shalt thou be with me in paradise." If Jesus was to rise on the third day, one would think we went to the subterranean receptacle. In Matthew 12:40, we are told, "For as Jonas was in three days and three nights in the whale's belly, so shall the sun of man be three days and three nights in the heart of the earth." And the Lord Jesus took the spirits under the earth to heaven. First Peter 3:18–19 says:

> For Christ also hath once suffered for sins, the just for the unjust, that he might bring us to God, being put to death in the flesh, but quickened by the Spirit. By which also he went and preached unto the spirits in prison.

Let's note that it says the spirits that are in prison and not the soul. In John 20:17, Mary was told by Jesus, "Touch me not; for I have not ascended to my father." We should also note John 7:34, "Ye shall seek me, and shall not find me: and where I am, thither ye cannot come."

So let us go to the word for thither, which is *sham*,[306] which means there (transferred to time). John is now transferred to the Lord's day in Revelation 1. If Jesus told his apostles they could not go where he was going, which is to the third heaven, I don't think any spirit of man is in heaven but in the middle of the earth. Our soul may be there, but there are three parts of a man: the spirit, the soul, and the body.

---

[306] Ibid., 1988.

Let us note 1 Thessalonians 5:23, "And the very God of peace sanctify you wholly, and I pray God your whole spirit and soul and body be preserved blameless unto the coming of our Lord Jesus Christ." Wholly is *holotles*,[307] which means complete to the end (i.e., absolutely perfect), from *holos*,[308] which means "whole" or "all" (i.e., complete). Note that it says the body is preserved unto the coming of the Lord, and not at his appearing. This is the "we which are alive and remain until the coming of the Lord" of 1 Thessalonians 4:17.

Matthew 24:13 says, "But he that shall endure unto the end, the same shall be saved." The word means complete, whole, all. Note as told in 1 Thessalonians 5:23, "whole spirit and soul and body be preserved" as three different entities. Let's also note Luke 1:46–47, "And Mary said, My soul doth magnify the Lord. And my spirit hath rejoiced in God my Saviour." This tells us that the Savior is the Savior of the spirit. The soul is the ability to commune with God, and the soul goes back to God. Let's note E. W. Bullinger's comment on the Greek word for spirit:

> We should note the Hebrew word that means to rejoin. I believe this means the soul and the spirit are rejoined. Note the Hebrew word meaning to make live. That means you are dead. Man (Psychologically) Spirit as imparted to man, making him "a living soul. When taken back to God, man becomes "a dead soul." The Hebrew Nephesh (soul) is translated "body" in Leviticus 21:11, Numbers 6:6, 19:11, 13.[309]

This is why Ezekiel tells us this in 18:4, "Behold, all souls are mine; as the soul of the father, so also the soul of the son is mine: the soul that sinneth, it shall die." The souls that go back to God are considered by God as dead. This is the second death when the soul and the spirit and the body are not resurrected together.

---

307 Ibid., 2122.
308 Ibid.
309 *Bullinger's*, 728.

Just as there are seven spirits of God, let us also note Revelation 20:5, "But the rest of the dead lived not again until the thousand years were finished. This is the first resurrection." Note the language "rest of the dead lived not until." They live again because they bore the earthly and they bore the heavenly.

Let us also note Acts 24:15, "And have this hope toward God, which they themselves also allow, that there shall be a resurrection of the dead, both the just and the unjust." The unjust dead live not again until the thousand years. Why are the unjust not resurrected? The answer is in 1 Corinthians 15:49: "And as we have borne the image of the earthly, we shall bear the image of the heavenly." At the Great White Throne Judgment, where death and hell delivered up the dead, they were judged every man according to their works. And how are they judged? The Lord says in Luke 12:47–48:

> And that servant, which knew his Lord's will, and prepared not himself, neither did according to his will, shall be beaten with many stripes, But he that knew not, and did commit things worthy of stripes, shall be beaten with few stripes.

The Lord Jesus received the stripes that were due for Christians' sins before he was put on the cross. Note that it says "prepared not himself" to reject what the Lord Jesus did.

If the souls that rule and reign with Christ did not take his mark and are beheaded, they would have to be on the planet to refuse it. And if this is the first resurrection, how could there be a pre-tribulation resurrection? We should note, "But the rest of the dead." It's only those who have died who have been resurrected, and here is where the soul and the spirit are made whole, not the ones alive. If you die without Christ, you don't rise until a thousand years later at the Great White Throne Judgment. The word for "resurrection" is the Greek *anastasis*,[310] which means a stand up again (i.e., literal), a resurrection after death. Strong's comment is: "Spoken of the future and general resurrection at

---

[310] *Strong's*, 2023.

the end of all things." We should note it is at "the end of all things," just was we are told "he that endured until the end, the same shall be saved."

We will see in the next set of verses what happened on that third day. Do we not think that this will happen the same way in the future? As Isaiah states, "the past reveals the future."

Matthew 27:52–54 says:

> And the graves were opened; and many bodies of the saints which slept arose, And came out of the graves after his resurrection, and went into the holy city, and appeared unto many. Now when the centurion and they that were with him, watching Jesus, saw the earthquake, and those things that were done, they feared greatly, saying, Truly this was the son of God.

We should notice that the centurion saw the bodies of the saints who slept arise. They saw the bodies, and did we notice the earthquake? This is how the Lord opens the graves of the dead. We should notice that the Lord will descend from heaven at the resurrection of the dead to meet the saints in the air and the saints are caught up to meet the Lord in the clouds. This could only mean that God is not on the throne when this happens. So how do the pre-tribulation resurrection pastors say the resurrection of the church happens in chapter 4 when the Lord is clearly on his throne in this verse and John is called up to the throne room in heaven and not meeting the Lord in the air? There is no collocation here.

The people who are resurrected to meet the Lord in the air are seen by the people who are left here. The true sign of the resurrection of the dead is when the earth mourns. All the earth mourns in Matthew 24:30, after the tribulation of those days, when the sun and the moon don't give their light. When this happens, the Jews and the nonbelievers in the world will realize that Jesus is the true God of heaven. There is no vanishing of the saints, as told to us by the pre-tribulation pastors. As Isaiah prophesies, "The past reveals the future." This is why Matthew 27:52–54 was written. Also, John is in the spirit; it does not tell us he received his new incorruptible body. Now let us look at this last trump in 1 Corinthians 15:52. That last trumpet is sounded in Revelation 11:15, which is the last of the trumpet judgments. Most pastors say that this last trumpet is not the last trumpet of God. Well, I think they are wrong, as we see in this next scripture.

Revelation 8:2 says:

> And I saw the seven angels which stood before God: and to them was given seven trumpets.

If God gives these angels these trumpets, this makes these trumpets the trumpets of God. The last one to sound is in 1 Corinthians 15:52, where we all shall be changed. Everyone on the planet will see this happen, and all of the tribes of the earth will mourn when they see this, just as in Revelation 11:11–12:

> And after three days and an half the spirit of life from God entered into them, and they stood upon their feet; and great fear fell upon them which saw them. And they heard a great voice from heaven saying unto them, Come up hither. And they ascended up to heaven in a cloud; and their enemies beheld them.

"Beheld" is *theoreo*,[311] which means to be a spectator of (i.e., discern). The people of the world see them ascend up to heaven, just as we read in Matthew 24:52–54. Once again, it's the "spirit of Life" that entered into the dead prophets.

In verse 13, we read, "And the same hour was there a great earthquake." This great earthquake is caused because the Lord has come down from heaven to meet the saints in the clouds and the earthquake is to open the graves of the dead. We should also note Matthew 27:51–53:

---

[311]   Ibid., 2087.

> And behold, the veil of the temple was rent in twain from the top to the bottom; and the earth did quake, and the rocks rent; And the graves were opened; and many bodies of the saints which slept arose, And came out of the graves after his resurrection, and went into the holy city, and appeared unto many.

This is an example of the future resurrection of the dead saints on the last day. The past reveals the future. There is no earthquake in Revelation 4. Another missing part of the prophecy is of the resurrection of the dead if it happens where the pre-tribulation pastors teach.

We should also note Ezekiel 37:1–10:

> The hand of the Lord was upon me, and carried me out in the spirit of the Lord, and set me down in the midst of the valley which was full of bones. And caused me to pass by them round about: and, behold, there were many in the open valley; and, lo, they were very dry. And he said unto me, Son of Man, can these bones live? And I answered, O, God, thou knowest. And he said unto me, Prophesy upon these bones, and say unto them, O ye dry bones, hear the word of the Lord. Thus saith the Lord God unto these bones; Behold, I will cause breath to enter into you, and ye shall live: And I will lay sinews upon you, and will bring up flesh upon you, and cover you with skin, and put breath in you, and ye shall live; and ye shall know that I am the Lord God.

Stop here. Let's note "carried me out in the spirit of the Lord." Let's reference this to Revelation 1:10, "I was in the Spirit on the Lord's day." Note the same language. This is a detailed description of how the Lord will raise the dead on the last day. The last three sentences tell us of the new resurrected bodies of those who have died. This is why the study in the Old Testament is important. This is how "the dead in Christ shall rise first." The next scripture tells us when this happens.

"So I prophesied as I was commanded: and as I prophesied, there was a noise [*qowl*,[312] which means from an unused root meaning to call aloud; a voice, a sound: aloud, lightness, proclamation, spark, thunder], and behold a shaking [*raash*,[313] which means vibration, uproar; commotion, earthquake, fierceness), and the bones came together, bone to his bone.

We should note these Hebrew meanings. First "to call aloud," second the "thunder," and third the "earthquake." Isaiah tells us what to look for when these things happen in 29:6: "Thou shall be visited of the Lord of hosts with thunder, with earthquake, and great noise, with storm and tempest, and the flame of devouring fire." This is the answer to our daily prayer "Thou kingdom come, Thy will be done on earth as it is in heaven" of Matthew 6:10. We will match these Old Testament scriptures to the New Testament to see just where the "call aloud, thunder, and the earthquake" takes place. Let's note the same language is given in Revelation 11:18–19:

And the nations were angry, and thy wrath has come, and the time of the dead, that they should be judged, and that thou shouldest give reward unto thy servants the prophets, and to the saints, and them that fear thy name, small and great; and shouldest them that destroy the earth. And the temple of God was opened in heaven, and there was seen in his temple the ark of his testament: and there were lightings, and voices, and thunderings, and an earthquake, and great hail.

Note the Hebrew meanings of voice, thunders, and earthquake are found in Revelation 11:18–19. The same language is used to connect the Old Testament with the New Testament. This is when the "dead in

[312] Ibid., 1960.
[313] Ibid., 1972.

Christ shall rise first." This happens immediately after the tribulation of those days, when the sun and the moon don't give their light, and then shall appear the Son of Man in heaven. We are told nine times in the scriptures that we are to wait for the Lord's appearing. When Isaiah warns of God's coming judgment to Judah, he tells us this. Isaiah 29:6 says, "Thou shalt be visited of the Lord of hosts with thunder, and with earthquake, and great noise, with storm and tempest, and the flame of devouring fire." The same detailed language is used in Revelation 11:19. This is the twenty-first-century church day of visitation.

Let's also note why there are thunderings, lightings, voices, and the earthquake in Revelation 11:19. The past reveals the future.

Exodus 19:16, 18 says:

> And it came to pass on the third day in the morning, that there thunders and lightings, and a thick cloud upon the mount, and the voice of the trumpet exceeding loud; so all the people that were in the camp trembled. And mount Sinai was altogether on a smoke, because the Lord descended upon it in fire: and the smoke thereof ascended as the smoke of a furnace, and the whole mount quaked greatly.

This tells us this is where the Lord descends from heaven in Revelation. Note the Lord "descended upon it in fire" and the New Testament equivalent is 2 Thessalonians 1:7–8, "When the Lord Jesus shall be revealed from heaven with his mighty angels. In a flaming fire taking vengeance on them that know not God." This is the Lord's appearing.

Let us also note in Exodus the reference to the "third day." I believe that the Lord God does everything for a reason. This is the precept upon precept study. That "third day" is given in Hosea 6:2, "After two days [two thousand years] will he revive us: in the third day he will raise us up, and we shall live in his sight."

If our calendar is right, does this mean the Lord's return can't be until the year 2033? This is why we can't set a date. We are not 100 percent sure our calendar year is right.

Note in Exodus the earthquake when the Lord appeared. And the vengeance of 2 Thessalonians when the Lord appears is found in Ezekiel 38:19–20, "For in my jealousy and in the fire of my wrath I have spoken, Surely in that day there shall be a great shaking in the land of Israel. And all men that are upon the face of the earth, shall shake at my presence." Another sign of Revelation 11:19 is lightnings. That's found in Matthew 24:27, "For as the lightnings cometh out of the east, and shineth even unto the west; so shall also the coming of the Son of Man be." This light will shine around the whole world. And when does this happen? Immediately after the tribulation of those days shall the sun be darkened, and the moon shall not give her light. The third "thunder" is in Revelation 10:3, 6, "And he cried with a loud voice, a when a lion roareth: and when he had cried, seven thunders uttered their voices. 'That there should be time no longer.' The last day is where the mystery of God should be finished." Let's note the meanings for the word "finish": "To bring about, complete, fulfill, accomplish, to end."[314] And another Greek word means "perfect, consummate. (The word is used of inaugurating as king, to confirm a kingdom, and so, the consummation of the martyrs, and the glorification of the saints)."

During the last day, John tells us four times, "I will raise him up on the last day," and the fourth "fierceness." This is Revelation 19:15, "And out of his mouth goeth a sharp sword, that with it he should smite the nations: and shall rule them with a rod of iron: and he treadeth the winepress of the fierceness and wrath of almighty God." All these verses together give us a vivid explanation of what to look for at the Lord's return. Now let's finish Ezekiel.

> And when I beheld, lo, the sinews and the flesh came upon them, and the skin covered them above; but there was no breath [life] in them. Then said he said unto me, Prophesy unto the wind, prophesy, Son of Man, and say to the wind, Thus saith the Lord God; Come from the four winds, O breath, and breath upon these slain, that they may live. So I prophesied

---

[314] *Bullinger's*, 287.

as he commanded me, and the breath came into them, and they lived, and stood upon their feet, an exceeding great army.

We should note that Ezekiel tells us God raises the tribes of Jacob from the grave to be an "exceeding great army." Note the detailed description on how the dead receive their new incorruptible bodies. He does this to fight in the battle of Armageddon. And Daniel tells us that is when Michael stands up to lead this battle. This is the difference between the dead church and the dead of the tribes of Jacob. The church meets the Lord in the clouds to instruct them on how to be a judge during their thousand-year reign.

Before we leave Ezekiel 37, I want to give you one more verse. Verse 14 says, "And I shall put my spirit in you, and you shall live, and I shall place you in our own land: then you shall know that I have spoken it." Back in chapter 7, I showed you the verse, "Will you save your souls, the souls that ye hunt to make they fly." I explained the soul flies to heaven before the tribulation. Now here in Ezekiel, God says he puts his "spirits into the dead." I believe the souls go back to God but the spirit goes to the middle of the earth. The second things of this is when the Lord God is going to bring all the living and dead tribes back to the land of Israel. And the third thing is this. This is the time this is going to happen: "I have spoken it." We see this language in Ezekiel 38:19: "For in my jealousy and in the fire of my wrath have I spoken, Surely in that day there shall be a great shaking in the land of Israel." I believe what God spoke was, "Come up hither," and God uses the earthquake to open the graves. This is when the Lord will be in the heavens above. Ezekiel 38:20 says, "All men upon the face to the earth shall shake at my presence."

This need for this great army is found in Zechariah 12:8–9:

In that day shall the Lord defend the inhabitants of Jerusalem; and he that is feeble among them at that day shall be as David; and the house of David shall be as God, as the angel of the Lord before them. And

it shall come to pass in that day, that I will seek to
destroy all the nations that come against Jerusalem.

Those who were raised from the dead made the exceedingly great
army of Ezekiel. We should also note 1 John 3:2, "Behold, now are we
the sons of God, and it doth not yet appear what we shall be: but we
know that, when he shall appear, we shall be like him; for we shall see
him as he is." Zechariah tells us, "In that day shall the Lord defend the
inhabitants of Jerusalem," and Ezekiel 38:18–20 tells us when Gog
comes against the land of Israel all men will shake at God's presence. We
should also note that the inhabitants of Jerusalem that are feeble will
be as David. They all have new bodies. This is just as in 1 Corinthians
15:51, which says, "Behold, I shew you a mystery; We shall not all
sleep, but we all [*pas*,[315] which means all, any, ever, the whole] shall be
changed." Everybody on the planet whose name is in the Lamb's Book
of Life will be changed, but those who are "not written in the Lamb's
Book of Life" are saved, as Revelation 21:24 states: "And the nations of
them which are saved out of it," out from the wrath of God. Life goes
on after the Armageddon battle. This is what you don't hear from most
pastors. This is more bad news for the environmental people of the
History Channel who produce the series *Life after People*. This is why
the Lord God says, "Man's knowledge is foolish."
Let us note Ezekiel 37:13–14:

And ye shall know that I am the Lord, when I have
open your graves, O my people, and brought you up
out of your graves. And shall put my spirit in you, and
ye shall live, and I shall place you in your own land:
then shall you know that I the Lord have spoken it,
and performed it, saith the Lord.

The Lord says in Ezekiel 38:19, "For in my jealously and in the
fire of my wrath have I spoken, Surely in that day there shall be a great
shaking in the land of Israel." That is when Gog shall come against

---

[315] *Strong's*, 2131.

the land of Israel. We should note in Ezekiel 37:9, "Come from the four winds, O breath, and breath upon the slain, that they may live." Note also it say "my spirit" and not the soul. And here again is the earthquake when this happens.

We will match this with Mark 13:27, "And then shall he gather his angels, and shall gather together his elect from the four winds, from the uttermost part of the earth to the uttermost part of heaven." Note the word for uttermost, *akron*,[316] which means the extremity. That extremity is under the earth. We should note that Mark tells us that God's angels gather his elect from the four winds. These are the same four winds that Ezekiel tells us that put the spirit into the dead that they may live. This tells us that only the dead are gathered at this time.

Mark tells us this happens in verse 24: "But in those days, after that tribulation, the sun shall be darkened, and the moon shall not give her light." Ezekiel tells us this happens in 34:12:

> As a shepherd seeketh out his flock in the day he is among his sheep that are scattered; so will I [God] seek out my sheep, and will deliver them out of all the places where they have been scattered in the cloudy and dark day.

Both prophets tell us it happens when the sky is dark.

We should also note Matthew 28:2, "And behold, there was a great earthquake: for the angel of the Lord descended from heaven, and came and rolled back the stone from the door, and sat upon it." This is to allow the Lord Jesus to be raised from the grave. In the same hour that the two witnesses are called up, there is a great earthquake. The dead are called up, for this is how the Lord will open the graves the second time, just as the mountain quaked when Moses met with God on Sinai. Verse 14 says, "the second woe is past: and, behold, the third woe cometh quickly." John tells us here that the first two judgments, the seal and the trumpet judgments, have been concluded. The third, which are the vials of the wrath of God, are coming upon man quickly.

[316] Ibid., 2017.

Let us look at what the Bible tells us happens when the seventh trumpet is blown. Let us remember the number seven is the number of a symbol of completion. This is just what the Bible tells us.

Revelation 11:15 says:

> And the seventh angel sounded; and there were great voices in heaven, saying, The kingdoms of this world have become the kingdoms of our Lord, and of his Christ; and he shall rule for ever and ever.

This is where the Lord takes control of the earth, for all the kingdoms are now under his control. But what else happens at this time? Revelation 11:18 says, "And the nations were angry, and thy wrath is come, and the time of the dead, that they should be judged, and that thou shouldest give the reward unto thy servant the prophets, and to the saints, and them that fear thy name small and great; and shouldest destroy them that destroy the earth." It is not until God's wrath has come that he will judge the dead and give the reward to his servants, the prophets and the saints. And this is the same message given by Bullinger in the word meanings for finish. That reward is at the marriage supper of the lamb.

Let's also note Revelation 11:18, "And the time that the dead that they should be judged, that thou shouldest give reward unto thy servants the prophets, and to the saints." The word is *nekros*,[317] which means dead (literal or figurative); also as a noun dead. Note the language—the dead should be judged and not the alive saints. The word "judge" is *krino*,[318] which means properly to distinguish (i.e., decide mentally or judicially); by implication to try, condemn, punish; avenge, conclude, damn. *Strong's Complete Word Study Concordance* comment on page 2104 is "to separate, distinguish, discriminate between good and evil, select, choose out of the good." And the word for reward is *misthos*,[319] which means pay for service (literal or figurative), good or bad; hire,

---

[317] Ibid., 2117.

[318] Ibid., 2104.

[319] Ibid., 2115.

reward, wages. And this discriminating against good and evil is the parable of the wheat and the tares.

And if I am correct in my interpretation of the Bible, this is also the time when the Old Testament tells us to "hide thyself for a little moment until the indignation be over past" in Isaiah 26:20. There is a reason for this. We should also note the words "to separate and discriminate between the good and evil." This is given in Matthew 13:49: "So shall it be at the end of the world: the angels shall come forth, and sever the wicked from among the just." Note Matthew said "at the end." The end comes when there is time no longer, the last day. That is found in Revelation 10:6–7: "There is time no longer. But in the days of voice of the seventh angel, when he begin to sound, the mystery of God should be finished." This means Revelation 10:6-7 happens at the same time as Revelation 11:18. This is the judgment of those of Matthew, Mark, and Luke who don't taste of death till they see the coming of the Lord. The dead are judged at the Lord's appearing, and those who remain are judged at his coming. The just are the meek who inherit the earth.

For pastors to preach that the whole church just vanishes before the tribulation is not scriptural, because the Lord Jesus states in Matthew 24:13, "All that endure until the end, the same shall be saved." According to *Strong's Concordance* the end here is *telos*,[320] which means properly the point aimed at as a limit, i.e. (by implication) the conclusion of an act or state. Can pre-tribulation pastors prove that the conclusion of the act which is the church age comes in Revelation 4?

Hosea 5:14–15 says:

> For I [God] will be unto Ephraim as a lion, and a young lion to the house of Judah: I even I will tear and go away, I will take away, and none shall rescue him. I will go and return to my place, till they acknowledge their offence, and seek my face: in their affliction they will seek me early.

---

[320] Ibid., 2163.

Are the Christians (Ephraim) of the world not expecting the soon return of our savior Jesus? He will return as the "Young Lion of the tribe of Judah" to the Jews of the "house of Judah" at the time of Armageddon. We should also notice that they will "seek me early" and at what time "in their affliction." Let us note the word for affliction is *tsar*,[321] which means a tight place (usually figurative) (i.e., trouble); adversary, distress, tribulation. The word "trouble" is the time of Jacob's trouble of Jeremiah 30. The tribulation is the time of tribulation in the book of Revelation. We should note here that God goes and returns to His place. That means he was here on earth before.

Hosea 6:1–3 says:

> Come and let us return unto the Lord: for he hath torn and he will heal us; he hath smitten, and he will bind us up. After two days will he revive us: in the third day, he will raise us up, and we shall live in his sight? Then shall we know, if we follow on to know the Lord: His going fort is prepared as the morning: and he shall come unto us as the rain, as the latter and former rain unto the earth.

Hosea tells us about the Lord's two visits of the earth when he says, "He shall come unto us as the rain, as the latter [to rule and reign for a thousand years] and the former [to die on the cross] unto the earth, and after two days [two thousand years] on the third day." He would revive us in the third day he will raise us up (resurrection), and we will live in His sight. Revive is *chayah*,[322] which means to live, whether literal or figurative; causative to revive, keep (leave), (make) alive, certainly, give (promise) life, (let, suffer to) life, nourish up, preserve (alive), quicken. The *Webster's Dictionary* meaning of revive is "to return to life or consciousness; to return to health and vigor; to produce again after an interval." It's the dead who are revived back to life. Note also that

[321] Ibid., 1956.
[322] Ibid., 1855.

the word means to keep alive. The word for "bind" is *chabash*,[323] which
means to wrap firmly; figurative to stop, to rule; bind (up), gird about,
govern, healer, put, saddle, wrap about. To bind in Hebrew means to
rule, govern, and heal. We should note that this rise up does not mean
to heaven but to bring the lost tribes of the house of Israel back to
the land of Israel. We should note the Hebrew word that means to
rejoin. I believe this means the soul and the spirit are rejoined. Note
the Hebrew word mean to make live. That means you are dead. Note
the Hebrew word meaning to govern. These rule and reign with Christ.
Note the Hebrew word meaning to heal.

We're told in Revelation 22:2:

> In the midst of the street of it [Jerusalem], and on
> either side of the river, was there the tree of life, which
> bare twelve manner of fruits, and yielded her fruit
> every month: and the leaves of the tree were for the
> healing of the nations.

We are also told Malachi 4:2, "But unto you that fear my name
shall the Sun of righteousness arise with healing in his wings." The
word "raise" is *zarach*,[324] which means; property, to irradiate, i.e., to rise
(as the sun); (specifically) to appear. The Lord is irradiating in Ezekiel
38:18 "that my fury shall come up to my face." And appear is Matthew
24:30 "and then shall the Son of Man in heaven." This places the wrath
of God immediately after the tribulation of those days, the sun will
be darkened and the moon shall give her light, and the powers of the
heavens shall be shaken.

In Ezekiel when the graves are opened, God puts his spirit in them.
In the book of Revelation when the two witnesses are called up, it
states the spirit of life from God entered them. In Luke 8:50, when the
Lord raised the daughter of one of the rulers of the synagogue, Jesus
said, "Fear not, believe only, and she shall be made whole." According
to *Strong's Complete Word Study Concordance,* the word "whole" in

---

323 Ibid., 1851.
324 Ibid.

Greek is *sozo*,[325] which is the same word as the word for "save". It is to save the spirit in the middle of the earth. His definition is to be safe (i.e., to deliver or protect), be (made) whole. When Jesus said, "Maid, arise," her spirit came again. Why does the Bible never say that the soul arises?

Can the soul and the spirit be two different indistinguishable (not clearly understood) individual (existing as an indivisible whole) things? John 6:33 says, "It is the spirit that quickeneth: the flesh profiteth nothing: the words that I speak unto you, they are spirit, and they have life." First Peter 3:18–19 says, "For Christ also hath once suffered for sins, the just for the unjust, that he might bring us to God, being put to death in the flesh, but quickened by the spirit: By which also he went and preached unto the spirits in prison." Both quicken are *zoopoieo*,[326] which means to (re-) vitalize, (literal or figurative). The word for prison is *phulake*,[327] which means a guarding, the act, the person; metaphorically a place where someone is watched, guarded, kept in custody. So is it just the spirit that goes to this prison, and the souls go back to God.

Let's note 1 Thessalonians 4:14: "For if we believe that Jesus died and rose again, even so them also which sleep [died] in Jesus will God bring with him." If the Lord Jesus is leaving from the throne, that means he is in heaven. These are the souls who were killed for the Word of God, which John told us about in Revelation. John sees the souls that were killed and that sat upon thrones, and they lived and reigned with Christ a thousand years in Revelation 20.

In 1 Thessalonians 4:14, we are told God will bring those that are in heaven and now in 1 Thessalonians 4:16, "And the dead in Christ will rise first." This is 1 Corinthians 5:5, "That the spirit may be saved in the day of the Lord." This is the resurrection of the spirit under the earth at the Lord's appearing when the soul and the spirit are reunited to be made whole. Then there are the people of 1 Thessalonians 5:23, "And I pray God your whole spirit and soul and body be preserved

[325] Ibid., 2161.
[326] Ibid., 2084
[327] Ibid., 2175.

blameless unto the coming of our Lord Jesus Christ." The people who are preserved blameless unto the coming of the Lord receive this in Acts 2:17, "And it shall come to pass in the last days, saith God, I will pour out my Spirit upon all flesh." These are the saints who never taste of death, as told by Matthew, Mark, and Luke.

First let's read Hebrews 4:12, "For the Word of God is quick, and powerful, and sharper than any two-edged sword, piercing even to the dividing [*merismos*,[328] which means a separation or distribution] asunder of soul and spirit. I believe that this does mean the soul and spirit can be separated. Is this why the dead in Christ are raised first? John 5:25 says, "Verily, verily, I say unto you, the hour is coming, and now is, when the dead shall hear the voice of the Son of God: and they shall hear shall live." Is it to unite the soul, which is heaven, with the spirit, which is the prison? Let us note again the word *zoopoieo*,[329] meaning quickened to (re-) vitalize." I believe this means to join together the soul with the spirit. Let us also note E. W. Bullinger's meaning for quicken "to make alive, give life, esp. of that which will last for ever, to give eternal life."[330] We read in Revelation 6:9, "And when He had opened the fifth seal, I saw under the alter the souls of men of them that were slain for the Word of God." Christians fight and die during the tribulation period, for the scriptures tell us, "He that killeth by the sword must be killed with the sword. Here is the patience and the faith of the saints."

We read in Revelation 7:14, "And I said unto him, Sir, thou knowest. And he said into me, These are they which came out of great tribulation, and have washed their robes, and made them white in the blood of the lamb." These who came out of the great tribulation have to wash their robes before they put them on. Also note that in Revelation 7:9 it says "souls of men" but Revelation 7:14 says "they." I believe they are not called souls because they are "dead souls," which will not receive a spirit. This is where Revelation 16:15 says, "Blessed is he that watcheth, and keepeth his garments, lest he walk naked, and

---

[328] Ibid., 2113.

[329] Ibid., 2084.

[330] *Bullinger's*, 618.

they see his shame." Note the words "these that came out of the great tribulation."

This tells us that Christians don't die during the great tribulation. This is Psalms 27:5: "For in the time of trouble he shall hide me in his pavilion: in the secret of his tabernacle he shall hide me, he shall set me upon a rock." This is Psalms 50:15: "And call upon me in the time of trouble: I will deliver (protect) thee, and thou shalt glorify me." The precept to this psalm is 2 Thessalonians 1:10: "When he shall come to be glorified in his saints, and to be admired in all them that believe (because our testimony among you was believed) in that day." This is Psalms 21:1: "The Lord hear thee in the time of trouble: the name of the God of Jacob [Jesus] defend thee." This is Psalms 81:7: "Thou callest in the time of trouble, I delivered (protected) thee; I answered thee in the secret place of thunder." They are protected by God at this time, and this is what makes the great tribulation great for Christians. The great tribulation is over. These are the people who have died during the wrath of God. Now let's look at some other scriptures.

Second Corinthians 4:14 says, "Knowing that he which raised up the Lord Jesus shall raise us up also by Jesus, and shall be present us with you." When this happens, let's note what is said. Second Corinthians 5:1–5 says:

> For we know that if our earthly house of this tabernacle were dissolved, we have a building of God, a house not made with hands, eternal in the heavens. For in this we groan, earnestly desiring to be clothed upon with our house which is from heaven: If so be that being clothed we shall not be found naked. For we that are in this tabernacle do groan, being burden: not for that we be unclothed upon, that morality might be swallowed up of life. Now he that hath wrought us for the selfsame thing is God. Who also hath given unto us the earnest of the Spirit.

Those who have accepted the Lord Jesus as their Savior will not be found naked because at the resurrection of the dead, morality will be swallowed up into eternal life. The souls of the dead that are in heaven are united with the spirit, which is beneath the earth on the last day.

The equivalent scripture in the Old Testament is Daniel 12:2: "And many of them that sleep in the dust of the earth shall awake, some to everlasting life, and some to shame everlasting contempt." And this is "a time of trouble, such as never was since there was a nation." This sounds like a resurrection of the dead after the great tribulation period.

And those called to the marriage supper of the lamb are spoken of in Revelation 19:8, "She should be arrayed in fine linen, clean and white: for the fine linen is the righteousness of the saints." Note those called to the supper should be arrayed in fine linen; they don't have to wash them. Note "arrayed" is *periballo*,[331] which means to throw all around (i.e., with clothing).

Now let's compare this to the Qur'an, chapter 22:24 on page 322:

> Allah will admit those who believe and act righteously into the Garden beneath which rivers flow. They will be given bracelets of gold and pearls to wear, and their raiment therein shall be silk.

If "fine linen is the righteousness of the saints" who are these that are wearing silk? It is small but another contradiction to the Bible. Muhammad got one thing right when he said beneath, but it will not be a garden.

Also note Revelation 14. The people who receive the mark of the beast receive the wrath of God. Note the language "the same" receive the wrath of God. It specifically says those who receive the mark of the beast. Now let's note verse 12, "Here is the patience of the saints: here are they that keep the commandments of God, and the faith of Jesus." And who are these who have "the faith of Jesus"? They would be the church. Now note verse 13, "Blessed are they which die in the Lord

---

4

from henceforth." Who are these who "die in the Lord" if it is not the church?

We also have this in Isaiah 57:15–16:

> For thus saith the high and lofty One that inhabiteth eternity, whose name is holy dwell in the high and lofty place, with him also with is of a contrite [*dakka*,[332] which means cushed (literal power, or figurative contrite): destruction] and humble [*shapal*,[333] which means depressed, literal or figurative] spirit, to revive [*chayah*,[334] which means to live, whether literal or figurative; preserve, quicken, save] the spirit of the humble, and to revive the heart [*leb*,[335] which means; the heart, the will and even the intellect] of the contrite ones.
>
> For I will not contend forever, neither will I be always wroth: for the spirit should not fail before me, and the souls that I have made.

We should note that the humble spirit is preserved, quickened, and saved, but there is a problem with contrite spirit's heart, which is the intellect of the contrite spirit. Is the intellect of the spirit the soul? Isaiah says, "The souls that I have made." We should also note, "For the spirit shall fail before me," and the souls I have made. Remember, God made his angels spirits. A third of the spirits rebelled with Satan against God and are the ones of whom Isaiah tells us, "The spirits fail before me." So God creates the soul of man when we attain this earthly body. Let's note this in 1 Corinthians 15:45, "And so it is written, The first man Adam was made a living soul; the last Adam was made a quickening spirit."

---

[332] Ibid., 1839.

[333] Ibid., 1993.

[334] Ibid., 1855.

[335] Ibid., 1888.

In Mark 12:30, the Lord says, "And thou shalt love the Lord thy God with all thy heart, and with all thy soul, and with all thy mind, and with all thy strength: this is the first commandment." We note the word "mind" is *dianoia*,[336] which means deep though, properly the faculty (mind or its disposition). It is from the word *nous*,[337] which means the intellect (i.e., mind). Compare to *psuche*,[338] which means breath (i.e., by implication) spirit. The mind is the spirit of man. There are two separate states of being. And we read that most of the people are killed in the battle of Armageddon, which are the armies. Does this not tell us that their souls make it to heaven but not their spirits?

Ezekiel tells us, "All souls are mine, the soul that sinneth, it shall die." E. W. Bullinger says, "When taken back to and by God, man becomes a dead soul."[339] Revelation 20:6 tells us, "Blessed and holy is he that hath part in the first resurrection: on such the second death hath no power." This makes the second death the soul in heaven without a spirit. First Corinthians 5:5 says "That the spirit may be saved in the day of the Lord Jesus."

It is written in 1 Timothy 4:10, "For therefore we both labour and suffer reproach, because we trust in the living God, who is the Saviour of all men, specially [*malista*,[340] which means most or particularly] of those that believe." If the Lord is the Savior of "all" men, doesn't this mean their souls are saved? It is only people who have eternal life on earth are the people whose spirits and souls are united.

This prophecy is given to the Babylonians in Jeremiah 51:57:

> And they shall sleep a perpetual [*owlam*,[341] which means properly concealed (i.e., vanishing point, always)] sleep, and not wake [*qutws*,[342] which means

---

[336]   Ibid., 2053.

[337]   Ibid., 2119.

[338]   Ibid.

[339]   *Bullinger's*, 728.

[340]   *Strong's*, 2110.

[341]   Ibid., 1933.

[342]   Ibid., 1960.

to wake (literal or figurative), arise, wake, watch. Identical ti *quwts*,[343] which means to clip off; used only as denominative; to spend the harvest season], saith the King, whose name is the Lord of hosts.

This tells us that the spirits of the Babylonians are in the grave for the thousand-year reign (to spend the harvest season) of the Lord Jesus. Their spirits don't rise until the great white throne judgment.
Isaiah 26:13–14 says:

O Lord our God, other lords beside thee have had dominion over us: but by thee only will we make mention of thy name. They are dead, they shall not live; they are deceased, they shall not rise [*quwm*,[344] which means to rise, to continue, remain]: therefore hast thou visited and destroyed them, and made all their memory to perish.

Isaiah tells us that people who have other lords do not rise when they die. Note it says "thou visited"; this is the time of visitation when the Lord will destroy those who destroy the earth. The people with other gods shall perish. This is the same message of Numbers 24:20: "And when he (Balaam) looked on Amalek, he took up his parable, and said, Amalek was the first of the nations; but in the latter end shall be that he perish for ever." This is the latter end when the descendants of Esau perish forever, at the time of the Lord's visitation.

We should also note in Psalms 37:9, "For evildoers shall be cut off; but those that wait upon the Lord, they shall inherit the earth." Evildoers is *raa*,[345] which means properly to spoil; figurative to make good for nothing (i.e., bad). The comment in *Strong's Complete Word Study Concordance* is, "A verb meaning to be bad, to do wrong. The

---

[343] Ibid.
[344] Ibid.
[345] Ibid., 1972.

root of the verb indicates breaking, in contrast to the word *taman*, which means to be whole."[346]

In all my years of listening to pastors, I have never heard the resurrection interpreted in this manner. I could be wrong or I could be right, but I will leave this to the Bible scholars to determine if this is correct. All I can say to the pre-tribulation resurrection pastors, such as John Hagee, when he says of his church, "Pack up, we're going up, in the twinkling of an eye to heaven before the tribulation," I say, "Unpack. You're not going up because God's judgments must begin at the house of God, the church." As stated in the past in Ezekiel 9:4, 6, "Set a mark upon the foreheads of the men and Slay utterly old and young, both maids, and little children, and women: but come not near any man upon whom is the mark; and begin at my sanctuary." The past reveals the future. I believe all these pastors miss the greater prophecy. Blessed are the meek, for they shall inherit the earth. This is given in the scriptures. As Jesus told his disciples in John 3:12, "If I have told you of earthly things, and ye believe not, how shall ye believe, if I tell you of heavenly things?"

Before we leave this, let's review Daniel 12:1–3:

> And at that time shall Michael stand up, the great prince that standeth for the children of thy people: and there shall be a time of trouble, such as never was since there was a nation even to that same time: and at that time thy people shall be delivered, every one that is written in the book. And many of them that sleep in the dust of the earth shall awake, some to everlasting life, and some to shame and everlasting contempt. And they that be wise shall shine as the brightness of the firmament; and they that turn many to righteousness as the stars for ever and ever.

This time of trouble is the great tribulation period, and it's at this time that Michael stands up his people and they are delivered.

---

[346]   Ibid.

Delivered is *malat*[347] which means to be smooth (i.e., by implication) to escape, preserve, save, speedily. But those who are in the dust of the earth awake. Awake is *quwts*,[348] which means to awake (literal or figurative); arise, wake, watch. It is identical to *quwts*,[349] which means to clip off, used only as a denominative from *qaytis*,[350] which means harvest, whether the product or the season.

Some of these arise into everlasting life, while others into shame and everlasting contempt. "Shame" is *cherpah*,[351] which means contumely, disgrace, the pudenda, rebuke. From *charaph*,[352] which means to pull off (i.e., by implication) to repose (as by stripping), specifically to betroth, blaspheme. Note the Hebrew word meaning disgrace, stripping, is the Old Testament equivalent of the New Testament verse given in Revelation 16:15, "Blessed is he that watcheth, and keepeth his garments, lest he walk naked, and they see his shame." Also note Revelation 7:14, "These are they which came out of great tribulation, and have washed their robes, and made them white in the blood of the lamb." And the word "contempt" is *deraown*,[353] which means an object of aversion. "And they that be wise." Wise is *sakal*,[354] which means to be circumspect, and hence, intelligent.

The wise in this resurrection are intelligent, and to be circumspect means to consider all circumstances and possible consequences. Now let's look at the word "spirit" in the Greek. It is *pneuma*,[355] which means vital principle or mental disposition. This means the spirit has the understanding or intellect, which means not all people in the resurrection will have a spirit. And the word "shame" in Hebrew means contumely. "Contumely" in *Webster's Dictionary* means, "Rude language

---

[347] Ibid., 1901.
[348] Ibid., 1960.
[349] Ibid.
[350] Ibid., 1961.
[351] Ibid., 1864.
[352] Ibid.
[353] Ibid., 1841.
[354] Ibid., 1984.
[355] Ibid., 2137.

and treatment arising from haughtiness and contempt." Why would not these souls receive this treatment? After they heard the message of the Lord Jesus and refused to accept him as Lord and Savior, and after he died on the cross for all of mankind's sins, they refused him.

This matches 2 Timothy 2:20–21:

> But in a great house (in my Father's house there are many mansions) there are not only vessels of gold and silver, but of wood and earth; and some to honour, and some to dishonour.

Note that Timothy says "some to honour," Daniel says "arise to everlasting life," Timothy says "some to dishonor," and Daniel says "others into shame and everlasting contempt."

Verse 21 says:

> If a man therefore purge [*ekkathairo*,[356] which means to cleanse thoroughly] himself from these, he shall be a vessel unto honour, sanctified, and meet [*euchrestos*,[357] which means easily used, (i.e., useful, profitable)] for the master's use, and prepared unto every good work.

Those who arise to everlasting lasting life who are honorable are profitable for the Master's (the Lord Jesus) use. They rule and reign with Christ a thousand years.

We should also note that Daniel tells us of a resurrection when there is the "time of trouble such as never was." It is just as Ezekiel 38:23, which says, "I [God] will magnify and sanctify myself and will be known in the eyes of many nations." "Sanctify" is *qadash*,[358] which means to clean (ceremonially or morally), appoint, consecrate, dedicate, defile, hallow, or proclaim. We should note the Hebrew word meaning to clean. Revelation 7:14 says, "These that came out of the

---

[356] Ibid., 2065.
[357] Ibid., 2083.
[358] Ibid., 1958.

great tribulation, and have washed their robes, and made them white in the blood of the lamb." We should note here that it states, "And have washed their robes, and made them white in the blood of the lamb." Christians already will have white robes waiting for them when they get to heaven.

Even in Habakkuk 3:16 we are told, "And I trembled in myself, that I might rest in the day of trouble: when He cometh up unto the people, he will invade them with his troops." Habakkuk tells us, "He will invade them with his troops" and Ezekiel tells us of "an exceedingly great army." Revelation 19:14 tells us, "And the armies which were in heaven followed him [the Lord Jesus] upon white horses, clothed in white linen, white and clean." But we should note the previous verse, "And he [the Lord Jesus] was clothed with a vesture dipped in blood: and his name is called the Word of God." For the battle is the Lord's.

Once again, we are told that in the day of trouble is when the Lord comes. "Cometh" here is *alah*,[359] which means to ascend; arise (up), (cause to) ascend up, at once, raise, recover, restore, (cause to) or burn. We should note when he comes, the Hebrew word means to ascend. The Lord descends from heaven and causes believers to ascend up (the dead or in this case the tribes of Israel, and not to heaven but back to the land of Israel, for the meek will inherit the earth) at once (in the twinkling of an eye). We should also note when the Lord comes in Habakkuk, it means "cause to burn," and Malachi tells us the same in 4:1:

> For, behold, the day cometh, that shall burn as a oven, yea, and all that do wickedly, shall be stubble: the day cometh shall burn them up, saith the Lord of hosts, that it shall leave neither root or branch.

And Isaiah tells us the same thing in 64:2: "As when the melting fire burneth. The fire causeth the water to boil, to make thy name known to thine adversaries, that the nations may tremble at thy presence!"

---

[359] Ibid., 1935.

This fire that burns happens at the Lord's presence. But there is this prophecy in Isaiah 43:2:

> When thou passeth through the water, I will be with thee; and through the rivers, I will be with thee: when thou walkest through the fire, thou shalt not be burned; neither shall the flame kindle upon thee.

We should also note that "fire that burneth" is against in Malachi "the wicked," and in Isaiah, it's against "thine adversaries." Those who are the Lord's are not burned, neither shall the flame kindle upon them. The tremble in Isaiah is *ragaz*,[360] which means to quiver (with any violent emotion, especially anger or fear), be afraid, stand in awe, provoke, shake, trouble.

When Shadrach, Meshach, and Aded-nego were put in the furnace by Nebuchadnezzar, this is how God delivered them in Daniel 3:27: "These men, upon the whose bodies the fire had no power, nor was a hair singed, neither were their coats changed, nor the smell of fire had passed on them." For God sent his angel and delivered his servants who trusted in him. The past reveals the future. Our trust in the Lord Jesus Christ will deliver us from the judgments of God, because our righteousness is according to our works.

Jeremiah tells us when the world will tremble in 10:10:

> But the Lord is the true God, he is a living God, and an everlasting king: at his wrath the earth shall tremble, and the nations shall not be able to abide his indignation.

In Revelation 16:15–16, we are told:

> Behold, I come as a thief and he gathered them into a place called Armageddon.

---

[360] Ibid., 1967.

This is when the indignation of the Lord happens, when the Lord comes as a thief at Armageddon. Now let's note what happens to those who were deceived and who received the mark of the beast.

Revelation 19:21 says:

> And the remnant [those that received the mark of the beast] were slain with the sword of him [the Lord Jesus] that sat upon the horse, which sword proceeded out of his mouth: and all the fowls were filled with their flesh.

So when are these people slain? Revelation 14:14 says, "And behold a white cloud, and upon the cloud one sat like unto the Son of Man, having a sharp sickle." People who are deceived by Satan do not inherit the earth. Let us not forget Luke 9:27: "But those mine enemies, which would not that I [the Lord Jesus] should reign over them, bring hither, and slay them before me."

We are told in Job 36:29–33 and 37:1–5:

> Also can any understand the spreadings of the clouds, or the noise [*t shu ah*,[361] which means a crashing or loud clamor; crying, noise, shouting, stir. From *show*,[362] which means from an unused root meaning to rush over, by implication devastation; desolation, destroy, destruction.] of his tabernacle. Behold, he spreadeth his light upon it, and covereth the bottom of the sea. For by them judgeth [*diyn*,[363] which means to rule, by implication to judge: also to strive; execute (judgment), judge] he the people; he giveth meat in abundance. With clouds, he covereth the light; and commandeth it not to shine by the cloud that cometh

---

[361] Ibid., 2002.
[362] Ibid., 1979.
[363] Ibid., 1839.

betwixt [*paga*,[364] which means to impinge, make intercession, intercessor, light (upon), meet (together), pray.] The noise thereof sheweth concerning the vapour [*alah*,[365] which means; to ascend)].

Stop here!

Let's review what we just read. We first notice clouds are being used as judgment. In these clouds is destruction by his tabernacle, or by them God is to rule and give the judgment. And God gives meat in abundance. Let's go to Luke 12:42, "Who is that faithful and wise steward, whom the Lord shall make ruler over his household, to give them their portion of meat in due season." So this is the meat given in abundance. And with the clouds, God covers the light, making the earth dark. And between there is the intercessor (Lord Jesus) where he meets together with his saints. Note also the Hebrew word meaning "to ascend." And now to chapter 37:

> At this my heart [*leb*,[366] which means the heart; used figuratively very widely for the feelings, the will and even the intellectual; likewise for the center of anything] trembleth [*charad*,[367] which means to shudder with terror; hence to fear; also to hasten; be (made) afraid, discomfit, quake, tremble], and is moved out of his place. Hearing attentively the noise of his voice, and the sound that goeth out of his mouth. He directeth it under the whole heaven, and his lightning unto the ends of the earth. After it a voice roareth [*sha'ah*,[368] which means to rumble or moan; mightily, roar]: he thundereth [*ra am*,[369]

---

[364] Ibid., 1944.
[365] Ibid., 1935.
[366] Ibid., 1888.
[367] Ibid., 1863.
[368] Ibid., 1974.
[369] Ibid., 1972.

which means; tumble (i.e., with be violently agitated; specifically to crash[of thunder]); figurative to irritate (with anger); roar thunder, trouble.] with the voice of his excellency: and he will not stay them when his voice [*qowl*,[370] which means to call aloud; a voice or sound; hold peace, proclamation, thunder] is heard.

Stop here!

Let's review what is said here. At the heart of or center of something, which I believe is the middle of the tribulation period, when the clouds darken the sun, as is stated in the previous verses, is when God is moved out of his place. And "his lightning unto the ends of the earth" here in Job is found in Matthew 24:27: "For as the lightnings cometh out of the east, and shineth even unto the west; so shall the coming of the Son of Man." This is because God is agitated and with anger. "And when his voice" to call aloud is the come up hither, the proclamation. Also note the Hebrew word meaning thunder. Note in Revelation when the seven thunders utter their voices that there is time no longer and the mystery of God should be finished. The secret Bible code the Jewish people are looking for is in the Bible as God gave it. I have read the book *The Bible Code* by Michael Drosnin. The only secret in the Bible is man's lack of study.

Throughout scripture, the Lord's presence is not until his wrath. Let's note the account of the Lord's wrath on Sodom and Gomorrah. In Genesis 18:1 it says, "And the Lord appeared unto him [Abraham] in the plains of Mamre." In verse 2, we will read that the Lord has two witnesses: "And he [Abraham] lifted up his eyes and looked, and, lo, three men stood before him." Does the Lord need two witnesses to justify to the residents in heaven that his punishment is just? They move Lot out of the cities to the city of Zoar. Verse 22 says, "Haste thee, escape thither; for I cannot do any thing till thou be come thither." Lot was still on the planet when the wrath of God came to cities of Sodom and Gomorrah. As Isaiah prophesies, "The past reveals the future." Almost all of the writers in the Bible tell us that God's presence is not

---

[370] Ibid., 1960.

known until the battle of Armageddon. In Revelation, he tells us this is when he comes as a thief. So how can these preachers say there is a pre-tribulation resurrection?

Isaiah 26:16, 19–21 says:

> Lord, in trouble have they visited thee, they prayer when thy chasten was upon them . . . Thy dead men shall live, together with my dead body shall thy arise. Awake and sing, ye that dwell in the dust; for thy dew is the dew of herbs and the earth shall cast out the dead. Come, my people, enter thou into thy chambers, and shut thy doors about thee: hide thy self as it were for a little moment, until the indignation be overpast. For, behold the Lord cometh out of his place to punish the inhabitants of the earth for their iniquity: the earth shall disclose her blood, and shall no more cover her slain.

> In that day the Lord with sore and great and strong sword shall punish the Leviathan the piecing serpent, ever leviathan that crooked serpent and they shall slay the dragon that is in the sea (Isa. 27:1).

"Thy dead men shall live together with my dead body shall arise, ye that dwell in the dust" is the resurrection of the dead. We should also note the time when this happens, "When thy chasten was upon them." Note also that it states in trouble with the Hebrew word meaning tribulation. Then he tells others to hide themselves for a little moment, until the indignation is past. Is the "hide thyself for a little moment" a message to the ten tribes of the House of Israel? This is how they are hid. In Psalms 27:5: "For in the time of trouble he shall hide me in his pavilion; in the secret place of his tabernacle shall he hide me." For behold, the Lord comes out of his place to punish the inhabitants of the earth. Let's note the word for punish is *paqad*,[371] which means

---

[371] Ibid., 1949.

to visit (with friendly or hostile intent), avenge, deliver to keep. This is the day of visitation the church has been looking for when the dead will hear the voice of the Son of Man. This is when the Lord descends from heaven with a shout.

We will match this in 2 Thessalonians 1:7–8:

> And to you who are troubled rest with us, when the Lord Jesus shall be revealed from heaven with his mighty angels. In flaming fire taking vengeance of them that know not God, and that obey not the gospel of our Lord Jesus Christ.

Let's note the words "know not God"; those are the Muslims. Let's also note that the Hebrew word meaning punish is to keep—to keep from the punishment as stated in Revelation 3:10: "Because thou hast kept the word of my patience, I also will keep thee from the hour of temptation."

And "in that day the lord with his sore and great and strong sword shall punish Leviathan," we are told in verse 4, "I would burn them together." Matthew 13:40 says, "As therefore the tares are gathered and burned in the fire; so shall it be in the end of this world." Verse 12 says, "And it shall come to pass in that day, ye shall gather one by one, O you children of Israel." This verse matches Matthew 24:40: "Then two shall be in the field; the one shall be taken and the other left." Let's note the word for taken is *paralambano*,[372] which means to receive near (i.e., associate with oneself); by analogy to assume an office. This assuming an office is to be a judge during the thousand-year reign of Christ. Verse 13 says, "And it shall come to pass in that day, that a great trumpet shall be blown, and worship the Lord in the holy mount at Jerusalem." This is the trumpet of 1 Corinthians 15:52: "for the trumpet shall sound, and the dead shall be raised incorruptible, and we all shall be changed."

Let us note here that this is when the Lord leaves heaven during his wrath to punish Satan and his followers, and in 27:1, we should notice

---

[372] Ibid., 2130.

that it says, "They." Are the "They" the Lord Jesus and the resurrected saints? And when does this happen?

Ezekiel 19:18–19, 23 says:

> And it shall come to pass at the same time when Gog shall come against the land of Israel, saith the Lord God, that my fury shall come up in my face. For in my jealousy and in the fire of my wrath have I spoken, Surely in that day there shall be a great shaking in the land of Israel. Thus I will magnify myself, and sanctify myself; and I will be known in the eyes of many nations, and they shall know that I am the Lord God.

Once again, we have the Lord leaving heaven when we are told, "I will be known in the eyes of many nations." And when will the people see the Lord? That is in Matthew 24:30:

> Immediately after the tribulation of those days shall the sun be darkened, and the moon shall give her light, and the stars shall fall from heaven, and the powers of heaven shall be shaken: and then shall appear the sign of the Son of Man in heaven.

This is when the Lord will descend from heaven with a shout at the start of Armageddon. This is when Isaiah, Ezekiel, Zechariah, Joel, Matthew, Mark, Luke, and Revelation all tell us the Lord comes and not in a secret pre-tribulation resurrection.

Revelation 19:15 says:

> And out of his mouth goeth a sharp sword, that with it he should smite the nations: and he shall rule them with the rod of iron: and he treadeth the winepress of the fierceness and wrath of almighty God.

Isaiah 13:9–13 says:

> Behold, the day of the Lord cometh, cruel both with
> wrath and fierce anger, to lay the land desolate; and
> he shall destroy the sinners thereof out of it . . . For
> the stars of heaven and the constellations thereof shall
> not give their light: the sun shall be darkened in its
> going forth, and the moon shall not cause her light to
> shine. And I will punish the world for their evil; and
> the wicked for iniquity; and I will cause the arrogancy
> of the proud to cease, and will lay low the haughtiness
> of the terrible. I will make a man more precious than
> fine gold; even a man than the golden wedge of Ophir.
> Therefore I will shake the heavens, and the earth shall
> remove out of her place, in the wrath of the Lord of
> Hosts, and in the day of his fierce anger.

We should notice that it is until the day of his wrath that the Lord
comes, and when he comes, it is with fierce anger, and he shall destroy
"the sinners" out of it when the sun and the moon are darkened. Isaiah
makes it very clear here that the sinners are destroyed and not the
righteous. Proverbs 11:30–31 says, "The fruit of the righteous is a tree
of life; and he that winneth souls is wise. Behold, the righteous shall
be recompensed in the earth: much more than the wicked and the
sinner." The tree of life will one day be in Jerusalem, and those who
win souls will have the right to it. Note also that it tells us here that
the righteous will be recompensed "in the earth." We should compare
this with Luke 19:27, where Lord Jesus says, "But those mine enemies,
which would not that I should reign over them, bring hither, and slay
them before me." Most pastors only teach that God is a God of love;
they are not telling the whole story. God is also a God of judgment,
and there are times when the Lord gets very angry. When he has had
enough, he acts.

Zechariah 14:1–3 says:

> Behold, the day of the Lord cometh, and thy spoil
> shall be divided in the midst of thee. For I will gather
> all nations against Jerusalem to battle; and the city
> shall be taken, and the houses rifled, and the women
> ravished; and half of the city shall go forth into
> captivity, and the residue of the people shall not be
> cut off from the city. Then shall the Lord go forth,
> and fight against those nations; as when he fought in
> the day of battle.

The word for forth is *yatsa*,[373] to go, appear, draw forth, escape, in the end, pluck out, be risen, or utter. Once again, we are told in scripture that when all nations gather against Jerusalem or Armageddon, this is when the Lord leaves heaven to fight against those nations. As we read here in the Hebrew meanings, he will appear, pluck out, escape, and utter. And when will this happen? When the Lord Jesus appears. Jesus tells us, "All that endure until the end, the same shall be saved."

Where else in scripture does the Lord come out of his place when the sun and the moon are darkened?

Revelation 6:12, 16–17 says:

> And I beheld when he had opened the sixth seal, and,
> lo, there was a great earthquake; and the sun became
> black as sackcloth of hair, and the moon became as
> blood . . . And said to the mountains and rocks, Fall
> on us, and hide us from the face of him that sitteth
> on the throne, and from the wrath of the lamb. For
> the great day of his wrath is come; and who shall be
> able to stand?

In this verse is a great earthquake, and the sun and the moon are dark. What happens when there is an earthquake? People fall down. This is why there is this question in this verse, "Who shall be able to stand?" Romans 14:4 says, "For God is able to make him stand."

---

[373] Ibid., 1876.

Psalms 76:7 tells us, "Who may stand in thy sight when once thy art angry?" Note the language "in thy sight" (sight—*paniym,*[374] meaning presence) and "once thy art angry," which is an equivalent message to "the great day of his wrath is come." We should note one of the meanings for *erchomai,*[375] for "come" is appear. Note the language "the face of him that sitteth on the throne." This is important. Then note, "And from the lamb," meaning a second person. There is also, "To hide us from the wrath of the lamb." This is the same message of Zephaniah 2:3, "Seek ye the Lord, all ye meek of the earth, which have wrought his judgments; seek righteousness, seek meekness: it may be ye shall be hid in the day of the Lord's anger." Let's also note here again that psalm tells us "to save all the meek of the earth." We should notice that it says "which have wrought his judgments." "Wrought" is *paal,*[376] which means to do or make, especially to practice; commit, ordain, work. We now know that the Lord does not leave heaven on the first day that the sun and the moon don't give their light.

Zechariah 12:9–10 says:

> And it shall come to in that day [the Day of the Lord], that I will seek to destroy all nations that come against Jerusalem. And I will pour upon the house of David, and upon the inhabitants of Jerusalem, the spirit of grace and supplication: and they shall look upon whom they have pierced, and they shall mourn for him, as one mourneth for his only son, and it shall be bitterness for him, as one that is in bitterness for his firstborn.

This day told here is when God destroys "all nations" that come against Jerusalem. And the New Testament equivalent is Revelation16:16, "And he gathered them together into a place called in the Hebrew tongue Armageddon." Verse 15 tells us, "Behold, I come

---

[374] Ibid., 1948.
[375] Ibid., 2079.
[376] Ibid., 1948.

as a thief." We should notice that the Lord's appearing is so grand that the people in Jerusalem can see his pierced hands and feet. Then they will realize they did kill their messiah almost two thousand years ago. We should note in Acts 2:17, "And it shall come to pass in the last days, saith God, I will pour out my spirit upon all flesh." This spirit is also poured out upon the house of David, and the inhabitants of Jerusalem, the Jews of the state of Israel.

Joel 2:1–2 says:

> Blow ye the trumpet in Zion, and sound an alarm in my holy mountain: let all the inhabitants of the land tremble: for the day of the Lord cometh, for it is nigh at hand; A day of darkness and of gloominess, a day of clouds and of thick darkness, as the morning spread upon the mountains; a great people and a strong; there hath not been ever like it, neither shall be any more after it, even to the years of many generations.

Let's compare Matthew 24:29–31 to Joel 1:1–2. In Matthew, it's, "The sun and the moon don't give their light." In Joel, it's "a day of clouds and of thick darkness." In Matthew, it's "Son of Man coming"; in Joel, it's "the Lord cometh, for it is nigh at hand." In Matthew, it's, "And he shall sent his angels with the sound of a trumpet"; and in Joel, it's "blow the trumpet in Zion." In Matthew, it's "all the tribes of the earth mourn," and in Joel, it's "the inhabitants of the land tremble." When two prophets use the same language, it's a good indication they mean the same event.

Joel 2:15–18 says:

> Blow the trumpet in Zion, sanctify the congregation, assemble the elders, gather the children, and those that suck the breasts: let the bridegroom go forth of his chamber, and the bride out of her closet. Let the priests, the ministers of the Lord weep between the porch and the altar, and let them say, Spare thy people, O Lord, and give not thine heritage to reproach, that

the heathen should rule over them: Wherefore should
they say among the people, Where is their God?
Then will the Lord be jealous for his land, and pity
his people.

And where else does the Lord get "jealous for his land"? In
Ezekiel 38:19: "For in my jealousy and in the fire of my wrath have I
spoken." There is also the prayer that says, "O God, spare thy people,
and not give thy heritage [the chosen people] to reproach, that the
heathen [Antichrist and his cohorts] should rule over them." The
word "bridegroom" is *chathan*,[377] which means a relative by marriage
(especially through the bride); figurative a circumcised child (as a
species of religious espousal); bridegroom, husband. We should also
note that the word for closet is *chuppah*,[378] which means a canopy:
chamber, closet, defense. We should also notice the sentence, "Where
is their God?" This refers to "Where is the promise of his coming?" in
2 Peter 3:4. Now to finish the verse:

And the same hour was there a great earthquake, and
the tenth part of the city fell and in the earthquake
were slain of men seven thousand: and the remnant
were affrighted, and gave glory to the God of heaven.
The second woes are past and behold the third woe
cometh quickly.

Stop here!
Look what else comes as quickly as the third woe. Before we go to
Revelation, we will look at what Isaiah has to say.
Isaiah 62:11 says:

Behold, the Lord hath proclaimed unto the ends of
the world, Say ye to the daughters of Zion, Behold,

---

[377]   Ibid., 1866.
[378]   Ibid., 1860.

thy salvation cometh, behold, his reward is with him,
and his work before him.

We read the exact message in Revelation. The word for the "end" is *qatseh*,[379] which means after, border, brink, edge end, (in) finite frontier. It is from *qatsah*,[380] which means to cut off (figurative) to destroy; (partial) to scrape off; cut of, cut short, scrape (off). The word for work is *pullah*,[381] which means labor, reward, wages, work. These Hebrew meanings are used in this next verse. We should note the "cut short," for the Lord shortens the days for his elect. In Isaiah there is "his reward is with him." When does this happen? At the end, the completion of the church age. Also note the Hebrew word meaning to destroy. The Lord will destroy those who destroy the earth when the seventh angel sounds the seventh trumpet and the dead are judged and give and reward his servants the prophets. There are also lightnings and voices and thunderings and an earthquake, all the signs that the Lord is near, as in this verse.

Daniel 11:45 and 12:1–2 says:

And He [the Antichrist] shall plant the tabernacles of his place between the seas in the glorious holy mountain; yet he shall come to his end, and none shall help him . . . And at that time Michael stand up, the great prince which standeth for the children of thy people: and there shall be a time of trouble, such as never was since there was a nation even to that same time: and at that time thy people shall be delivered, every one that shall be found written in the book. And many of them that sleep in the dust of the earth shall awake, some to everlasting life, and some to shame and everlasting contempt.

---

379 Ibid., 1962.
380 Ibid.
381 Ibid., 1948.

We should note that it is not until this "time of trouble" that God's people will be delivered. Delivered is the word *malat*,[382] which means properly to be smooth (i.e., by implication) to escape; causative to release or rescue, speedily. This Hebrew word meaning speedily is a reference to, "Behold, I [God] come quickly, and my reward is with me" in the book of Revelation. It's not until this time that "them that sleep in the dust of the earth shall awake." "Awake" is *quwts*,[383] which means to awake (literal or figurative); arise, watch.

I believe this shame and everlasting contempt are the souls without spirits of men who have not believed in the Lord Jesus and the Christians who have no works, or their works are burned in the judgment seat of Christ, and without the Lord Jesus, they would not make it to heaven. The *Webster's Dictionary* meaning for the word "contempt" is, "The feeling one has toward something he considers worthless or vile; scorn." The word for contempt is *draown*,[384] which means an object of aversion. Is this the way Christians will feel when they get to heaven and have done nothing to spread the gospel of the Lord? Is this why "all that call upon the name of the Lord, shall be saved"? They have no works but on their dying bed confess in Jesus and are saved.

And we should note in Jeremiah 51:39, "In their heat I will make their feasts, and I will make them drunken, that they may rejoice, and sleep a perpetual sleep, and not wake, saith the Lord." Let us first note that Jeremiah prophesies this against the Babylonians. Heat is the word *chom*,[385] which means to be hot. Perpetual is the word *owlam*,[386] which means properly concealed (i.e., the vanishing point); general time out of mind (past and future) (i.e., practical) eternity. We should note that the Hebrew word for perpetual and the word "old" in Genesis are the same. We read in Jeremiah that there are spirits (out of mind because the mind is the spirit of man) that sleep and are not awakened. They stay in the dust of the earth where it is hot (hell).

---

[382] Ibid., 1901.
[383] Ibid., 1960.
[384] Ibid., 1841.
[385] Ibid., 1857.
[386] Ibid., 1933.

We should note Ezekiel 18:4, "Behold all souls are mine; as the soul of the father, so also the soul of the son is mine: the soul that sinneth, it shall die." This is where the great white throne judgment comes in. Revelation 20:13–15 says:

> And the sea gave up the dead which were in it; and death and hell delivered up which were in them: and they were judged according to their works. And death and hell were cast into the lake of fire. This is the second death. And whosoever was not found written in the book of life was cast into the lake of fire.

First Corinthians 3:12–14 says:

> Now if any man build upon this foundation gold, silver, precious stones, wood, hay, stubble; Every man's work shall be made manifest: for the day shall declare it, because it shall be revealed by fire; and the fire shall try every man's work of what sort it is. If any man's work abide which he hath built thereupon, he shall receive a reward. If any man's work shall be burned, he shall suffer loss; But he himself shall be saved; yet so as by fire.

I believe those whose works are burned and shall suffer loss are the souls in Daniel 12 that come to shame and everlasting contempt. I believe that loss is the spirit of man. His soul may be saved but not his spirit. They are called up with some to everlasting life in Daniel, and in 1 Corinthians, they are those who receive a reward. And we should note also in 1 Timothy 4:10, "We trust in the living God, who is the Saviour of all men, specially of those that believe."

Isaiah 13:9–11, 13 says:

> Behold, the day of the Lord cometh, cruel with wrath and fierce anger, to lay the land desolate: and He shall destroy the sinners out of it. For the stars of heaven

and the constellations thereof shall not give their light: the sun shall be darkened in his going forth, and the moon shall not cause her light to shine. And I will punish the world for their evil, and the wicked for their iniquity; and I will cause the arrogancy of the proud to cease, and the earth shall be moved out of her place, and will lay low the haughtiness of the terrible. Therefore, I will shake the heavens, and the earth shall move out of her place, in the wrath of the Lord of Host, and in the day of his fierce anger.

We should notice that the "day of the Lord cometh" is at his wrath. This is done when the sun and moon do not give their light. God is in heaven until he comes to destroy the sinners out of the earth. We should note Hebrews 12:26: "Whose voice then shook the earth: but now he hath promised, saying, Yet one more I shake not the earth only, but also heaven." The only time this "shaken" happens is in the days of God's fierce wrath. Here is your global weather change: "the earth shall be moved out of her place." We are told in Matthew 27:51, "And, behold, the veil of the temple was rent in twain from the top to the bottom; and the earth did quake, and the rocks rent." We should note that when the Lord gave up his earthly body and was back in his spirit body, the earth quaked.

Isaiah 24:17–23, 25:7–9 says:

Fear, and the pit, and the snare, are upon thee, O inhabitants of the earth. And it shall come to pass, that he who fleeth from the noise of the fear shall fall from the pit; and he that cometh up out of the pit shall be taken in the snare, for the windows from on high are open, and the foundations of the earth do shake. The earth is utterly broken down, the earth is clean dissolved, the earth is moved exceedingly. The earth shall reel to and fro like a drunkard, and be removed like a cottage; and the transgression thereof shall be heavy upon it; and it shall fall, and not rise again. And it shall come to pass in that day, that the Lord shall punish the host of the high ones that are on high, and the kings of the earth upon the earth. And they shall be gathered together, as prisoners are gathered in the pit, and shall be shut up in the prison, and after many days shall they be visited. Then the moon shall be confounded, and the sun ashamed, when the Lord of Host shall reign in mount Zion, and in Jerusalem, and before his ancient gloriously.

And he will destroy in this mountain the face of the covering cast over all people, and the veil that is spread over all nations. He will swallow up death in victory; and the Lord God will wipe away tears from off all faces; and the rebuke of his people shall he take away from off all the earth: for the Lord hath spoken it. And it shall be said in that day, Lo, this is our God; we have waited for him, and he will save us: this is the Lord; we have waited for him, we will be glad and rejoice in his salvation.

First note here that when the "windows on high are open," judgment from God comes. Note Genesis 7:11–12, "The same day were all fountains of the great deep broken up, and the windows of heaven were opened. And the rain was on the earth forty days and forty nights." Revelation 12:15–16 says:

And the serpent [Satan] cast out of his mouth water as a flood after the woman [Israel], that he might cause her to be carried away of the flood. And the earth helped the women, and the earth opened her mouth, and swallowed up the flood which the dragon cast out of his mouth.

Satan tries to destroy Israel the same way God killed the giants on the earth that were produced by the sons of God, the angels, which were Satan's angels.

Then we should note that the earth shall reel to and fro. This tells us of a great earthquake that shakes the whole earth. In verse 21, note, "And it shall come to pass in that day." That day is the day of the Lord. The Lord will punish the host of the high ones that are on high. The high ones are found in Obadiah 1:1, 3, "Thus saith the Lord concerning Edom. The pride of thine heart hath deceived thee, thou that dwellest in the clefts of the rock, whose habitation is high; that said in his heart, Who shall bring down to the ground?" He will also punish the kings of the earth. They will be "shut up in the prison." This is the prison of hades, for it says and after many days, they shall be visited. Those many days are the thousand-year of the reign of Christ. This is when God brings those in hell to the great white throne judgment. Then in verse 23, once more we told that the sun and the moon are darkened. Then the Lord will reign on mount Zion, on the Temple Mount. Also note Isaiah's, "We have waited for him, and he will save us," and the equivalent verse in the New Testament, "All that endure until the end, the same shall be saved."

The Lord will destroy the veil that is spread over all of the nations, which God will swallow up death in victory. The New Testament equivalent scripture is given in 1 Corinthians 15:54, "So when this corruptible shall have put on incorruption, and the mortal shall put on immortality, then shall be brought to pass the saying that is written, Death is swallowed up in victory." The mortals who put on immortality are the "we which are alive and remain until the coming of the Lord" of 1 Thessalonians 4:17.

In 25:7, Isaiah tells us, "He [God] will destroy in this mountain the face of the covering cast over all the people, and the veil." The word for veil is *massekah*,[387] which means properly a pouring over (i.e., fusion of metal); by implication a libation league. It is from the word *nasak*, which means a primitive root; to pour out, especially a libation, or to cast (metal); by analogy to appoint a king. This libation (libation

---

[387] Ibid., 1903.

in *Webster's Dictionary* means an act of pouring a liquid as a sacrifice as to a deity) league is the Muslims and their mosque. A new king is anointed. The book of Revelation tells us when the Lord becomes King of the whole earth. Revelation 11:15 says, "And the seventh angel sounded; and there were great voices in heaven saying, The kingdoms of this world are become the kingdoms of our Lord, and of Christ; and he shall rule for ever and ever."

It's done when there is a veil over all the earth, just as we are told in Matthew 24:29–30. That veil is what causes the sun and the moon not to give their light. Note that the Lord punishes "the host of the high ones that are on high" and not the meek of the earth and the rebuke (*cherpah,*[388] which means contumely, disgrace) of his people is taken off the earth. They are the meek who inherit the earth. I think it is also important to note that twice we are told, "We have waited for him." If there was a pre-tribulation resurrection, there would be no waiting. We are told here again about the shaking of the earth before the great darkness. This is the Old Testament prophecy that is given in the New Testament.

Where else in the Bible does it say, "He will swallow up death in victory"? First Corinthians 15:52–54 says:

> In a moment, in the twinkling of an eye, at the last trump: for the trumpet shall sound, and the dead shall be raised incorruptible, and we shall be changed. For this corruptible must put on incorruption, and this mortal must put on immortality. So when this corruptible shall have put on incorruption, and this mortal shall immortality, then shall be brought to pass the saying that which is written, Death is swallowed up in victory.

The saying that is written is in Isaiah 25:8, and this happens when there a "veil that is spread over all nations meaning darkness." The New Testament prophecy is backed up by the Old Testament. It confirms that

---

[388] Ibid., 1864.

the resurrection of the dead does not happen in Revelation 4 because there is no alive church resurrection. This is not in the scriptures. It says in 1 Corinthians that the dead are raised incorruptible and the living "shall be changed." The meek who inherit the earth put on immortality. This is how death is swallowed up in victory. We get this victory as stated in 1 John 5:4–5: "For whatsoever is born of God overcometh the world: and this is the victory that overcometh the world, even our faith. Who is he that overcometh the world, but he that believeth that Jesus is the son of God." The tribulation period is the twenty-first-century Christians' test period to overcome the world.

Matthew says, "He that endure unto the end, the same shall be saved." The end comes when the seven thunders utter their voices, where we are told "that there should be time no longer" and "the mystery of God should be finished." This means you will rule and reign with Christ a thousand years.

Joel 2:1, 3, 10–11, 30–32 says:

> Blow ye the trumpet in Zion, and sound an alarm in my holy mountain; let all the inhabitants of the land tremble; for the day of the Lord cometh, for it is nigh at hand . . . A fire devoured before them, and behind them a flame burneth: The land is a Garden of Eden before them, and behind them a desolate wilderness; yea, and nothing shall escape them . . . The earth shall quake before them; the heavens shall tremble: The sun and the moon shall be dark, and the stars shall withdraw their shining . . . And the Lord shall utter His voice before his army: For his camp is very great: For He is strong that executeth His word: for the day of the Lord is great and very terrible; and who can abide in it? . . . And I will shew wonders in the heavens and in the earth, blood, and fire, and pillars of smoke . . . The sun shall be turned into darkness, and the moon into blood before the great and terrible day of the Lord come . . . And it shall come to pass, that whosoever shall call upon the name of the Lord

> shall be delivered: for in mount Zion and in Jerusalem
> shall be deliverance, as the Lord had said, and in the
> remnant the Lord shall call.

I take these scriptures literally, that they say exactly what they mean. We should note here that Joel says that the sun and the moon are darkened before the great and terrible day of the Lord. According to *Strong's Concordance* the word "great" is the Hebrew word *gadowl*,[389] which means or (shortened). It is from *gadal*,[390] which means properly to twist (i.e., to be) (causative make) large (in various senses, as in body, mind, estate or honor and pride); advance, boast, bring up, exceed, excellent. This is another example of the Old Testament's importance in end-time prophecies, for the Hebrew word meaning to shorten matches this. We are also told in Matthew 24:22, "Except those days shortened, there should no flesh be saved: but for the elect's sake those days shall be shortened." The word for shorten is *koloboo*,[391] which means to dock (i.e., figuratively), abridge, shorten. It is from the word *kolazo*, which means (dwarf); properly to curtail (i.e., figuratively) to chastise (or reserve for infliction); punish. If the Lord is going to shorten the days for his elect, they would have to be on the planet.

And the word for terrible is the word *yare*,[392] which means to fear; moral to revere; causative to frighten. We should also note the word for deliverance is *pleytah*,[393] which means an escaped portion; escape remnant. The word for remnant is *sariyd*,[394] which means a survivor; alive, left, remain. The word for call is *qara*,[395] which means to call out to, famous, guest, invite. Note the Hebrew word meaning survivor and remain. It refers to we who are alive and remain till the coming of the Lord.

---

[389] Ibid., 1831.
[390] Ibid., 1832.
[391] Ibid., 2102.
[392] Ibid., 1877.
[393] Ibid., 1947.
[394] Ibid., 1995.
[395] Ibid., 1963.

Joel tells us here that there will be an escaped remnant (that will not be in fear) (and we which are alive and remain till the coming of the Lord), and the Lord will shorten the days. Note in Joel, "And the Lord shall utter his voice before his army." The Lord utters with his voice, "Come up hither" to the dead, just as we have read in Ezekiel where the four winds put the spirit into the dead that they may live to fight in the battle of Armageddon. Also note in verse 3, "a fire devoureth before them and behind them," but the land of Israel will be like the Garden of Eden. This is why Ezekiel also tells us after the battle of Armageddon that there are people employed to bury the bones of all those who came against Israel.

Another important part of this passage in Joel is, "The earth shall quake and the heavens shall tremble." This message is given in Hebrews 12:26–29:

> Yet once more I shake not the earth only, but also heaven. And at this word, Yet once more, signifieth the removing of those things that are shaken, as of those things that are made, that those things that cannot be shaken may remain. Wherefore we receiving a kingdom which cannot be moved, let us have grace, whereby we may serve God acceptably with reverence and Godly fear.

Note here that after the shaking, those who "may remain" will serve God with reverence.

"For our God is a consuming fire." Note those of Hebrews 12:26–29 that "those things that cannot by shaken may remain" are those of 1 Thessalonians, and we who are alive and remain till the coming of the Lord have met the Lord in the air, which, as Hebrews says, receive the kingdom of God on earth and serve him. Hebrews tells us, "Our God is a consuming fire," and 2 Thessalonians tells us the Lord comes "in a flaming fire taking vengeance on them that know not God, and obey not the gospel of Jesus Christ."

Also note the same language of Joel, "And I will shew wonders in the heavens and in the earth, blood, and fire, and pillars of smoke."

These are recorded in Acts 2:19, "And I will shew wonders in heaven above, and signs in the earth; blood, and fire, and vapors of smoke." When two or more prophets use the same language to predict a special happening, it means the same happening.

There is also the trumpet of God told to us here that is blown in Zion (Jerusalem). There is this "the Lord will utter his voice (Come Up Hither)." The same come up hither is spoken when the two prophets are called up in Revelation 11:12.

Joel 3:9, 14–16 says:

> Proclaim ye among the Gentiles, prepare war, wake up the mighty men, let all the men draw near; let them come up . . . Multitudes, multitudes in the valley of decision: For the day of the Lord is near in the valley of decision. The sun and the moon shall be darkened, and the stars shall withdraw their shining . . . And the Lord shall roar out of Zion and utter his voice from Jerusalem.; and the heavens and the earth shall quake; but the Lord will be the hope of his people, and the strength to the children of Israel.

The multitudes in the valley of decision are in the battle of Armageddon. Joel tells us the day of the Lord is near. This is when Revelation tells us, "I come as a thief, and he gathered them to Armageddon." The sun and the moon are darkened when the Lord will roar out of heaven. This is in Matthew 24, where it says, "The sun and the moon are darkened, and then shall appear the Son of Man in heaven. And utter his voice from Jerusalem." Where in scripture is the Lord's voice heard in Jerusalem? In Revelation 11:12 it says after the two witnesses are killed in Jerusalem, "And they heard a voice from heaven saying come up hither." In Joel, there is an earthquake. Then in Revelation 11:13, it says, "And the same hour there was a great earthquake." That is to resurrect the dead. In verse 18, the dead are judged. Then let us note verse 15 where the seventh trumpet is sounded. This is the last trumpet of 1 Corinthians 15:52 when the dead are raised and we all shall be changed. Note the difference of the last verse: "the hope of his people." I believe this is the church and the children of Israel. In Joel 2–3, there is so much information, with each chapter giving us a little different information to give the full prophecies. This again is the precept upon precept, line upon line study needed to get these prophecies correct. This is also affirmed in Acts 2:16–17, 19–21:

> But this is the day that which was spoken by the prophet Joel . . . And it shall come to pass in the last days, saith God. I will pour out my spirit upon all flesh . . . And I will shew wonders in heaven above, and signs in the earth beneath: blood, and fire, and vapour of smoke . . . The sun and the moon into darkness, before that great and notable day of the Lord come . . . And it shall come to pass, that whosoever shall call upon the name of the Lord shall be saved.

We should note here that the important reference made to understand this scripture is in Joel. In Acts, we are told again that the sun and the moon are darkened before the great and notable day of the Lord. That is when whosoever calls upon the name of the Lord will be saved. "Saved" is *sozo*,[396] which means to save (i.e., deliver or protect) (literal or figurative); heal, preserve. This is where the Lord will pour out the Holy Spirit upon all flesh. It is written in Joel 2:28, "And it shall come to pass afterward, that I will pour out my spirit upon all flesh: and your sons and your daughters shall prophesy, and you old men shall dream dreams, your young men shall see visions." "Young" is *bachuwr*,[397] which means properly selected, i.e. youth. I believe these young men given in Joel are the same 144,000 remnant of all the children of Israel who are sealed by God to take the gospel to the world. Revelation 14 says, "These are they which were not defiled with women; for they are virgins." When does this happen? It's for the last days. Are these last days just before the Last Day? And who is the

---

[396]   Ibid., 2161.
[397]   Ibid., 1822.

Lord pouring out his spirit to, if it is not the church? This means the church is on the planet in the last days.

Let's refer to Revelation 1:9, which says, "I, John, who also am your brother, and companion in tribulation." John was transferred to the tribulation period. Verse 10 says, "I was in the spirit on the Lord's Day." Is this "day of the Lord" of Joel and Acts the same day as Revelation 1:10, "The Lord's day"? John was transported in time to the Day of the Lord. We should also note Daniel 6:27, which says, "He delivered and rescueth, and he worketh signs and wonders in heaven and in earth, who hath delivered Daniel from the power of the lions." Daniel was delivered, and he was still on the earth. We are also told in 2 Peter 2:9, "The Lord knoweth how to deliver the godly out of temptation, and to reserve the unjust unto the Day of Judgment to be punished." The Lord can deliver Daniel. Second Peter says, "The Lord knoweth how to deliver the godly out of temptation," where there are signs and wonders in heaven and the earth, just as in Acts 2.

Zephaniah 1:14–16 says:

> The great day of the Lord is near, it is near, and
> hastened greatly, even the voice of the day of the Lord
> the mighty men shall cry there bitterly . . . That day
> is a day of wrath, a day of darkness and gloominess, a
> day of clouds and thick darkness. A day of the trumpet
> and alarm against the fenced cities, and against the
> high towers.

At the voice of the day of the Lord (the come up hither), the mighty men will cry there bitterly the same as Matthew 24:30, "And then shall appear the Son of Man in heaven: then shall all of the tribes of the earth shall mourn?" Is not the "A day of darkness and gloominess, a day of clouds and thick darkness" the same as Matthew 24:29, "Immediately after the tribulation of those days shall the sun be darkened and the moon shall not give her light"?

Is not the "a day of the trumpet" the same as 1 Corinthians 15:52, "In a moment, in the twinkling of an eye, at the last trump"? Is this not also the, "And he shall sent his angels with the sound of a trumpet" of

Matthew 24:31? Is not the alarm against the fenced cities, the security fence that Israel is putting up around the state of Israel, and the high towers a reference to the United States as the land of un-walled villages of Ezekiel 38? We should also note where else there is this darkness. Mark 15:33 says, "And when the sixth hour was come, there was darkness over the whole land until the ninth hour while our Lord was being crucified on the cross."

Zephaniah 2:2–3 says:

> Before the decree bring forth, before the day pass as a chaff, before the fierce anger of the Lord come upon you, before the day of the Lord's anger come upon you . . . Seek ye the Lord, all ye meek of the earth, which have wrought His judgments seek righteousness, seek meekness: it may be ye shall be hid in the day of the Lord's anger.

As we read here in scripture, there are those who are hid in the day of the Lord's anger. The "hid" are the meek who shall inherit the earth. The word "decree" is *choq*,[398] which means an enactment; hence an appointment (of time, space, quantity, labor, or usage); appointed, set time, statutes, task. So before the set time of the Lord's return to the earth, we are to seek righteousness, seek meekness, so that the meek are hidden from the Lord's anger. Just as when judgments came to the house of Judah before the Babylonian captivity, the Lord seals his people. Remember also that the Lord hid Jeremiah in his day from judgment. When the Pharisees went to cast stones at Jesus, the Lord hid himself in the midst of them and passed by.

Malachi 4:1–5 says:

> For, behold, the day cometh, that shall burn as an oven; and all the proud, yea, all that so wickedly, shall be as a stubble; and that day that cometh shall burn them up, saith the Lord of Host, that it shall leave

---

[398] Ibid., 1861.

them neither root or branch. But unto you that fear my name shall the Sun of righteousness arise with healing in his wings; and ye shall go forth, and grow up as calves of the stall. And ye shall tread down the wicked; for they shall be ashes under the soles of your feet in the day that I shall do this, saith the Lord of Host. Remember the Lord of Moses, my servant, which I commanded unto him in Horeb for all Israel, with the statutes and judgments. Behold, I will send you Elijah the prophet before the coming of the great and dreadful day of the Lord: And he shall turn the heart of the fathers to the children, and the heart of the children to their fathers, lest I come and smite the earth with a curse.

We should note here that Elijah the prophet comes before the "great and terrible day of the Lord." And it shall burn as an oven. How does it burn as an oven? When the captain and his fifty men come to kill Elijah, this is told in 2 Kings 1:12: "And Elijah answered and said unto them, If I be a man of God, let fire come down from heaven, and consume thee and the fifty. And the fire of God came down from heaven, and consumed him and his fifty." The two witnesses in the book of Revelation will have the same power. Revelation 11:3, 5 says:

And I will give power unto my two witnesses, and they shall prophecy a thousand two hundred and threescore days, clothed in sackcloth. And if any man will hurt them, fire proceedeth out of their mouth, and devoureth their enemies: and if a man will hurt them, he must in the same manner be killed.

Malachi tells us, "For they shall be ashes under the soles of their feet."

We heard this same language in Zechariah 14:12, "And this shall be the plague wherewith the Lord will smite all the people that have fought against Jerusalem; Their flesh shall consume away while they stand upon their feet." We see it again in Ezekiel 38:22, "And I will plead against him with pestilence and with blood, and upon many people that are with him, an overflowing rain, and great hailstones, fire, and brimstone." We also see it in Revelation 16:21, "And there fell upon men a great hail out of heaven."

We should note Joel 2:3, "A fire devoureth before them, and behind them a flame burneth: the land is a Garden of Eden before them, and behind them a desolated wilderness; yea and nothing shall escape them." Who is this against but the wicked who come against Jerusalem? They shall be as ashes under the soles of your feet in the day that God does this. The result is in Ezekiel 39:15, "And the passengers that pass through the land, when any seeth a man's bone, then shall he set a sign by it, till the buriers have buried in the valley of Hamon-Gog."

Malachi 4:2 says, "But to those that fear my name the Sun of righteousness [the Lord] will arise with healing in his wings." Arise is the word *zarach*,[399] which means properly, to irradiate (i.e., to rise), specifically to appear. The word "irradiate" in the *Webster's Dictionary* means, "To cast rays of light upon; illuminate, to enlighten intellectually or spiritually." The world will be illuminated in 2 Thessalonians 2:8, "And then shall that Wicked be revealed, whom the Lord shall consume with the spirit of his mouth, and shall destroy with the brightness of his coming." "Wicked" is *anomos*,[400] which means lawless, not subject to (the Jewish) law. And the wicked are told to us in Luke 19:14 when the Lord says, "But his citizens hated him [Jesus], and sent a message [the message of Muhammad's], saying, We will not have this man [Jesus, but Allah] to reign over us." The Lord appears with healing in his wings, and this healing is told to us in Revelation 22:1, "From the throne of God there was the tree of life and the leaves of the tree of life were for the healing of the nations." This healing of the nations is also given in Zephaniah 3:15–20:

399 Ibid., 1850.
400 Ibid., 2026.

The Lord hath taken away thy judgments [*mishpat*,[401] which means properly a verdict (favorable) pronounced judicially, especially a sentence or formal decree (human or divine law, individual or collective) including the act, the place, the suit, the crime and the penalty; abstract justice], he hath cast out thine enemy [the declared enemy, Muhammad]: the King of Israel, even the Lord, is in the midst of thee: thou shalt not see evil any more.

In that day [the day of the Lord] it shall be said to Jerusalem, Fear thou not: and to Zion, Let not thine hands be slack. The Lord thy God in the midst [*qereb*,[402] which means nearest part (i.e., whether literal or figurative, e.g. the middle of the battle). From *qarab*, which means to approach, be at hand, be near].

Stop here! When is the middle of the battle, and when will the Lord be near? Matthew 24:30 says:

Immediately after the tribulation [just before the great tribulation] of those days shall the sun be darkened and the moon shall not give here light, and the stars shall fall heaven, and the powers of the heavens shall be shaken: And then shall appear the Son of Man in heaven.

Continue on with Zephaniah:

Of thee is mighty; he will save, he will rejoice over thee with joy; he will rest in his love, he will joy over thee with singing. I will gather them that are sorrowful

---

[401] Ibid., 1912.
[402] Ibid., 1963.

[*yagah*,[403] which means afflict, cause grief, grieve] for the solemn [*mow ed*,[404] which means properly an appointment (i.e., a fixed time or season); specifically a festival; conventionally a year; by implication, an assembly (as convened for a definite purpose)] assembly, who are of thee, to whom the reproach of it was a burden.

Behold, at that time I will undo all that afflict thee: and I will save her that halteth [*tsela*,[405] which means a limping or fall (figurative); adversity. *Webster's Dictionary* meaning of limp is to fall short, lacking in strength or firmness.], and gather her [unto Judah shall the gathering of the people be of Genesis 49:10] her that was driven out [the ten lost tribes of the house of Israel]; and I [God] will get them praise and fame in every land where they were put to shame. At that time will I bring you again, even in the time that I gather you: for I will make you a name and a praise among all the people of the earth, when I turn back your captivity [God considers all the lands of all the tribes of house of Israel captivity if they're not in their own land] before your eyes, saith the Lord.

Revelation 11:13–14 says:

And the same hour was there a great earthquake, and the tenth part of the city fell and in the earthquake were slain of men seven thousands: and the remnant were affrighted, and gave glory to the God of heaven. The second woe is past; and behold the third woe comes quickly.

---

[403] Ibid., 1869.

[404] Ibid., 1895.

[405] Ibid., 1955.

I do not think John put this here because we don't know how to count. Also note "a great earthquake." The earthquake is to open the graves of the dead. We should note that the third woe comes quickly, but there is something else that comes quickly.

Revelation 22:12 says:

> And, behold, I come quickly and my reward is with me, to give every man according as his work shall be.

We are also told of when the resurrection of the dead saints happens. It is on the last day, for John tells us in John 6:39–40, 44:

> And this is the father's will which hast sent me that all which he hast given me I should lose nothing, but shall raise him up at the last day. And this is the will of him that sent me, that everyone which seeth the son, and believeth on him, may have everlasting life: and I will raise him up at the last day . . . no man can come to me, except the father which hast sent me, draw him: and I will raise him up at the last day.

John tells us again in John 12:48:

> He that rejected me, and receiveth not my words, hath one that judgeth him: the word that I have spoken, the same shall judge him in the last day.

Who has rejected the Lord but the atheists, Muslims, and all the other ungodly people of the world?

John also says in John 12:46:

> I am come a light into the world, that whosoever believeth on me should not abide in darkness.

If those who believe in the Lord Jesus do not abide in darkness, this would be just as the days that the judgments came to Egypt, when there were three days of darkness. It was so dark that they did not move for three days, but the children of Israel had light. Let us note Exodus 10:22: "thick darkness in all the land of Egypt." The word for darkness is *choshek*,[406] which means the dark, hence (literal) darkness.

John tells us that the Lord Jesus will rise up (come up hither) on the last day. To raise here is *anistemi*,[407] which means to stand up (literal or figurative, transitive or intransitive); arise, lift up, raise up (again), stand up (right). To rise up again means you're dead. Since John mentions this four times, do we not think that this is something he wants us to pay attention to? If this is the case, we must look for the last day in scripture, and the last day is not found in Revelation 4. So where in scripture is the last day?

Revelation 10:4–7 says:

> And when the seven thunders had uttered their voices, I was about to write: and I heard a voice from heaven saying unto me, Seal up those things which the seven thunders uttered, and write them not. And the angel which I saw stand upon the sea and upon the earth lifted up his hand to heaven, And sware by him that liveth for ever and ever, who created heaven, and the earth, and the things that therein are, and the sea, and the things that are therein, that there shall be no time longer. But in the days of the voice of the seventh angel, when he shall begin to sound, the mystery of God should be finished, as he hath declared to his servants the prophets.

Let us note that in the days of the voice of the seventh angel, he will begin to sound that there will be time no longer, "the last day." We

---

[406] Ibid., 1865.
[407] Ibid., 2025.

should note there are days of the thunders. The days of thunders are in Daniel 12:11–12:

> And from the time that the daily sacrifice shall be taken away, and the abomination that maketh desolater set up, there shall be a thousand two hundred and ninety days [three and a half years]. Blessed is he that waiteth, and cometh to the thousand three hundred and five and thirty days.

These forty-five days are the days of thunder. This is where the wrath of God comes. We should note that the ones who make it to the 1,335th day are blessed. Jesus tells us in Matthew 5:4, "Blessed are they that mourn: for they will be comforted." And the equivalent message is in Matthew 24:30, "And then shall appear the Son of Man in heaven: and then shall all the tribes of the earth shall mourn."

Just as Jesus states, "Those that endure till the end shall be saved," the meek inherit the earth. The mystery of God should be finished in the church age. "Thunder" is *bronte*,[408] which means to roar: thunder. The Lord roars in Jeremiah 25:30, "The Lord shall roar from on high, and utter his voice from his holy habitation; he shall mightily roar upon his habitation." He also roars in Amos 3:16, "The Lord also shall roar out of Zion; and utter his voice from Jerusalem." And why does he utter his voice from Jerusalem? To call up the two prophets who were killed by the Antichrist. One of the words for thunder is *raam*, which means to tumble (i.e., to be violently agitated); figurative to irritate.

So where does God get agitated and irritate? Ezekiel 38:18-19 says:

> And it shall come to pass at the same time when Gog shall come against the land of Israel, saith the Lord God, that my fury shall come in my face. For in my jealously and in the fire of my wrath have I spoken.

---

[408] Ibid., 2044.

Surely in that day there shall be a great shaking in the
land of Israel.

And the earthquake in Ezekiel is given to us in Revelation 11:13,
"And the same hour was there a great earthquake, and the tenth part of
the city fell, and in the earthquake were slain of men seven thousand:
and the remnant were affrighted, and gave glory to the God of heaven."
This happens after verse 12, "And they heard a great voice from heaven
saying unto them, come up hither. And they ascended up to heaven in
a cloud."

Now let us note John 11:24, "Martha saith unto him, I know that he
shall rise again in the resurrection at the last day." We should note here
that Martha knew it was not until the "last day" that the resurrection
would happen. This "last day" was given to us by John four times.
The word for this last "day" is *eschatos*,[409] which means farest, final (of
place or time); end of, last, latter end, uttermost. It is a noun, probably
from EK (1537), on page 2064 form, in the sense of farthest; the
extreme, most remote, spoken of place and time. We should also note
Revelation 10:6, "Time no longer." The word *chronos*[410] is a reference
to this is time, "Which designates a fixed or special occasion." I would
say the special occasion is the resurrection of the dead. Let's note other
scripture that proves this. First Corinthians 15:23-24 says:

But every man his own order: Christ the first fruits;
afterward they are Christ's at his coming. Then cometh
the end, when the kingdom to God, even the father;
when he shall put down all rule and all authority and
power.

We should note that Paul tells us the coming of the Lord is when
there is resurrection of the dead in his own order. We should also note
that he tells us, "Then cometh the end, the last day." Just as Jesus raised
the dead after his three days and nights in the middle of the earth, the

---

[409]   Ibid., 2080.
[410]   Ibid., 2180.

spirits of people are in the middle of the earth from the first day of Jesus Christ's resurrection till this resurrection. Ezekiel tells us in 18:4, "Behold, all souls are mine." Revelation 6:9 says, "I saw under the altar the souls of them that were slain for the Word of God." They don't see the spirits of men.

John tells us in John 5:28, "Marvel not at this; for the hour is coming, in which all that are in the graves shall hear his voice." It must be the spirit of man that is in the grave (under the earth). First Corinthians 5:5 says, "To deliver such a one unto Satan for the destruction of the flesh, that the spirit may be saved in the day of the Lord Jesus." "Save" is the word *sozo*,[411] which means to save (i.e., deliver or protect) (literal or figurative); heal preserve, be (made) whole. The saved people will be made whole soul and spirit. "Then cometh the end." And when this happens, he will put down all authority and power. And when does this happen in the book of Revelation?

Revelation 11:15 says:

> And the seventh angel sounded; and there were great voices in heaven, saying, The kingdoms of this world are become the kingdoms of our Lord, and of his Christ; and he shall reign for ever and ever.

The pre-tribulation resurrection pastors should be able to explain how Revelation 4 is the last day and the end and prove this is not the last trumpet of the seventh angel, the last trumpet of 1 Corinthians 15:52.

John 6:54 says:

> Whosoever eateth my flesh, and drinketh my blood, hath eternal life: and I will raise him up at the last day.

It is not until the last day when the resurrection of the saints happens. By the way, I do this every Sunday when I attend church. I

---

411 Ibid., 2160.

take the bread and drink the "grape juice," which is of the Lord. But before I do this, I ask for forgiveness for my sins. I believe that if you have any unconfessed sin, you should not partake of the Lord's Supper. We should also note 1 Corinthians 7:5, "Defraud ye not one to other, except it be with consent for a time, that ye may give yourselves to fasting and prayer; and come together again, that Satan tempt you not for your inconsistency."

The Lord speaks in Matthew 17:21, "Howbeit this kind goeth not out but by prayer and fasting." Mark also tells us why the disciples couldn't rebuke the foul spirit. Jesus tells them, "Come forth by nothing but by prayer and fasting." Do you as Christians fast at all? Is this why your prayers are not answered, because you don't fast?

Revelation 15:1–2, 5–8 says:

> And I saw another sign in heaven, great and marvelous, seven angels having the seven plagues; for in them is filled up the wrath of God . . . And I saw as it were a sea of glass mingled with fire: and them that had gotten victory of the beast, and over his image, and over his mark, and over the number of his name, stand on the sea of glass, having the harps of God.

Stop here!

When John is looking down from heaven, when the Lord meets the saints in the air, it would probably look like they are standing on a sea of glass. We should also note Revelation 4:6, which says, "And before the throne there was a sea of glass like unto crystal." Is this what John saw that was great and marvelous? The word "sign" is *semeion*,[412] which means an indication, especially ceremonial, or supernatural; miracle, sign, token, wonder. This is the same sign spoken of in Matthew 24:30, "Immediately after the tribulation of those days shall the sun be darkened and the moon shall not give her light, and the stars shall fall from heaven, and the powers of the heavens shall be shaken: and then

---

[412] Ibid., 2151.

shall appear the sign of the Son of Man in heaven." This is where this ceremony and miracle happens.

The word "marvelous" is *thaumastos*,[413] which means wonder at (i.e., by implication) wonderful; marvel (-lous). It is from *thaumazo*,[414] which means to wonder; by implication to admire; admire, have admiration. This comes from *thauma*,[415] which means wonder. The comment in *Strong's Complete Word Study Concordance* states, "Apparently from a form of *theaomai*, prolonged form of a primary verb; to look closely at, i.e., (by implication) to perceive (literal or figurative) by extension to visit; behold, look (upon)."[416] Compare this to *optanomai*,[417] which means to gaze (i.e., with wide-open eyes, as at something remarkable). We should note the Greek word meaning "to visit." Throughout the Old Testament, when the judgments came on the people, it's called "the time of their visitation." Consider the following examples. Isaiah 10:3 says, "And what will ye do in the day of visitation, and in the desolation which shall come from afar?" Isaiah 29:6 says, "Thou shall be visited of the Lord of hosts with thunder, and with earthquake, and great noise, with strom and tempest, and the flame of devouring fire."

Let us note that this marvelous event is told to us by Micah and Zechariah. Micah 7:15–16 says:

> According to the days of thy coming out of Egypt will I [God] shew unto him marvelous things. The nations shall see and be confounded at all their might: they shall lay their hand upon their mouth, their ears shall be deaf.

We should note the reference to the days of the great plagues that were upon Egypt. The equivalent message is given in Revelation 15:1 where the seven last plagues of the wrath of God are poured out upon

---

413 Ibid., 2086.
414 Ibid.
415 Ibid.
416 Ibid.
417 Ibid., 2123.

the earth. It also states, "I saw as it was a sea of glass mingled with fire." I believe this is the resurrection of the dead. Note Revelation15:1, "And I saw a sign in heaven, great and marvelous." This sign is the same sign as in Matthew 24:30, "And then shall appear a sign of the Son of Man in heaven." In verses 18 and 19, we are told:

> Who is a God like unto thee, that pardoneth iniquity, and passeth by the transgression of the remnant of his heritage? he retaineth not his anger for ever, because he delighteth in mercy. He will turn again, he will subdue our iniquities; and thou wilt cast all their sins into the depths of the sea.

Zechariah 8:6–7 says:

> Thus saith the Lord of hosts; If it be marvelous in the eyes of the remnant of this people in these days should it also be marvelous in mine eyes? saith the Lord of hosts. Thus saith the Lord of hosts; Behold, I [God] will save my people from the east country, and from the West Country.

Let us compare the "save my people from the east, and from the west country" of Zechariah to the "land of unwalled villages" and the "land of Israel" in Ezekiel 38. "These days" of Zechariah has its equivalent message in the New Testament in Matthew 24:29, "Immediately after the tribulation of those days" where the sun and the moon don't give their light. Then the Son of Man shall appear in heaven. This is what is marvelous in the eyes of the remnant of this people in Zechariah. And this people of Zechariah are the people told to us in 1 Thessalonians 4:15, "And we which are alive and remain until the coming of the Lord."

The word "marvelous" is the word *pala*,[418] which means properly perhaps to separate (i.e., distinguish) (literal or figurative); by implication

---

[418]   Ibid., 1946.

to be (causative make) great, difficult, wonderful; accomplish. Note the Hebrew word meaning to separate. This recalls the parables of the wheat and the tares and the just and the unjust. Could the "mingled with fire" be the Lord who is a consuming fire? Hebrews 12:29 tells us, "For our God is a consuming fire."

Revelation 4:8 says:

> And the four beasts had each of them six wings about him; and they were full of eyes within: and they rest not day and night saying, Holy, Holy, Holy, Lord God Almighty, which was, and is, and is to come.

Does John put this in the book to tell us something? I think so. Revelation 8:1 says:

> And when he opened the seventh seal, there was silence in heaven about the space of half an hour.

If there is silence in heaven, then the four beasts are not saying, "Holy, Holy, Holy, the Lord God Almighty," and if no man is able to enter the temple of God, that should tell us the Lord is not there. Isaiah 26:21 says: "The Lord cometh out of his place," and 1 Thessalonians 4:16 says, "For the Lord himself shall descend from heaven." Could this space of about a half an hour found in Daniel 12:10–11?

> And from the time that the daily sacrifice shall be taken away, and the abomination that maketh desolate set up, there shall be a thousand two hundred and ninety days. Blessed is he that waiteth, and cometh to the thousand three hundred and five and thirty days.

Could these forty-five days in Daniel be the Revelation 8:1 space of half an hour, the days of the wrath of God? The space of half an hour in heaven is talked about in Revelation 9:5:

And to them it was given that they should not kill
them, but that they should be tormented five months:
and their torment was as the torment of a scorpion,
when he striketh a man. Blessed is he that waited.

This is the "seek meekness; it may be shall be hid in the day of the
Lord's anger" of Zephaniah 2:3. And this is the "we which are alive
and remain until the coming of the Lord" of 1 Thessalonians 4:15.
These are the people of Revelation 22:14: "Blessed are they that do
his commandments that they may have right to the tree of life, and
may enter in through the gates into the city." These are the, "Blessed
are the meek: for they shall inherit the earth" of Matthew 5:5. This is
the message the Bible is telling us. We should note that the scorpions
torment just those who don't have the seal of God in their foreheads.

Isaiah 26:20–21 says:

Come, my people, enter thou into my chambers, and
shut thy doors about thee: hide thyself as it were for a
little moment until the indignation be overpast. For,
behold, the Lord cometh out of his place to punish
the inhabitants of the earth for their iniquity.

Zephaniah 2:3 says:

Seek ye the Lord, all ye meek of the earth, which
have wrought his judgments; seek righteousness, seek
meekness: it may be ye shall be hid in the day of the
Lords anger.

The *Webster's Dictionary* meaning for wrought is "made with great
care." So are the judgments of God not made with great care not to
affect his people when his judgments affect the earth? Note it says here
"enter thou into my chambers." That chamber that "my people" enter
is given in Psalms 27:5, "For in the time of trouble he shall hide me in
his pavilion: in the secret place of his tabernacle shall he hid me." The
same message is given in Revelation 21:3: "Behold, the tabernacle of

God is with men, and he shall dwell with them, and he shall be their God." This is when the Lord shall descend from heaven with a shout, with the voice of the archangel and the trumpet of God, and the dead in Christ shall rise first. This is when Isaiah 26:21 tells us when the Lord comes out of heaven. This is when we who are alive and remain until the coming of the Lord shall be caught up with them (the dead) in the clouds, to meet the Lord in the air; so shall we ever be with the Lord. As we read when the judgments of God fell on Egypt, they did not affect the Hebrews. So why would the judgments in the book of Revelation not do the same? Those who are meek of the earth and are hidden in the day of the Lord's anger are the meek who are spoken of in scripture.

Has the church missed the bigger picture? That bigger picture is that the meek inherit the earth, which is just what the Lord told us to pray about in the Lord's Prayer: "Thy kingdom come. Thy will be done on earth as it is in heaven." We should also note Psalms 37:9, "For evildoers shall be cut off: but those that wait upon the Lord, they shall inherit the earth." Psalms 37:29 says, "The righteous shall inherit the land, and dwell therein for ever." Psalms 37:34 says, "Wait on the Lord, and keep his ways (commandments), and he shall exalt thee to inherit the land: when the wicked are cut off, thou shall see it." If "thou shall see" when the wicked are "cut off" or destroyed, that would mean the righteous are on the planet. Psalms 37:3–8 says, "But the transgressors shall be destroyed: the end of wicked shall be cut off." Then Psalms 37:39 tells us, "But the salvation of the righteous is of the Lord: he is their strength in the time of trouble (tribulation)." And this is just what we will read in this next verse. Let's read Matthew 25:31–34, 41:

> When the Son of Man shall come in his glory, and all the holy angels with him, then shall he sit upon the throne of his glory: And before him shall be gathered all nations: and he shall separate them one from another, as a shepherd divideth his sheep from the goats: And he shall set his sheep on his right hand, but the goats on the left. Then shall the King say unto them on his right hand, Come, ye blessed of

my father, inherit the kingdom prepared for you from the foundations of the world: then he will also them on his left hand, Depart from me, ye cursed, into everlasting fire, prepared for the devil and his angels.

If Christians are not on the planet when the Lord returns, who are these sheep? Why is there a separation from the goats? Well, the goats are those who don't have their faith in the Lord Jesus, and we read what happens to them. And this is the same message given in the psalms where the wicked are cut off and the meek will inherit the earth. And we should notice that Lord Jesus says he will gather from all nations. As we will read in the next verse, "And the nations which are saved." This tells us that there are nations saved from the wrath of God during the tribulation period.

Revelation 21:24, 27 says:

And the nations of them which are saved and walk in the light of it: and the kings of the earth do bring their glory and honour into it. And the gates of it shall not be shut at all by day: for there shall be no light there. And they shall bring their glory and honour of the nations into it. And there shall in no wise enter into it any thing that defileth, neither whatsoever worketh abomination, or maketh a lie: but they which are written in the Lamb's book of Life.

Let us note the definition of the word "saved" in Greek in Revelation 21:24, which is *sode*,[419] which means to save (i.e., deliver or protect) (literal or figurative); heal, preserve, save (self), do well, be (made) whole. It is from *sos* (n.f.) safe, delivered, to save, make whole, preserver, safe from danger, loss, destruction. Note the Greek word meaning "be made whole" and "protected." The dead are made whole by the spirit, which is under the earth, when it is united with the soul that John saw in heaven. The ones protected are given in 1

---

[419]   Ibid., 2181.

Thessalonians 5:23: "And the very God of peace sanctify you wholly: and I pray God your whole spirit and soul and body be preserved blameless unto the coming of our Lord Jesus Christ." Note it says the body is preserved until when? The coming of the Lord. We should also note here that there are people whose names are "written in the Lamb's Book of Life" still on the earth. Note it says, "And the nations of them which are saved." Not all nations receive the wrath of God because they don't come against Jerusalem.

These people who "maketh a lie" in Revelation are not allowed to bring their honor and glory to it, which is the temple of God in Jerusalem at his return. This is not the big lie of Muhammad because his people are destroyed from being a people. We should also note in Matthew 25, where the Lord tells us who inherits eternal life. You may be an every-Sunday churchgoer, but if you don't have compassion for the poor, where is your faith? I saw a man once who had a sign, "Will work for food." Well, I stopped and told him I had some yard work I needed help with. He said to me, "I don't do yard work." Did I give that man a dime? No. I will help those who will help themselves, for the Bible tells us that if a man wants to eat, he should work.

Isaiah 45:17–19 says:

> But Israel shall be saved in the Lord with an every lasting salvation: ye shall not be ashamed nor confounded world without end. For thus saith the Lord that created the heavens; God himself from the earth and made it; he hath established it, he created it not in vain, he formed it to be inhabited: I am the Lord; and there is none else. I have not spoken in secret, in a dark place of the earth: I said not unto the seed of Jacob, Seek ye me in vain: I the Lord speak righteousness, I declare things that are right.

We should note Isaiah tells us "all Israel" shall be saved. This includes the unbelieving Jews of the world. We should also note this "world without end." We should also note, "I have not spoken in secret, in a dark place of the earth." The prophet Muhammad received his revelation, but in a cave, a dark place. God has not spoken in dark places, so who gave Muhammad his revelation? We should note, "I am the Lord, and there is none else." If there is no one but the Lord, who are the Muslims praying to? To the environmental people, the Lord states, "He formed the earth to be inhabited." So to the environmental people, God says the earth is his creation to be inhabited forever. There is not an earth that the History Channel states in *Life after People*.

We are also told in 1 John 2:18:

> Little children, it is the last time: and as ye have heard that Antichrist shall come, even now are there many Antichrists; whereby we know that it is the last time.

John tells us here that there are many Antichrists in the world during all periods of man, but there will be the true Antichrists at the end of the age. If we look back into history, there were many leaders who tried to rule the world. They have brought death and destruction since man has been upon the earth. This will continue until the return of the Lord. John goes on to tell us that we know that the end is very near when the Antichrist is here and the Lord's return is very near. This dealing with Antichrist includes the twenty-first-century "little children."

Matthew 24:6, 13–14 says:

> And ye shall hear of wars and rumor of wars: see that ye be not troubled: for all these things must come to pass, but the end is not yet . . . but he that shall endure unto the end, the same shall be saved . . . And this gospel of the kingdom shall be preached, in all the world for a witness unto all nations; and then shall the end come.

We are told there will be rumors of war in the last days, and the world of Islam is bringing these passages to pass. And we are told in scripture that we are to endure to the end. This is one of the most important verses in scripture that the church must understand. We are told here that we are to endure until the end. The end is after the gospel of the kingdom is preached unto all the world, and that is done when the sealed servants of God that number one hundred and forty-four thousand do it. The end comes when the seven thunders utter their voices in Revelation 10:4 where we are told in verse 6, "There is time no longer" and in verse 7, "The mystery of God should be finished." This is the end when there is time no longer. Since this is when the end comes as the Lord has declared to his servants the prophets, this makes the pre-tribulation rapture pastors false prophets. If you see the news of today, are we not in the wars and rumor of wars that our Lord tells us of Matthew 24?

Revelation 6:9–11 says:

> And when he opened the fifth seal, I saw under the altar the souls of them that were slain for the Word of God, and for the testimony which they held: And they cried with a loud voice saying, how long, O Lord, holy and true, dost thou not judge and avenge our blood of them that dwell on the earth: and white robes were given unto everyone of them, and it was said unto them, that they should rest yet for a little season, until their fellow servants also and their brethren, that they should be killed as they were, should be fulfilled.

We should note here in the fifth seal judgment that John sees those who were slain for the Word of God, and he does not see any "resurrection" saint. More saints are to die, as they were killed. Nowhere in the book of Revelation does John see any saint who can be said that the Lord took them in a "resurrection" until Revelation 14:4, "These [the 144,000] were redeemed from among men, being the first-fruits unto God and to the lamb." What part of "first-fruits" do we not understand? The word for redeemed is the word *agorazo*,[420] from

---

[420] Ibid., 2012.

the word *agora*,[421] and this is akin to *egeiro*,[422] which means to waken (transitive or intransitive) (i.e., rouse) (from sleep, from disease, from death); awake, lift (up), raise (again). If these are the first to be raised again from the dead, then there is no pre-tribulation resurrection or alive church resurrection. Note the language, "White robes were given unto everyone of them." Those who come out of the great tribulation period have to "wash their robes and make them white in the blood of the lamb." Why is the Muslin world more prepared to die for their religion than Christians? We should note Psalms 116:15, "Precious is the sight of the Lord is the death of his saints." When I die, I pray that God thinks I am precious in his sight.

Revelation 12:17 says:

> And the dragon was wroth with the woman, and went to make war with the remnant of her seed which keep the commandments of God, and have the testimony of Jesus Christ.

The dragon is the devil, the woman is Israel, the seed is those who try to keep the commandments of God, and the church is those who have the testimony of Jesus Christ. In the scriptures, we have read that the people who have the "testimony of Jesus" are the ten tribes of the house of Israel.

Revelation 14:12–13 says:

> Here is the patience of the saints: here are they that keep the commandments of God, and the Faith of Jesus, and I heard a voice from heaven saying unto me, write, blessed are they which die in the Lord from henceforth: yea saith the spirit, that they rest from their labours, and their works do follow them.

---

[421]   Ibid.

[422]   Ibid., 2060.

If these who have "the faith of Jesus" are not the church, I do not know who they are. Maybe the pre-tribulation resurrection pastors know. We know who is still trying to "keep the commandments" by not accepting the Lord Jesus as their Savior. We should notice that their works follow them. So does this mean that the grace period has ended?

Romans 5:2–3, 9 says:

> By whom also we have access by faith into his grace wherein we stand, and rejoice in the hope and glory of God. And not only so, but we glory in tribulation also; knowing that tribulation worketh patience . . . Must more then, being justified by his blood, we shall be saved from the wrath through him.

The "tribulation that worketh patience" here in Romans is the same as the "here is the patience of the saints" of Revelation 14:12. This is the "wrath through him" of Romans, the same wrath of Revelation 15: "Seven angels having the seven last plagues, for in them is filled up the wrath of God." The word *hupomone*[423] is Greek for the word "patience" given in Romans 5:3 and means cheerful (or hopeful) endurance, constancy, enduring, patience, continuance (waiting). The comment on this is: "Specifically patience as a quality of mind, the bearing of evils and suffering with tranquil mind."[424] This does not sound like a pre-tribulation resurrection. We should note that one of the word meanings is waiting. Let's note Isaiah 40:31, "But they that wait upon the Lord shall renew their strength; they shall mount up with wings as eagles; they shall run, and not be weary; and they shall walk, and not faint."

First Thessalonians 1:10, 5:9 says:

> And to wait for his son from heaven, whom he raised from the dead, even Jesus, which delivered us from

---

[423] Ibid., 2170.
[424] Ibid.

the wrath to come. For God hath not appointed us to wrath, but to obtain salvation by our Lord Jesus Christ.

He does not say here that we are delivered from tribulation. Let us note the meaning of appointed: "to put, set place; then generally to bring a thing into a place; an so bring in a situation."[425] We should notice it says here, "To wait for his Son." We are told in Psalms 37:34, "Wait on the Lord." Psalms 40:1 says, "I waited patiently for the Lord." Psalms 27:14 says, "Wait on the Lord; be of good courage, and he shall strengthen thine heart: wait, I say, on the Lord." "Wait" is the word *qavah*,[426] which means to bind together (i.e., collect); (figurative) to expect; gather, patiently, tarry. "Delivered" is the word *rhuomai*,[427] which means to rush or draw (i.e., rescue). And the same language that is used in the psalms is used in the previous verses of Romans, Revelation, and Isaiah. In 1 Thessalonians, Psalms, and Isaiah, we are told that those who wait on the Lord, the Lord will strengthen or rescue. And we are to wait for the Lord when Psalms 37:39 says, "But the salvation of the righteous is of the Lord: he is their strength in the time of trouble." Trouble means tribulation. We are to do this again in Psalms 41:1 and 50:15.

I cannot find one verse in scripture that says we are saved from tribulation, but it does promise to keep us from the wrath of God. God does not have to take us off the planet to do that.

Luke 8:10–13 says:

> Unto you it is given to know the mysteries of the kingdom of God: but to others in parables; that seeing they might see, and hearing they might not understand. Now the parable is this: the seed is the Word of God. Those by the wayside are they that hear; then the Devil cometh, and taketh away the word out

---

[425] *Bullinger's*, 60.
[426] *Strong's*, 1959.
[427] Ibid., 2149.

of their hearts, lest they believe and be saved. They on the rock are they, which, when they hear, receive the word with joy; and these have no root, which for awhile believe, and in time of temptation fall away.

Who is the Lord speaking to if not the church? If the church was resurrected off the planet before the devil shows up, this would not be in scripture. Unless we are deeply rooted in our faith in Jesus, when the devil comes and tempts us with the pleasures of this life, will we have the faith to overcome the devil? Let's note the time of temptation. "Temptation" is the word *peirasmos*,[428] which means a putting to proof (by experiment [of good or evil], solicitation, discipline, or provocation); by implication adversary; temptation. It is from *periazo*,[429] which means to test (i.e., endeavor), scrutinize, entice, or discipline. For "to fall away," we go to *Strong's Complete Word Study Concordance,* and the word is *aphistemi*,[430] which means to remove (i.e., active) instigate to revolt; usually (reflexive) to desist or desert. This is why teaching the pre-tribulation resurrection is wrong. People who believe this will be the people who have roots. There are these promises from God to help those that are his.

Luke 10:19–20 says:

Behold, I give you power to tread on serpents and scorpions, and over all the power of the enemy: and nothing shall by any means hurt you. Notwithstanding in this rejoice not, that the spirits are subject unto you; but rather rejoice, because your names are written in heaven.

To be given power over something must mean that there will be people affected by these serpents, but God's people have power over them. Note what the scripture says here: "because your names are written in heaven." It states again that we have all the power over the

---

[428]   Ibid., 2133.

[429]   Ibid.

[430]   Ibid., 2039.

enemy. "Enemy" is the word *echthros*,[431] which means hateful; usually as a noun, an adversary (especially Satan); enemy, foe. Where are these serpents and scorpions mentioned in scripture? Revelation 9:3–4 says:

> And there came out of the smoke locusts upon the earth: and unto them was given power, as the scorpions of the earth have power. And it was commanded them that they should not hurt the grass of the earth, neither any green thing, neither any tree; but only those men which have not the seal of God in their foreheads.

God's people are still on the earth at this time, and to protect them, God puts a seal in their foreheads because their names are written in heaven. This is the same seal when the Lord brought the judgments to the house of Judah in Ezekiel 9:4, "Set a mark upon the forehead of the men that sigh and that cry for all the abominations that be done in the midst thereof."

We should also note Isaiah 5:5, "And now go to; I will tell you what I will do to my vineyard [Israel]: I will take away the hedge thereof, and it shall be eaten up; and break down the wall thereof, and it shall be trodden down." We see here that the hedge that protected all of Israel was taken away by God. Jesus tells us just when that hedge is taken away. In Mark 12:1–11, the Lord says:

> A certain man [that man was Jesus] planted a vineyard [that vineyard was Israel] and set a hedge [*phragmos*,[432] which means a fence, or enclosing barrier (literal or figurative); hedge, partition] about it, and digged a place for the winevat [*hupolenion*,[433] which means vessel or receptacle under the press (i.e., lower winevat)], and built a tower, and let out to

---

[431] Ibid., 2083.
[432] Ibid., 2174.
[433] Ibid., 2170.

husbandman [*georgos*,[434] which means a land worker
(i.e., farmer)], and went into a far country.

Verses 2–5 tell us that God sent to Israel prophets for them to do
right, but they beat some and killed some. Starting in verse 6:

Having yet therefore one son [Jesus], his wellbeloved,
he sent him also last unto them, saying, They [Jews
of Israel] will reverence my son [Jesus]. But those
husbandmen said among themselves, This is the heir;
come, let's kill him, and the inheritance shall be ours.
[The high priest and the Pharisees have Jesus crucified.]
And they took him, and killed him, and cast him out
of the vineyard [earth]. What shall therefore the Lord
of the vineyard do? He will come and destroy the
husbandmen, and will give the vineyard unto others.

In 1 Thessalonians 4:16, we are told that the Lord shall descend
from heaven, and the dead in Christ shall be raised and in 5:2 "as a
thief in the night." The Lord comes as a thief when he gathers them to
the battle of Armageddon of Revelation 16:16. The Lord comes as a
thief for the "resurrection of the dead." The Old Testament equivalent
scripture when the Lord shall descend is Ezekiel 38:18, 20: "And it
shall come to pass at the same time when Gog shall come against the
land of Israel, saith the Lord God, that my fury shall come up in my
face. And all men that are upon the face of the earth shall shake at my
presence."

First Thessalonians 5:2–4 says:

For yourselves know perfectly that the day of the
Lord so cometh as a thief in the night . . . For when
they say, peace and safety; then sudden destruction
cometh upon them, as travail upon a woman with
child; and they shall not escape. But ye brethren are

---

[434]   Ibid., 2046.

not in darkness, that that day should overtake you as
a thief . . .

This day of peace and safety will only come when the Antichrist makes the peace agreement. This darkness of 1 Thessalonians where that day will not overtake the church is the same darkness of Matthew 24:30 where it's immediately after the tribulation of those days where there is a sign in heaven, and then shall appear the Son of Man. All hell breaks out after this.

Isaiah 41:22 says:

Let them shew the former things, what they be, that
we may consider them, and know the latter end.

This is the judgment on the house of Judah in 586 BC to be taken into Babylonian captivity. Isaiah tells us that to know the latter end, God shows the former things. The conditions are described in Ezekiel 32:7–8:

And when I shall put thee out, I will cover the heaven,
and make the stars thereof dark; I will cover the sun
with a cloud, and the moon shall not give her light.
All the bright lights of heaven will I make dark over
thee, and set darkness upon thy land, saith the Lord.

When God's judgments come, darkness happens. It happened then, and it will happen again at the end of the age, as spoken of in Matthew 24:30, "Immediately after the tribulation of those days shall the sun be darkened, and the moon not give her light. And then shall appear the Son of Man." Here is another example of things done in the past that reveal the future.

Exodus 9:23–24 says:

And Moses stretched forth his rod toward heaven:
and the Lord sent thunder and hail, and fire ran along
upon the ground; and the Lord rained hail upon the

land of Egypt. So there was hail, and fire mingled with the hail, very grievous, such as there was not like it in the land of Egypt since it became a nation.

Exodus 7–11 contains God's judgments upon Egypt. But the land of Goshen, where the Hebrews were, was not affected. That should tell us that the judgments in the book of Revelation will not affect us but only those God's judgments are against. Note Revelation 21:24, "And the nations of them which are saved shall walk in the light of it." There will be nations saved from the wrath of God. Note that the second to the last judgment is a day of darkness.

Exodus 10:22–23 says:

And Moses stretched forth his hand toward heaven; and there was a thick darkness in all the land of Egypt three days. They saw not one another, neither rose any from his place for three days: but all the children of Israel had light in their dwellings.

This is the same way God shortens the days for the elect's sake. Notice that they did not rise for three days, but the children of Israel had light. We should also notice that they did not move for three days because of the darkness. Here comes the last judgment, which is the judgment against the firstborn of Egypt. The children of Israel were instructed to put the blood of the lamb on the lintel and on the two side posts, and the Lord would not let the destroyer come into their house.

Exodus 12:29 says:

And it came to pass that at midnight the Lord smote all the first born in the land of Egypt.

Notice that it was at midnight when the Lord did this, and when the final judgment came the Lord himself got involved. Where else is it prophesied that the Lord will come at midnight?

Matthew 25:6 says:

> And at midnight there was a cry made, Behold, the
> bridegroom cometh; go ye out to meet him.

Before the night is over, Pharaoh says to Moses, "Go ye serve the Lord," and the children of Israel were delivered out of Egyptian bondage. So shall it be in the latter days, after the day of darkness. The people under the blood of the lamb will be delivered from the destroyer.

We should also note that in the time of the Exodus, there are two witnesses in Moses and Aaron who were against Pharaoh, just as there are two witnesses against the Antichrist in Revelation. Where does man expect to survive a nuclear attack but in the holes of the earth? We should note here that Micah tells us God delighted in mercy and has compassion upon us, and as our Lord told us, our sins will be cast into the depths of the seas, never to be remembered. What a great and forgiving God the Lord of heaven is. And I say praise the Lord.

Let's look what the History Channel's *The Exodus, Exposed* says happened at the Exodus. In the year 1500 BC, the island of Santorini, an island off the coast of Greece, erupted, causing soot and ash to come down on Egypt. Archaeologists have found pumice in Egypt they can trace to the island of Santorini in diggings that date back to the year 1500 BC. In Egypt is the Puwer Payprus, which states, "Darkness caused by ash cloud." In 1947 the "Ahmose" Stele was found in Egypt, which states, "Great storm and darkness." It puts this in the time of the reign of Ahmose. Ahmose means "the brother of Moses."

But there is this problem. Josephus states, "It was then one thousand and sixty-two years, six months, ten days from the departure out of Egypt; and from the Deluge to the destruction of the temple."[435] If the destruction of the temple was around 586 BC, adding 1,062 years to this brings the exodus to around 1648 BC. But the National Geographic Channel says on one program that some scientists say the eruption happened as early as 1620 BC. Which one of the scientists is right? With Josephus detailing to the day, it makes me think he

---

[435] Whitson, *The New Complete Works of Josephus*, 346.

had access to records we don't have today. But the programs on the History Channel and the National Geographic Channel both agree that Santorini pumice is found in Egypt.

My biggest problem is they try to say it was just by chance that all these things happened naturally, taking God out of the picture. But they also miss one of the greatest miracles of these plagues. The plagues did not affect the Hebrews, and this is the greatest miracle of all. But scientists also state that because of the river being turned red, all the following plagues would happen naturally, just as Moses prophesied. This tells us that the Father God controls mother earth. They did get one thing right. Father God will use the natural forces of the earth to bring judgment to man. As Isaiah states, "The past reveals the future." Does God use the same method in the fifth trumpet judgment where, "There arose a smoke out of the pit; as the smoke of a great furnace; and the sun and the air were darkened by reason of the smoke of the pit"? Is Pharaoh an example of the Antichrist that persecutes "the woman," which is Israel, in the book of the Revelation?

I have just seen on the Science Channel a program about the island of Krakatoa. When it blew in 1883, these were the effects on the area around the islands. There was darkness during the daylight hours. There were multiple earthquakes. A ship's captain in the area reported that his compass did not work because of the electrical charges that were caused by the eruptions. I believe this is how the Lord will smite the arrows, as told to us in Ezekiel 39. These electrical charges will cause the guidance systems of these missiles to fail. All of these things happen in the book of Revelation before the coming of our Lord. Even the Islamic prophet predicted this would happen before the coming of the Mahdi, but their Mahdi is the Antichrist. It is apparent to me that Islamic predictions are more correct than the teachings of the pre-tribulation resurrection pastors.

Using Isaiah's way to understand Bible prophecy, line upon line, this is the conclusion I have come up with. It is mentioned at least eight times in scripture that the, "Sun and moon darkened, and the stars do not give its light" (Isa. 23:10; 24:23; Joel 2:10; 2:30; 3:14; Acts 2:20; Matt. 24:29; Mark 13:4). What does the next sentence say?

He shall swallow up death in victory (Isa. 25:8).

And the Lord shall utter his voice before his army (Joel 2:11).

Whosoever shall call upon the name of the Lord shall be delivered (Joel 2:31).

And the Lord shall roar at of Zion, and utter his voice from Jerusalem, and the heavens and the earth shall shake: but the Lord will be the hope of his people, and the strength of the children of Israel (Joel 3:16).

That whosoever shall call upon the name of the Lord shall be saved (Acts 2:21).

And then shall appear the sign of the Son of Man in heaven (Matt. 24:29).

And the stars of heaven shall fall, and the powers that are in heaven shall be shaken. And then shall they see the Son of Man coming in the clouds with great power and glory (Mark 13:25–26).

Does this not show us that this is the resurrection of the dead? Does this not reveal that there is a day in the future when this day happens? There is this "great day" that is the resurrection of the dead, and "terrible and dreadful day" that is the wrath of God. It is after the sun and the moon don't give their light in Matthew 24. Let's note Joel 3:16, which tells us that "the Lord shall utter his voice from Jerusalem." This is the equivalent to Revelation 11:12, "And they heard a voice from heaven saying unto them, Come up hither," when the two witness who were killed in Jerusalem are called. Then Revelation tells us in verse 13, "And the same hour was a great earthquake." The earthquake is to open the graves of the dead in Ezekiel 38.

This is the Lord's appearing of Matthew 24 that Paul writes to all the churches to look for. After the seventh vial of the wrath of God, there is this: "And there were voices, and thunders, and lightnings; and there was a great earthquake, such as was not since men were upon the earth." This talks about the Lord's return to the earth, the coming of Matthew 24, where there are some standing here who will not taste of death till they see the coming of the Lord. Zechariah 14:4 tells us, "And his feet shall stand on that day upon the mount of olives, which is before Jerusalem," where there is a great earthquake. This is when Zechariah 14:5 states, "And the Lord my God shall come, and all the saints with thee."

Isaiah tells us in 60:2, "For behold, the darkness shall cover the whole earth, and gross darkness the people: but the Lord shall arise upon thee, and his glory shall be see upon thee." It is the darkness that covers the whole earth when the Lord shall arise. It is dark to reveal "whom the Lord shall consume with the spirit of his mouth, and destroy with the brightness of his coming" of 2 Thessalonians 2:8. In Matthew 24:27, it says, "For as the lightning cometh out of the east, and shineth even unto the west; so shall the coming of the Son of Man be." But there are two types of darkness: one that covers the whole earth, and the darkness of Revelation 16:10: "And the fifth angel poured out his vial upon the seat of the beast; and his kingdom was full of darkness; and they gnawed their tongues for pain." We should note that this judgment only affects the seat of the beast and his kingdom.

Now let's go to the parable of the ten virgins. Are the ten virgins a reference to the ten lost tribes of the house of Israel? Is the oil for the lamps a reference to the knowledge of the Lord's return during the time of "the sun and the moon darkened"? Note verse 6, "And at midnight there was a cry made, behold, the bridegroom cometh; go ye out to meet him." Is it at midnight not to let us know the sky is dark? During this darkness, only half of the church will be looking for the Lord's return because of the teachings of the pre-tribulation resurrection. In verse 13 it says, "Watch therefore, for ye know neither the day nor the hour wherein the Son of Man cometh," but we can know when to start watching. First Thessalonians 5:4 says "But ye brethren, are not in darkness, that that day overtake you as a thief."

Note Exodus 12:29, "And it came to pass, that at midnight the Lord smote all the firstborn in the land of Egypt, from the first born of Pharaoh that sat on the throne unto the first born of the captive that was in the dungeon; and all the firstborn of cattle." Is there a connection between, "And at midnight there was a cry made; go ye out to meet him" and "that at midnight the Lord smote all the firstborn in the land of Egypt"?

Can this thick darkness where God was in Exodus 20:21 be an example of the Lord's return?

The darkness of Amos 5:20:

> Shall not the day of the Lord be darkness, and not light? Even very dark.

The darkness of Zephaniah 1:15:

> That day is a day of wrath, a day of trouble and distress, a day of wasteness and desolation, a day of darkness and gloominess, a day of clouds and thick darkness.

The darkness of Isaiah 60:2:

> For, behold, the darkness shall cover the earth, and gross darkness the people: but the Lord shall arise upon thee, and his glory shall be seen upon thee.

The darkness of Matthew 24:29–30:

> Immediately after the tribulation of those days shall the sun be darkened and the moon shall not give her light, and the stars shall fall from heaven, and the power of the heavens be shaken: And then shall appear the sign of the Son of Man in heaven

The darkness of Revelation 9:2:

And he opened the bottomless pit, and there arose a
smoke out of the pit, as the smoke of a great furnace;
and the sun and the air were darkened by reason of
the smoke of the pit.

In Exodus 24:18, "Moses went into the midst of the cloud," and
God was an example of the rapture of the dead. Also note that it was
for forty days and forty nights.

Let's note Daniel 12:11–12:

And from the time that the daily sacrifice shall be taken
away, and the abomination that maketh desolate set
up, there shall be a thousand two hundred and ninety
days. Blessed is he that cometh to the thousand three
hundred and five and thirty days.

With all these scriptures devoted to a time when there is this great
darkness, you would think they were put here for a reason. There has
to be something very important that happens when this occurs. This is
when the Lord will descend from heaven with a shout. How have these
Bible scholars overlooked this happening?

Is this forty-five days the days of the wrath of God, the time period
of the caught up dead who are in the clouds before the Lord's return?
Are the "Blessed is he that waiteth" and those hid in the day of the
Lord's anger a reference to the meek who inherit the earth?

Let's also note Deuteronomy 4:11–12:

And ye came near and stood under the mountain:
and the mountain burned with fire unto the midst
of heaven, with darkness, clouds, and thick darkness.
And the Lord spake unto you out of the midst of
the fire; ye heard the voice of the words, but saw no
similitude, only heard the voice.

Let's compare these verses with Zephaniah 1:14–15:

The great day of the Lord is near, it is near, and hasteth greatly, even the voice of the day of the Lord. The mighty man cry there bitterly. That day is a day of wrath, a day of trouble, and distress, a day of wasteness and desolation, a day of darkness and gloominess, a day of clouds and thick darkness.

Note that God speaks out of darkness, clouds, and thick darkness in both Deuteronomy and Zephaniah. In Zephaniah, it states the great day of the Lord is near, "the Lord's return to the earth," and the voice of the day of the Lord, "Come up hither."

Deuteronomy 4:26–31 says:

I call heaven and the earth to witness against you this day, that ye shall soon utterly perish from off the land where unto ye go over Jordon to possess it; ye shall not prolong your days upon it, but shall be utterly destroyed. And the Lord scatter you among the nations, and ye shall be few in number among the heathen, whither the Lord shall lead you. But if from thence thou shalt seek the Lord thy God, thou shalt find him, if thou seek him with all thy heart and with all your soul. When thou are in tribulation, and all these things come upon thee, even in the latter days, if thou turn to the Lord thy God, and shalt be obedient unto his voice; For the Lord thy God is a merciful God; He will not forsake thee, neither destroy thee, nor forget the covenant of thy fathers which he sware unto them.

Note: God has the future outlined from the beginning. God is going to scatter all of the tribes of Israel, and the "the Lord shall lead them" until the time of the tribulation of the latter days. We should also note that God says they will be few in number. There are over a billion Chinese people; there are over a billion in India; there are over a billion

Muslims in the world today who have not accepted Jesus as their Lord. There are also the Russian people who don't even believe in God. There are also the European people who have left the church. We might not be the country the Lord wants us to be, but there is in America much work being done for the Lord. We have over one hundred million people in this country who are God-fearing, church-going Christians who believe in the Lord, and they say that our destruction is coming.

I cannot believe this will happen. Someone has to inherit the earth, and if the Christian people of the world today do not, then who will? Jesus tells us in Matthew 7:13–14:

> Enter ye in at the strait gate: for wide is the gate, and broad is the way, that leadeth to destruction, and many be which go in there at: Because strait is the gate, and narrow is the way, which leadeth unto life, and few there be that find it.

Isaiah tells us that our works are as filthy rags unto the Lord, but if we have faith in the Lord, he will forgive us and protect us. Are we the light to the world that is taking the gospel to the whole world? They all should believe in our Lord. Even then, we do not do the job well enough, for the Bible tells us in Revelation 7:4:

> And I heard the number of them which were sealed; and there were sealed an hundred and forty and four thousand of all the tribes of the children of Israel.

These are the sealed servants of God during the tribulation period who take the gospel to the whole world, for God is not willing that any should perish but that all should come to repentance. Note the reference to "the tribes of the children of Israel," which were sealed. These are the lost tribes of the house of Israel that the Lord Jesus told to preach the gospel to in Matthew 10:6 and 15:24. These are the people of Deuteronomy 4:27, "And the Lord shall scatter you [house of Israel] among the nations." Also note Deuteronomy 4:30–31, "When thou art in tribulation, even in the latter days, if thou turn to the Lord thy God, and shalt be obedient unto his voice; (For the Lord thy God is a merciful God) he will not forsake thee, neither destroy thee." The tribulation of the latter days of Deuteronomy is the tribulation of Revelation 7:4 where it states, "The tribes of the children of Israel." The God I know leaves no one behind. I do not know why anyone would want a pre-tribulation rapture, because the meek who inherit the earth inherit all things and have eternal life with our Lord and Savior. This is why I pray daily the prayer of Matthew 6:10: "Thy kingdom come. Thy will be done on earth, as it is in heaven."

Revelation 7:1 says:

> And after these things I saw four angels standing on the four corners of the earth, holding the four winds of the earth, that the wind should not blow on the earth, nor on the sea, nor on any tree.

This tells us that the vials of the wrath of God affect only those who take the mark of the beast. God causes the winds to quit blowing to keep the ash only in certain areas.

When the mountain called Saint Helen's erupted in the 1980s, the people were covered in soot and ash and did not see the sun for three days. Is this an example of how the Lord will shorten the days for the elect's sake? Is this the smoke of the pit of Revelation that gnawed their tongues for pain in fifth vial?

Note Revelation 18:4:

> And I heard another voice from heaven saying, Come out of her my people, that ye be not partakers of her sins, and that ye receive not of her plagues.

This tells us that the plagues only affect certain areas. And if there are "my people" still on the earth at this time, there was no rapture of the church before the "wrath of God" happens. Are these people the "the meek that inherit the earth"? The word is *laos*,[436] which means;

---

[436] *Strong's*, 2106.

a people meaning of "my people" in Revelation 18:4, "Specifically of the Jews as the people of God's choice. Figuratively, of Christians as God's spiritual Israel." I believe when *Strong's* says here, "God's spiritual Israel," he should have said "house of Israel." I believe that the western hemisphere is where the house of Israel went after the Assyrian captivity.

Verse 21 says:

> And there fell upon men a great hail out of heaven, every stone about the weight of a talent: and the men blasphemed God because of the plague of the hail; for the plague thereof was exceeding great.

Note Joshua 10:11:

> And it came to pass, as they fled from before Israel, and were going to Beth-Horon, that the Lord cast down great stones from heaven upon them unto Asekah, and they died: They were more which died with hailstones than they whom the children of Israel slew with the sword.

This is just what our Lord does in Revelation 16:21, "And there fell upon men a great hail out of heaven, every stone about the weight of a talent," and Ezekiel 38:22, "And I will plead against him with pestilence and with blood; and I will rain upon him, and upon his bands, and upon the many peoples with him, and overflowing rain, and great hailstones, fire, and brimstones." As we read in Joshua, God used hailstones, and more are killed by the hailstones from God, and they did not affect the children of Israel. This is the same method God will use at the battle of Armageddon. The past reveals the future.

Revelation 14:1, 3–4 says:

> And I looked, and, lo, a lamb stood on mount Zion, and with him an hundred forty and four thousand, having his father's name written in their foreheads.

> And they sung as it were a new song before the throne, and before the four beasts, and the elders: and no man could learn that song but the hundred and forty and four thousand which were redeemed from the earth. These are they which were not defiled with women; for they are virgins. These were redeemed from among men, being the first fruits unto God and to the lamb.

These being the first fruits that were redeemed from the earth among men unto God and the lamb could only mean that the rapture of the dead has not happened yet. What about "first fruits" does the pre-tribulation pastor not understand? And I will repeat this as many times as I can. If there is a pre-tribulation rapture, then rip this passage out of your Bible. Even after the one hundred and forty-four thousand are taken back to heaven, this happens.

Revelation 14:6–7, 9–10, 12 says:

> And I saw another angel flying in the midst of heaven, having the everlasting gospel to preach unto them that dwell on the earth, and to every nation, and kindred, and tongue, and people, Saying with a loud voice, Fear God, and give glory to him; for the hour of his judgment is come: and worship Him that made heaven, and earth, and the sea, and the fountains of water. And the third angel followed them, saying with a loud voice, If any man worship the beast and his image, and receive his mark in his forehead, or in his hand, the same shall drink of the wine of the wrath of God, which is poured out without mixture into the cup of his indignation: and he shall be tormented with fire and brimstone in the presence of the holy angels, and in the presence of the lamb. Here is the patience of the saints: here are they that keep the commandments of God, and the faith of Jesus.

As we see here in these scriptures, Satan is going to have so much opposition. Let us read what the *Webster's Dictionary* meaning is of the word "opposition": "A configuration in which one celestial body is opposite another in the sky or in which elongation is near or equal to 180 degrees." That celestial body is the angels with the 180-degree message against Satan on the planet. We should also note that those who take the mark of the beast receive the wrath of God in the presence of the lamb and his holy angels. And here is the warning to the church: "Here is the patience [*hupomone*,[437] which means cheerful (or hopeful) endurance, constancy; enduring, patience] of the saints: here are they that keep the commandments of God, and the faith of Jesus." Did you notice the Greek word meaning enduring? Jesus tells, "But he that shall endure unto the end, the same shall be saved. And this gospel of the kingdom shall be preached in all the world for a witness unto all nations; and then shall the end be." We read here in Revelation 14 that the angels accomplish that mission. If those who have their faith in Jesus are warned not to take the mark of the beast, they have to be on the planet.

Revelation 20:6 says:

> Blessed and holy is he that hath part in the first resurrection: on such the second death hath no power, but they shall be priests of God and of Christ, and shall reign with him a thousand years.

Note: If the rapture of the dead happens in Revelation 4:1, who are these who have "the faith of Jesus" in Revelation 14:12? We should note here also that after the hundred and forty-four thousand are in heaven that an angel is going to warn people not to take the mark of the beast. No one is going to accidentally take the mark of the beast by a national ID card. We should note also that the warnings are not to take the mark of the beast, for if they do, they will receive the wrath of God and not the judgments of the seal and trumpet judgments.

Psalms 34:15–19 says:

---

[437]   Ibid., 2170.

The eyes of the Lord are upon the righteous, and his ears are open unto their cry. The face of the Lord is against them that do evil, to cut off the remembrance of them from the earth. The righteous cry, and the Lord heareth, and delivered them out of their troubles. The Lord is nigh unto them that are of a broken heart; and saveth such as be of a contrite spirit. Many are the afflictions of the righteous: but the Lord delivered out of them all.

In this psalm it tells us that the "righteous cry" and the Lord hears. This is told again in Luke 18:7, "And shall not God avenge his own elect, which cry day and night unto him, though he bear long with them." Many are the afflictions of the righteous. What does the book of Revelation say? In 17:7 it states, "God shall wipe away all tears from their eyes." The psalmist tells us that the Lord hears, and delivers them out of the troubles (tribulation). "Contrite" is the word *dakka*,[438] which means crushed. This is why there is this verse in Luke 18:8: "I tell you that he will avenge them speedily. Nevertheless when the Son of Man cometh, shall he find faith [crushed] on the earth?"

Proverb 1:27–28, 33 says:

When your fear cometh as destruction, and your destruction cometh as a whirlwind; when distress and anguish cometh upon you. Then shall they call upon me, but I will not answer; They shall seek me early, but they shall not find me: But whoso hearkened unto me shall dwell safely, and shall be quiet from fear of evil.

We should note here that it says when distress and anguish come upon you and you call upon the name of the Lord, God will not answer. Luke 17:22 says, "The days will come, when ye shall desire to see one

---

[438] Ibid., 1839.

of the days of the Son of Man, and ye shall not see it." But let's read the promise: "Whoso hearken unto me [God] shall dwell in safety, and shall be quiet from the evil." "Quiet" is the word *shaan*,[439] which means to loll (i.e., be peaceful); be at ease, rest.

Proverb 2:5, 7–8, 12–13, 16–17 says:

> Then shalt thou understand the fear of the Lord, and find the knowledge of God. He layeth up sound wisdom for the righteous: He is a buckler to them that walk uprightly. He keepeth the paths of judgments, and preserveth the way of the saints. To deliver thee from the way of the evil man, from the man that speaketh forward things; Who leave the paths of uprightness, to walk in the ways of darkness; To deliver thee from the strange women, even from the stranger which flattereth with her words; Which forsaketh the guide of her youth, and flattereth with the covenant of God.

Proverbs 1 and 2 tell us that in the time of trouble, the Lord will preserve the way of the saints and deliver the saints from the evil man (Antichrist). "Preserveth" is the word *shamar*,[440] which means properly to hedge about (i.e., guard); generally to protect, attend to. That same hedge was about Job so that the devil could not affect him. The same hedge in Ezekiel 13:5 where the lying prophets were condemned: "Ye have not gone up into the gaps, neither made up the hedge for the house of Israel to stand in the battle in the day of the Lord." The New Testament equivalent verse is in Romans 14:4, "For God is able to make him stand." That hedge has the equivalent verse in Ephesians, "Put on all the armour of God to fight the wiles of the devil." And who could this strange woman of verse 16 be?

Revelation 17:5–7 says:

---

439 Ibid., 1975.
440 Ibid., 1990.

> And upon her forehead was a name written, Mystery,
> Babylon the great, the mother of harlots and
> abominations of the earth. And I saw the woman
> drunken with the blood of the saints, and with the
> blood of the martyrs of Jesus; and when I saw her,
> I wondered with great admiration. And the angel
> said unto me, wherefore didst thou marvel? I will
> tell thee the mystery of the woman, and of the beast
> that carrieth her, which hath the seven heads and ten
> horns.

We should notice that even John was fascinated with the woman, and John gets rebuked by the angel for his great admiration. This is the Vatican in Rome, because verse 9 tells us, "The seven heads are seven mountains, on which the woman sitteth." They will answer to God for all the people they tortured and killed during the Dark Ages. Let's note Mark 13:22–23: "For false Christs and false prophets shall rise, and shall shew signs and wonders, to seduce, if it were possible, even the elect. But take ye heed: behold, I have foretold you all things." We should note here that it says, "If it were possible" to seduce the elect. "Elect" is the word *eklektos*,[441] which means by implication favorite; chosen.

We should note here also that there is another warning about false prophets. These false prophets are the teachers of the people who worship a God other than the Lord Jesus Christ. Second Thessalonians 1:8 states "them that know not God." If the false Christ is the Antichrist who will show signs and wonders but can't seduce the elect, the elect would have to be on the planet. Mark even says, "I have foretold you all things." This is a warning to the people who read this Bible. This is a warning to the church that when this man who does the great sign and wonders appears, we are to realize just who he is and not fall for his false promises.

We should also note this is 1 John 2:18: "Little children, it is the last time: and as ye have heard that the Antichrist shall come, even now

---

[441] Ibid., 2066.

there are many Antichrists; whereby we know that it is the last time." John was warning the church in his days that there are many Antichrists in the world, and there will be until the true Antichrist comes in the last days. The church in John's day overcame the Antichrist because "ye have known the Father." That is how the twenty-first-century church will overcome the Antichrist. The past reveals the future.

Proverbs 3:11–12, 24–26, 33, 35 says:

> My son, despise not the chastening of the Lord; neither be weary of his correction: For whom the Lord loveth he corrected; even as a father the son in whom he delighted. When thou liest down thou shalt not be afraid: yea, thou shalt lie down, and thy sleep shall be sweet. Be not afraid of sudden fear, neither of the desolation of the wicked, when it cometh. For the Lord shall be thy confidence, and shall keep that foot from being taken. The curse of the Lord is in the house of the wicked; but he blesseth the habitation of the just. The wise shall inherit glory: but shame shall be the promotion of fools.

The Lord tells us here that when the sudden fears come, God will bless the habitation of the just, so be not afraid. Solomon tells us, "Despise not the chastening of the Lord." This chastening is the judgments of the book of Revelation. The church is told to endure till the time of the end. Is the tribulation period the time when God corrects his people? We should also note here that the "curse of the Lord is in the house of the wicked." Once again, we are told, "Be not afraid of the sudden fear." Why? When it comes, the desolation is upon the wicked. Note also that the shame shall come upon the fools. Note Psalms 14:1, "The fool hath said in his heart, There is no God." A fool in the Bible is a person who does not believe in God, as we have seen in many scriptures where God's wrath is going to be directed.

Habakkuk 3:2, 4 says:

O Lord, I have heard thy speech and was afraid: O
Lord, revive thy work in the midst of years, in the
midst of the years make known: in wrath remember
mercy. And his brightness was the light; He had horns
coming out of his hands; and there was the hiding
of his power. Before him went the pestilence, and
burning coals went forth at his feet.

Note: At the time of God's wrath, there is the "hiding of his power."
Is the way God hid power revealed in Exodus 20:21, "And Moses drew
near unto the thick darkness where God was," and Psalms 18:9, "He
bowed the heavens also, and came down: and darkness was under
his feet"? The burning coals, the plague of the hail, is mentioned in
Revelation 16:21, "And there fell upon men great hail out of heaven."
Nahum 1:2–3, 5, 7–8 says:

God is jealous, and the Lord revengeth, the Lord
revengeth, and is furious; The Lord will take
vengeance on his adversaries, and reserveth wrath for
his enemies. The Lord is slow to anger, and great in
power, and will not at all acquit the wicked: The Lord
hath his way in the whirlwind and in the storm, and
the clouds are the dust of his feet. The mountains
quake at him, and the hills melt, and the earth is
burned at his presence, yea, the world, and all that
dwell therein. The Lord is good, a strong hold in the
day of trouble; and he knoweth them that trust in
him. But with an overrunning flood he will make
an utter end of the place thereof, and darkness shall
pursue his enemies.

We should note here that God's wrath is only against his adversaries,
and that darkness pursues his enemies. This is the darkness of the smoke
of the pit in Revelation 9; the fifth trumpet judgment. We should also
compare the "day of trouble" in Nahum with the "day of trouble" in
Jeremiah 30. We should also note once again that the clouds are the

dust of his feet. We should also note that God is jealous. Why is God jealous, and when does God seek his revenge? We go to Joel 3:2, "I [God] will gather all nations, and will bring them down into the valley of Jehoshapat [Armageddon] and I will plead with them there for my people and for my heritage Israel whom they have scattered among the nations, and parted my land."

I hear all the time that no one knows when the resurrection of the dead happens. I believe that is far from the truth. All these scriptures were given for us to know. And this next verse in Isaiah tells us why.

Isaiah 9:11–14 says:

> And the vision of all is become unto you as the words of a book that is sealed, which men deliver to one that is learned, saying, Read this, I pray thee: and he saith, I cannot; for it is sealed: And the book is delivered to him that is not learned, saying, Read this, I pray thee: and he saith, I am not learned. Wherefore the Lord said, Forasmuch as this people draw near me with their mouth, and with their lips do honour me, but have removed their heart far from me, and their fear toward me is taught by the precept of men: Therefore, behold, I will proceed to do a marvelous work among this people, even a marvelous work and a wonder: for the wisdom of their wise men shall perish, and the understanding of their prudent men shall be hid.

The Lord did not give us this book so we are not to know his plan for the end of time. Maybe if we spent as much time reading and studying the Bible as we do watching television, this book would not be this great mystery to us. As Isaiah states in chapter 29, "Read this I pray thee," not to tell us that we can know when the end times are about to happen if we just read this book that has been delivered to us. "And he saith, I am not learned"; that sounds just like the church of God today. I hear people say we cannot know when the end times come, for God has forbidden it. This is why men had to meet in secret to study the Bible during the Dark Ages. If they were caught by the Catholic

Church, they would be tortured or killed. This is why Nostradamus wrote in quatrains. But thank God this is far from the truth today. He further states that people "Draw near with their mouth." Yes, I attend church on Sunday, but that is the only time I have to study the Word of God or spend time praying and just having a personal relationship with the God who has given us all the blessings of this life here and with the life that is to come through him. Even though we don't have time for God, he tells us that he will proceed to do his marvelous work. This same message in given in the next verse.

Matthew 13:11 says:

> Because it is given unto you to know the mysteries of the kingdom of heaven, but to them it is not given. For whosoever hath, to him shall be given, and he shall have more abundance: but whosoever hath not; from him shall be taken away even that he hath.

The Lord tells us that we are to know the mysteries of God if we just study his Word. The more you study, the more knowledge will be given to you. The least of what you know, even the little that you do know, will be taken away. This is why the study of God's Word should be important to everyone who has put his or her trust in the Lord. I know many churches say you don't need to study the Old Testament because the Lord ended that part of scripture. They are so wrong, because without the Old Testament, you cannot understand what God did in the past or how he will act in the future.

To the skeptical person who says our Bible lost its translation over the years, you are just in denial of what the Bible tells us. God would not let this happen. He would want every church age to know just what his message is to all the churches of God from the first century to the twenty-first century. All will understand, and all will have the knowledge of the Lord. God, as we know him who is the Lord, puts his messages into plain and simple language English, so that all Christians can understand. Is most of the Christian world of the English-speaking language?

This concludes my interpretation of what I see is the time of resurrection of the dead. If I am wrong and there is a pre-tribulation rapture, or the living church rapture is in heaven before the tribulation period, then rip all these passages out of the Bible. Isaiah says in 26:9, "When thy [the Lord's] judgments are in the earth, the inhabitants of the world will learn righteousness." If I am wrong, then rip out all the scriptures that tell us to wait for his appearing and coming. Rip out all the scriptures that tell us that the meek will inherit the earth. Rip out of the Bible all the scriptures that tell us that the Lord will appear when there is a great darkness that covers the earth. This is why I used so many of the Old Testament prophets, because they tell us exactly when the Lord descends from heaven and why. Rip out of your Bible all the scriptures that tell the church to endure until the end. And let us no longer pray, "Thy Kingdom come. Thy will been done on earth as it is in heaven," because the church wants to be raptured to heaven. I have just taken all these scriptures out of context, because the Lord will secretly take the church off the planet. That will make the environmentalists happy. I hate to disappoint them, for when the Lord comes back, man will live on this planet forever.

But some people tell us that the meek will not inherit the earth because man's carbon footprint is destroying the earth and God did not make the earth for man. We are to give back this planet to the animals. But since man is an animal since we evolved from apes, why would the world be saved without man? Animals put off greenhouse gases. I almost forgot that this book is just a bunch of fables, as told to us by Mr. Strauss of the 1800s. Darwin tells us we evolved from apes because God didn't create man. How stupid can I be to think this book is the Word of God when there is no God? I want to thank Mr. Strauss and Mr. Darwin and the atheists of the world, along with the environmentalists and evolutionists, for their great insight and knowledge. They are much smarter than these men who wrote the Bible who received their knowledge from the Master of the universe.

Closing Comments

You HAVE JUST READ all the verses and my comments, and this is how I came to my interpretation of the Bible. If I repeated myself, it is because sometimes you have to hear scripture over and over again to understand its meaning, just like you cannot just pick up the Bible and read it once to get the full meaning. The Bible repeats itself so that Bible prophecy is clear to all who want to know. It has taken me many hours of study to come to these conclusions. I did this because I love to study God's Word. It took me ten years of study and about ten years to put the scriptures together to write this book. If my interpretation of the Bible is correct, with the use of the history books, I don't see how anyone can say that the Bible is not truly the Word of God. Remember the old saying, "If the shoe fits, wear it." I believe this book matches history and the Bible perfectly.

I believe I prove that the so-called pre-tribulation rapture is false theology. Amos tells us in 3:7, "Surely, God will do nothing, but he revealeth his secret unto his servants the prophets." If "the Lord shall descend from heaven with a shout, with the voice archangel and the trumpet of God, and the dead in Christ shall be raised first," find the verse for the living church in the scriptures. Find the verse that says that God descends from heaven before his wrath. And most of all, find the Greek word rapture in either *Strong's or Bullinger's* concordances. Most of all, I exposed all these greedy, lying pastors who take scripture out of context for their personal gains.

The world is not going to end on December 21, 2012, as the Mayans predicted. Can we as a civilized society stop the battle of Armageddon from happening? That would depend on the Muslim society. Will God turn away his judgments upon man in the book of Revelation? That also depends on man himself, as I said at the very first part of this book. This book is about sin and God's dealings with it.

With American society, and most of the world, promoting abortion, same-sex marriage, the worldwide greed for money, the treatment of have-nots of the world, and the general decline of morality will bring God's judgment. I believe the biggest mistake Americans are making is turning their backs to God. Taking the Bible out of schools was the biggest mistake for the young people. Handing them a condom instead of a Bible sends these young people the wrong message. Professors in college teach young men and women there is no God, that we just evolved from apes. This is wrong. Judges are not even allowing prayer before a sporting event or at the start of class; this is wrong. America and the whole world are going in the wrong direction.

My original intent after this study was to take these verses to the pastors around my city, and as stated before, I mailed this study out to pastors around the country, with no response. I was hoping they would quit teaching the pre-tribulation rapture theory, because that is all it is—a theory. I do not see it based in biblical prophecy. This is why I wrote this book and named it *The Big Lie, Exposed*, because I expose many untruths. The truth must be told to the Christian world, and they must prepare for the bad things that are about to happen.

There is no pre-tribulation rapture. It is not in scripture. So when the tribulation comes, the church should be ready to help their fellow members deal with these troubles. Proverbs tells us in 11:30–31:

> The fruit of the righteous is a tree of life; and he that winneth souls is wise. Behold the righteous shall be recompensed [*shalam*,[442] which means; to be safe (in mind, body or estate); figurative to be completed; by implication to be friendly, make good, make

---

[442]   Ibid., 1987.

restitution, restore reward] in the earth: much more
the wicked and the sinner.

We should note here that the righteous will be safe in mind, body, or estate "in the earth." If you or I win souls for the Lord, in the tribulation period, we will eat of the tree of life and live forever. This is the message pastors should be teaching. This is the Old Testament equivalent verse to 2 Corinthians 1:4, "Who comforteth us in all our tribulation, that we may be able to comfort them which are in any trouble." We should remember that the "tree of life" will be in Jerusalem, as given in the book of Revelation. We should also note that with the Lord, there are always conditions for blessing.

Part of the following messages about the fall of the Roman Empire I got out of *A History of Civilization* by Brinton, Christopher, and Wolff. Reading the history of the fall of the Roman Empire sounds like what America is today. Mothers during the days of the Roman Empire didn't want to bring up their children but left it to serving maids. Mothers back then were too busy going to the gladiatorial shows, to the plays, and to the horse racing. Rome, like America, liked imported food and luxury items. They also had the very rich and the very poor. The very rich lived very conformably, while the poor lived in wooden tenements. The social problems that plagued Romans also plague Americans, and that included divorce. Even back then, fathers had no rights to bring up their children. Like today and during the Roman Empire days, the poor had no regular jobs but relied on public charity. The poor during the Roman Empire days had free access to the bath houses, circuses, and the chariot races.

A History of Civilization writes about the *History of the Decline and Fall of the Roman Empire* by Edward Gibbon. Let us note what it says on page 136: "Another example of disagreement over intangibles is the theory advanced by Professor Rostovtsev, a distinguished historian of the early twentieth century. Rostovtsev contended that Rome collapsed when her underprivileged masses sought a share of the high living standards and cosmopolitan culture of the ruling class. This revolt of the masses caused the bitter class tensions evident during the military anarchy and the reign of Diocletian." Not much has changed in two thousand years. There was class warfare then, and there is class warfare now. During the Dark Ages, it was done by the sword. Today, it's done by taxation.

As today, during those days, everyone was looking for a handout by the government. In John Kennedy's inauguration speech, he said, "Ask not what your country can do for you but what you can do for your country." This statement by President Kennedy, to me, is one of most powerful statements ever made to the American people. Now all you hear is what your country can do for you. Why will no other Democrat president stand up against the enemies of America, as President Kennedy did when Russia put in nuclear weapons in Cuba? John Kennedy was also a big supporter of the Jewish state. After he was elected president, he provided the state of Israel with Hawk missiles. This got his brother Bobby Kennedy killed by Sirhan Sirhan, a Palestinian, a few years later. Have the Democrats forgotten this?

Let us face another fact: Franklin Roosevelt's Social Security system was the biggest Ponzi scam ever planned by man. The only way the government could provide for a retirement system is more people had to die than live to provide this money. With the baby-boomers about to retire, Social Security is in big trouble. The Lord God had the perfect retirement system that would not fail. It's called children. The Fifth Commandment was, "Honour thy father and thy mother: that thy days may be long upon the land which the Lord giveth thee." The government's replacement of the family unit that God commanded did more to destroy God's system. This is the plan by the progressive liberals.

This is what it said in an *A History Of The Modern World* by R R. Palmer, Second Edition, revised with the collaboration of Joel Colton, on page 607: "In religion, liberals thought each individual should adopt any faith, or no faith as he chose, and that the church and clergy should play little or no role in public affairs." This is why it is written in Isaiah 32:5, "The vile [*nahal*,[443] meaning stupid, wicked, foolish] person shall be no more be called liberal." To have no faith goes against the greatest of the commandments spoken by the Lord Jesus Christ, and that is to

---

[443]   Ibid., 1914.

love your God with all your heart and all your soul—to put God first in your life. For Isaiah to tell us this in his time that in the future man would think this way should prove he was inspired by God.

I voted in my first presidential election when Jimmy Carter got elected. I voted for him. He was the worst president America ever had. His handling of the Iran crisis was a complete failure. When Ayatollah Khomeini took the American captives and held them for almost a year (444 days), all that was done was a failed rescue attempt. This weakness gave the Islamic people their first taste of victory against America. Ronald Reagan was next, and he failed when he did nothing to the terrorists who killed over two hundred of our marines in Lebanon, although he was on his mission to destroy the Russian "evil empire." He cut and ran from Islamic terrorism. That was the second taste of victory over America.

George Bush was next. He did well in defeating Iraq in the first Gulf War, but he did not complete the job because of pressure from the rest of the world. I became very worried about him when he stated over and over again this "New World Order." We, as Christians, know who the ruler of the "new world government" is, and he is the Antichrist. I knew he was toast and would not be re-elected for this stupid statement. Then there was President Clinton, who did more to destroy our military force than any president in history outside of Jimmy Carter. Under his administration, the military budget was cut to the extreme, in the so-called peace dividend. This is just what he did. He did nothing against the Arab world, which made numerous attacks against Americans. This was the third taste of victory against America.

After September 11, 2001, I thought Americans would come together because they would realize there is an enemy out there with a goal to destroy us, just as the generation before united when the attack came on Pearl Harbor. I have not seen of any film clips that stated that President Roosevelt was a failed president by the Republicans because of the attack on Pearl Harbor as the Democrats are saying today about President Bush. In the movie *Mid-Way*, after the attack on Pearl Harbor, the Japanese commander says, "We have just awakened a sleeping giant." Americans went to sleep after the war was over.

Are the Democrats so obsessed with being in power that they would aid the enemy by destroying President Bush? Go ahead, Democrats, tell the radical Muslims they are winning the war. This is just going to fuel their fire for their hatred against America and any country not Muslim. When we think we are weak, they will think they are strong. The attacks will come. The Democrats tried doing all they could to tie President Bush's hands in the war on terrorism.

Does anybody not see the hatred the Muslim world has for the state of Israel, England, and America? You can talk until you are blue in the face, but this is not going to change the minds of radical Islam. The failure of the past presidents to deal with Islamic terrorism has brought us to this. Do we want another attack on this country because of our failure to act against Arab terrorism? To fail by not attacking is the problem. Finally, with George Bush, we had a president willing to take the fight to the terrorists. He did not care that the polls said; this was not what the American people wanted to do to respond to Islamic terrorism. To cut and run from Iraq and the terrorists is to give the Muslim world another victory in their battle against the little Satan, which is Israel, and the big Satan, which is America. It is also apparent that most of the world does not want to deal with Islamic terrorism, and the American people have the same mentality, just as I found out on November 7, 2006.

On November 7, 2006, Americans gave the cut-and-run Democrats back the power in Congress and the Senate. The polls said it was because of the war in Iraq, the fifth victory for Islamic terrorism. The American people have spoken. This gives Islamic terrorism fuel for their aggression against America because they think America is weak. Just look what is happening in France and in Britain. Their main problem is the Muslim population. We should also remember the July 7, 2005, subway bombers who killed fifty-two people and injured around seven hundred who were born in England, and they had no loyalty to the English people they killed who were their fellow citizens. Their loyalty is only to Allah. The one thing forgotten by our immigration department is that the people who come to America must pledge allegiance to be Americans first. That will never happen to a true Muslim. His allegiance is to Allah and Allah only. The destruction of Israel and America is their goal.

Wake up, America. This is the big difference between Muslims and Christians. Christians believe in life, and the Islamic religion wants them to die for Allah. What a stark difference. But the Lord Jesus tells us not to battle with them ourselves. This battle is the Lord's. This is the time for Christian people to try and teach the peaceable Muslims that their God is not able to save them or give them eternal life except the only true God, the Lord Jesus Christ, and be the, "Blessed are the meek; for they shall inherit the earth."

Who can we depend on? Just watch the news. We are alone in this battle. This is why you must study history, because history repeats itself. In *The History of the World* by J. M. Roberts on page 770, Mr. Roberts tells us which thoughts are the thoughts of our first president George Washington:

> The great rule of conduct for us in regard to foreign nations is, in extending our commercial relations, to have with them as little political connection as possible. Our detached and distant situation invites and enables us to pursue a different course. It is our true policy to steer clear of permanent alliances with any portion of the foreign world. Moreover, Washington also warned his countrymen against assumptions of permanent or special hostility or friendship with any other nation.

Even George Washington knew we could not depend on our allies when the chips are down, for he says to have little political connections with Europe. What insight George Washington and the rest of the founding fathers of this country had. Thank our God for George Washington.

Look what is happening in the world today. Most of the world hates America and Israel, just as Washington told us. Is this why he was the father of this country, just as Abraham was the father of the countries to come? I believe the Lord brings into power certain people who do the things God wants to happen. I think our founding fathers knew who they were, and this is how America got its symbol of the eagle. They took it right out of Daniel 7 where the lion had eagles' wings till the eagles' wings were plucked. They know that the symbol for England was the lion and they were going to fight for independence from them. Taxes started this fight. Some of our founding fathers were Masons. I believe they knew they were the descendants of the house of Israel and that America would bring to pass Bible prophecy. In my next manuscript I plan to prove America is in the Bible. This should prove to most people the prophecies were written by the men of God.

We should also note that Americans had to fight for the land they acquired, just as the tribes of Israel did when God led them out of Egyptian bondage. Just what split Israel into two different countries? Jeroboam was going to increase the yoke (taxes) on the people of Israel more than Solomon. What splits Americans today but taxes? Democrats want to take from the rich, or better said, anyone with a job, and give it to people who don't want to work. I think it is ironic that Israel split and had a northern kingdom and a southern kingdom just as America split in the days of the American civil war into the north against the south.

It is going to take real leadership and a man of high moral standing for America to survive the coming days and not one saying he is against the war that was started by our enemies who are out to destroy us. And before we act, we should get permission from the rest of the world. Here is where the word "stupid" comes into play again. Why should we have to get permission from anyone to protect and defend this country? Why do we fight among ourselves instead of the people out to destroy us? It should not be whose political party controls America! This is the same cut-and-run that is taught in the churches of God when they are told not to worry, God is going to rapture them out of here before the tribulation, instead of being soldiers for Christ as stated in 2 Timothy 2:3, "Thou therefore endure hardness, as a good soldier of Christ Jesus."

I was in my church the Sunday after the attack on America on 9/11. It was filled with people I had never seen before. I also noticed that the new people quit coming after just a few weeks. Did they feel that the threat was gone and they were no longer in danger and had no need for God? Is this time of trouble that brings people back to God the "tribulation period"? What will it take for the people of God to return to him so that he can bless them? Does it take disastrous action from God to bring his people back to his house? This is but one reason I believe the church goes through the tribulation period. For the past forty years, politicians have gotten elected by what your country can do for you. Americans want free education, free health care, free drugs, and the list goes on, while the national debt continues to rise. Will America ever return to responsible spending, or will it lead the country into bankruptcy? Will this be the way the Antichrist controls the world, by doing away with this debt?

The Lord warned us of this when he told us not to take the mark of the beast. It's because it's the economy, stupid. Will Americans ever get out of debt? Americans owe three trillion dollars in credit-card debt. Will America elect a true Christian to lead this country who will not let that happen? Will America stand with Israel during the coming trouble ahead? Will Americans go out and vote for a Christian who knows the Bible so he or she will not let the Antichrist control America? Will Christian Americans ever stand up to the ACLU and say to them that America is a Christian nation and we want God back in our schools, back in our public buildings, and back into all phases of our lives? And most of all, do Americans want Christ back in our celebration of Christmas? We need Christmas, not this stupid "holiday celebration." In our public schools, it's now called the "winter break."

Or better yet, maybe someone should hire the ACLU to file a lawsuit against the federal and state offices for closing down on Christmas day. This should include the courts around the country also because we must have a separation of church and state. Closing these offices, courts, and schools down for the day acknowledges a said religion. That religion is the birth of Christ. We must not let this happen. We must not ask a person in court to tell the truth, "so help me God," because that acknowledges God. We should do away with Thanksgiving Day also. We have no God to thank for our blessings. We did this all on our own thanks to our ancestors, the ape men, since we just evolved from apes.

We also need to end the federal and state tax deductions to churches, because this acknowledges a religion. Let us become a completely pagan nation. Since we do not acknowledge God (the Lord Jesus), there is no reason state or federal offices or any business should close on Sunday. Last of all, we must take the word "God" off our money because we no longer trust God, and all laws that relate to Christian values must end. This will make it legal to kill your child at any age, because a woman should have a right to choose. Do we not see how stupid this is?

I can say this for the Muslim religion: their governments are not debating on whether two people of the same sex can marry. They don't approve of abortion and birth control, and they are not promoting this worldwide in the name of health care. They are not filling their children with drugs for mind control, just mind control to kill Jews and Christians. They are not making movies with actors blaspheming God's name. No wonder they think they are on a religious jihad. Just look at how ungodly America and Europe have become. Are the Christians ever going to fight back, or have we become the Laodicean church—the church that was lukewarm, not hot or cold for the Word of God? I hear these stupid people say we as a country can't acknowledge a said religion because they don't want to offend anyone.

Well, the founding fathers of this country said our rights are guaranteed by our creator. There is no creator but the Lord Jesus. I feel sorry for those who are ashamed of the Lord Jesus, for Jesus says in his own words in Luke 9:26–27:

> For whosoever shall be ashamed of me and my words, of him shall the Son of Man be ashamed, when he shall come in his own glory, and in his Father's, and of the holy angels. But I tell you the truth, there be some standing here, which shall not taste of death, till they see the kingdom of God.

I would just as soon end the whole celebration of the season as to take the Lord out of Christmas since Americans have made this holiday a pagan holiday by its promotion of Santa Claus instead of the Lord. I think we should notice that Satan and Santa are almost spelled alike. Both take the Lord out of the picture. Parents would serve their children better if they told them, "These gifts were provided for you by the Lord." Here is what the Bible tells us about the pagan Christmas tree. Jeremiah 10:3–5 says:

> For the customs of the people are vain: for one cutteth a tree out of the forest, the work of the hands of the workman, with the ax. They deck it with silver and with gold; they fasten it with nails and with hammers that it not move. They are upright as the palm tree, but speak not: they must needs be borne, because they cannot go. Be not afraid of them; for they cannot do evil, neither also is it in them to do good.

Does this not sound like our Christmas tree today? And if this custom was vain then, it is vain now.

Churches have even made Easter a pagan holiday by having church-sponsored Easter egg hunts, which is another pagan custom. There will be only one holiday when the Lord returns and maybe the one we should follow now. This is given in Zechariah 14:16, "And it shall come to pass, that every one that is left of all the nations which came against Jerusalem shall even go up from year to year to worship the King, the Lord of hosts, and to keep the feast of tabernacles." Zechariah goes on to say in verse 19, "This shall be the punishment of Egypt, and the punishment of all nations that come not up to keep the feast of tabernacles." The plagues that were put upon Egypt will be the plagues the Lord will put on all nations during the thousand-year reign of the Lord. So why do Christian churches not celebrate this holiday? It is important to the Lord.

We celebrate Christian holidays the way we do because, "It's the economy, stupid." If Christian Americans would sit out one Christmas and not buy a single present or do anything that is related to Christmas, we would hurt the big merchants' pocketbooks. How fast do you think our politicians would act to put the Lord Jesus back into Christmas? How fast will we change the mind of some of these left-wing judges who say it is unconstitutional to acknowledge our Lord if we start having these judges impeached? Where is the Christian freedom of speech? Bible prophecy is coming to pass because the Lord Jesus stated in Matthew10:22, "And ye shall be hated of all men for my name's sake." This is why I wrote this manuscript. This is why Isaiah 32:5 says, "The vile person shall be no more called liberal." It's these judges who rule against the knowledge of the Lord Jesus Christ. Knowledge of the Lord is your only salvation. Stand up, Christians. To do this, you must have backbone. The Lord said in Matthew 10:33, "Those that do deny me, I will deny before my father which is in heaven."

Are you denying the Lord when you want our Lord out of this celebration? I think you do. Taking Christ out of Christmas makes this holiday celebration a pagan holiday. Do you not want to offend an Arab because of his belief? I do not care if an Arab person does not participate in our holiday, because I am not going to participate in his pagan holiday. Either we stand with the Lord or we don't. This is your choice.

If your religion tells you to hate America, I tell you this: get out. We see throughout this country that Muslim people are killing more Christian and Jewish Americans and the press likes to play down the fact that they are Muslims. I don't care if I am not politically incorrect. The time is coming when you will have to choose. If you are against the Lord and Savior, I am against you. I know who the God of heaven is, and it is not the God of Islam. My trust is in the Lord Jesus, and it should be for all Americans. I even hear people say all religions lead people to heaven. This is not true. Those people live for all eternity in everlasting shame and contempt. Those who believe in the Lord Jesus Christ live for all eternity on the earth in the presence of the Lord.

I think the pope of Rome should question Islam, "What does your religion teach?" Open the Bible in any Muslim country and see what happens to you. To do that gets you the death sentence. If they can't tolerate any symbol of religion outside of Islam in their country, maybe we should not tolerate the teaching of Islam in a Christian country. We can justify not allowing mosques to be built in this country because of what is taught in the Qur'an, and that is to kill Christians and Jews. If the Muslim world hates the Christians this much, maybe they should stay out of this Christian nation, which we are in America. Go home.

Go back to your country if you do not like America and our Christian beliefs. Go back to the seventh century. This is where your religion takes you.

This was told to them by the prime minister of Australia. God bless this man to make the first stance against Arabs in his country. He told them to fit into their society or get out. Even some of our universities in this country have sold out our Christian beliefs and accepted money from the Arab world to teach the Qur'an. They say it is Middle Eastern studies. Where is the ACLU? Why have they not filed a lawsuit against these universities, as they have against the teachings of the Christian religion? Will some people do anything for the almighty dollar?

I have seen enough Islamic television to know they teach to hate and to kill Jews and Christians. Palestinian children are shown maps of the Middle East. There is no Israel on those maps, just a Palestinian state. This is taught in the schools as well as in their mosques across the whole Middle East. I was watching a program a few years ago of small Palestinian children in a classroom. They would come to the head of the class and state, "I want to be a martyr for Allah by killing Christians and Jews." The Qur'an states in chapter 4 on page 83, "Kill yourselves in striving for the cause of Allah or go forth from your homes for the same purpose." This is what their religion teaches. It is the religion of hate, and Americans should open their eyes to the facts. If that happens, I believe that God will bless America and bring peace to our true brethren, the Jews of Israel. Scripture tells us in 2 Chronicles 7:14:

> If my people, which are called by my name, shall humble themselves, and pray, and seek my face, and turn from their wicked ways, then will I hear from heaven, and will forgive their sin, and I will heal their land.

It is time for America to return to God and ask him for forgiveness. This is the chance for the global-warming scientists to do something about "weather change." Turn from your wicked ways, and the Lord God will heal it. I believe part of the Muslim world has declared war on any country that is not Islamic. The only peace between these people will be made by the Antichrist. Even if we leave Iraq, the war will come to us here. We should not depend on the United Nations' countries for any help. We must realize that we, meaning England, America, and Israel, must stand firmly together in the coming days. My last message to you is to support Israel until the "last day," for if we stand with the Jews, which were of the same bloodline as the Lord and are the chosen people of *God,* we will be victorious in the last days. We will be the meek who inherit the earth. God bless America was never as important a statement to make as it is today. I know that I am saved and will inherit the earth and heaven; will you?

Bibliography

Brinton, Crane. *A History of Civilization: Volume One: to 1715.* 1, England Cliffs: Prentice-Hall, Inc., 1960.

Bullinger, E. W. *A Critical Lexicon and Concordance to the English and Greek New Testament.* Grand Rapids: Kregel Publications, 1999.

Bullinger, E. W. "Meaning of Numbers in the Bible: The Number 7." BibleStudy.org. Barnabus Ministries / BibleStudy.org, 2011. Web. 7 Jun 2011. <http://www.biblestudy.org/bibleref/meaning-of-numbers-in-bible/7.html>.

Bullinger, E. W. "Meaning of Numbers in the Bible: The Number 10." BibleStudy.org. Barnabus Ministries / BibleStudy.org, 2011. Web. 7 Jun 2011. <http://www.biblestudy.org/bibleref/meaning-of-numbers-in-bible/10.html>.

Corsi, Jerome R. "Discovery backs theory oil not 'fossil fuel'." WorldNetDaily (2011). Web. 7 Jun 2011. <http://www.wnd.com/news/article.asp?ARTICLE_ID=59991>.

Estulin, Daniel. *The True Story of the Bilderberg Group.* 2 ed. Walterville: TrineDay LLC, 2009.

Griffin, G. Edward. *The Creature from Jekyll Island.* Appleton, Wisconsin: American Opinion Publishing, 1994.

Khan, Muhammed Z. *The Qur'an.* North Hampton Olive Branch Press, 2005.

Palmer, R. R. *A History of the Modern World.* 2 ed. New York: Alfred A. Knopf, Inc., 1961.

Roberts, J. M. *A New History of the World.* Oxford: Oxford University Press, 1976.

Strong, James. *Strong's Complete Word Study Concordance,* KJV Expanded Edition. Word Study Series. Warren Baker. Chatanooga: AMG Publishers, 2004.

Tungate, Mel. "Tungate Evolution-LDS." Tungate.com. Mel Tungate, 01/08/1999. Web. 7 Jun 2011. <http://www.tungate.com/ Evolution.htm>.

Whiston, William. *The Complete Works of Josephus.* Grand Rapids: Kregel Publications, 1999.

Wilson, Ambrose John. "The Sign of the Prophet Jonah and its Modern Confirmations." Princeton Theological Review 25.4 (1927). Princeton Seminary Library. Web. 7 Jun 2011. <Tungate, Mel. "Tungate Evolution-LDS." Tungate.com. Mel Tungate, 01 08 1999. Web. 7 Jun 2011.>.

"The Supreme Court's Christian History of America." VFTOnline. org. Vine & Fig Tree, n.d. Web. 7 Jun 2011. <http://vftonline.org/ EndTheWall/TrinityHistory.htm>.

Webster's Dictionary.